D0687547

Self-taught Chess for Beginners and Intermediates

Self-taught Chess for Beginners and Intermediates

MILTON FINKELSTEIN

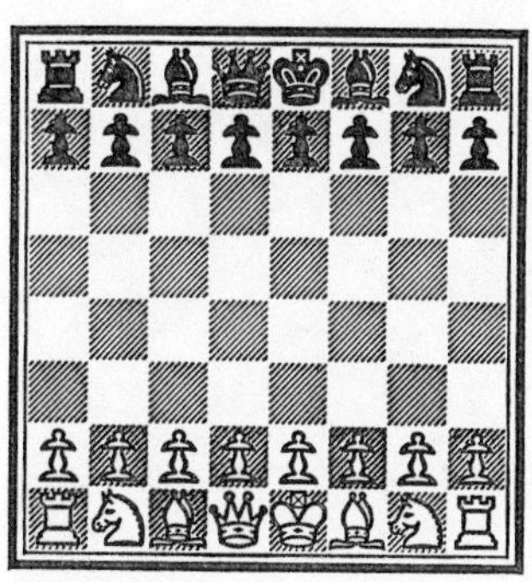

Doubleday & Company, Inc.
Garden City, New York
1975

ISBN 0-385-09793-X
Library of Congress Catalog Card Number 74-18794

Printed in the United States of America

Contents

The author expresses his special thanks and appreciation to United States Chess Federation Life Master Asa Hoffmann for his careful reading of the manuscript and his suggestions for its improvement.

Foreword

The game of chess, which has been developing for thousands of years, has long been one of the pastimes associated with the superior mind and the great intellect, the "egghead." This is a pity, for chess has thereby lost millions of possible players—people who, once they learned the game, would enjoy it for a lifetime.

The fact is that chess is a simple game, difficult only for those who have reached mastery and wish to demonstrate this mastery in competition with other experts. This is what you must learn to become a good chess player—one good enough to enjoy the game and to play it for fun:

1. The six different kinds of moves possible by the six different kinds of pieces on the chessboard.
2. A small number of objectives that will help you understand how to win the enemy King—the object of the game.
3. A set of principles that will help you understand how to use your pieces to win the pieces of your opponent, and thus make easier the task of winning his King.

You do not need any previous knowledge of chess to read this book. All you need is a chessboard and a little time—time in which to *learn chess by the Self Taught method.*

Part One

Introduction to Chess

The Chessmen

Most sets of chessmen follow a pattern of construction called the "Staunton pattern." The printed symbols for chess pieces used in this book are intended to look like the chess pieces themselves.

BLACK WHITE

The King. Each player has one King. It is usually the tallest piece. It sometimes has a cross on its upper end.

The Queen. Each player has one Queen. It is almost as high as the King, and usually has a crown-shaped upper end.

The Rook. Each player has two Rooks. The Rook looks like a corner of an ancient castle.

The Knight. Each player has two Knights. The Knight looks like the head of a horse.

The Bishop. Each player has two Bishops. The Bishop looks like the hat worn by high church officials. It usually has a slit near its upper end.

The Pawn. Each player has eight Pawns. These little foot-soldiers are the smallest pieces on the chessboard.

DIAGRAM 1

The Board and the Chessmen

Let's begin by looking at the chessboard. Set it before you so that it looks like the chessboard at the left. (Diagram 1)

Facts to Remember About the Chessboard

1. Notice that the board is placed so that there is a White square at the lower right corner.
2. The board contains 64 squares, alternately colored light and dark. For convenience, the light-colored squares are called **White** squares; the dark-colored squares are called **Black** squares.
3. The board contains Ranks, Files, and Diagonals. The diagram at the right (Diagram 2) demonstrates what these are.

DIAGRAM 2

   a. A **Rank** is a line of squares running from left to right across the chessboard.
   b. A **File** is a line of squares running up and down the board at right angles to the ranks.
   c. A **Diagonal** runs across the board, following across squares of the same color.
4. Notice the color of squares adjacent to one another. On a Rank or a File, the color changes from square to adjacent square. On a Diagonal, the color of the next square is the same as the color of the square on which you begin.

5. Except for one piece, as you shall see, the chessmen move along Ranks, Files, or Diagonals.

Setting up the Chessmen

Set the chessmen up as shown in the diagram on page X. Note that:

1. The White pieces are set up on one side of the board; the Black pieces are set up on the other side of the board. The two sides of the board are labeled White and Black. It is customary in chess to call the player who has the white pieces "White"; the player of the black pieces is called "Black."
2. The pieces are placed on the first two ranks in front of White and Black. The eight Pawns are lined up on the second rank. The Rooks, Knight and Bishops are placed at both sides, working in toward the middle of the first rank. The King and Queen are placed in the center of the first rank.
3. The Queen is always placed on its own color—the White Queen on a White square; the Black Queen on a Black square.

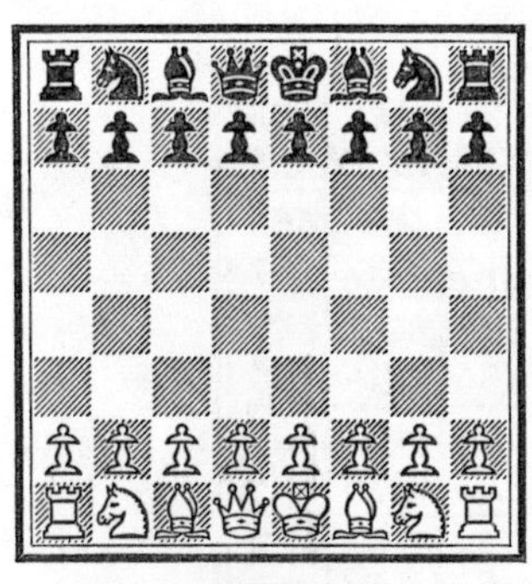

DIAGRAM 3

How the pieces are set up for the beginning of a game.

Chess Notation

We cannot describe the moves of chess, or present the principles that will explain the game to you, unless we have some simple method of describing the squares of the chessboard and the chessmen. This system is called *chess notation.* It requires:

1. *Abbreviations for the pieces.* In this book, and in most of the other books on the game, the following abbreviations are used:

K = King	**Kt** = Knight
Q = Queen	**B** = Bishop
R = Rook	**P** = Pawn

Thus, whenever we use the letter K, we are referring to the King. Whenever we use the letter R, we mean the Rook. From this point on we will be using this system of *notation.*

2. *Symbols for the squares on the chessboard.* The squares on the chessboard are named according to the rank and file on which they stand. The ranks are numbered 1 to 8; the files are given the name of the piece which stands on the first rank at the beginning of the game. The board is divided vertically into two halves—the King's side and the Queen's side, and the R, Kt, and B on the King's side are called KR (King's Rook), KKt (King's Knight) and KB (King's Bishop). In the same way, the R, Kt and B on the Queen's side are called QR (Queen's Rook), QKt (Queen's Knight) and QB (Queen's Bishop).

QR1 QR8	QKt1 QKt8	QB1 QB8	Q1 Q8	K1 K8	KB1 KB8	KKt1 KKt8	KR1 KR8
QR2 QR7	QKt2 QKt7	QB2 QB7	Q2 Q7	K2 K7	KB2 KB7	KKt2 KKt7	KR2 KR7
QR3 QR6	QKt3 QKt6	QB3 QB6	Q3 Q6	K3 K6	KB3 KB6	KKt3 KKt6	KR3 KR6
QR4 QR5	QKt4 QKt5	QB4 QB5	Q4 Q5	K4 K5	KB4 KB5	KKt4 KKt5	KR4 KR5
QR5 QR4	QKt5 QKt4	QB5 QB4	Q5 Q4	K5 K4	KB5 KB4	KKt5 KKt4	KR5 KR4
QR6 QR3	QKt6 QKt3	QB6 QB3	Q6 Q3	K6 K3	KB6 KB3	KKt6 KKt3	KR6 KR3
QR7 QR2	QKt7 QKt2	QB7 QB2	Q7 Q2	K7 K2	KB7 KB2	KKt7 KKt2	KR7 KR2
QR8 QR1	QKt8 QKt1	QB8 QB1	Q8 Q1	K8 K1	KB8 KB1	KKt8 KKt1	KR8 KR1

DIAGRAM 4

Notice that each square has two names—one as read from the White side; the other as read from the Black side. *In chess notation, each player considers his moves as made from* his *side.* He therefore names the squares concerned from his side. Thus, White's K1 is the same as Black's K8. An easy way to remember the name of a square is to think of the number 9. White's 4th rank is Black's 5th rank; Black's 3rd rank is White's 6th rank, etc.

Diagram 5 will give you an opportunity to make sure that you understand this system of chess notation. There are ten squares on which heavy letters have been printed. Name the squares with capital letters from the White side. Name the squares with lower-case letters from the Black side. The answers appear at the bottom of this page.

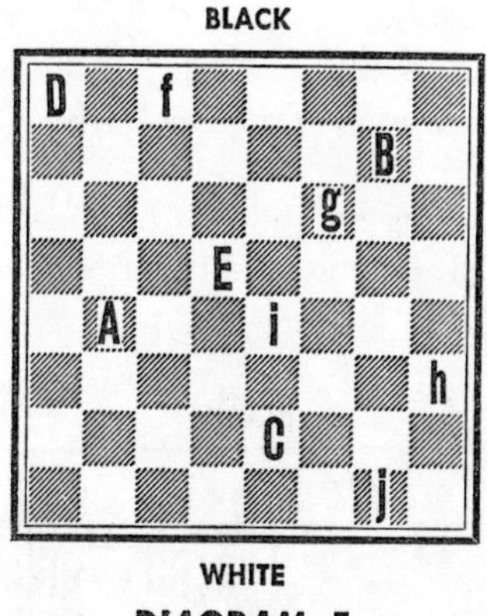

DIAGRAM 5

NAMING THE PIECES DURING THE GAME

The names of the squares, as shown in Diagram 4, never change. However, the names of the pieces sometimes do. For example, a Pawn placed on K2 at the beginning of a game is called the KP. If, in the course of the game, this Pawn should move off the K file, for example, onto the Q file, it is then called the QP. Pawns get their names from the files on which they stand at any given moment during a game.

Pieces are sometimes identified by the square on which they stand. Suppose two pieces of the same kind (two Rooks or two Knights, for example) can each move to the same square. We identify the one which is to move by naming the square from which it is moving. Diagram 6, will make this point still clearer.

A—QKt4
B—KKt7
C—K2
D—QR8
E—Q5

f—QB1
h—KR6
g—KB3
i—K5
j—KKt8

As we will see later, it is possible for a Rook to move as many squares as the player desires along an open file. In this case, it is desired to move a Rook to the square Q5. Both of the White Rooks can make this move. We must therefore identify the Rook which is to move. This is done by naming first the square *from* which the move is made and then the square *to* which the move is made. A dash is used to indicate the movement. Thus, if we move the Rook from Q1 to Q5, we write:

R(Q1)—Q5

In the same way, if we move the Rook from Q8, we write:

R(Q8)—Q5

With the help of chess notation, it becomes possible to keep a record of the moves of a game, and to write chess books which can then be read by others.

DIAGRAM 6

How Do the Chess Pieces Move?

White and Black take turns moving in chess. *White always has the first move.* Each player moves one piece at a time, with the exception of *Castling*, which will be discussed later.

Diagram 7 illustrates the move of the King. The King moves one square in any direction. In the diagram, the King is at K4. He has eight squares open to him—Q3, Q4, Q5, K3, K5, KB3, KB4, and KB5. The King stands now in the center of K4. He can be moved to any one of the other squares named and would be placed in the center of that square. If he were placed at the side of the board,

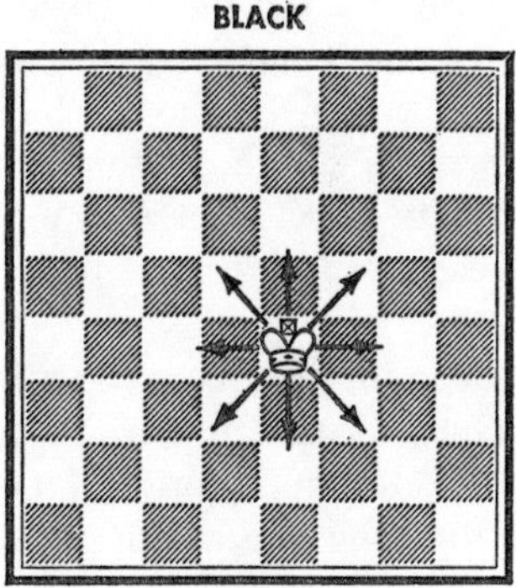

DIAGRAM 7

say at KR5, he could move only to five different squares. If placed at a corner square, like QR1, he would have only three available squares to which to move.

Rules Regarding the Movement of the King

1. The King cannot move into a square occupied by one of his own men. Only one piece can occupy any square on the chessboard at any one time.
2. The King can capture an undefended enemy piece in any square to which the King can move—that is, a square adjacent to the square on which the King is standing. Diagram 8 illustrates the capturing move.

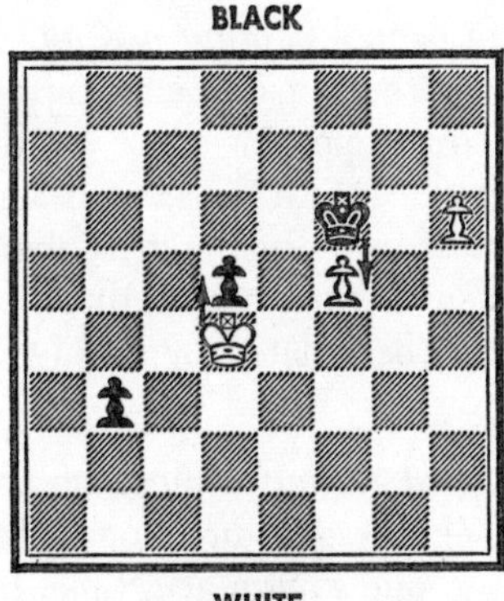

DIAGRAM 8

White to move can capture the Black Pawn on Q5. This would be written **K × P**, the letter × standing for "captures" or "takes." Black to move can take the White Pawn on his KB4. Here again the move would be written **K × P.** Note that White cannot take the Black Pawn on White's QKt3, for it is more than one square away. For the same reason, Black cannot take the White Pawn on Black's KR3.

3. The King cannot move into a square in which he will be under possible capture. Thus, if two Kings are placed as in Diagram 9, neither one can move into the squares K4, Q4, or QB4. To do so would be to place the King in a position where the enemy King could capture it.

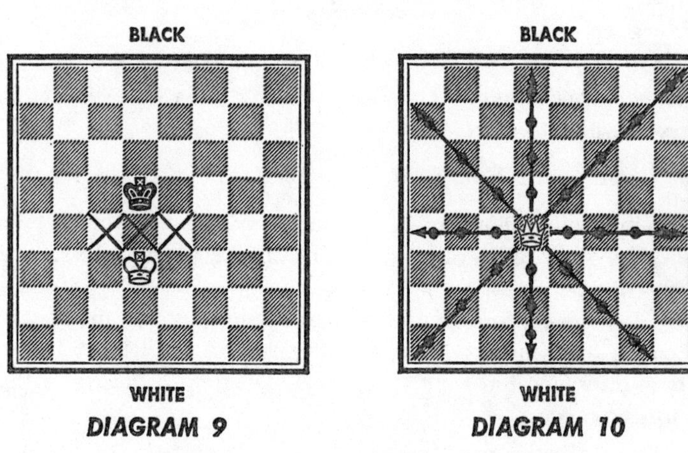

DIAGRAM 9 *DIAGRAM 10*

Remember: *A King cannot capture a King,* for it can never get close enough to do so without itself being captured.

The King is the most important piece on the chessboard. The object of the game is to capture the enemy King. When the King is captured, the game is over. In practice, the King is never captured, but the game ends when his capture cannot be prevented. This condition, called "checkmate," or simply "mate," will be discussed in detail later on.

The Queen is the most powerful piece on the chessboard. Like the King, it can move in eight directions. Unlike the King, the Queen is not limited to one square at a time, but can move as far as possible, or as many squares along one line as the player desires. In Diagram 10, the White Queen is placed on Q4. She can move to 27 different squares, each indicated by a dot. These include:

a. 7 squares on the 4th rank
b. 7 squares on the Q file
c. 7 squares on one diagonal and 6 on the other.

Here are four of the possible moves that could be made by the Queen in Diagram 10. Check each by referring to the diagram.

Q—QR1 Q—KKt7 Q—KB4 Q—KR4

If you had any difficulty in finding these squares, then spend a little more time to familiarize yourself with the notation as shown on Diagram 4.

Rules Regarding the Movement of the Queen

1. The Queen can capture any enemy piece. (A Queen can be so placed that it cannot be prevented from taking the enemy King on its next move. This would be "checkmate," the end of the game. In the same way, every other piece can be so placed that its next move will be the forced capture of the enemy King.) In capturing a piece, the enemy piece is removed from the board and its square taken by the Queen. All other captures, by any chess piece, follow the same rule. *Remove the other piece* and *replace it with your piece.*
2. The Queen is best placed near the center of the board. The great power of the Queen is based upon its ability to get from one part of the board to another. It can do this most easily when it is placed at or near the center of the board.
3. The Queen cannot jump over any pieces.

Rules Regarding the Movement of the Rook

The Rook is next in power to the Queen. It can move in four directions, as shown in Diagram 11. It moves as far as possible, or as far as you wish to move it. Note in Diagram 11 that it can move to any one of 14 squares, all along the rank and file on which it is standing. If we measure the value of a chess piece by its ability to move around the chessboard, then a Rook is a little more than half as powerful as a Queen; two Rooks are a little more powerful than a Queen.

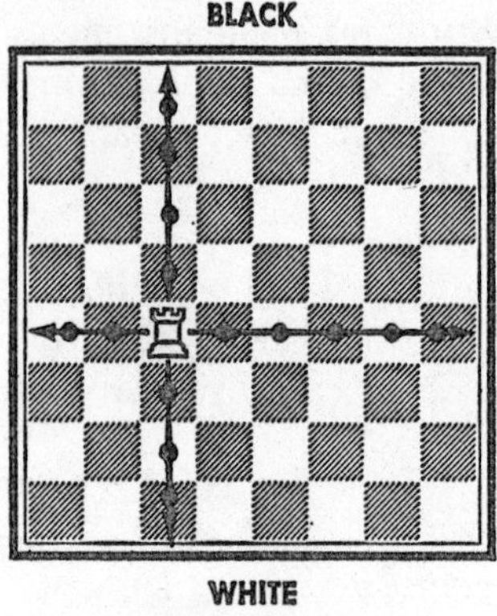

DIAGRAM 11

Rules Regarding the Movement of the Bishop

The Bishop is a little less powerful than the Rook. Its movement is along the diagonals only. From a center square, as in Diagram 12, it commands 13 squares. For a square like QR1 it commands only 7. Its average control of the board is 9 or 10 squares.

Since there are two Bishops, one acting on White squares and the other acting on Black squares, we can say that the Bishops are able to control the entire board. That is, there is no square to which a Bishop may not move. Since each Bishop is confined to squares of its own color, they cannot possibly interfere with one another.

DIAGRAM 12

Rules Regarding the Movement of the Knight

The Knight is about equal in power to the Bishop, even though it can control only eight squares at a time. The reason for this is that the Knight can cover the whole board, not only half of it like the Bishop.

Speaking in mathematical terms, the move of the Knight is in the pattern set by the moves of the Rook and Bishop. The Rook move is at right angles to the rank or file. The Bishop move is half that

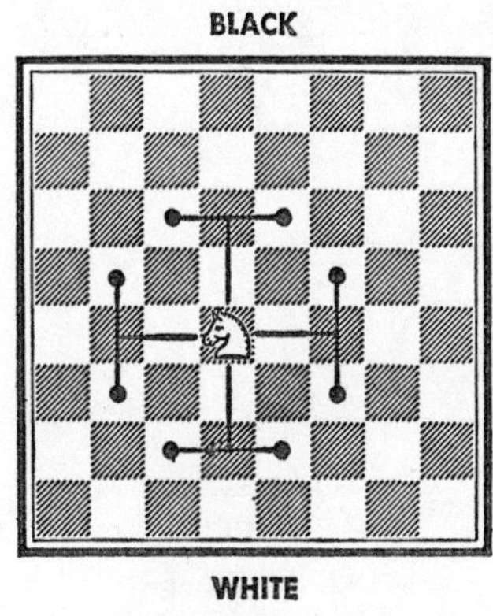

DIAGRAM 13

angle—one of 45 degrees. The Knight move is half that—one of 22½ degrees. It is illustrated in Diagram 13.

The Knight is at Q4. Its move is like the letter L—two squares on a rank and then one more square on a file; or two squares on a file and then one square on a rank. The color of the square on which it stands changes every time it moves. In Diagram 13, the Knight can move to K2, KB3, KB5, K6, QB6, QKt5, QKt3, and QB2. In moving to these squares, the Knight can jump over any piece standing on a square adjacent to K4—all it needs is a place on which to land.

Thus, in the original position of the pieces (Diagram 3), the Pawns and the Knights are the only pieces that can move. Take the White Knights as an example. They can move to KR3, KB3, QB3 and QR3.

Another way to consider the Knight's move is to think of it as going to any of the vertices of an octagon whose center is the square on which the Knight is standing.

Rules Regarding the Movement of the Pawn

The Pawn is the weakest of all the forces on the chessboard. Its movement is forward only, one square at a time, as illustrated in Diagram 14. However, the Pawn can move either one or two squares forward on its first move. This is true for each Pawn.

DIAGRAM 14

When a Pawn reaches the eighth rank on any file, it must then be exchanged for another piece—a Queen, Rook, Bishop or Knight. This piece replaces the Pawn, and immediately acts as if it were one of the original pieces of the type selected. Thus, you can have three or more Queen, Rooks, Bishops or Knights at one time during a game of chess. This power of being promoted to a more powerful piece is called *Queening*, and makes the proper playing of your Pawns an important part of successful chess play.

Castling

Once in a game each player is permitted to move two pieces at the same time. This move is called *castling*, and follows these rules:

1. Neither the King nor the Rook has been moved.
2. There are no pieces between the King and Rook on the first rank.
3. The King is not in check—that is, no enemy piece is at the

moment attacking the King and threatening to capture it on the next move.

4. No enemy piece controls either of the two squares next to the King and in the direction of the Rook. Thus, the King will not move across or into a check. Diagrams 15, 16, 17, and 18 illustrate Castling.

Castling is a single move. Its purposes are:

1. to place the King in a position of greater safety;

BLACK

WHITE

DIAGRAM 15

BLACK

WHITE

DIAGRAM 16

Position of King and Rook after Castling on King side.

BLACK

WHITE

DIAGRAM 17

BLACK

WHITE

DIAGRAM 18

Position of King and Rook after Castling on Queen side.

2. to bring the Rook out of its corner and into a position where it can become more active.

Diagrams 19, 20, 21, show positions in which Castling is not possible.

Notation for Castling: Castling on the King side is indicated by O—O. Castling on the Queen side is indicated by O—O—O.

BLACK

WHITE

DIAGRAM 19

White cannot Castle because the Rooks have already moved. Black cannot Castle because the King has already moved.

BLACK

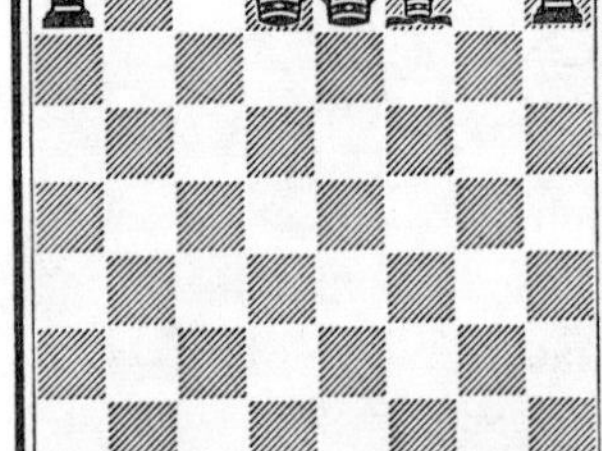

WHITE

DIAGRAM 20

Neither side can Castle because pieces stand in the way; they are blocking the movement of the King and the Rook.

BLACK

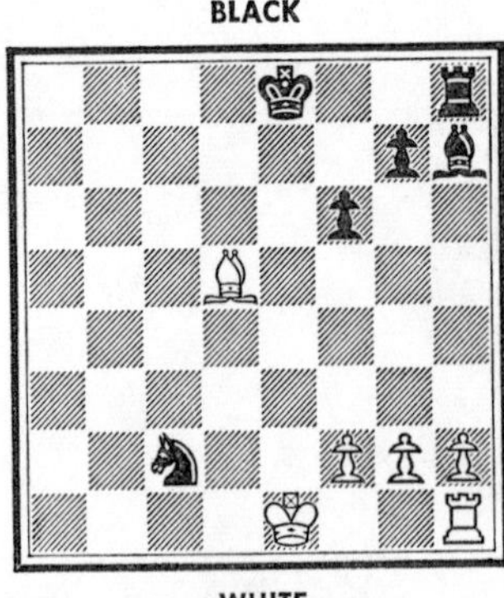

WHITE

DIAGRAM 21

BLACK

WHITE

DIAGRAM 22

In Diagram 21, White cannot Castle because his King is in check (by the Knight). Black cannot Castle because the King would move into check (by the Bishop). In Diagram 22, every White piece can make at least one capture.

Capturing

We have made several references to "capturing." Let us now examine the several rules relating to this key idea in chess.

1. Except for the Pawn, every piece captures as it moves.

(That is, it can take any piece or Pawn that stands on any square to which it can move.)

In Diagram 22, every White piece can make a capture. These are listed below.

a. K × Kt (the King can take the Knight at KB6).
b. Q × Kt (R2) (the Queen can take the Knight at KR2).
c. Q × Kt (B6) (the Queen can take the Knight at KB6).
d. R × Kt (the Rook can take the Knight at KR2).
e. R × P (the Rook can take the Pawn at QB2).
f. B × P (the Bishop can take the Pawn at QR6).
g. Kt × P (the Knight can take the Pawn at QR6).

In each case the captured piece would be removed from the board and its place taken by the capturing piece.

Diagram 23 further illustrates capturing.

It is White's turn to move. The White Queen can make four captures:

BLACK

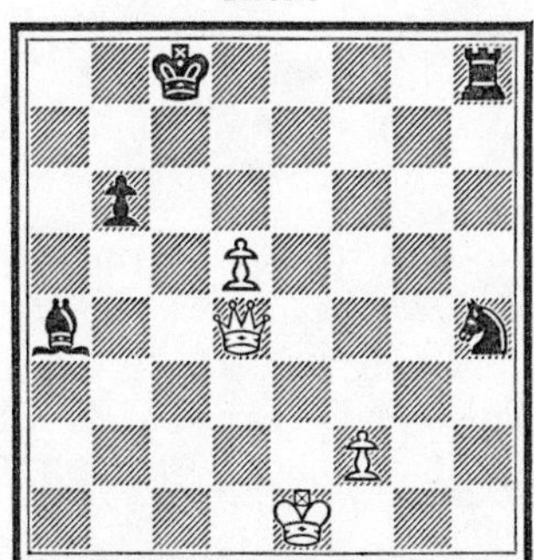

WHITE

DIAGRAM 23

a. Q × B (White Queen takes Black Bishop at QR4).
b. Q × Kt (White Queen takes Black Knight at KR4).
c. Q × P (White Queen takes Black Pawn at QKt6).
d. Q × R (White Queen takes Black Rook at KR8. When this

capture is made, the Black King is then in check. That is, White, to move again, would be able to take that King. Check is indicated by the letters *ch,* and sometimes by a plus sign.

Note that the White Queen cannot move to QR7, for it cannot pass over the Black Pawn on QKt6. For the same reason, it cannot move to KKt1 (Pawn on KB2 blocks the way) or to Q6, 7 or 8 (Pawn on Q5 bars the way).

The Pawn changes its direction of movement when making a capture. It moves forward, but captures diagonally, in a V-like manner. Diagram 24 illustrates the way in which a Pawn can take an enemy Pawn or piece.

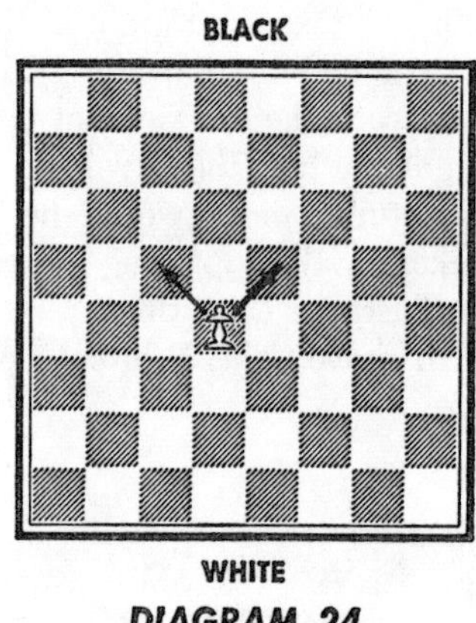

DIAGRAM 24

Diagram 25 further illustrates capturing by the Pawn. White Pawns can make the following captures:

a. P × Q (White Pawn on Q3 can take the Black Queen on QB4. The Queen would be removed from the board and its place taken by the Pawn.)

b. P × P (White Pawn on Q3 can take the Black Pawn on K4).

c. P × Kt (White Pawn on KB4 can take the Black Knight on KKt5).

The Pawn on QB2 cannot make any captures. Neither can the Pawn on K3. If it were Black's turn to move, the only Pawn that could take anything would be the Pawn on Black's K5, which could take the White Pawn on Black's Q6.

DIAGRAM 25

Diagrams 26 and 27 illustrate Queening. White to move in Diagram 26 can play P × R(Q), the Pawn taking the Black Rook and, as in Diagram 27, becoming a White Queen. The Pawn could also become a Rook, Bishop or Knight.

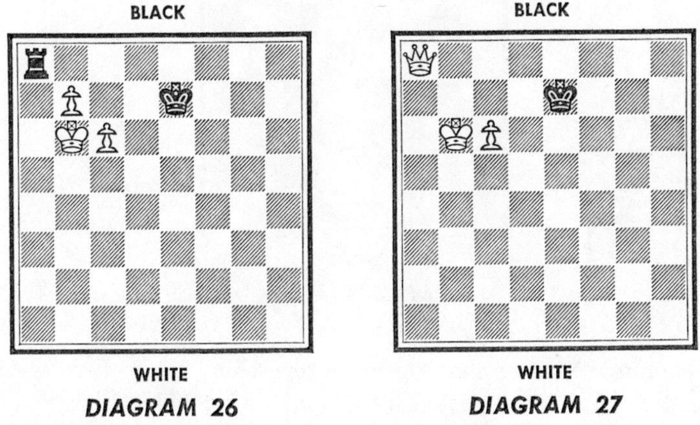

DIAGRAM 26 DIAGRAM 27

Diagrams 28, 29 and 30 illustrate a special move of the Pawn. This move is called capturing *en passant* (in passing), which is usually written *P* × *P e.p.* Diagram 28 shows a White Pawn on its original square. If it were to move one square forward, to Q3, the Black Pawn could take it. In the early years of chess, Pawns were able to move only one square forward. When the rules of chess were changed to permit a Pawn to move two squares forward on its first move, the rule of *en passant* was also adopted.

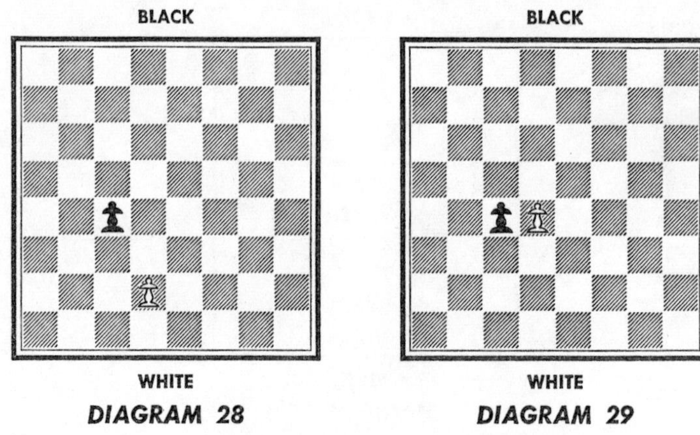

DIAGRAM 28 DIAGRAM 29

DIAGRAM 30

Diagram 29 shows the position after White has moved P—Q4. The White Pawn has passed the Q3 square on which Black would have been able to capture it. Diagram 30 shows what Black can then do. Black has played *P × P e.p.* He has captured the White Pawn as if it had moved only one square.

The <u>En Passant</u> Rule

1. Only Pawns may capture *en passant.*
2. A Pawn on the fifth rank may capture an enemy Pawn on an adjacent file if it makes a double move to its fourth rank. The

capture is made as if the enemy Pawn had moved only one square forward.

3. An *en passant* capture must be made at once. You cannot wait a move or more before capturing *en passant.*
4. Unless it is the only possible move, an *en passant* capture is a voluntary decision—to be made if you wish. Capturing *en passant* is the only exception to the rule that a capturing piece occupies the square of the piece it has captured.

Check

A *check* is a move which attacks the enemy King. The King may not be permitted to remain in check. There are three possible ways of getting out of check, illustrated in Diagram 31.

DIAGRAM 31

1. *Move the King out of Check.* The Black King is attacked by the White Queen. It can move to Q2, K2 or B2 to escape.
2. *Block the Check* by placing (interposing) a piece along the line of attack. The Black Knight can move to B1 to do this.
3. *Capture the Checking Piece.* The Black Knight can take the Queen. Removing the Queen from the board would end the attack on the Black King.

Hints on Getting Out of Check:

1. See if you can capture the checking piece first.
2. You cannot interpose a piece if you are attacked by a Knight or

a Pawn. You must either capture the Knight or Pawn or move your King away.

Checkmate (Mate)

The purpose of the game is to capture the enemy King. This is called *checkmate.* A King is checkmated when it cannot escape from check. That is, it is in check and will be in check again next move no matter what move is made in defense. A checkmate is a check from which a King cannot escape. The diagrams which follow illustrate some of the ways in which checkmate can be effected.

BLACK

WHITE

DIAGRAM 32

1. *Checkmate by attack on the rank.* White to move in Diagram 32 could play R—Q8 mate. The White Rook on Q8 would be attacking the Black King. The King could not move out of check. No Black piece can be interposed. The White Rook cannot be captured. No matter what Black does, his King will be captured on the next move. The game is over, and White has won.

   (The same result would occur if a White Queen were on the Q file instead of the Rook, for Q—Q8 would also be mate.)

   Black to move would checkmate White after R—Kt8. The White King could not move out of check. There is no way in which White can capture the Black Rook. The only possible move would be to interpose the White Rook by playing R—Q1. Black would then play R × R and the White King is mated.

BLACK

WHITE

DIAGRAM 33

2. *Checkmate by attack on the diagonal.* White is mated in the position shown in Diagram 33. The Black Queen attacks the White King. The King cannot escape.
   a. White cannot capture the checking piece.
   b. White cannot block the check by interposing a piece.
   c. The White King cannot move out of check. The only moves possible for the White King are K—Q1 (where the Black Knight would capture it) and K—Q2 (where it will still be taken by the Black Queen).

BLACK

WHITE

DIAGRAM 34

3. *Checkmate with a Knight.* Diagram 34 illustrates what is known as a "smothered mate." The Black King is surrounded by its own

pieces and cannot move. The White Knight's attack on the Black King cannot be opposed in any way. The Knight cannot be captured. No piece can be placed in the way of a Knight check. Black is mated.

4. *Checkmate by a supported piece or Pawn.* Black can win in two ways in Diagram 35.
   a. Black can play P—R7 mate. The Black Pawn on R7 attacks the White King. The King cannot take this Pawn, for it would then be moving into check by the Black Queen. No other piece can capture the Pawn. The King cannot move out of check, for K—B1 is impossible because the Black Bishop on Black's B5 would capture the King.
   b. Black can play Q—R7 mate. White still cannot escape by K—B1. Nor can he capture the Black Queen. To do so would result in capture by the Black Bishop on Black's K4.

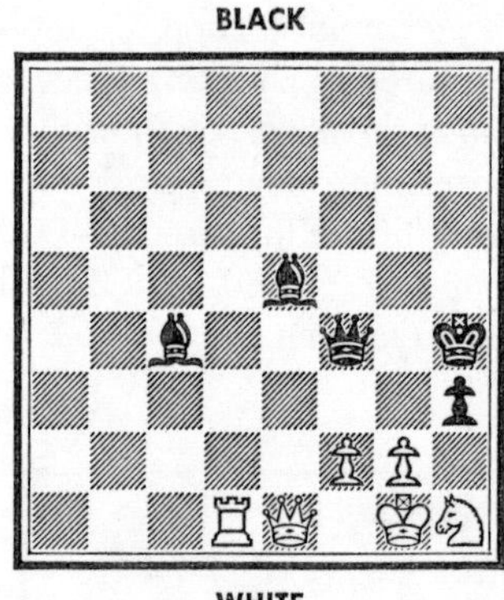

DIAGRAM 35

STALEMATE

There is another kind of mate, which does not lose, but results in a drawn game. A drawn game is one which is won by neither player. This is called *stalemate.*

Stalemate occurs when the player whose turn it is to move cannot make any move without placing his King in check. The King is not in check at the time. Diagram 36 illustrates stalemate.

It is White's turn to move. However, there is no possible move for White.

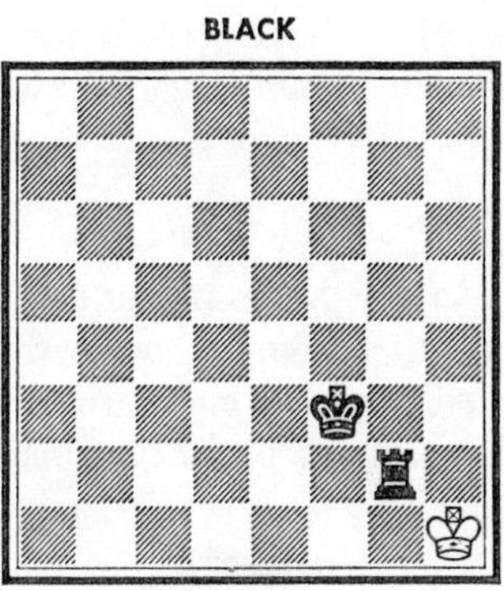

BLACK

WHITE

DIAGRAM 36

a. K × R is impossible because the White King would then be captured by the Black King.

b. K—R2 is impossible because Black would play R × K.

c. K—Kt1 is impossible because Black would play R × K.

White is not in check in the diagrammed position. However, White cannot move without moving into check. The game, therefore, ends in a draw, for White is stalemated. The possibility of stalemate often makes it possible for a player with fewer pieces to prevent his opponent from winning the game. Diagram 37 is based upon a position which arose in a game between American chessmasters Carl Pilnick and Samuel Reshevsky.

BLACK

WHITE

DIAGRAM 37

It is White's move. He plays Q—B2. When Black answers with Q × Q, White is stalemated, and the game is drawn.

Perpetual Checks

Imagine a position in which one player can check the other endlessly. Neither side can then win, for the moves will repeat forever. Such a condition, called *perpetual check*, results in a draw. Diagram 38 illustrates how such a drawn game can occur.

DIAGRAM 38

It is White's turn to move. He is far behind, and is threatened by mate in short order. Were it Black's turn to move, then Q—KKt6 or R—K7 would each lead to mate. But White can save the game by playing Q—Q8*ch.* Black will then have to play K—R2, upon which White can play Q—R5*ch.* Black would then have only one move, K—Kt1. White returns to Q8 and shuttles back and forth between Q8 and QR5. Black cannot escape these checks, and the game is drawn.

How to Use this Book

This book is intended for two kinds of chess players:

1. People who cannot yet play chess and who want to master the basic ideas of chess.
2. People who play the game and want to improve their playing ability.

The book can be used in two different ways:

1. Beginners should play over the games twice. The first time you play the moves, pay special attention to the "Rule to Remember" sections. Study them. Learn them. They will help you to improve your game.

The second time you play over the games, work through the notes carefully. These notes—the comments following the moves—will help you understand why chess masters play the moves they do. These are the moves you will be trying in your own games. It is important for you to know *why* you make any chess move.

2. More experienced players may know the "Rules to Remember" sections. Check them anyway, to refresh your chess knowledge. Pay close attention to the introduction to each game. Try to see the *plan* of the winning player. Make sure you understand the idea behind each chess opening. The games in this book were selected to give you an insight into successful chess ideas.

More experienced players should play through the games and notes. Then select the opening ideas which most interest you. A player who knows a few openings well will do better than someone who knows only a little about many openings. Practice using a few selected openings until you have met many of the situations that occur with them.

This book tries to teach by example. The games included in this book have been selected to provide these examples. Each one has one or more chess lessons to teach. Those lessons are pointed out in the notes and in the "Rule to Remember" sections.

White may choose from 20 possible opening moves. Black then has 20 possible replies. There are thousands of combinations of moves possible after only 2 or 3 moves have been made by each player. Only a small number of these sets of moves are used by chess players. Each set of moves has been given a name—usually that of the player who introduced it into master play, or that of the place in which it was first or most commonly played.

For the games in this book, you will receive the basic information listed below.

1. You will be told the name of the opening.
2. You will be told when and where the game was played.
3. You will be told who played *White* and who played *Black*.
4. In the comments which precede each game, you will be told:
   a. Something about the idea behind the chess opening.

   b. White's plan in the game.
   c. Black's plan in the game.
   d. What the game helps you understand about chess.
5. More than 300 diagrams illustrate the games. Use these to check your positions. If you find a difference between your chessboard and a given diagram, then replay the moves to that point.

How to Use the Quiz Sections

There are four quizzes in this book.

Quiz One (pages 243–46) reviews some of the key tactical ideas in winning chess games. Try it several times: when you have completed the first ten games of the games section, when you complete the 25 games beginning with *1.* P—K4, and when you have completed the book.

Quiz Two (pages 247–48) reviews simple mates. You cannot win chess games unless you understand each idea illustrated by this quiz. Try Quiz Two every week or two until you can recognize these basic mating positions.

Quiz Three (pages 249–52) is a more advanced examination of basic mating ideas. Try it when you feel you have mastered Quiz Two. Check it from time to time to make certain you can recognize the idea illustrated by each of the positions.

Quiz Four is a final test of your chess knowledge. It will tell you how well you understand the ideas presented in this book, and can permit you to rate yourself. Do Quiz Four at any time. By the time you complete this book, your score on the quiz should demonstrate that *Self-taught Chess* has really brought you to the point where you can compete with other players!

Pages 261–70 contain the answers to the Quiz Section, with explanations of the reasons for correct answers.

Part Two

Games Section

1 King's Gambit

Vienna, 1903

White	*Black*
G. Maroczy	M. Tchigorin

The Opening

In the King's Gambit, White offers the KBP. If Black takes it (*1.* P—K4, P—K4; 2. P—KB4, P × P), White tries to develop an attack on the K-side.

White's Plan

In this game, White concentrates on developing his pieces. He uses the open K file and KB file to organize an attack on the Black King.

Black's Plan

Black seems to feel that he can defend himself, and loses valuable time in attacking and taking first one Knight and then the other.

What to Watch for

White, fully developed, uses his open lines to crash through, sacrificing more material in the process.

This is one of the most instructive games ever played, for it illustrates one important chess idea after another. Most significant of these for the beginner is the value of getting your pieces into play!

1.	**P—K4**	**P—K4**
2.	**P—KB4**	**P × P**

White's offer of a Pawn in the opening is called a *gambit*. The King's Gambit is an opening preferred by players who enjoy attack, and who can comprehend complicated positions. When Black takes the Pawn he willingly submits to the coming attack—if he tries to keep the Pawn. In this game, Black takes all he can get—and gets more than he bargained for!

3.	**Kt—KB3**	**P—KKt4**
4.	**B—B4**	**P—Kt5**
5.	**Kt—B3**	

White has been developing his pieces, while Black continues to grasp for material gain. The offer of a piece made by

---

RULE TO REMEMBER

a. Developing the pieces means getting the pieces into play. A piece which moves from its original square to where it can attack the enemy position is said to be *developed. Try to develop your pieces!*

b. Open files are files on which pieces can move freely. An *open* file has no Pawns of your own or your opponent's on it. A *half-open* file has an enemy Pawn on it, but none of your own. *Try to get open files. Try to prevent your opponent from getting them.*

c. A *sacrifice* is an offer of a Pawn or a piece. Usually, the Pawn or piece is given away for a reason—such as gaining time to attack elsewhere, or getting your opponent to move his King to an exposed position. *Do not sacrifice any Pawn or piece unless you have a clear reason for it.*

White in this position is called the *Muzio Gambit*. White's advantage in development is worth the piece.

5.	P × Kt
6. Q × P	P—Q3
7. P—Q4	B—K3

RULE TO REMEMBER

Try to get your pieces into play! White here has 3 pieces in play; Black has none.

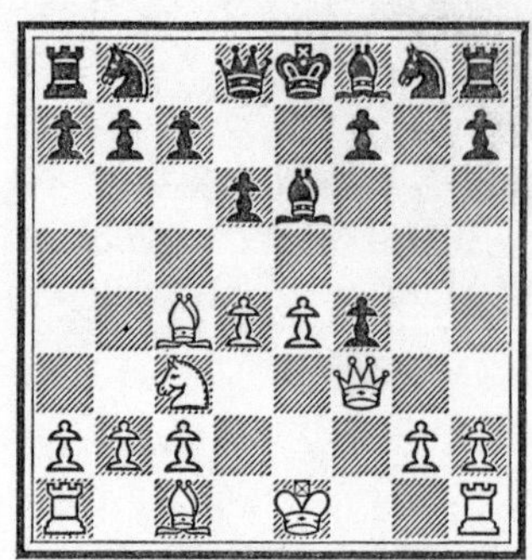

(Look at your chessboard. Do you have this position on it? If so, you understand chess notation, and have been making each move correctly. Otherwise, play through the moves again to reach this position.)

8. Kt—Q5	P—QB3

RULE TO REMEMBER

Black is playing poorly. He should have played a move like . . . . Kt—QB3, to get a piece into play. Try to get your pieces into play!

---

9. O—O

White continues to develop his pieces. Black goes after more material.

9.	P × Kt
10. P × P	B—B4
11. B × P	B—Kt3

RULE TO REMEMBER

Extra material cannot win the game if your opponent's pieces are in play and yours are not. Black has two pieces for a Pawn, but White's pieces are all ready to attack!

12. B—Kt5*ch*	Kt—Q2
13. QR—K1*ch*	

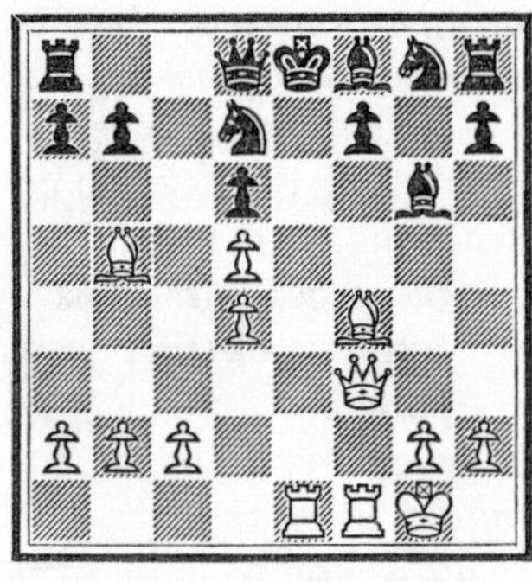

White's development is complete. Every piece will now join in the attack on the enemy King.

13.	B—K2
14. B × P	K—B1 ?

RULE TO REMEMBER

When your King is under attack, try to create an "escape square." Black here should have tried . . . . Q—Kt3. The Queen would then attack both White Bishops. At the same time, the square Q1 would have become available to the Black King.

15. R × B *!*

By taking with the Rook, White is able to keep the pin on the Black Knight with his next move.

15.	Kt × R

RULE TO REMEMBER

A *pin* exists when one piece prevents another piece from moving. The Black Kt is on the same diagonal as the Black King. The White Bishop attacks the Knight. The Knight cannot move away, for White's Bishop would then take the King. The Bishop thus *pins* Black's Knight.

Try to *pin* your opponent's pieces!

***Avoid* the pinning of your own pieces!**

16. R—K1	K—Kt2

Otherwise White will play *17.* B × Kt*ch* and win the Black Queen.

17. B(Q6) × Kt	Q—R4

Black attacks B and R. White's next move defends both, and also threatens B × Kt.

18. Q—K2	Kt—B1
19. B—B6*ch*	K—Kt1

19. . . . . K × B ? would lead to mate in one move by *20.* Q—K5 mate.

RULE TO REMEMBER

Don't be afraid to give away a piece if your opponent's King comes under attack if he takes it. The offer of a Bishop by White's 19th move is called a *sacrifice.*

The ? mark in 19. . . . . K × B ? means it is not the best move. The *!* mark on 22. Q—K7 *!* means it is a very good move.

---

20. **Q—K5** **P—KR3**

Black would lose at once by *20.* . . . . Q × B, because of *21.* B × R and the threat of mate on Kt7 to follow.

An interesting line of play might then be *20.* . . . . Q × B; *21.* B × R, Kt—K3; *22.* P—QB4, Q—R4; *23.* P—QKt4, Q—B2; *24.* P × Kt, Q × Q; *25.* B × Q, P × P; and White's two extra Pawns lead to an easy win.

21. **B × R** **P—B3**

Otherwise it is mate in one on Kt7.

22. **Q—K7** *!*

A final sacrifice.

22. . . . . **K × B**
23. **Q × P*ch*** **K—Kt1**
24. **R—K7** **Resigns**

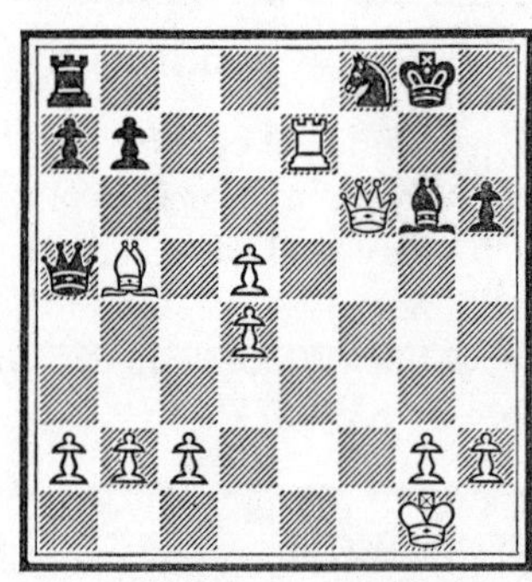

This is the final position of the game. Do you have the same position on your chessboard? If you do, then you are ready to continue with the pages of chess instruction that follow. If not, study the pages in the first section of this book that explain chess notation.

Now let's return to the game. *Why did Black resign?*

Black can do no more than to delay the mate for a few moves. Mate follows on Kt7.

White threatens 25. Q—Kt7 mate. Let's look at what Black can try:

a. If *24.* . . . . B—B2; *25.* Q × B*ch*, K—R1; *26.* Q—Kt7 mate.

b. If *24.* . . . . Kt—K3; *25.* Q × B*ch*, K—R1; *26.* Q—R7 mate.

c. If *24.* . . . . Q—K8*ch*; *25.* R × Q delays the mate for a few moves but cannot save Black's game.

This game won the First Brilliancy Prize in the Vienna Gambit Tournament of 1903. It is an excellent illustration of the dangers faced by Black in the King's Gambit.

2 Falksbeer Counter-Gambit

Mahrisch-Ostrau, 1923

White	*Black*
R. Spielmann	S. Tarrasch

The Opening

White tries to play the King's Gambit. Black replies by offering a gambit in return. This opening, the *Falksbeer Counter-Gambit,* is one of the strongest defenses to the King's Gambit (*1.* P—K4, P—K4; 2. P—KB4, P—Q4). Black gives up a Pawn to gain a grip on the center squares.

White's Plan

In this game, White wins a piece, but at the cost of permitting his opponent to attack.

Black's Plan

Black's offer of a piece on the 8th move was a well-prepared bit of analysis. Tarrasch, long one of the world's greatest chess players, demonstrated again and again the value of planned surprises, such as the one in this game.

What to Watch for

White, although a piece ahead, finds his development cramped. Black succeeds in setting up an attack on the King side.

1.	**P—K4**	**P—K4**
2.	**P—KB4**	**P—Q4**
3.	**P × QP**	**P—K5**
4.	**P—Q3**	**Kt—KB3**
5.	**P × P**	**Kt × KP**

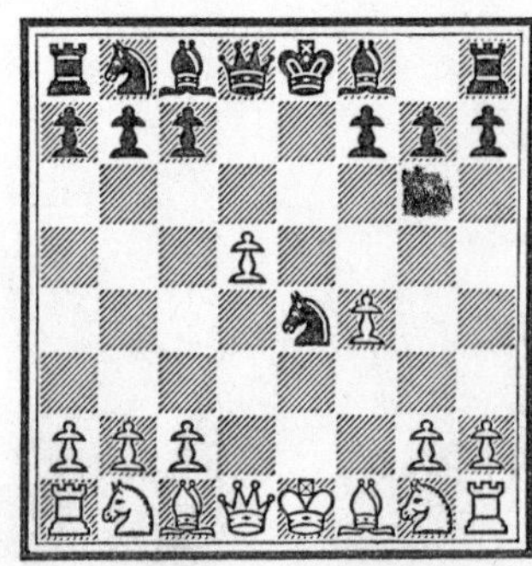

White is a Pawn ahead. Black has a somewhat more solid position, and now threatens to win material by *6.* . . . . Q—R5*ch*, and, if *7.* P—Kt3, Kt × P; *8.* P × Kt, Q × R. This threat is often seen in positions where a player has advanced the KBP.

VALUE OF THE PIECES

A Knight is worth about 3 Pawns.

A Bishop is worth a little more than 3 Pawns.

A Rook is worth about 5 Pawns, or a Bishop plus 2 Pawns, or a Knight plus 2 Pawns.

A Queen is worth a little less than 2 Rooks, or about the same as 3 minor pieces.

(Knights and Bishops are called *minor pieces.*)

---

6. **Kt—KB3** **B—QB4**

Threatening 7. . . . . Kt—B7. White's reply is not best, although it was considered good until the present game. 7. B—B4 would lead to an equal game. If 7. B—B4, Kt—B7; 8. Q—K2*ch,* Q—K2; 9. R—B1.

7. **Q—K2** **B—B4**
8. **P—KKt4** *?*

This move wins a piece, but loses too much time. (Better is Kt—QB3).

8. . . . . **O—O** *! !*
9. **P × B** **R—K1** *!*
10. **B—Kt2**

Black threatens Kt—B7, attacking Q and R simultaneously.

RULE TO REMEMBER

When chess players speak of "time," they mean "moves." A *loss of time* means that you have allowed your opponent to make more moves developing pieces than you have. You have a *gain of time* when you are able to get more pieces into play than your opponent.

---

10. Kt—K5 would not have been enough to prevent this attack, for Black would reply *10.* . . . . Q—R5*ch* and would then win with Kt—B7*ch.* One possible line of play would be: *10.* Kt—K5, Q—R5*ch; 11.* K—Q1, Kt—B7*ch; 12.* K—Q2, Q × P*ch; 13.* K—B3, Q—Kt5 *mate.* Such lightning attacks are common in positions characterized by open lines around the King.

10. . . . . **Kt—B7**
11. **Kt—K5** **Kt × R**
12. **B × Kt** **Kt—Q2** *!*

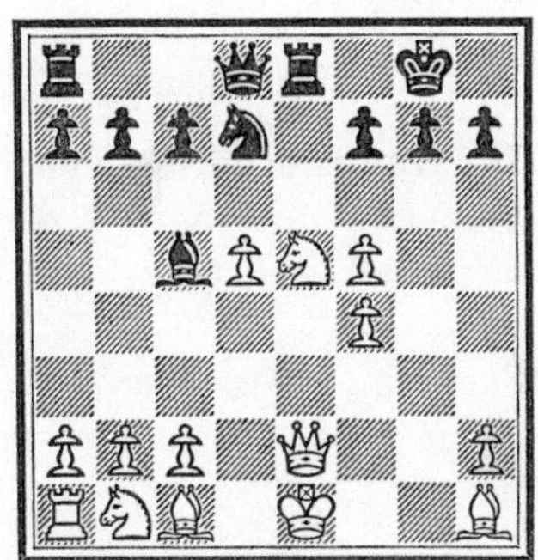

12. . . . . P—KB3, threatening to win the White Knight, would allow *13.* P—Q6 *!* and, if . . . . P × Kt; *14.* Q—B4*ch*, K—R1; *15.* Q × B, to White's advantage.

13. **Kt—QB3**	**P—KB3**
14. **Kt—K4**	**P × Kt**
15. **Kt × B**	**Kt × Kt**
16. **P × P**	**Q—R5*ch***
17. **K—B1**	

17. K—Q1 would allow Black to play *17.* . . . . Q—Q5*ch; 18.* B—Q2, R × P; to Black's advantage.

17.	**R—KB1**
18. **K—Kt1**	

The KBP cannot be defended. If *18.* Q—B3, Q—B5*ch; 19.* K—Kt1, Q × BP; followed by *20.* . . . . R × P.

18.	**Q—Q5*ch***
19. **B—K3**	**Q × KP**
20. **R—K1**	**Kt—Q2**

Black now threatens R(R1)—K1, to again attack White's B.

21. **Q—B4**	**K—R1**
22. **B—K4**	**R(R1)—K1**

RULE TO REMEMBER

The White Bishop is pinned. If it moves away from K4, then Black's Rook will take White's Rook.

When you pin a piece, try to attack it with more than one piece!

23. **B—Q4**	**Q—B5**
24. **R—K2**	

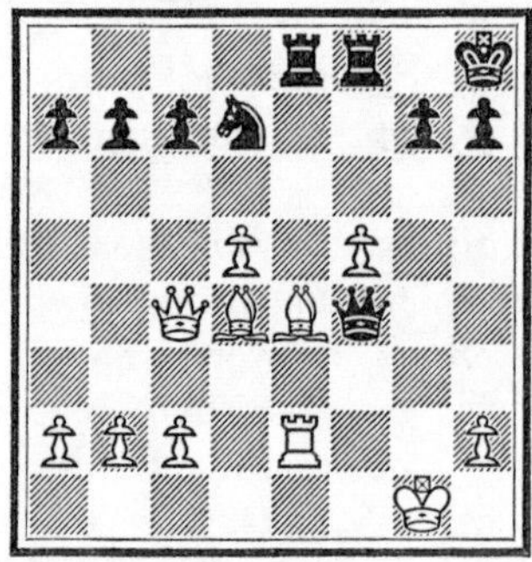

A last gasp trap! If Black plays *24.* . . . . R × B; *25.* R × R, Q × R; then White wins the Queen by *26.* B × P*ch* and *27.* Q × Q.

24.	**Kt—B3**
25. **B × Kt**	**P × B**
26. **P—KR3**	**R—Kt1*ch***

Resigns

If 27. K—R1, Q—B8*ch; 28.* K—R2, Q—Kt8 mate. If *27.* R—Kt2, Q × B. White resigns because he knows that the advantage of a Rook is decisive.

RULE TO REMEMBER

An extra Rook is enough to win. Set up this position:

White King at White's KB3
White Rook at White's QB2
Black King at Black's Q4

White wins by forcing the Black King to the side of the board.

1.	K—B4	K—Q5
2.	R—Q2*ch*	K—B6
3.	K—K3	K—B5
4.	R—Q3	K—B4
5.	R—Q4	K—B3
6.	K—K4	K—B4
7.	K—K5	K—B3
8.	R—Q5	K—B2
9.	R—Q6	K—Kt2
10.	K—Q5	K—B2
11.	K—B5	K—Kt2
12.	R—B6	K—Kt1
13.	K—Kt6	K—R1
14.	R—B8 mate	

Try other positions, and use the same method. An extra Rook should win every time!

3 Kings's Gambit Declined

Manhattan Chess Club, 1959

White	*Black*
M. Finkelstein	P. Brandts

The Opening

The King's Gambit can also result in a quiet positional game. Black can, by *1.* P—K4, P—K4; 2. P—KB4, B—B4, decline the gambit.

White's Plan

In this game, White concentrates on limiting the scope of Black's pieces, and on applying pressure on both sides of the board.

Black's Plan

Black tries to open the game, but is hindered by the limited mobility of his pieces.

What to Watch for

Black permits White to obtain a passed Pawn, which is forced through to Queen.

1.	P—K4	P—K4
2.	P—KB4	B—B4
3.	Kt—KB3	P—Q3
4.	P—Q4	P × P
5.	B—Q3	

A gambit after all! White calculates that the doubled Pawn on the Queen file leaves Black's game cramped.

RULE TO REMEMBER

A *positional game* is one in which the players do not attack until they have developed their pieces. The pieces are usually prepared for action behind the player's Pawns.

An *open game* is one in which the players open lines for quick attack.

A *passed Pawn* is a Pawn which cannot be blocked in its advance by any enemy Pawn. Watch the White *Queen's* Rook Pawn in this game.

5.	. . . .	Kt—QB3
6.	O—O	B—KKt5
7.	P—KR3	B × Kt
8.	Q × B	Q—Q2

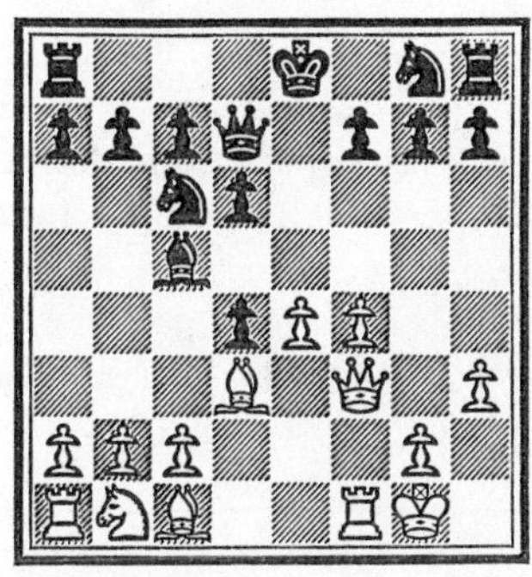

Black must decide where he is to put his King. *8.* . . . . Q—Q2 prepares for Q-side castling, and White shifts the action to the Q-side.

RULE TO REMEMBER

Doubled Pawns exist when a player has two Pawns on the same file. Black has a doubled Pawn on the Queen file in this game.

Try to avoid doubled Pawns!

Try to force your opponent to have doubled Pawns!

---

9. P—R3	P—QR3
10. P—QKt4	B—Kt3
11. Kt—Q2	Kt(Kt1)—K2

RULE TO REMEMBER

When you have castled on one side and your opponent has castled on the other side, try to direct your attack against his King.

---

12. B—Kt2	O—O—O
13. K—R1	P—B4

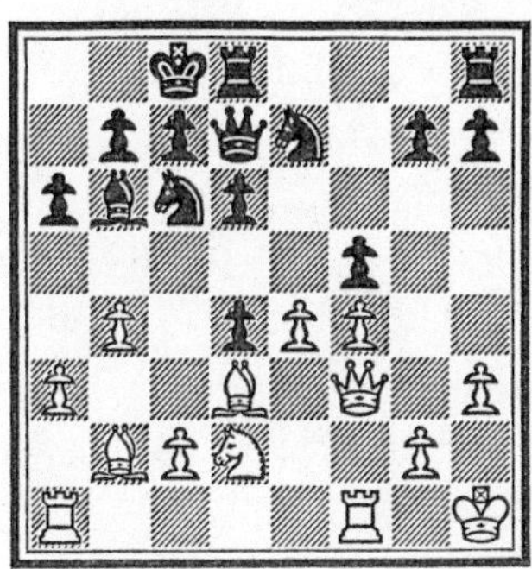

14. P—Kt5	P × KtP
15. B × P(Kt5)	P × P
16. Kt × P	P—Q4
17. Kt—B2	Q—B4
18. P—QR4 *!*	

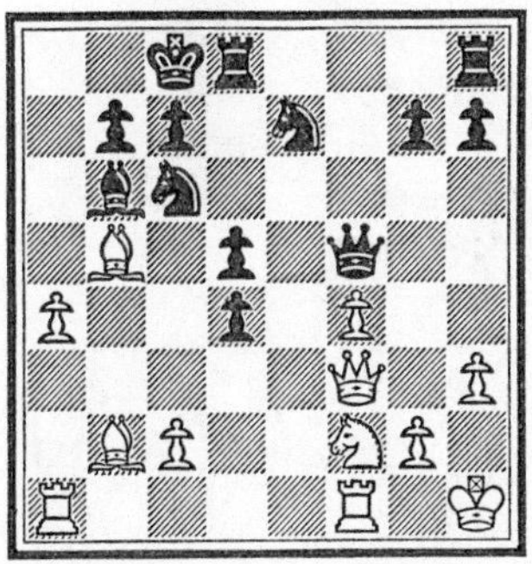

Black could lose his Queen on *18.* . . . . Q × P(B7), because of *19.* Kt—Q3, Q—Q7; *20.* R—B2, Q—K6; *21.* Q—Kt4*ch*, K—Kt1; 22. R—K1. Or, *19.* Kt—Q3, Q—Q7; *20.* R—B2, Q—R4; and the Queen is out of play. The Pawn is not worth taking.

18.	....	Kt—R4
19.	B—R3	Kt(K2)—B3
20.	Kt—Q3	Kt—B5
21.	KR—K1	KR—K1
22.	B × Kt(B6)	P × B
23.	B—Kt4	

White has been permitted to establish a passed Pawn. Black should now play 23. .... R × R*ch; 24.* R × R, B—R4. A passed Pawn should be blocked as soon as possible.

23.	....	R—K6
24.	Q—Kt4	Q × Q
25.	P × Q	R(1)—K1 ?

25. .... R × R*ch; 26.* R × R, B—R4 is still best.

26.	R(K1)—QKt1	R—K7
27.	P—R5	B—R2
28.	B—B5 *!*	B × B
29.	Kt × B	R × BP
30.	P—R6	Kt—Kt3
31.	P—R7 *!*	

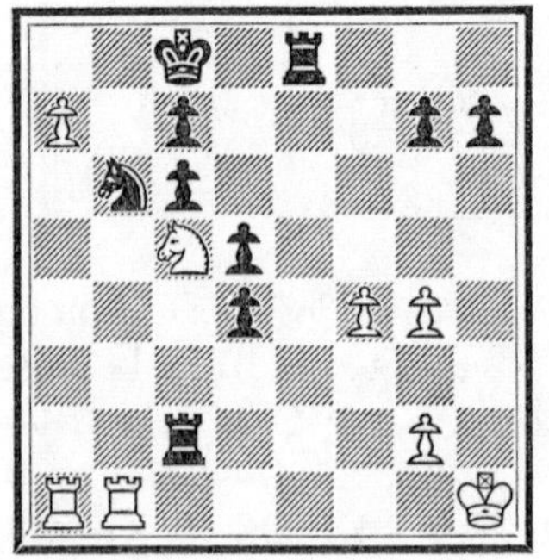

Black cannot prevent the Queening of the Pawn. White

RULE TO REMEMBER

A question mark (?) after a move means it is not the best move.

An exclamation point (!) after a move means it is a very good move.

---

can, therefore, make the two sacrifices which follow:

31.	....	R × Kt
32.	R × Kt *!*	K—Q2

If *32.* .... P × R; *33.* P—R8(Q)*ch* will win.

33.	R—Kt8	R—K7
34.	P—R8(Q)	R(B4)—B7
35.	R—Q8*ch*	Resigns

If *35.* .... K—K2; *36.* R—K8*ch* and *37.* R × R leaves Black a Queen behind without any play.

RULE TO REMEMBER

An extra Queen is enough to win. Set up this position:

White King at White's QR1

White's Queen at White's QR8

Black King at Black's K4

White wins by forcing the Black King to the side of the board. The trick is to place the Queen a Knight's move away from the Black King, and then to parallel the King's moves.

1.	Q—B6	K—B4	*9.*	Q—K3	K—R7
2.	Q—Q6	K—Kt4	*10.*	Q—Kt5	K—R6
3.	Q—K6	K—B5	*11.*	K—Kt2	K—R7
4.	Q—Q5	K—K6	*12.*	K—B2	K—R6
5.	Q—B4	K—B6	*13.*	K—Q2	K—R7
6.	Q—Q4	K—Kt6	*14.*	K—K2	K—R6
7.	Q—K4	K—B7	*15.*	K—B2	K—R7
8.	Q—Q3	K—Kt7	*16.*	Q—R4 mate	

4 Giuoco Piano

Gijon, 1951

White	*Black*
N. Rossolimo	M. Euwe

The Opening

The Giuoco Piano Opening (also called the "Italian Game" or the "Slow Game") has long been popular. It permits the gradual development of the pieces to good squares, and leads to many lines of play in which combinations can occur. It is recommended as a good opening with which to gain experience. After the opening moves *1.* P—K4, P—K4; *2.* Kt—KB3, Kt—QB3; *3.* B—B4, B—B4; White can try to gain control of the center of the board by *4.* P—B3 and *5.* P—Q4.

White's Plan

White in this game was the champion of France. He gives up a Pawn on his 15th move in an attempt to open up a blocked position, and then makes the mistake of opening up a line of attack against his King.

Black's Plan

Black was the chess champion of the world from 1935 to 1937. In this game, he slowly and successfully develops his pieces, taking full advantage of the several inaccuracies in White's play.

The Outcome

The game ends with a fine combination in which two Rooks and a Knight mate in the middle of the chessboard.

RULE TO REMEMBER

A *combination* is a series of forced moves, usually including a sacrifice, leading to a win of material.

A *mating* combination is one which leads to a checkmate.

1.	**P—K4**	**P—K4**
2.	**Kt—KB3**	**Kt—QB3**
3.	**B—B4**	**B—B4**
4.	**P—B3**	**Q—K2**

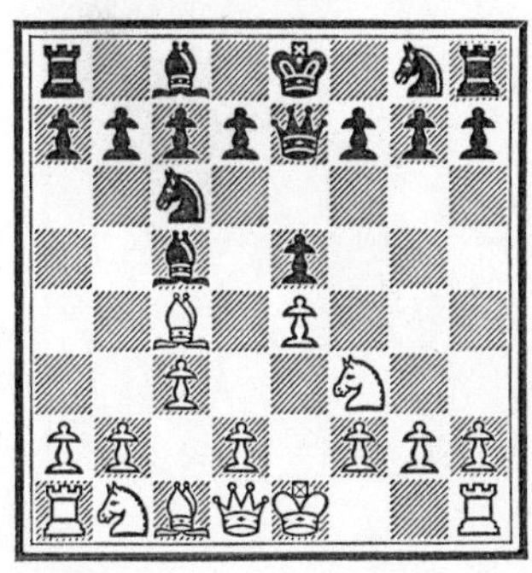

Black plans a closed game. White wants an open game, but is forced to strengthen his position before trying to open up any lines.

5. P—Q4 B—Kt3

RULE TO REMEMBER

The temporary loss of a Pawn in the opening is not to be feared *if*

1. **You gain in development for it—at least two and if possible three moves.**
2. **The Pawn can be regained in the next few moves.**

If Black here plays 5. . . . . P × P, White should play 6. O—O, and if Black tries to hold the extra Pawn by 6. . . . . P × P; 7. Kt × P leaves White fully developed. 6. . . . . Q × P would be a poor move because 7. R—K1 pins and wins the Black Queen.

---

6. O—O P—Q3
7. P—KR3

Played to prevent . . . . B—KKt5, for the White KKt is needed to support the Pawn on Q4.

7. . . . . Kt—B3
8. R—K1 O—O
9. Kt—R3

This Kt is aiming for the square Q5, via B2 and K3.

9. . . . . K—R1 !

Black moves the K off the diagonal so that he can later play . . . . P—KB3, further strengthening his control of his K4 square.

RULE TO REMEMBER

***Control* is an important idea in chess. Black here wants to keep the game closed. He feels that it will remain closed so long as there is a Black Pawn on Black's K4. He therefore protects the square K4 with as many pieces as he can.**

Try to control the square or squares you expect to be important in the game!

---

10. Kt—B2 Kt—Q1

Vacating the B3 square so that the White Knight destined for Q5 can be driven away by a Pawn.

11. P—QKt3 B—K3
12. B—Q3 Kt—Kt1

RULE TO REMEMBER

Discovered Attack: This occurs when you have two pieces on the same rank, file, or diagonal. There is also an enemy piece on the same line.

In the game, White can win a Pawn by *13.* P × P, P × P, *14.* Kt × P. However, the Black Queen and Bishop would then be on the same file as the White Knight. Black could play *14.* . . . . B × RP, and the Queen on Black's K2 would be attacking White's Knight. Discovered attack!

Watch out for discovered attacks before you move a piece onto a line containing two enemy pieces!

13. Kt—K3	P—KB3
14. Kt—Q5	Q—B2*!*

RULE TO REMEMBER

When a piece is attacked by a less valuable piece, it should be moved away. Move it to the square on which it can most easily be brought into play.

In this position, Black attacks White's Kt twice. White defends it once. Black threatens to win a Pawn by *15.* . . . . B × Kt, *16.* P × B, Q × P.

15. P—B4

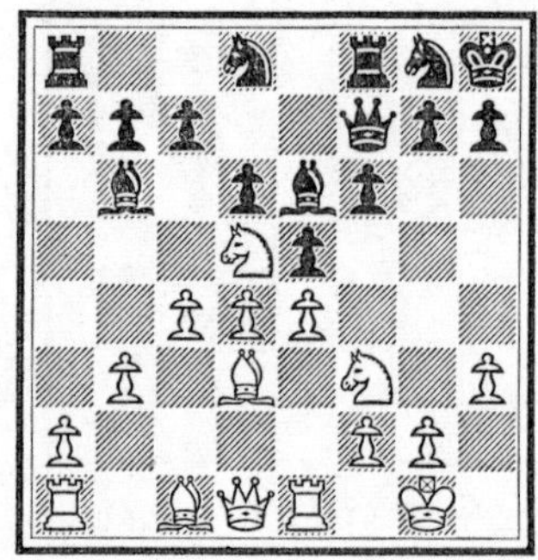

15. Kt × B, RP × Kt; *16.* P—B4 would have been better. White prefers to keep his Kt.

15.	B × QP
16. Kt × B	P × Kt
17. B—B2	P—B3
18. Kt—B4	P—QB4

Black decides to hold on to the Pawn.

19. Q—Q3	P—KKt4*!*

White's last move threatened trouble after *20.* P—K5, when *21.* Q × P mate would become possible (a discovered attack!). Black's *19.* . . . . P—KKt4 enables the Q on KB2 to protect against this mate.

20. Kt—Q5	Kt—B3
21. Q—Kt3	Kt—K4

RULE TO REMEMBER

When you control a square, you may sooner or later be able to occupy it with a piece. The Black Kt on K4 in this game is an example of this idea.

Black now has his extra pawn plus a solid position in the center of the board. Given time, he will be able to break through on the K-side after moves like Kt—K2, R—KKt1, QR—KB1, and then P—B4. White decides to take the initiative at all costs.

RULE TO REMEMBER

To take the initiative **is to make a series of attacking moves.**

To have the initiative **is to be able to make attacking moves.**

---

22. P—KR4

Better is 22. P—B4. As played, White permits the opening of the KKt file without compensation. It is not enough just to attack an advanced pawn. With 22. P—B4, the KB file might have become a line of attack for White.

RULE TO REMEMBER

Knight Forks: **A fork is the attacking of two pieces at the same time. A fork can win material. When one attacked piece moves away, the Knight can take the other pieces.**

If Black could play . . . . Kt—B6*ch*, he would be attacking Q and K at once. The Black Q pins the White Pawn on KKt2. White could not take the Kt. The White K would have to move and Black would then play . . . . Kt × Q.

---

22.	P × P*!*
23. Q × P	Q—Kt3

Now Black gains time by a series of little threats; at present 24. . . . . Kt—B6*ch* would win the White Queen.

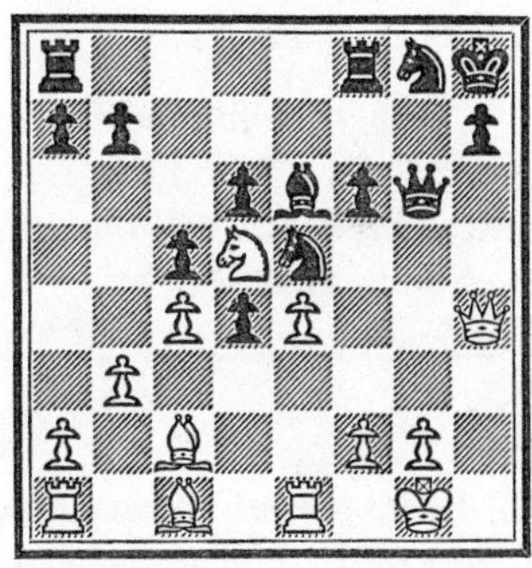

24. K—R1	B × Kt
25. BP × B	Kt—K2
26. P—B4	R—KKt1

Again forcing White to defend; the threat is Q × P mate.

RULE TO REMEMBER

When one of your pieces is attacked, see if you can counterattack before you move the piece away. If White now takes the Kt, he will be mated. The counterattack prevents White from winning the Kt!

---

27. Q—R3	Kt—Kt5

Another threat, this time to win the Queen by . . . . Kt—B7*ch* (a Knight Fork). Note that White hasn't the time to complete his development, or to organize an attack, while each Black move tightens the pressure.

28. **K—Kt1** **Kt × P!**

RULE TO REMEMBER

A Pawn can be pinned just as a piece can. If White here plays P × Kt, then Black will take the B on White's QB2!

---

29. **B—Q3**

29. P—B5 would appear to win a piece, but fails after *29.* . . . . Q—K1. (The White Pawn on K4 is pinned!)

29. . . . . **Kt(Q4)—K6**

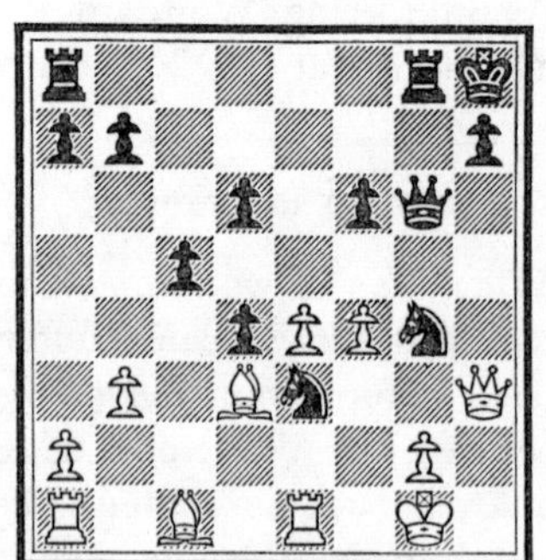

30. **B—Q2**
30. . . . . **Kt—KB7!!**

The Kt must be taken! A beautiful move. (Notice the Knight Fork!)

31. **K × Kt** **Q × P*ch***
32. **Q × Q** **R × Q*ch***
33. **K—B3** **R(R1)—KKt1!**

Black threatens mate in one, and White must prepare an escape for the King.

34. **P—K5**

There is no escape. On *34.* P—B5, R(1)—Kt6*ch*, *35.* K—B4, Kt—Kt5; *36.* B—K2, Kt—K4! wins.

RULE TO REMEMBER

When the enemy King has no possible moves, you can then checkmate it by attacking it. In the position reached in the note to White's 34th move, Black would win by playing . . . . R—Kt5*ch*, and if White played B × R, the other Rook would recapture with mate.

Now Black can mate in two moves.

34. . . . . **R(1)—Kt6*ch***
Resigns

For *35.* K—K4 is followed by *35.* . . . . P—B4 mate or *35.* . . . . P—Q4 mate.

5 Two Knights Defense

Amsterdam, 1922

White	*Black*
M. Euwe	R. Reti

The Opening

The Two Knights Defense is a good way for Black to decline the Giuoco Piano. After the opening moves *1.* P—K4, P—K4; 2. Kt—KB3, Kt—QB3; 3. B—B4, Kt—B3 White can attempt an immediate attack by *4.* Kt—Kt5 or by *4.* P—Q4.

White's Plan

White delays the recapture of a piece in this game, instead spending time in an attack against the Black King.

Black's Plan

Black was one of the great players and teachers of the '20s and early '30s. He finds and executes a mating attack which involves the sacrifice of everything except the two pieces he needs for the mate.

What to Watch for

The game demonstrates how a Queen which invades the 8th Rank can be the cause of disaster—for the reason that it can be attacked by a Rook, while a second piece is attacking the King position.

1. **P—K4**	**P—K4**
2. **Kt—KB3**	**Kt—QB3**
3. **B—B4**	**Kt—B3**
4. **P—Q4**	

If *4.* Kt—Kt5, attacking the Black KBP with B and Kt, Black's best is *4.* . . . . P—Q4; 5. P × P, Kt—QR4; *6.* B—Kt5*ch*, P—B3; 7. P × P, P × P—a gambit line in which Black's superior

---

RULE TO REMEMBER

Opening moves must be planned. You can often give up material in the opening, and regain it quickly. However, you must plan a few moves ahead to get away with this.

---

development gives him an equal game.

4.	**P × P**
5. **O—O**	**Kt × P**
6. **R—K1**	**P—Q4**
7. **B × P**	**Q × B**
8. **Kt—B3**	

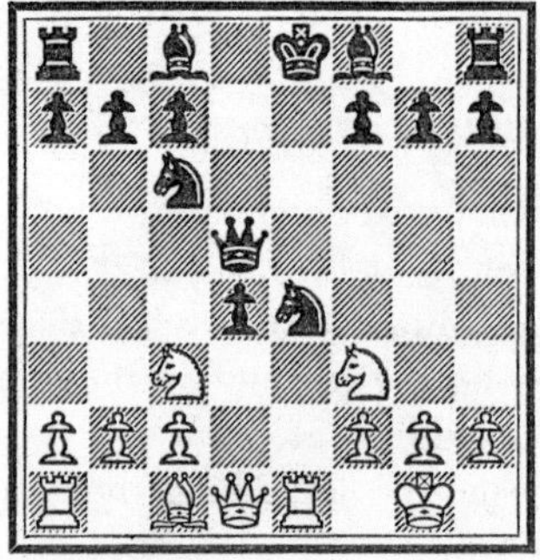

Black cannot play *8.* . . . . P × Kt because of *9.* Q × Q. He moves the Q to a safe corner.

In this position the Black P on Q5 is *pinned.* The White Kt *forks* Black's Q and Kt. White *planned* this when he played his first 7 moves.

8.	**Q—QR4**
9. **Kt × P ?**	

It is best to take the Knight while it is available. Thus, 9. Kt × Kt, B—K3; *10.* Kt(4)—Kt5, O—O—O; *11.* Kt × B, P × Kt; *12.* R × P leads to an even game. Weak for Black would be *9.* Kt × Kt, B—K2?; *10.* B—Kt5, regaining the Pawn and completing White's development.

9.	**Kt × Kt**
10. **Q × Kt**	**P—KB4 !**

The Kt is defended, and Black is temporarily a piece ahead. *11.* P—KB3 is not possible because Black would win the Q by B—QB4 (a pin!). White cannot play *11.* Kt × Kt either, because of *11.* . . . . Q × R mate. He therefore hits at Q8.

11. **B—Kt5**	**Q—B4 !**

The exchange of Queens would leave Black a piece ahead. White is forced to continue an inadequate attack.

12. **Q—Q8*ch***	**K—B2**
13. **Kt × Kt**	**P × Kt**
14. **QR—Q1**	

Necessary to prevent *14.* . . . . Q × P*ch !; 15.* K × Q, B—B4*ch; 16.* K moves, R × Q; after which Black has an easy win with his extra piece. Now the R protects the Q at White's Q8.

14.	**B—Q3 !**

Black sees the attack to come,

RULE TO REMEMBER

An extra piece is usually enough to win. Sometimes an extra Pawn is enough to win.

How? Just exchange pieces until you are left with the extra piece or Pawn(s) ahead. Then force a Pawn through to make another Queen. As we have seen, an extra Queen quickly forces checkmate.

---

and returns some material to put the White Q out of play.

15. **Q × R** **Q × B**

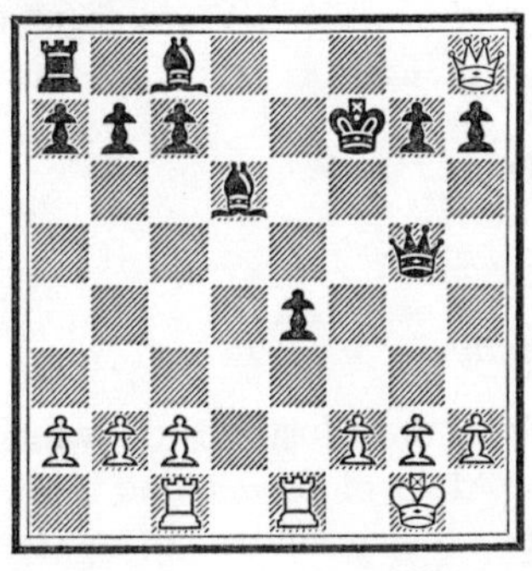

Black now threatens *16.* . . . . B—R6, and White will either be mated by *17.* . . . . Q × P mate or will lose his Queen.

16. **P—KB4**

Black cannot take this Pawn. If *16.* . . . . Q × P; *17.* R—KB1 (a pin!). If *16.* . . . . B × P, *17.* R—Q8. If *16.* . . . . P × P (e.p.); *17.* Q—K8*ch,* K—B3; *18.* Q—Q8*ch,* K—Kt3; *19.* Q × Q*ch,* K × Q; *20.* P × P, and a long ending would follow which Black could probably win. But Reti prefers to play for the mate.

RULE TO REMEMBER

When you have a choice between winning material or mating, always choose the mate! On *21.* K—B1, Black could take the R on White's Q1. However, mate by *21.* . . . . Q—B6 and *22.* . . . . Q—B7 is better!

---

16. . . . . **Q—R5**
17. **R × P** **B—KR6 ! !**

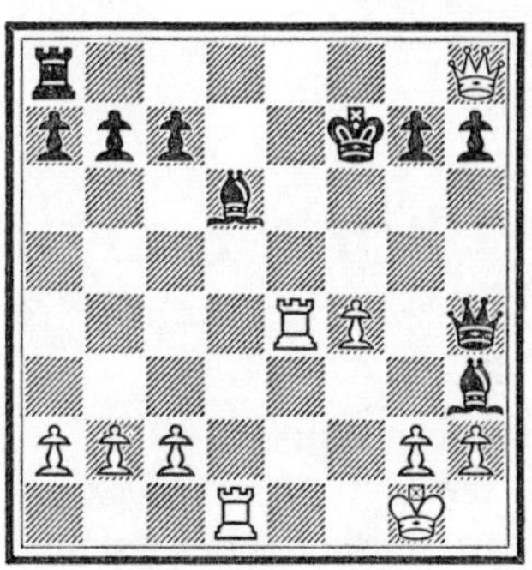

Sacrifices such as this cannot be made unless the moves which are to follow are clearly understood. Black saw everything which follows before giving up the Rook.

18. **Q × R**

There is no other move. If *18.* P—KKt3, Q—R4.

18. . . . . **B—B4*ch***
19. **K—R1**

If *19.* R(either one)—Q4, B × R*ch;* *20.* R × B, Q—K8 mate.

19. . . . . **B × P*ch !***
20. **K × B** **Q—Kt5*ch***
21. **Resigns**

Mate is forced. If *21.* K—R1, Q—B6 mate. If *21.* K—B1, Q—B6*ch;* *22.* K—K1, Q—B7 mate. Another mating idea would have been *20.* . . . . Q—B7*ch;* *21.* K—R3, Q—B6*ch;* *22.* K—R4, B—B7*ch;* *23.* K—Kt5, P—R3*ch;* *24.* K—B5, Q—R4 mate.

6 Four Knights Game

Scheveningen, 1913

White	*Black*
Edward Lasker	F. Englund

The Opening

The Four Knights Game is considered to be a positional opening. After *1.* P—K4, P—K4; 2. Kt—KB3, Kt—QB3; 3. Kt—B3, Kt—B3 the players have equal positions. If both players continue to develop carefully, a drawish position results. When either player breaks the symmetry, as in this game, a sharp struggle results.

White's Plan

White, in this game, concentrates on development, and is able to use it to generate a sudden mating attack.

Black's Plan

Black has a chance to simplify in the early moves, but does not take advantage of it. Instead, he brings his Queen out, is forced to lose time moving it about, and then falls into a trap.

Comment

The game illustrates the value of rapid development, and is one of the few examples in master play of a mate by two Bishops.

1. **P—K4**	**P—K4**
2. **Kt—KB3**	**Kt—QB3**
3. **Kt—B3**	**Kt—B3**
4. **B—Kt5**	**Kt—Q5**
5. **Kt × P**	**Q—K2**
6. **Kt—B3**	

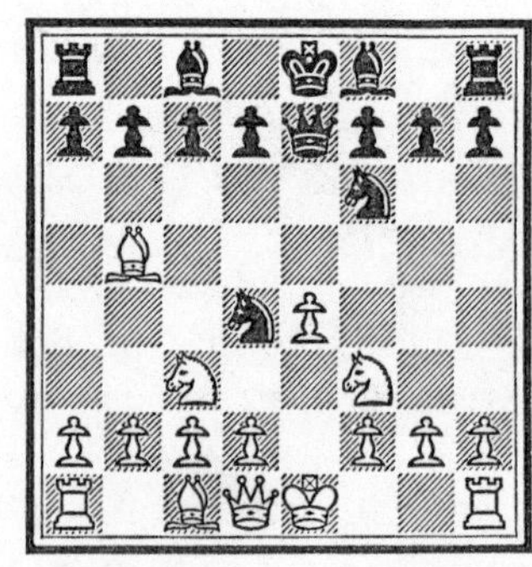

Black can here simplify by *6.* . . . . Kt × B; 7. Kt × Kt, Q × P*ch; 8.* Q—K2, Q × Q*ch; 9.* K × Q, *10.* Kt—Q4, to be followed by *11.* P—QR3. Instead, he gives White time to develop.

6.	Kt × P ?
7. O—O	Kt × Kt
8. QP × Kt	Kt × Kt*ch*

Black could not take the B because of 9. R—K1 winning the Queen (a pin!).

9. Q × Kt	Q—B4
10. R—K1*ch*	B—K2
11. B—Q3	P—Q4
12. B—K3	

The Queen chase begins.

12.	Q—Q3
13. B—KB4	Q—KB3
14. Q × P*!*	

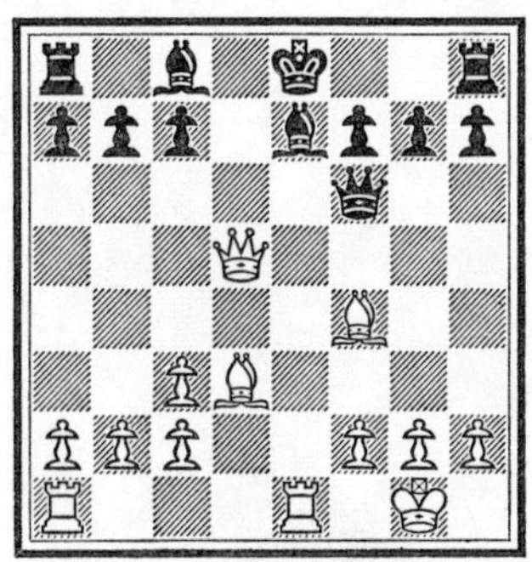

Black cannot take the Bishop. If *14.* . . . . Q × B; *15.* B—Kt5*ch*.

a. If *15.* . . . . K—B1; *16.* Q—Q8*ch!;* B × Q; *17.* R—K8 mate.

b. If *15.* . . . . P—B3; *16.* B × P*ch !*, P × B; *17.* Q × P*ch*, K—B1; *18.* Q × R, and Black will soon lose.

RULE TO REMEMBER

Do not place your Queen in the middle of the board while your opponent's pieces are able to attack it. You will then lose time moving the Queen, while your opponent's pieces move into better positions.

---

14.	P—B3
15. Q—K4	B—K3
16. R—K3	B—QB4
17. B—K5	Q—R3

There is no other square for the Queen. If *17.* . . . . Q—Kt3; *18.* Q—KR4, Q—R3; *19.* Q × Q wins a Rook after *19.* . . . . P × Q, *20.* B × R.

18. R—Kt3	B—KB1
19. R—Q1	

Setting the trap

19.	O—O—O

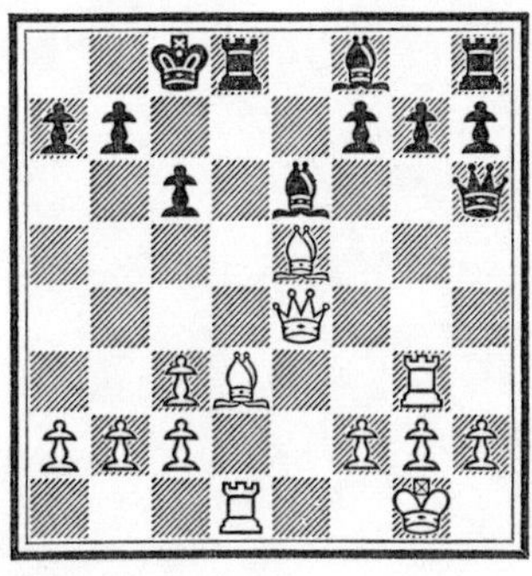

20. Q × P*ch!* P × Q
21. B—R6 mate

RULE TO REMEMBER

Avoid getting your major pieces out of play. Try to keep them in contact with your King position. They will be needed to help defend the King.

7 Ruy Lopez

Moscow, 1951

White	*Black*
E. Geller	P. Keres

The Opening

The Ruy Lopez is the most popular of all regular K—Pawn openings. After *1.* P—K4, P—K4; 2. Kt—KB3, Kt—QB3; White plays *3.* B—Kt5. The resulting position permits endless variation. Black can here play such moves as P—QR3, Kt—B3, B—B4, P—Q3, Kt—Q5 and P—B4—each of which leads to a different style of game. The line of play illustrated by this game is called the Morphy Defense—one of the best replies to White's 3rd move.

White's plan

White, one of Russia's leading players, seeks complications. In the process, he wins a piece at the cost of having a Q and R out of play.

Black's Plan

Black, an Esthonian master who is one of the best grandmasters in the world, also seeks complications. He finds them, and succeeds in winning through a deep positional combination.

Comment

The game is an excellent example of a sustained attack under pressure.

CHESS PLAYERS TO REMEMBER

Paul Morphy, of New Orleans, was America's most gifted player in the 1850s. He was the strongest player in the world, known for the brilliancy of his play and his ability to develop his pieces for quick attack. He retired from chess at the beginning of the Civil War. He introduced the defense for Black used in this game. It is still Black's most popular defense to the Ruy Lopez.

Ruy Lopez was an early Spanish player, best known for his successful use of the opening which bears his name.

---

1. P—K4	P—K4
2. Kt—KB3	Kt—QB3
3. B—Kt5	P—QR3
4. B—R4	

White cannot win the KP. If *4.* B × Kt, QP × B; *5.* Kt × P, Q—Q5. It is best to withdraw the B and maintain the pressure on the Black Knight.

4.	Kt—B3
5. O—O	B—K2

RULE TO REMEMBER

Black cannot win the KP by *5.* . . . . Kt × P because of *6.* R—K1. When Black's Knight moves away, White can play Kt × P.

---

6. R—K1	P—QKt4
7. B—Kt3	P—Q3
8. P—B3	

This prepares for P—Q4 and also provides a square for the B now on Kt3.

8.	O—O
9. P—KR3	

To prevent Black's B—Kt5.

9.	Kt—QR4
10. B—B2	P—B4

RULE TO REMEMBER

***Try to prevent pins!* Moves like P—KR3 prevent a B from pinning the KKt.**

---

11. P—Q4	Q—B2
12. Kt(Kt1)—Q2	

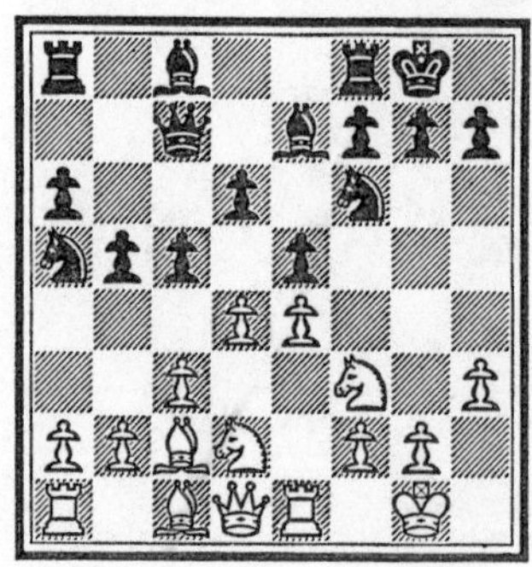

12.	BP × P
13. P × P	B—Kt2
14. Kt—B1	

14. P—Q5 closes the center and relieves the tension. Both players would then have to regroup their pieces in preparation for action on the K side. White prefers to keep the QP where it can influence the center squares (K5, QB5, Q5).

RULE TO REMEMBER

The *center* of the chessboard is a group of 8 squares; they are QB4, QB5, Q4, Q5, K4, K5, KB4, KB5. When you control these squares, or most of them, you can place your pieces in the center of the board. Pieces placed in the center can go to any other part of the board. Attacks can be made with greater ease.

Try to control the center squares!

---

14. . . . .   R(R1)—B1
15. B—Kt1

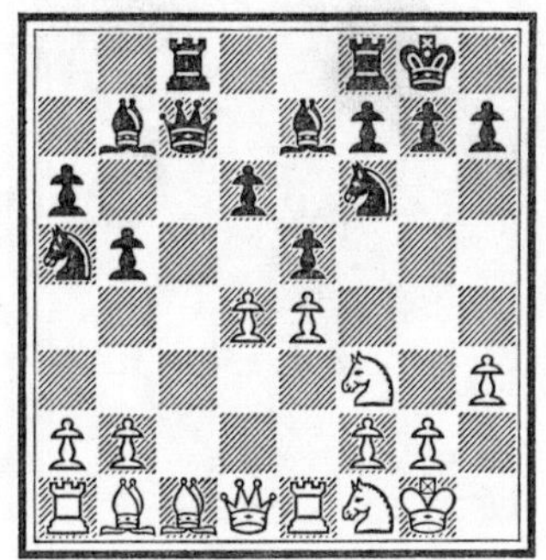

Black threatened *15*. . . . . Q × B. If the B moved to Q3, then *15*. . . . . P—Q4; *16*. P × QP, P —K5; *17*. B × P, Kt × B; *18*. R × Kt, B × P and Black has an easy development. The isolated QP should fall, and, by moves like Q—Kt2, R—B2, KR—B1, Black should develop a Q-side attack.

15. . . . .   P—Q4
16. P × QP   P × QP
17. B—Kt5   P—R3 ?
18. B—R4 ?

White misses a chance for a brilliancy. He could have played *18*. B × P !, P × B; *19*. Q—Q2, and then:

a. *19*. . . . . K—Kt2; *20*. Kt—Kt3.

b. *19*. . . . . Kt × P; 20. Q × RP, P—B4; *21*. R—K6.

c. *19*. . . . . B × P; *20*. Q × RP, B × Kt; *21*. Kt—Kt3 and mate on Kt7 should follow.

RULE TO REMEMBER

An *isolated* Pawn is a Pawn which cannot be protected by another Pawn. Thus, there is no Pawn on an adjacent file.

An isolated Pawn is a weakness because your opponent can place a piece in front of it. You cannot then drive the piece away with a Pawn.

Try to avoid isolated Pawns unless they are passed Pawns!

---

18. . . . .   Kt × P
19. Q—Q3

Threatening mate on R7.

19. . . . .   P—Kt3
20. B—Kt3   B—Q3
21. B × B   Q × B
22. Q—Q2

White attacks the Kt on R5 and the Pawn on KR6. One must fall, and the Black position would crumble. However, Keres has planned well!

22. . . . .   Kt—KB5 ! !

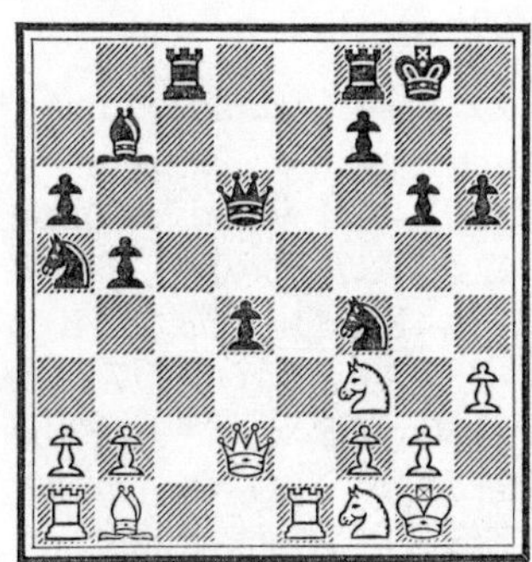

23.	Q × Kt(R5)	B × Kt*!*
24.	P × B	Kt × P*ch*
25.	Kt—Kt2	Kt—B5*ch*
26.	K—Kt1	Kt—R6*ch*
27.	K—Kt2	Kt—B5*ch*

Black has gained some time on his clock by repeating moves.

RULE TO REMEMBER

Master chess is played under time limit rules. The time limit varies from 15 to 20 moves an hour. A special double stop-clock keeps a record of the time consumed by each player. If a player goes overtime (he fails to make the required number of moves in the permitted time), he loses the game. Master players often "gain time" by repeating moves, as in this game.

---

28. **K—Kt1** **Q—Q4**

Black threatens Q—R4, Q—R6 and Q—Kt7 mate, in addition to the immediate Q X BP and Q—Kt7 mate.

29. **Kt—Kt3**

29. B—K4 would permit Q—R4 etc.

29. R—K4 would lose after Q—Kt4*ch*; *30.* Kt—Kt3, R—B8*ch*; *31.* R—K1, Q—R5; *32.* R × R, Q—R6; *33.* any, Q—Kt7 mate.

29. Q—Q2 would lose the Q after *29.* . . . . Q—Kt4*ch*; *30.* Kt—Kt3, Kt—R6*ch*.

29. . . . . **P—Q6*!***

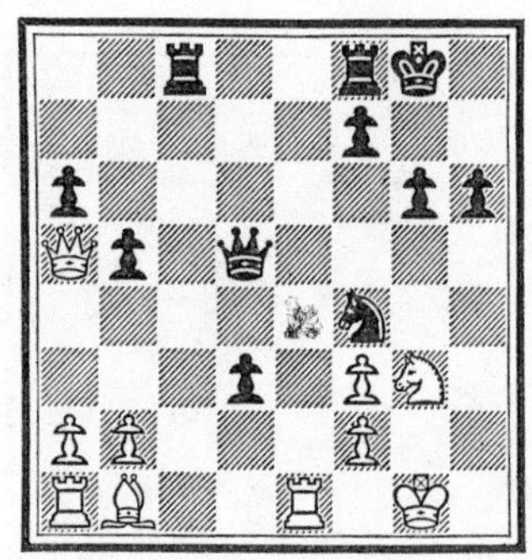

Locking in the White Bishop and Rook.

30. **Kt—K4**

Hoping for Kt—B6*ch* (the Black K and Q would be forked).

30. . . . . **Q—KB4**

Again threatening Q—R6.

31. **Q—Kt4**

A last gasp. If *31.* . . . . Q—R6; *32.* Kt—B6*ch*, K—Kt2; *33.* Q × Kt.

31. . . . . **R(KB1)—K1**
32. **Resigns**

White cannot meet the threat of R × Kt and Q—Kt5*ch* or Q—Kt4*ch*. If *32.* Kt—Kt3, Q—R6; *33.* R × R*ch*, R × R; *34.* Q × Kt, R—K8*ch* and mate next move (*35.* Kt—B1, R × Kt mate).

8 Ruy Lopez

Nottingham, 1936

White	*Black*
Sir George Thomas	J. R. Capablanca

The Opening

In the Ruy Lopez, White can often simplify and move towards the endgame by seeking early exchange. However, you should not try to play endings until you have mastered the principles of endgame play. If your opponent is a better endgame player than you are, he can find and use the slightest advantage.

White's Plan

White plays cautiously in this game. He gives up a Pawn without compensation, and then simplifies to a lost ending. His play shows the disadvantages of playing without a plan.

Black's plan

Black was a former world champion—a Cuban grandmaster who lost fewer games in his chess career than any other player. He wins a Pawn after a White error in the opening. He then turns the extra Pawn into a winning advantage through exchanges of material.

Comment

The game is an important illustration of endgame play with the Rook.

1. P—K4	P—K4
2. Kt—KB3	Kt—QB3
3. B—Kt5	P—QR3
4. B—R4	P—Q3
5. B × Kt*ch*	P × B

RULE TO REMEMBER

***Opening Trap:* An opening trap is a plan to win material by making moves which allow your opponent to make a mistake. If White had made the mistake of playing 5. P—Q4, then one of the oldest opening traps could have occurred. It is called the Noah's Ark Trap.**

Noah's Ark Trap

_1._ P—K4, P—K4; 2. Kt—KB3, Kt—QB3, _3._ B—Kt5, P—QR3; _4._ B—R4, P—Q3; _5._ P—Q4?, P—QKt4; _6._ B—Kt3, Kt × P !; _7._ Kt × Kt, P × Kt; _8._ Q × P, P—QB4 _!; 9._ Q—Q5 (threatening Q × R or Q × BP mate), B—K3; _10._ Q—B6_ch_, B—Q2; _11._ Q—Q5, P—B5. Black wins the B for 2 P's.

---

6. **P—Q4** **P—B3**

Black realizes the importance of keeping a Pawn on K4, where it can become the basis for later play on Q5, K5 and KB5.

7. **B—K3**

White fears that Black will play 7. . . . . P—Kt3 and 8. . . . . B—Kt2, with pressure against the center. In reply, he wishes to play 8. Q—Q2, setting up a double attack on the KR6 square. Thus, if both sides played these moves, Black would be unable to play 9. . . . . Kt—K2 intending *10.* . . . . O—O, for White would play 9. B—R6 to remove the Black Bishop on Kt2. In view of this threat, Capablanca decides to develop in a different way.

7. . . . . **Kt—K2**
8. **Kt—B3** **Kt—Kt3**

Keeping in mind the possibility of . . . . Kt—B5 at some later stage of the game as well as a possible . . . . Kt—K4.

9. **Q—Q2** **B—K3**

Black wants to play . . . . P—Q4, and prepares for it with this move.

10. **P—QKt3 ?**

White permits Black to play P—Q4, giving away control of the center. *10.* R—Q1 would have been better, so that *10.* . . . . P—Q4 would be answered by *11.* P × KP, P × P(K4), *12.* P × P, P × P; *13.* Kt × QP, winning a P.

10. . . . . **P—Q4 *!***

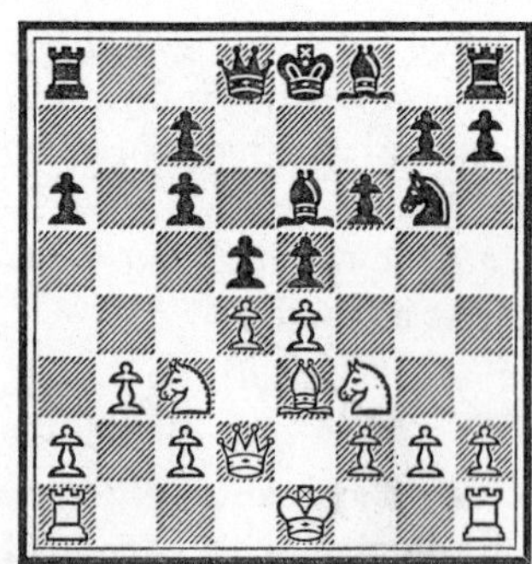

11. **O—O ?**

This move will lose a Pawn. Better would have been *11.* P × QP, BP × P; *12.* P × P, P × P; *13.* Kt—QR4, P—K5; *14.* Kt—Q4, B—Q2; *15.* B—Kt5, although Black would still have the better game.

11. . . . . QP × P
12. Kt(QB3) × P B—Q4
13. Kt—Kt3

White cannot protect the Knight by *13.* Q—Q3 because of *13.* . . . . P—KB4 and *14.* . . . . P—K5.

13. . . . . B × Kt
14. P × B Kt—R5*!*

With this move Black must win a Pawn. The Knight threatens Kt × P*ch* with an attack on the Queen. If *15.* Q—K2 or Q1, then Black plays Q—Q4. The continuation then might be:

15. Q—K2, Q—Q4; *16.* Kt—K4, Q—K3; *17.* KR—Q1, Q—R6; *18.* Q—B1, Kt × P*ch; 19.* K—R1, Q × P mate.

15. Q—Q3 Kt × P*ch*
16. K—R1 Kt × QP
17. Q—K4 Q—Q4

The remainder of the game demonstrates how to win when a Pawn ahead.

RULE TO REMEMBER

When you are a Pawn or more ahead, you can usually win by equal exchanges of pieces.

Exchange when you are ahead! This makes your advantage in material more important.

Avoid exchanges when you are behind!

RULE TO REMEMBER

Use your King as a fighting piece in the endgame. There are only a few pieces left in an ending. There is less danger that your King will be checkmated. When Black plays *21.* . . . . K—B2 in this game, the K is protecting the Pawn on KKt2 and also preparing to come into the center later on.

18. Q × Q P × Q
19. B × Kt P × B
20. QR—Q1 B—B4

White will win one Pawn back in any event. Black prefers to bring his Bishop out rather than to play *20.* . . . . P—QB4.

21. Kt—B5 K—B2

RULE TO REMEMBER

Place your Rooks on open files in the endgame. This gives them full scope. It permits them to move into the enemy position.

22. Kt × QP	KR—K1
23. P—QB3	R—K4
24. R—Q3	QR—K1

RULE TO REMEMBER

***Double your Rooks!* When two Rooks are so placed that one protects and supports the other, we say that they are "doubled." Doubled Rooks are one of the most powerful tools of the successful player!**

Black has completed his preparations for the breakthrough. White's only chance would be to counter the pressure on the open file, perhaps by K—Kt2—B3 and R—K3. Instead, he wastes another move and weakens his Q-side Pawns.

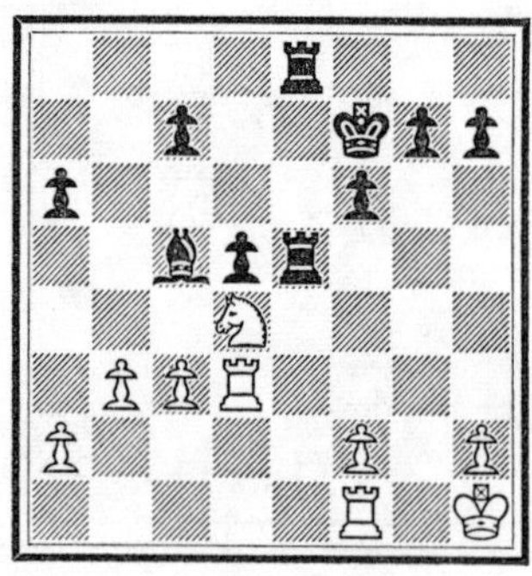

25. P—QR4	B × Kt
26. R × B	

White keeps his Pawns together. If *26.* P × B, R—K8 and, after the exchange of Rooks, Black brings his King in to attack the Q-side Pawns.

26.	P—QB4
27. R—Q2	R—QKt1
28. R—QKt1	P—QR4

Now the White Rook must remain on the Kt file to protect the Pawn on QKt3.

RULE TO REMEMBER

***The Backward Pawn.* A backward Pawn is one that is not supported by another Pawn and, like the White Pawn on QKt3 in this game, cannot advance without being lost.**

***Avoid* backward Pawns!**

***Attack* the backward Pawns of your opponent!**

29. K—Kt2	K—K3
30. R—B2	K—Q3
31. P—B3	P—Kt4
32. K—Kt3	P—R4

Black now threatens *33.* . . . . P—B4, and then *34.* . . . . R—K6 and *35.* . . . . P—Kt5.

33. P—R4 P × P*ch*
34. K × P R—K6
35. K—Kt3

Both White Rooks are pinned down to the defense of the Q-side Pawns.

35. . . . . P—B5 *!*
36. P—Kt4 P × P
37. P × P

If *37.* R × P, R × P *!* wins a Pawn.

37. . . . . R—Kt6
38. Resigns

Black wins the QKtP. White can try *38.* R—Q1, R(Kt1) × P; *39.* R(2)—Q2, R—Q6; *40.* R × R, P × R; *41.* R × P, R × P, after which Black's extra Pawns will win.

RULE TO REMEMBER

Set up the position after the final note of this game. How does Black win?

1. He advances his RP to R5. White must play his K to R3 to prevent the further advance of the Black RP.

2. He then advances his K to B4 and B5. Then he pushes the QP forward.

3. The Black QP will become a Queen, which makes the win easy. Otherwise, White will have to give up his Rook for the QP. Then Black will be a Rook ahead—an easy win.

---

9 Ruy Lopez

Moscow, 1956

White	*Black*
D. Bronstein	B. Sliva

The Opening

In recent years attempts have been made to use the Ruy Lopez as an attacking opening—one in which White can develop quickly and open lines for attack. In such approaches to the opening, White plays P—Q4 as soon as possible.

White's Plan

White, in this game, is one of Russia's strongest players, who once played a tie match for the world's championship. His opening plan is to plant a Pawn on Q4, to develop fully, and then to break through on the K or Q side.

Black's Plan

Black also develops quickly, but makes the mistake of opening up his K-side.

Comment

The game features an extended attack on the Black King position, in which Black repeatedly finds a defense but finally succumbs.

1.	**P—K4**	**P—K4**
2.	**Kt—KB3**	**Kt—QB3**
3.	**B—Kt5**	**P—QR3**
4.	**B—R4**	**P—Q3**
5.	**P—B3**	**B—Q2**
6.	**P—Q4**	**B—K2**

Black wants to hold control of K4, and plans to place his B on KB3.

7.	**O—O**	**B—B3**
8.	**B—K3**	**Kt(Kt1)—K2**
9.	**Kt(Kt1)—Q2**	**O—O**

RULE TO REMEMBER

The Exchange: **When you win a Rook for either a Bishop or a Knight, you gain an advantage. This advantage is called *the exchange.* (*See move 15.*)**

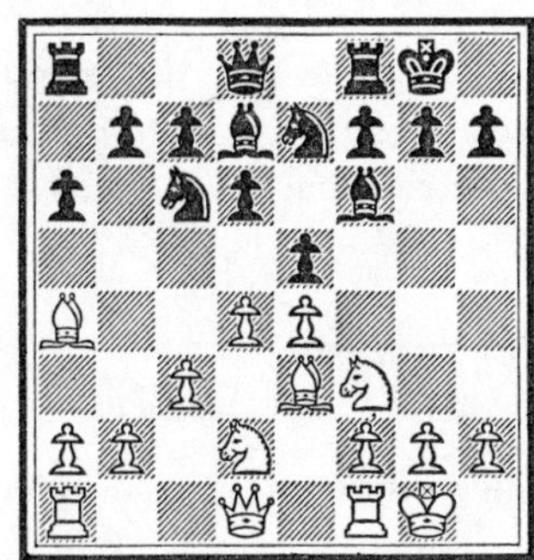

10. **P—QR3** **Kt—Kt3**
11. **P—QKt4** **R—K1**
12. **B—B2** **P—R3**
13. **Kt—Kt3**

White is fully developed and ready to attack on either wing. For example, *14.* P—Q5, followed by P—B4 and P—B5. Or, on the K-side, *14.* Q—Q2, followed by Kt—K1, Kt—Q3 and P—KB4. Black decides to block the K-side.

13. **. . . .** **B—Kt4**
14. **Kt × B** **P × Kt**
15. **P—KKt3** ***!***

White invites *15.* . . . . B—R6, to which he will reply *16.* Q—R5*!*, B × R; *16.* R × B, and the attack will be worth the exchange. Black's Pawn on Kt4 will fall, and White would then play P—KB4 to open up the K-side.

15. **. . . .** **P—B3**

15. . . . . B—R6, despite its dangers, was preferable. *15.* . . . . P—B3*?* opens the diagonal for attack against the King.

16. **Q—R5** ***!*** **Kt(B3)—K2**

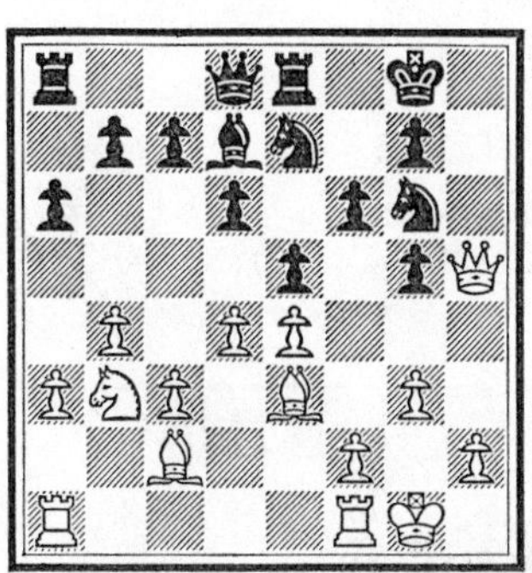

17. **Kt—B5** ***! !***

White takes immediate advantage of the open diagonal. Black cannot take this Knight, for:

a. 17. . . . . P × Kt; *18.* B—Kt3*ch*, K—B1; *19.* P × KP, P × P(K4); *20.* B × BP, and Black cannot prevent mate after *21.* Q × Kt.

b. 17. . . . . P × Kt; *18.* B—Kt3*ch*, P—B5; *19.* B × P*ch*, K—

RULE TO REMEMBER

When material is even, and you are under attack, try to exchange pieces. Usually, it is easier to defend when there are fewer pieces on each side.

That is what Black tries to do in this game. Unfortunately, his position was too vulnerable for this "simplification" to succeed.

B1; *20.* P × P, B—Kt4; *21.* B—R2, P—Kt3; *22.* P × P, P × P; *23.* Q—R6 mate.

17.	**B—B3**
18. **B—Kt3*ch***	**P—Q4!**
19. **R(R1)—Q1**	**P—Kt3**
20. **Kt—Q3**	**KP × P**
21. **B × P(Q4)**	**K—B2**

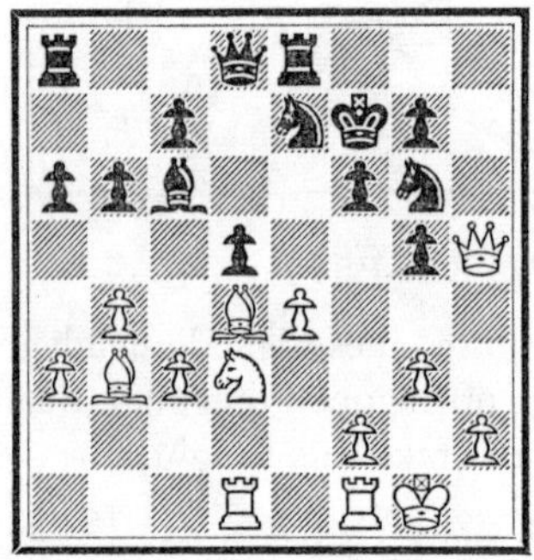

Black has blocked the attack but a new one awaits as soon as White can regroup the pieces.

22. **P—KB4**	**R—R1**
23. **Q—K2**	**P × BP**
24. **Kt × P**	**Kt × Kt**
25. **R × Kt**	**Q—QB1**

Black hopes for a counter-attack after *26.* . . . . Q—R6. But White smashes through before Black can do this.

26. **P × P**	**B × P**
27. **B × P (B6)!**	

Threatening mate by *28.* Q × Kt*ch*, K—Kt3; *29.* Q × P*ch*, K—R4; *30.* Q—Kt5 mate. Black hasn't enough time to defend himself against this threat and still counter the pressure on the QR2—KKt8 diagonal.

27.	**P × B**

RULE TO REMEMBER

Place your pieces on open lines when possible! White's sacrifice of the B on KB6 opened up a discovered attack by the Rook on Q1. Now White will take the B on his Q5.

---

28. **R× B!**	**Kt × R**
29. **B × Kt*ch***	**Resigns**

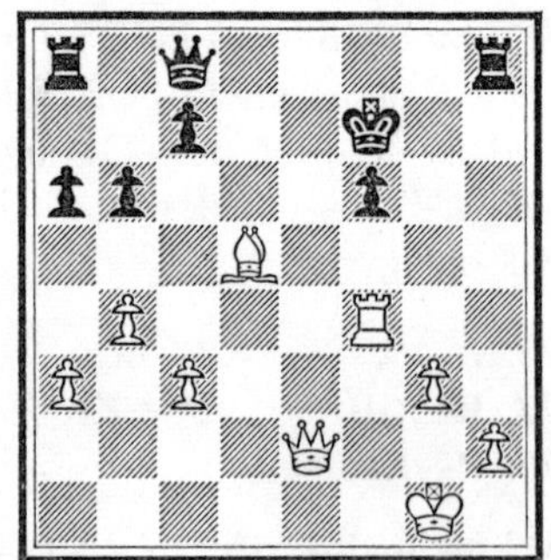

Mate cannot be avoided.

a. *29.* . . . . K—B1; *30.* R × P*ch*, K—Kt2; *31.* Q—K7 mate.

b. *29.* . . . . K—Kt2; *30.* Q—K7*ch*, K—Kt3 or R6; *31.* Q × P*ch* and *32.* R—R4 mate.

c. *29.* . . . . K—Kt3; *30.* Q—K4*ch*, P—B4; *31.* R—Kt4*ch*, K—B3; *32.* Q—Q4*ch*, K—K2; *33.* R—Kt7*ch*, K—K1; *34.* B—B6*ch*,

Q—Q2; *35.* B × Q*ch,* K—Q1 or B1; *36.* Q—B6 mate.

d. 29. . . . . K—Kt3; *30.* Q—K4*ch,* K—Kt2; *31.* Q—K7*ch* and *32.* Q × P*ch* etc. . . . . . .

It is important for students of chess to work out the probable lines of play whenever reaching such points of resignation as that in this game. For example, how does White mate if in note (c) above, White plays 35. Q × Qch and Black then plays K—B1?

10 Ruy Lopez

Zurich, 1959

White	*Black*
R. Fischer	P. Keres

The Opening

This game is longer than most modern tournament encounters. Black makes a minor error, and White sinks his teeth into the position. The closed positional Ruy Lopez means constant tension, in which each player must beware of several threats at once.

White's Plan

White is the incredible Bobby Fischer, a sixteen-year-old grand-master when this game was played, and world champion thirteen years later. He plays to open his opponent's King-side and, when he wins a Pawn, moves into a difficult ending, requiring very exact play.

Black's Plan

Black, one of the world's great attacking players, is human, and makes a few second-best moves in this game. He then tries to play for a draw.

Comment

The game demonstrates how to win a Bishop and Pawn ending. The finish is especially instructive.

1.	P—K4	P—K4
2.	Kt—KB3	Kt—QB3
3.	B—Kt5	P—QR3
4.	B—R4	Kt—B3
5.	O—O	B—K2
6.	R—K1	P—QKt4
7.	B—Kt3	O—O
8.	P—B3	P—Q3
9.	P—KR3	Kt—QR4
10.	B—B2	P—B4
11.	P—Q4	Q—B2
12.	Kt(Kt1)—Q2	BP × P
13.	P × P	B—Kt2
14.	Kt—B1	R(R1)—B1

To this point, both players are following the game between Geller and Keres (Number 7 in this book). This line is one of the most commonly played in the Ruy Lopez. But Fischer, unlike Geller, does not lock in his QR.

15. B—Q3

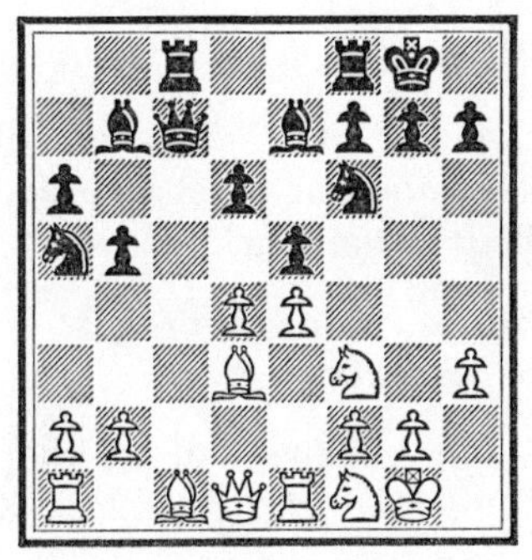

15. . . . . Kt—B3 ?

The first of the second-best moves. *15.* . . . . P—Q4; *16.* P × QP, P—K5; *17.* B × P, Kt × B; *18.* R × Kt, B × P; *19.* R—K1, B—KB3; *20.* B—K3, KR—Q1 would regain the QP or *15.* . . . . P—Q4; *16.* P × KP, Kt × P; *17.* Kt—Kt3, P—B4; *18.* P × P e.p., B × P; *19.* Kt × Kt, P × Kt; *20.* B × P, KR—Q1 would give Black an attack well worth the Pawn.

16. Kt—Kt3 *!* R(KB1)—K1

If Black goes after the QP by . . . . P × QP, then *17.* Kt—B5, and, if *17.* . . . . P—Q4; *18.* P × P, Kt × P; *19.* Kt × B*ch*, Kt(Q4) × Kt; *20.* B × P*ch !*, K × B; *21.* Kt—Kt5*ch*, K—Kt3; *22.* Q—Kt4, P—B4; *23.* Q—R4, R—KR1; *24.* R—K6 mate!

17. Kt—B5 B—B1
18. B—Kt5 Kt—Q2
19. R—QB1

White has mobilized his strength on the K-side. Here he threatens *20.* P—Q5 to win a piece, and forces Black's Queen further away from the K side.

19. . . . . Q—Kt1
20. B—Kt1

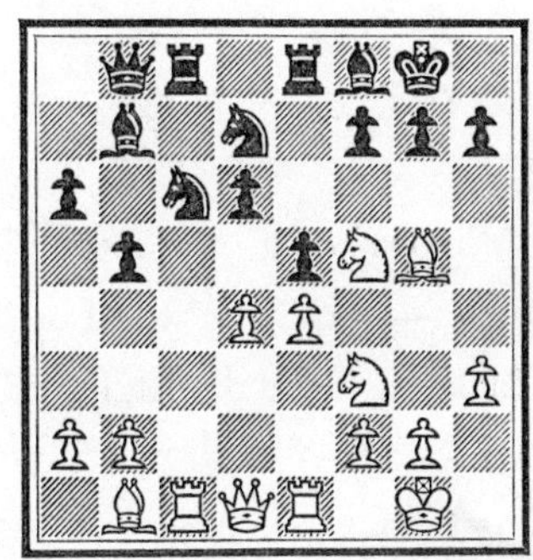

White's control of the board is becoming menacing, and Black decides to exchange a few pieces before White can begin action on the K-side.

RULE TO REMEMBER

A *brilliancy* is the word applied to a move which is correct, unexpected, and which leads to a definite advantage. Most often, a brilliancy is some kind of sacrifice, or the beginning of a combination of moves involving a sacrifice.

---

20.		**Kt × P**
21. **Kt(B3) × Kt**		**R × R**
22. **B × R**		**P × Kt**

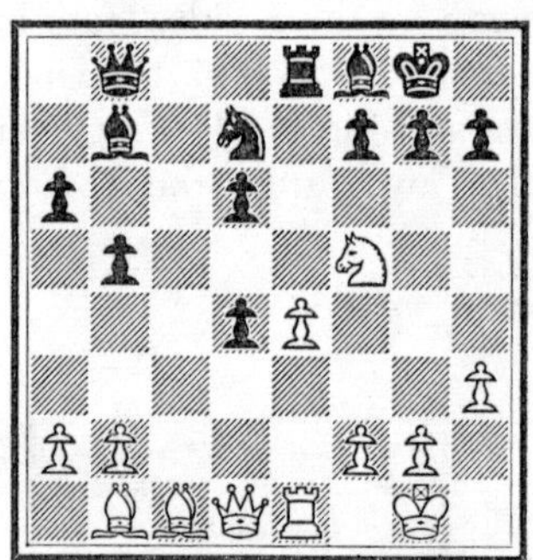

But White finds a brilliancy!

23. **Kt—R6*ch*!**	**P × Kt**

Black must take the Kt, for 23. . . . . K—R1 would allow *24.* Kt × P*ch*.

24. **Q—Kt4*ch***	**K—R1**
25. **Q × Kt**	**B—Q4**

Black makes a quick defense of the K position.

26. **Q—B5**	**R—K4**
27. **Q—B3**	**P—B4*!***

A strong counter. Note that Black's Bishop still cannot be taken because of . . . . R × R*ch*.

28. **B—B4**	**R—K1**
29. **Q—R5**	**B × KP**
30. **P—B3*!***	**B—B3**
31. **R—QB1*!***	

Avoiding the exchange of Rooks, attacking the Bishop, and still attacking Black's Pawns.

31.	**B—Q2**
32. **B × RP*!***	

White eliminates the Bishop that best protects the Black K position.

32.	**R—K3**
33. **B × B**	**Q × B**

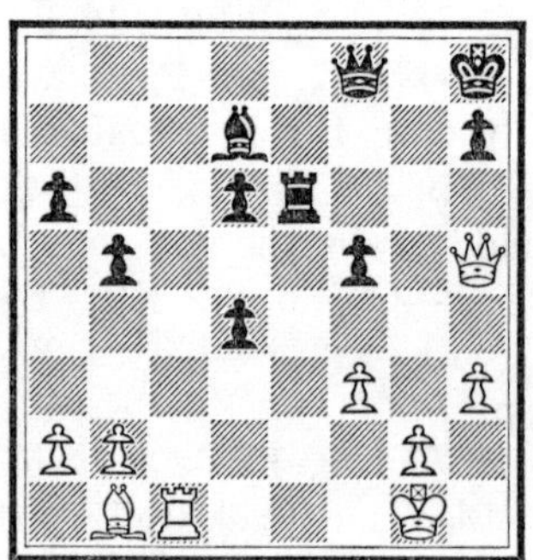

34. **Q—R4**

Black's BP could not be taken.

a. 34. B × P, R—R3*!* (Discovered attack!)

b. 34. Q × BP, R—K8*ch* (Discovered attack!)

34.	**Q—B3**
35. **Q × Q*ch***	**R × Q**
36. **K—B2**	

RULE TO REMEMBER

Look for pins in every position! The White Pawn on K4 is pinned. On White's *26.* P × B, Black wins by *26.* . . . . R × R*ch*; *27.* K—R2, R × B.

White's plan is now to pick off the badly placed Black Pawns; Black will try to steer to a drawable ending. *36.* R—B7 is tempting, but fails against *36.* . . . . R—B2; *37.* B × P, R × B; *38.* R × B, R—Q4 *!*; *39.* K—B1, P—Q6; *40.* K—K1, R—K4*ch !*; *41.* K—Q2, R—K7*ch*; *42.* K × P, R × KKtP, when Black rather than White will have winning chances.

36. . . . . K—Kt2
37. **R—B7** **R—B2**
38. **K—K2** **P—B5**

So that, if 39. K—Q3 ?, B—B4*ch*. Black feels that he can hold the position if he can get his K to the center before White does.

39. **R—R7** **K—B3**
40. **R × P** **R—K2*ch***
41. **K—B2**

The King's future is on the K-side.

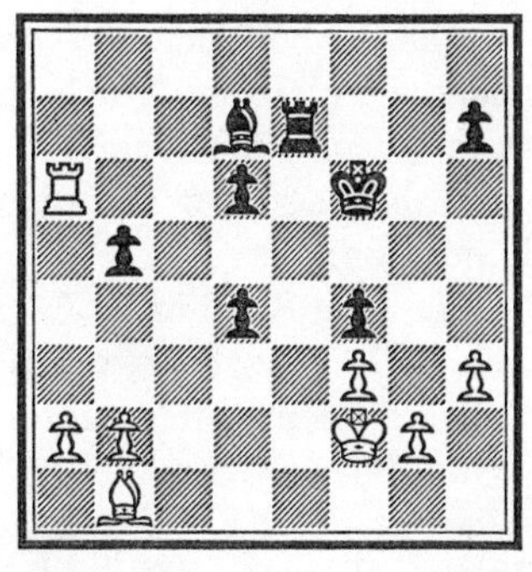

41. . . . . **B—K3**
42. **R × P** **K—K4**
43. **R—B6** **B—Q4**
44. **R—KR6**

44. R—B5? would lose after *44.* . . . . K—Q3; *45.* R × P, B—B5; *46.* R—KB5, R—K7*ch*; *47.* K—Kt1, R—K8*ch*; *48.* K—B2, R × B.

44. . . . . **R—QB2**
45. **R—R5*ch*** **K—Q3**
46. **R—R6*ch*** **K—K4**
47. **R—R5*ch*** **K—Q3**

Both players gain time on the clock.

48. **R—B5** **R—B8**
49. **B—Q3** **R—Q8**

49. . . . . B—B5 ? would fail against *50.* R × BP, B × B; *51.* R × P*ch* and 52. R × B. (Double attack!)

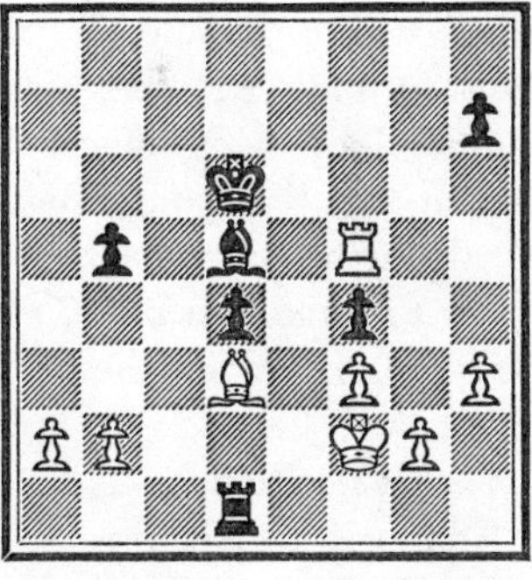

50. **K—K2** **R—KKt8**
51. **K—B2** **R—Q8**
52. **K—K2** **R—KKt8**
53. **R—Kt5** **B × RP**
54. **B × KtP** **R—Kt8**
55. **K—Q3** **P—R3**
56. **R—R5**

The Rook cannot go after the RP via R—Kt6*ch*, because Black will play K—B4, supporting the QP and attacking the B.

56.	R × P
57. K × P	R × P
58. R × P*ch*	K—K2

RULE TO REMEMBER

A single passed RP cannot be forced through to Queen in an ending where K and P play against a lone K. The player with the lone King places his King on the R1 square before the advancing Pawn. There is no way to force him out. Try it after you have finished this game.

Use this position:

White K on KKt5
White P on KR5
Black K on KR1

The Black K cannot be forced out of the way. The best White can do is to force a *stalemate*. Try it. (See page 24 for a description of *stalemate*.)

The Black Pawn is going to fall. However, the ending may still be a draw if the advance of the White Pawns can be blocked. The King here moves into position before the Pawns.

59. K—K4	R—Kt4
60. B—R6	B—B2
61. B—B8*!*	

White's plan is clear. He wants to answer *61.* . . . . R—R4 with *62.* R—QKt6, and the KRP is still safe. Remember that the KRP cannot win, and that, with B of the wrong color, White cannot win after *61.* . . . . R—R4; *62.* R × R, B × R; *63.* K × P, B × P*!*

61.	R—Kt3
62. R—R7	K—B1
63. B—Kt4	

RULE TO REMEMBER

You cannot win with the combination of K, B, and RP against K if the Bishop cannot command the square on which the P is to Queen. Check this after you finish this game. You reach this position:

White K on KKt6 or KR6
White B anywhere on the board, on a white square.
White P on KR7
Black K on KR1

If the B were on a black square, White could win.

Threatening *64.* R × B*ch*, K × R; *65.* B—R5, with an easily won ending. (The extra Pawn will become a Queen).

63. . . . . **R—Kt2 ?**

Keres weakens. He should have played *63.* . . . . R—Kt3; *64.* K × P, K—Kt1, and the White Pawns can still be stopped.

64. **R—R6** **R—Kt3 ?**

You should keep as much material as you can when one or two Pawns behind in an ending. Now White sees his winning line.

65. **R × R !** **B × R*ch***
66. **K × P** **K—Kt2**
67. **K—Kt5** **B—Q6**
68. **P—B4** **B—K5**

Remember that Black will draw if he can exchange his B for the White BP.

69. **P—R4** **B—Q6**
70. **P—R5**

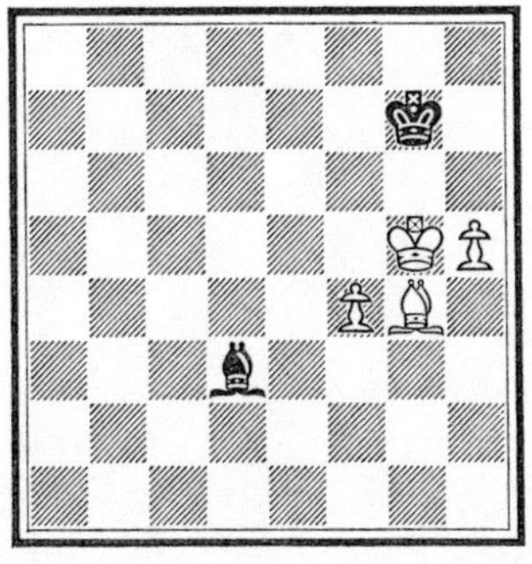

70. . . . . **B—K5**
71. **P—R6*ch*** **K—R1**
72. **B—B5**

The problem: to advance the KBP without its capture. The method: to drive the Black Bishop off the diagonal. If 72. . . . . B × B, White Queens a Pawn quickly.

72. . . . . **B—Q4**
73. **B—Kt6** **B—K3**
74. **K—B6** **B—B5**

So that he can play B—Q6 if *75.* . . . . P—B5.

75. **K—Kt5** **B—K3**
76. **B—R5 !** **K—R2**
77. **B—Kt4 !**

If *77.* . . . . B × B; *78.* K × B, K × P; *79.* K—B5 wins!

77. . . . . **B—B5**
78. **P—B5** **B—B2**
79. **B—R5** **B—B5**
80. **B—Kt6*ch*** **K—Kt1**
81. **P—B6** **Resigns**

White wins by playing his King to K7 and then placing his Bishop on K6. For example:

81.	**P—B6**	**B—R7**
82.	**K—B4**	**B—Kt6**
83.	**K—K5**	**B—R7**
84.	**K—Q6**	**B—Kt6**
85.	**K—K7**	**B—R7**
86.	**B—R5**	**K—R2**
87.	**B—Kt4**	**K × P**

88. **B—K6, and the BP will Queen.**

11 Ruy Lopez

Lublin, 1942

White	*Black*
A. Alekhine	K. Junge

The Opening

Many players make the mistake of attempting early attacks against stronger opponents. When facing the champion of the world, such an attack will fail unless it is properly prepared—for every aggressive opening move in the opening is made instead of a normal developing move—and weaknesses result which an Alekhine knows how to exploit!

White's Plan

The move *6.* Q—K2 which Alekhine plays here is called the Worall attack in the Ruy Lopez. White expects the Q file to be opened, and wishes to place a Rook there.

Black's Plan

Black opens the game too early, offering a Pawn which White refuses. Black is soon burdened with meeting several threats at once, and crumbles quickly, after White advances a Pawn to KB6.

What to Watch for

The game demonstrates how the control of open lines can lead to the quick mobilization of your forces. Note how the Bishop on the diagonal QR2—KKt8 and the Rooks combine with the Queen in the final attack.

1. P—K4	P—K4
2. Kt—KB3	Kt—QB3
3. B—Kt5	P—QR3
4. B—R4	Kt—B3
5. O—O	B—K2
6. Q—K2	

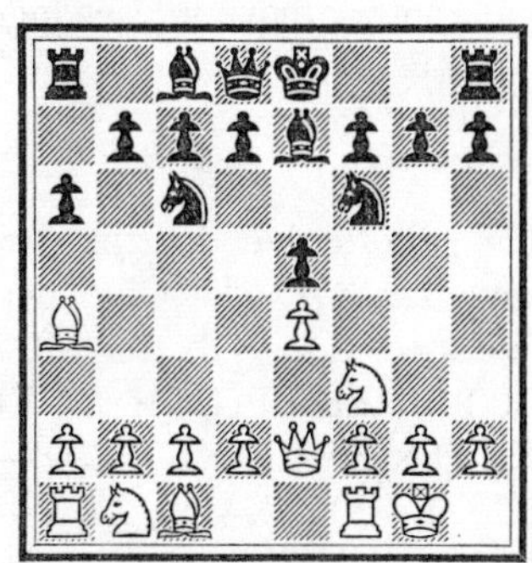

The Worall attack. White threatens. *7.* P—Q4, and if *7.* . . . . P × P; *8.* P—K5.

6. . . . . **P—QKt4**
7. **B—Kt3** **O—O**

Now on *8.* P—Q4, P × P; *9.* P—K5, Kt—K1. But *7.* . . . . P—Q3 was better for Black.

8. **P—B3** **P—Q4**

A Pawn is offered, which White cannot really afford to capture. If *9.* P × P, Kt × P; *10.* Kt × P, Kt—B5 *!; 11.* Q—K4, Kt × Kt; *12.* P—Q4 *!,* B—Kt2; *13.* Q × B, Kt—K7*ch; 14.* K—R1, Kt × B; *15.* R × Kt, Kt—Q6; *16.* R—B1, P—B4 *!* and Black's superior development leads to a lasting attack.

9. **P—Q3**

White protects the KP and opens up the diagonal for the B. Meanwhile, Black's P sits on Q4, and the line in the previous note, based on *10.* . . . . Kt—B5, is no longer possible. Black must spend another move in exchanging on K5.

9. . . . . **P × P**

The alternative to the exchange is *9.* . . . . P—Q5, when White's position is better after *10.* P × P, Kt × P(Q5); *11.* Kt × Kt, Q × Kt; *12.* Kt—B3, P—B4; *13.* B—K3, Q—Q1; *14.* P—B4!

10. **P × P** **B—KKt5**

RULE TO REMEMBER

Where should you place your Bishop? Try to place it where it pins a Knight. Black's move . . . . B—Kt5 here pins the White Kt on KB3. If the Queen moves away—to such a square as QB2—then Black can play B × Kt and leave White with a doubled Pawn.

---

11. **P—KR3** **B—R4**
12. **B—Kt5** **Kt—K1**
13. **B × B** **B × Kt**

If *13.* . . . . Q × B; *14.* B—Q5, Q—B3; *15.* P—KKt4, B—Kt3; *16.* Kt × P*!* is the threat. Black hopes to prevent this by removing the Kt first and then capturing at K2 with his Kt.

14. **Q × B** **Kt × B**

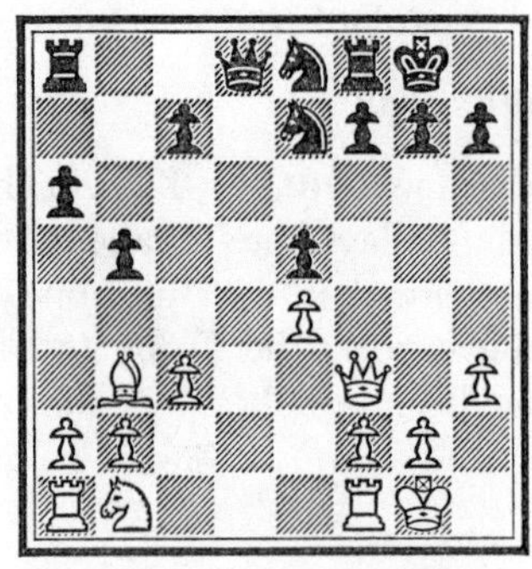

The opening attack has been halted, and Black finds himself cramped on his first and second ranks. Now White takes the Q file.

15. **R—Q1** **Kt—Q3**
16. Kt—Q2 **P—QB3 ?**

A weak move, for now the Kt must be protected by the Q. Black should have sought a means of applying pressure, such as *16.* . . . . K—R1 and *17.* . . . . P—KB4.

17. **Kt—B1** **Q—B2**
18. **P—QR4 !** **R(R1)—Q1**
19. **Kt—Kt3** **Kt(K2)—B1**
20. **P × P** **RP × P**

Now White has 4 lines of attack open—the R file, the Q file, the diagonal for the B, and the KB file for the Queen.

21. **Kt—B5 ! !**

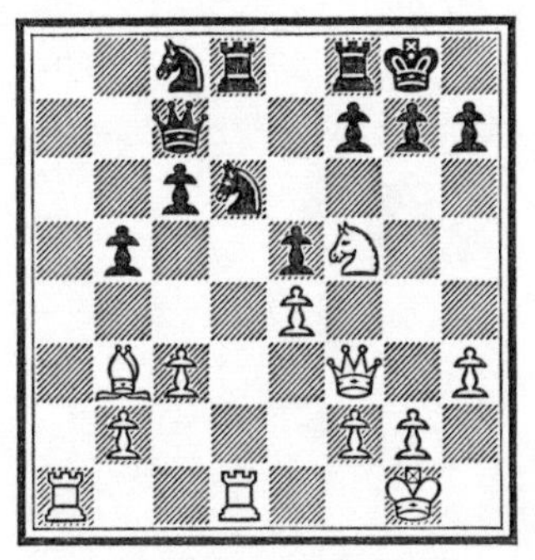

A move which subtly attacks in several ways.

a. The Kt bears on Black's KKt2, with the White Queen ready to join in.

b. The Black Kt on Q3 is attacked again.

c. The Kt supports the possible advance of White's K-side Pawns.

21. . . . . **Kt—Kt3**

Black seeks to block the game with *22.* . . . . Kt(Kt3)—B5.

22. **Q—K3 !**

Another move with more than one meaning.

a. *23.* Kt × Kt, R × Kt; *24.* R × R, Q × R; *25.* Q × Kt.

b. If *22.* . . . . Kt(Q3)—B5; *23.* Q—Kt5, P—Kt3; *24.* B × Kt, Kt × B; *25.* R × R, R × R; *26.* Kt—K7*ch*, K—Kt2; *27.* R—R7 !, Q × R; *28.* Kt—B5*ch* and *29.* Q × R mate.

RULE TO REMEMBER

A piece which must protect two or more other pieces is said to be *overloaded.* The Black Queen here protects both Black Knights. When both of them are attacked, the Queen must leave the defense of one.

Do not overload your pieces!

When your opponent has an overloaded piece, try to attack each of the protected pieces.

---

22. . . . . **Kt × Kt**

22. . . . . Kt(Kt3)—B5 would fail after *23.* B × Kt, Kt × B; *24.* Q—B5, Kt × P; *25.* Kt—K7*ch*, K—R1; *26.* R × R, R × R; *27.*

To prevent B—B2 and Q × P mate. However . . . .

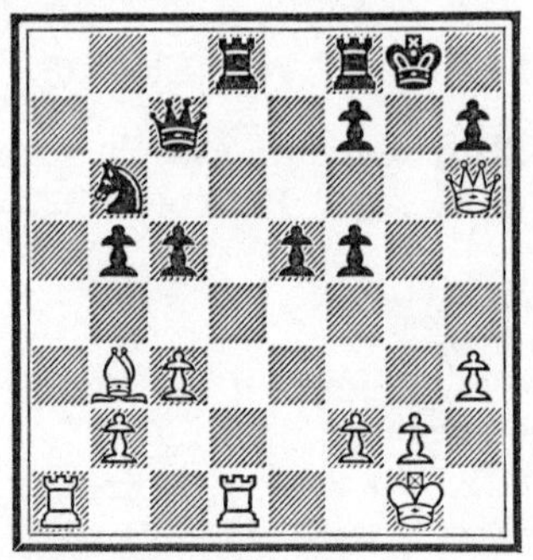

R—R7, Kt—Q6; *28.* R × Q, Kt × Q; *29.* Kt × P, when White would win one or more Pawns.

23. **P × Kt** **P—B4**

Trying for *24.* . . . . P—B5, to block the Bishop's diagonal. But White opens up another one.

24. **P—B6 *!*** **P × P**

Otherwise White plays Q—Kt5! If *24.* . . . . P—Kt3; *25.* Q—R6 wins.

25. **Q—R6** **P—B4**
26. **B × P*ch !!*** **Q × B**

Forced, for *26.* . . . . K × B loses the Q after *27.* Q × P*ch*, and *26.* . . . . R × B fails because of *27.* Q—Kt5*ch* and *28.* R × R. Of course, *26.* . . . . K—R1 allows *27.* Q—B6 mate.

27. **R × R** **Kt—R5**

Black cannot recapture the Rook. If *27.* . . . . R × R; *28.* Q—Kt5*ch* (double attack), K—B1; *29.* Q × R*ch* (another double attack!), K—Kt2; *30.* Q × Kt leaves White a Rook ahead.

28. **P—QKt3** **Resigns**

The Kt must move, and then:
a. If *28.* . . . . Kt × P; *29.* QR—R8 leads to mate.
b. If *28.* . . . . Kt—Kt3; *29.* R—R7, Q × R; *30.* R × R mate or *30.* Q × R mate.

12 Ruy Lopez

1949 Russian Championship

White	*Black*
V. Smyslov	V. Lyublinsky

The Opening

The Ruy Lopez generally turns out to White's advantage if the game opens up quickly. Black, therefore, tries to develop before opening up the game. This game shows how White can force the game despite Black's attempts to hide behind a shell.

White's Plan

Vassily Smyslov was world chess champion for a year, when he beat Botvinnik in their 1957 match. He lost the title in the return match a year later. In this game, he demonstrates a champion's ability to attack. His plan is to set up King-side threats based on possible mate along the KR file.

Black's Plan

Black, a strong Soviet master, seems to be playing for a draw. He sets up a solid position that apparently cannot be opened. However, his pieces have little scope, and his planning fails when faced by one of the world's finest chess imaginations!

The Outcome

In this game, White leaves a Knight *en prise* (subject to capture) for a dozen moves, and wins the game when he finally does move it!

1.	**P—K4**	**P—K4**
2.	**Kt—KB3**	**Kt—QB3**
3.	**B—Kt5**	**P—QR3**
4.	**B—R4**	**P—Q3**
5.	**P—B3**	**B—Q2**
6.	**P—Q4**	**Kt—B3**

Black is playing a closed defense. He will avoid action until he has placed his pieces where he wants them.

7.	**QKt—Q2**	**B—K2**
8.	**O—O**	**O—O**
9.	**R—K1**	**B—K1**

Black has plenty of time. White cannot open up the game, and development can continue.

10. **B—Kt3** **Kt—Q2**
11. **Kt—B1** **B—B3**

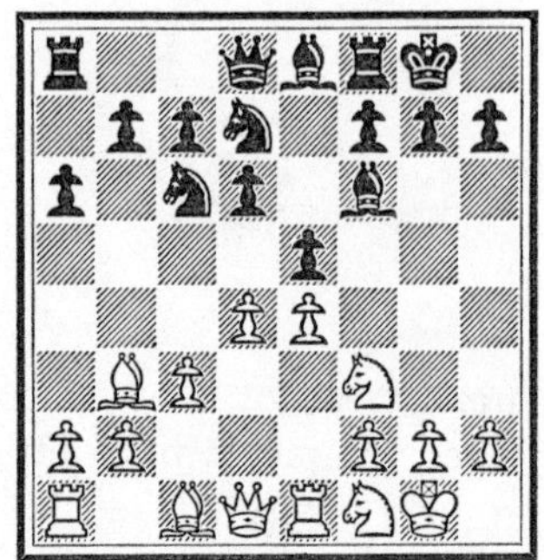

This last Black move has been questioned by Russian analysts. They feel *11.* . . . . . K—R1 and *12.* . . . . . P—B3 to be more in keeping with Black's previous play. But White could then plan for P—KB4 and P—KB5, with strong pressure.

12. **Kt—K3** **Kt—K2**

Otherwise White will play Kt—Q5, and the B at B3 will be exchanged. If Black plays *12.* . . . . P—KKt3; *13.* Kt—Q5, B—Kt2; then White has *14.* B—Kt5, further weakening the Black position.

13. **Kt—Kt4**

RULE TO REMEMBER

Bishops are usually a little stronger than Knights. That is why masters often try to exchange a Knight for a Bishop.

The Bishop still goes—or at least the threat to exchange it is there to bother Black.

13. . . . . **Kt—KKt3**
14. **P—Kt3**

To prevent a possible . . . . Kt—B5 and to prepare for the advance of the KRP.

14. . . . . **B—K2**
15. **P—KR4** **Kt—B3**
16. **Kt—Kt5**

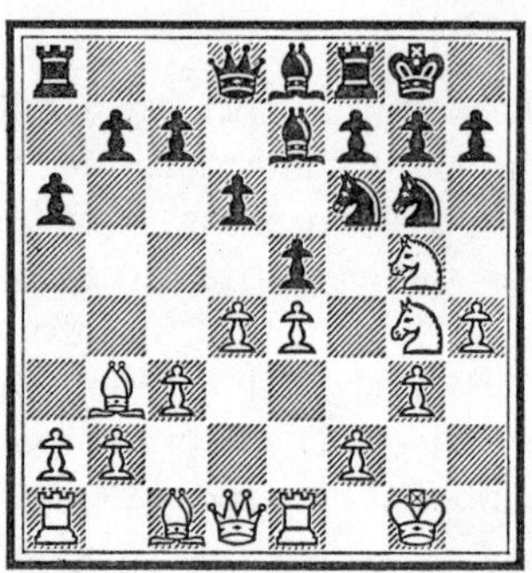

This Kt at Kt5 will be the key to the rest of the game.

16. . . . . **P—R3**
17. **Kt × Ktch !**

White opens the way for the entry of his Queen.

17. . . . . **B × Kt**

17. . . . . P × Kt(B3) loses because of *18.* Kt—R3, K—Kt2; *19.* P—R5, Kt—R1; *20.* Q—Q2, and Black's K-side crumbles. For example, *20.* . . . . P—KB4; *21.* Q × P*ch*, K—Kt1; *22.* Kt—Kt5,

B × Kt; 23. B × B, followed by B—B6 and Q—Kt7 mate.

18. **Q—R5** *!* **Kt—R1**

The White Knight cannot be captured. *18.* . . . . . P × Kt; *19.* P × KtP, B—K2; *20.* Q × Kt (the B on Kt3 prevents the capture of the Q), and Black cannot prevent White's K—Kt2, R—R1, and mate on R7 or R8.

19. **P × P** **P × P**
20. **B—K3** **Q—K2**

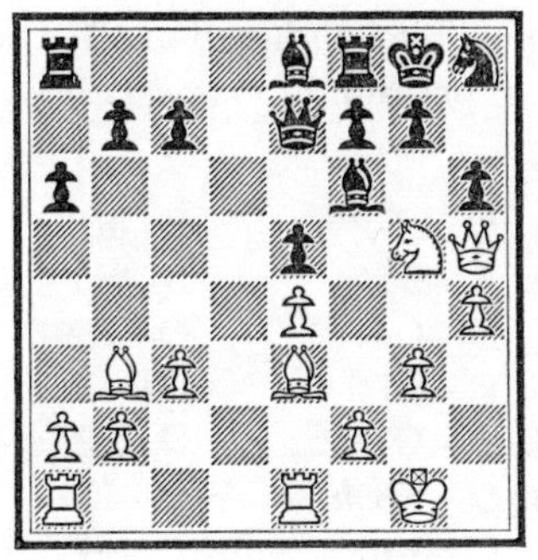

P × Kt is still bad. Thus, *20.* . . . . . P × Kt; *21.* P × P, P—KKt3; *22.* Q—R4, B—Kt2; *23.* K—Kt2 and *24.* R—R1 (threatens mate by Q—R7*!*).

21. **B—Q5** *!* **P—B3**

Now *21.* . . . . . P × Kt leads to *22.* P × P, P—KKt3; *23.* P × B, P × Q; *24.* P × Q and a Rook falls. *21.* . . . . . P—B3 leaves the Black B at K1 locked in.

22. **B—Kt3** **B—Q2**
23. **R(R1)—Q1** **R(R1)—Q1**
24. **R—Q2** **B—B1**

The Kt still cannot be taken, for the line indicated in the last note is still there!

25. **R(K1)—Q1** **R × R**

Otherwise White will play *26.* R × R, R × R; *27.* R × R, Q × R; *28.* Kt × P.

26. **R × R** **Q—B2**
27. **B—B5**

Now, if *27.* . . . . . P × Kt; *28.* B × R, K × B; *29.* P × P, and B and Kt are attacked.

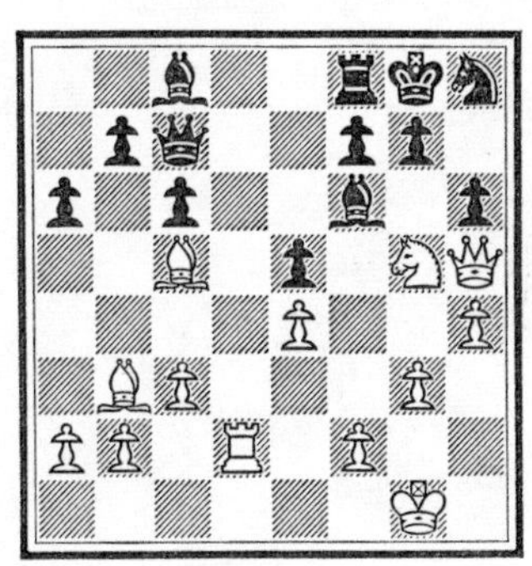

27. . . . . . **R—Q1**
28. **R × R*ch*** **B× R**
29. **Kt × P** *! !*

The "sacrifice" is only temporary, as White's next move demonstrates. Of course, White had to see to the end position before making his 29th move.

29. . . . . Kt × Kt
30. B—Kt6 ! Q—Q2

For 30. . . . . Q × B allows 31. Q × Kt*ch*, K—R2; 32. P—R5, and mate on KKt8 cannot be prevented unless Black surrenders his Queen.

31. B × B K—R2
31. B × Kt Q × B(Q1)
32. B—Kt6*ch* Resigns

White wins the KP and then wins by forcing his KP through. Black has no defense to this threat.

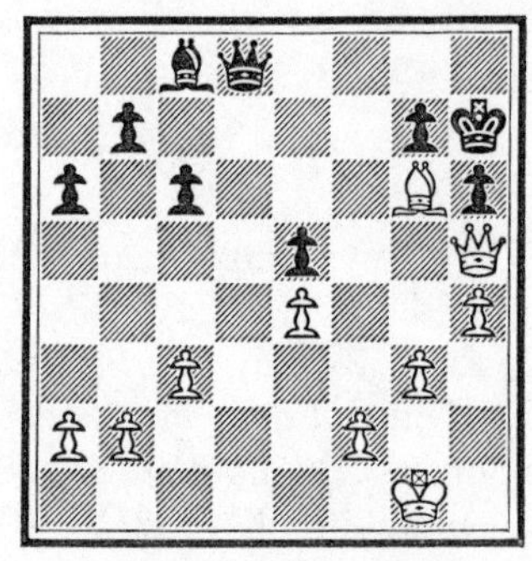

RULE TO REMEMBER

Work out the steps in forcing a passed Pawn through. Here is a possible continuation after the final position of Game 12.

32. . . . . K—R1
33. Q × KP B—Kt5
34. B—B5 B—B6
35. Q—Q4 Q—K2
36. P—K5 Q—KB2
37. Q—Q7 Q × P
38. Q—K8*ch* Q—Kt1
39. Q—Kt6

and the Pawn marches on to Queen.

13 Ruy Lopez

Moscow, 1935

White	*Black*
N. Riumin	M. Botvinnik

The Opening

Our last look at the Ruy Lopez is a game of great complexity. You are advised to play the game through, and then go through it a second time with the notes.

White's Plan

White plays the Worall attack, but confuses two approaches. This line involves either steady development or an early attempt to open the Q side by P—QR4 after Black has played P—QKt4. Riumin tries both methods at once, and gives Black time to develop a K side attack.

Black's Plan

Botvinnik was on the rise in 1935, showing those fighting qualities that made him the Russian champion and later the world champion. He locks up the game and then attacks on the King side.

What to Watch for

The attack in this game involves pressure on the KKt file, in combination with a series of threats by the minor pieces.

1.	**P—K4**	**P—K4**
2.	**Kt—KB3**	**Kt—QB3**
3.	**B—Kt5**	**P—QR3**
4.	**B—R4**	**Kt—B3**
5.	**O—O**	**B—K2**
6.	**Q—K2**	**P—QKt4**
7.	**B—Kt3**	**P—Q3**
8.	**P—B3**	

8. P—QR4 is probably better. Black then plays 8. . . . . R—QKt1; 9. P × P, P × P and White has control of the QR file for his Rook.

8.	**. . . .**	**O—O**
9.	**P—Q4**	**B—Kt5**
10.	**R—Q1**	**P × P**
11.	**P × P**	**P—Q4**

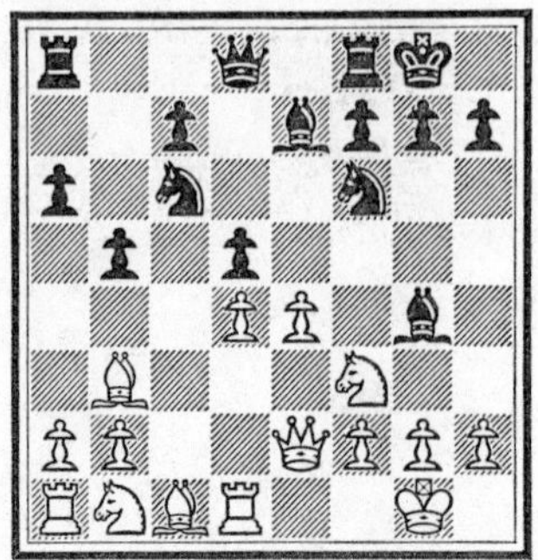

12. **P—K5** **Kt—K5 !**

The Kt is firmly planted on K5. One threat now is *13.* . . . . . Kt—Kt4, and White must give up his B for the Kt, for *13.* . . . . . Kt—Kt4; *14.* Kt(Kt1)—Q2 will allow *14.* . . . . . Kt × QP. White now tries to relieve the pin on his KKt.

13. **P—KR3** **B—R4**
14. **P—QR4 ?**

White changes his mind and attempts Q-side action. Best was to develop by *14.* Kt—B3, when the double attack on Black's QP would force *14.* . . . . . Kt × Kt.

14. . . . . **P—Kt5 !**

Black refuses to open up the game, and, with this move, further locks up White's Q-side. Now the threat of 15. . . . . Kt—R4 is added to White's worries.

15. **P—R5**

White is forced to waste another move to make certain that Black's Kt does not invade the Q-side.

15. . . . . **K—R1**

Preparing for the advance of the KBP, which is not possible now because White could then play Q × Kt. (If *15.* . . . . P—B3; *16.* Q × Kt, and the QP is unable to capture the Q).

16. **P—Kt4** **B—Kt3**
17. **Kt—R2**

White's position is badly cramped. Black threatens P—B3 or P—B4, and there is no immediate defense. White, therefore, sets up Pawn moves such as P—KB3 and P—KB4—5. But Kt—R2 just lets the Black B in.

17. . . . . **B—R5 !**

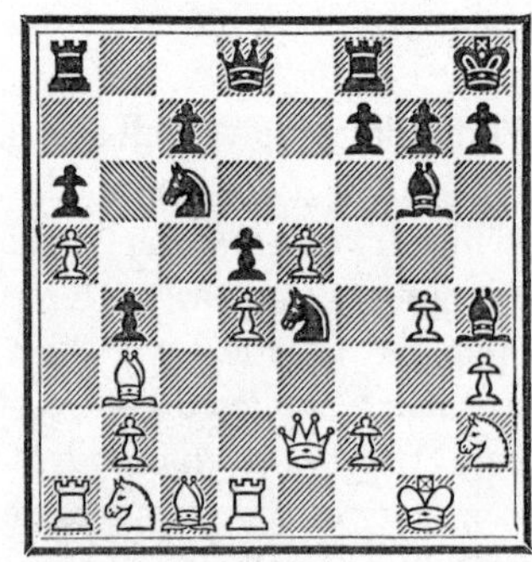

18. **B—K3**

To defend the KBP.

18. . . . . **P—B4**
19. **P—B4**

Otherwise Black will drive the B back by *19.* . . . . P—B5. *19.*

P × P; B × P would leave the White K position bare.

19. . . . . **B—Kt6**

Threat—to win a P by *20.* . . . . P × P; *21.* P × P, B × P. (Note how 20. . . . P × P would discover an attack on White's KBP by the Black Rook on KB1.)

20. **P—Kt5** **P—R3 !**

White's Q-side remains undeveloped, while Black's threats have forced weakening P moves. Now the KKt file will be opened.

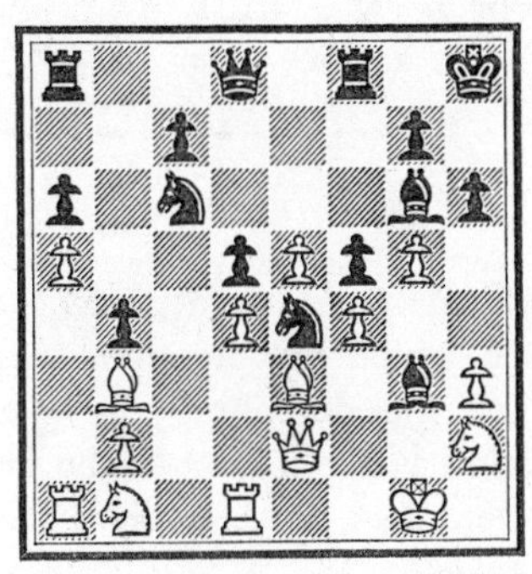

21. **P × P** **P × P**
22. **Kt—Q2** **Kt—K2 !**

An important move, for it defends the QP and gives additional support to the K-side. Had the Kt remained at QB3 it might later have been attacked along the QB file.

23. **K—R1** **Q—K1**

More threats! *24.* . . . . B—R4 will be played, and the K1—R5 diagonal is open on the Q-side. White must pull his pieces over to defend on the K side.

24. **R—KKt1** **B—R4**

RULE TO REMEMBER

Gain time by attacking your opponent's major pieces. In this game, White was threatening to simplify by *25.* Kt × Kt, B × Kt; *26.* Kt—B6!, R × Kt; *27.* P × R, B × R; *28.* P × Kt, B × B; *29.* Q × B, and White should win. Instead, *24.* . . . . B—R4 throws White on the defensive.

---

25. **Kt(R2)—B3** **R—KKt1**
26. **Kt—B1** **Q—B2**

For White cannot take the B. If *27.* Kt × B, Kt × Kt*ch* and White must play *28.* R × Kt, giving up the exchange and then another Pawn. White is in a strait-jacket!

27. **B—Q1** **R—Kt2**
28. **R—B1** **P—B3**

Which takes care of the threat of any action on the QB file.

29. **R—B2** **QR—KKt1**

The mobilization of Black's forces is complete. Black now threatens such annoyances as *30.* . . . . B × P; *31.* R × R, Q × R; *32.* B × B, B × Kt*ch*; *33.* Q × B, Q—Kt8 mate.

30. **R—Kt2**

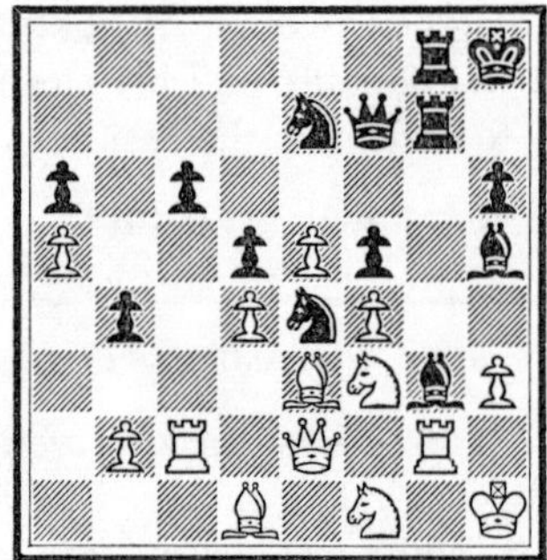

30.	**B × P**

Black goes ahead, for *31.* B × *B* allows *31.* . . . . R × R, while *31.* R × R, Q × R still threatens the mate on KKt8.

31. **Q × P**

The White Queen rushes away from the pins. Q—K1 would be better although Black then has *31.* . . . . B—Kt6 and, if *32.* Q × P, P—B5 will let the Black Q or Kt in via KB4.

31.	**R × R**
32. **R × R**	**R × R**
33. **K × R**	**Q—Kt3*ch***
34. **K—R1**	

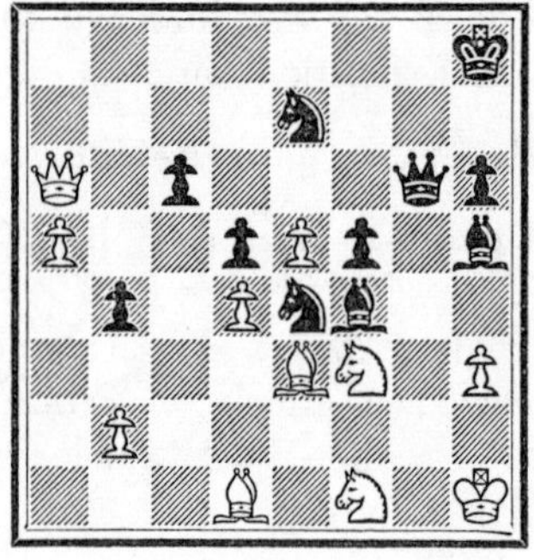

34.	**B × B**
35. **Kt × B**	**Kt—B7*ch***
36. **K—R2**	**Kt × B**
37. **Resigns**	

For *37.* Kt × Kt, B × Kt; and Black is a piece ahead.

RULE TO REMEMBER

When you are attacking a piece which is defended, then attack the defending piece as well! If you can remove the defender, then the first piece can be taken!

---

14 French Defense

World Championship Match, 1954

White	*Black*
V. Smyslov	M. Botvinnik

The Opening

White generally gets a good game in openings beginning *1.* P—K4, P—K4. Black has a long struggle to obtain equality. The records show that games between equally matched players which begin *1.* P—K4, P—K4 are more often won by White. Black therefore turns to other first moves than *1.* . . . . P—K4, of which *1.* . . . . P—K3, the French Defense, is one of the most popular.

White's Plan

Smyslov plays aggressively in this game, seeking and finding complications. A passed Pawn is his key to victory.

Black's Plan

Botvinnik makes a weak Kt move which ties up his K-side and loses valuable time. The only plan he can then follow is a desperate but insufficient defense.

Comment

The game features a Q sacrifice which turns out to be a very short term loan.

1. **P—K4**	**P—K3**
2. **P—Q4**	**P—Q4**
3. **Kt—QB3**	**B—Kt5**

These are the characteristic moves of the opening as it is played today. There are many other approaches, such as:

a. 1. P—K4, P—K3; 2. P—Q4, P—Q4; 3. P—K5

b. 1. P—K4, P—K3;2. P—Q4, P—Q4; 3. P × P

c. 1. P—K4, P—K3; 2. P—QKt3, P—Q4; 3. B—Kt2, P × P; 4. Kt—QB3, Kt—KB3; 5. P—KKt4*!*

d. 1. P—K4, P—K3; 2. P—Q4, P—Q4; *3.* Kt—QB3, Kt—KB3, 4. B—Kt5 or *4.* P—K5.

e. 1. P—K4, P—K3; 2. P—Q4, P—Q4; 3. Kt—Q2

f. 1. P—K4, P—K3; 2. Q—K2

The student is advised to try out each of these, for only by playing them can their several different lines of development become clear.

4. **P—K5** **P—QB4**

This attack on the QP is an essential part of the French Defense. Black wants to open the QB file for a Rook.

5. **P—QR3** **B—R4**

Or *5.* . . . . B × Kt*ch;* *6.* P × B, Kt—QB3

6. **P—QKt4** *!*

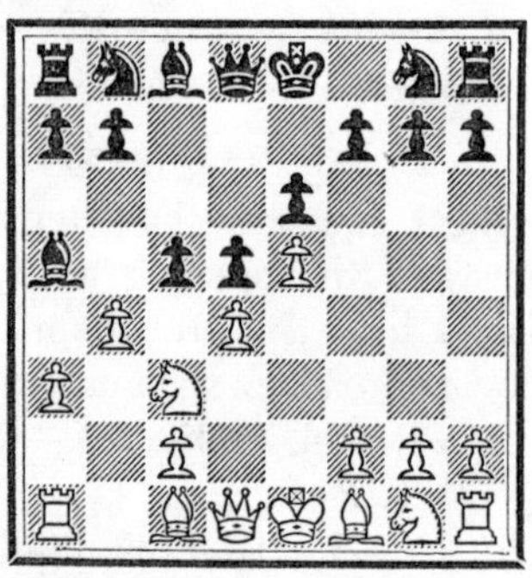

White seeks complications at once. If *6.* . . . . P × KtP; *7.* Kt—Kt5 *!* P × RP*ch;* *8.* P—B3, and White's attack will get under way quickly by such moves as R × P, Kt—Q6*ch,* and B—Q3.

6. **. . . .** **P × QP**
7. **Q—Kt4 !**

The attack is on, for Black must now lose time defending his KKtP, by . . . . K—B1 or . . . . P—KKt3, or else lose it in the attempt to gain a little time.

7. **. . . .** **Kt—K2**
8. **P × B** **P × Kt**
9. **Q × KtP** **R—Kt1**
10. **Q × P**

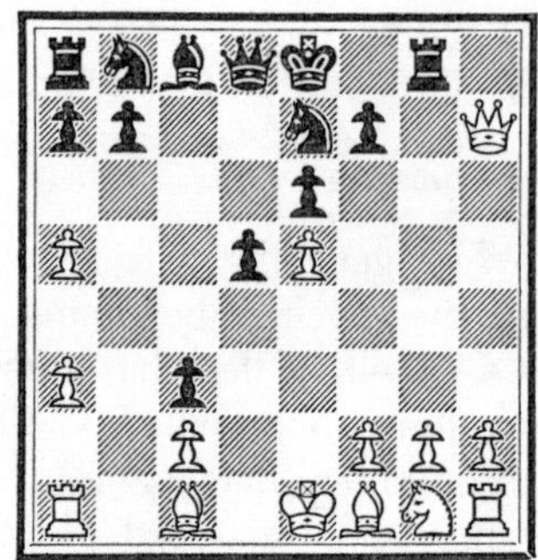

White has obtained a passed Pawn on the KR file. If Black contents himself with slow development, this P will advance to Queen. Every move must therefore contain a threat, so that White will be too busy to find time for moves of the KRP.

10. **. . . .** **Kt—Q2**
11. **Kt—B3** **Kt—B1** *?*

But this is not really a threat. The Q would move away anyway, and now Black needs another move to get the Kt at B1 into play. Better was *11.* . . . .

Q—B2, attacking the KP a second time.

12. **Q—Q3** **Q × P**
13. **P—KR4**

The Pawn begins its march!

13. **. . . .** **B—Q2**
14. **B—Kt5 *!***

Played to prevent *14.* . . . . O—O—O, when *15.* B × Kt wins a piece. The KRP still threatens to advance.

14. **. . . .** **R—B1**
15. **Kt—Q4**

Freeing the KBP for an advance to B4, and also holding open the possibilities of Kt—Kt3 or Kt—Kt5.

15. **. . . .** **Kt—B4**

Black invites *16.* Kt × Kt, P × Kt; which would permit *17.* . . . . Kt—K3 and *18.* . . . . Kt × B or *18.* . . . . Kt—B4.

16. **R—QKt1 *!***

White is willing to give up the QRP in exchange for the QKtP. For example, *16.* . . . . Q × P; *17.* Kt ×Kt, P × Kt; *18.* R × P, and the Russian master Kotov points out that White would win after *18.* . . . . R × B; *19.* P × R, Q—B8*ch*; *20.* Q—Q1, Q × P (Kt4); *21.* Q × P, Q—B8*ch*; *22.* Q—Q1, Q—B5; *23.* R—R3*!*

16. **. . . .** **R—B5**
17. **Kt × Kt** **P × Kt**
18. **R × P *!***

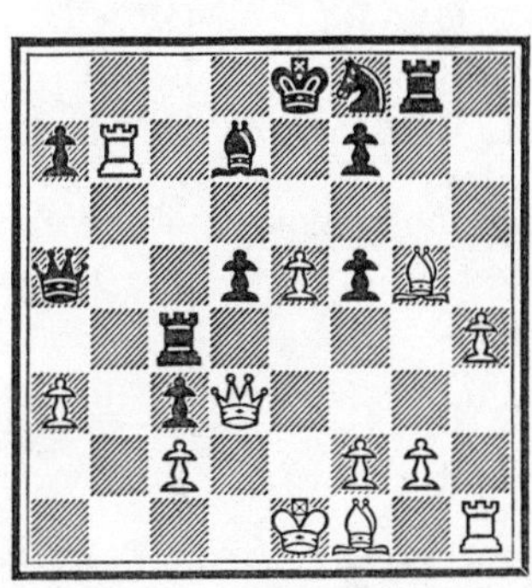

A move with a hidden sting. White has decided to sacrifice his Queen—for a few moves, at least. When he regains it, the position will be simplified, and

---

RULE TO REMEMBER

Once you have established a passed Pawn, plan your game about the advancement of that Pawn!

In this game, White had his passed Pawn after move 10. He began moving it forward on move 13. He played B—KKt5, planning a later B—B6 to guard the Pawns' queening square. Finally, he kept a Rook at KR1 to support the Pawn in its advance. The game was over 15 moves after the passed Pawn had been established!

---

the key plan—to advance the KRP—will become alive again.

18.	R—K5*ch*
19. Q × R *!*	QP × Q
20. R—Kt8*ch*	B—B1
21. B—Kt5*ch*	Q × B

The only move, for the K is caught in the crossfire of the two B's.

22. R × Q	Kt—K3
23. B—B6	

Now the RP is free to march on to R8.

23.	R × P
24. P—R5	B—R3
25. P—R6	Resigns

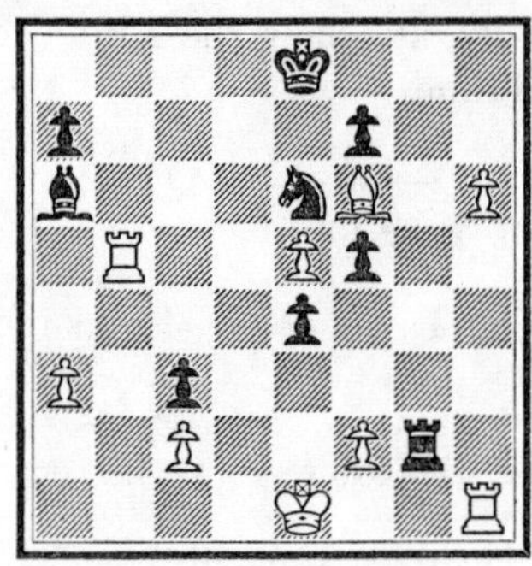

The Pawn cannot be stopped. If *25.* . . . . B × R; *26.* P—R7. If *25.* . . . . Kt—B1; *26.* R—Kt8*ch*, K—Q2; *27.* R × Kt, followed by the Pawn's advance. If *25.* . . . . Kt—Kt4; *26.* B × Kt, R × B; *27.* P—R7 and again the Pawn must queen.

15 French Defense

Moscow, 1944

White	*Black*
V. Smyslov	M. Botvinnik

The Opening

The French Defense demands the most exact play by White. Black threatens to open the game by exchanging one or more of White's center Pawns. Black then gains pressure on the Q-side, or locks it up and switches his pieces to the K-side. Unless White seeks moves that threaten, and in this way limit Black's responses, the position may be opened before White has completed his development. This game sees Black succeeding in that way. It is considered one of the best examples of Black success with the French Defense.

White's Plan

White changes plans during the opening, permitting Black that slight gain of time which makes a counterattack possible. If a single rule of opening play could be attempted, it might be: "Keep applying pressure by threats and threats of threats."

Black's Plan

This was one of the games which won Botvinnik his reputation for calmness under attack. See especially his 15th and 20th moves. He defends carefully but always with an eye for a chance to counterattack.

Comment

The game illustrates the attack against an uncastled King.

1. **P—K4**	**P—K3**
2. **P—Q4**	**P—Q4**
3. **Kt—QB3**	**B—Kt5**
4. **P—K5**	**P—QB4**
5. **P—QR3**	**B × Kt*ch***

For White's play after 5. . . . . B—R4, see Game 14.

6. **P × B**	**Kt—K2**
7. **P—QR4**	

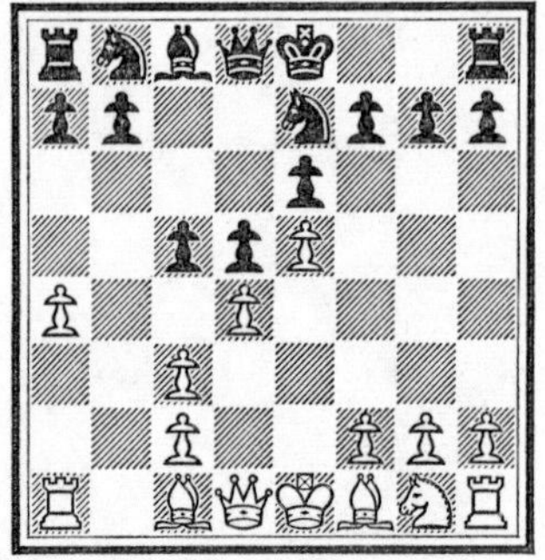

White plans B—R3, with pressure on the diagonal.

7. . . . . Kt(Kt1)—B3
8. Kt—B3 Q—R4

The Queen is strongly posted on R4. It attacks two Pawns, and ties down White's pieces to their defense. And the road is kept open for a quick trip to the K side via Q1.

9. B—Q2

A change of plans. The B should have been saved for B—R3, and *9.* Q—Q2 played.

9. . . . . P—B5*!*

RULE TO REMEMBER

Make a plan of attack early in the game. Then check each move to see if it is proper as part of your plan. If you change your plan, make sure the new plan has an objective you can achieve.

Locking in the White KB and closing up the Q-side. White should (and does) initiate immediate action on the K-side.

10. **Kt—Kt5** **P—KR3**
11. **Kt—R3**

The Kt maneuver has freed the KBP and KKtP for action. The threat now is Kt—B4 and Kt—R5 as well as P—KB4.

11. . . . . **Kt—Kt3**
12. **Q—B3***?*

Another change of plan. *12.* P—KB4 and *13.* P—KKt4 would be better.

12. . . . . **B—Q2**
13. **Kt—B4** **Kt × Kt**
14. **Q × Kt** **Kt—K2***!*

Preparing for the next move.

15. **P—KR4** **B × P***!*

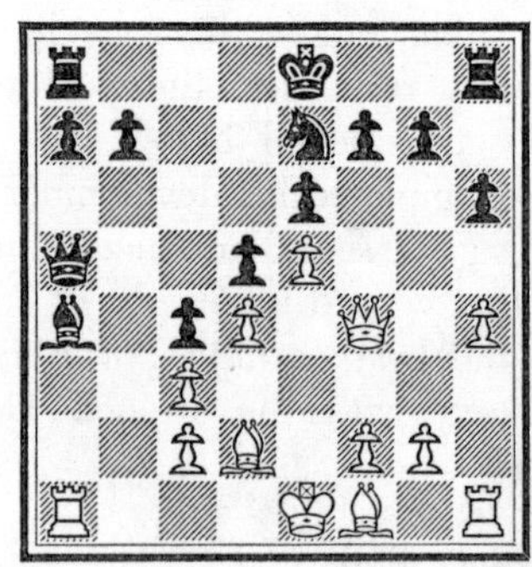

The Bishop is pinned, but White cannot take advantage of its position.

16. **P—R5**

Smyslov builds his attack, but would have done better to play *16.* B—K2, preparing *17.* B—Q1.

16. . . . . **Q—Kt4 !**

Now Black threatens B × P as well as Q—Kt7 if White plays *17.* R—B1.

17. **K—Q1** **R—QB1**
18. **B—B1**

To avoid *18.* . . . Q—Kt7 at any future time.

18. . . . . **R—B3**
19. **B—K2** **R—R3 !**

Now White must defend against *20.* . . . . B × P*ch*, which would win the exchange after *21.* K × B, R × R.

20. **K—Q2** **O—O**
21. **P—KKt4**

Black has castled into the storm, and Smyslov hastens to provide one. White now plans either P—Kt5 or B—R3.

21. . . . . **P—B3 !**

But Black meets all threats at once. Now *22.* B—R3 is met by *22.* . . . . B × P*!* *23.* B × Kt, Q—Kt7*!*, and White will lose at once. And, if *22.* B—R3, B × P*!*; *23.* K × B, Q—Kt6*ch;* *24.* K—Q2, R × B wins.

22. **P × P** **R × P**

White might have done better to play *22.* Q—Kt3, for the continuation after *22.* . . . . P × P; *23.* P—Kt5, Kt—B4; *24.* Q × P is better than what now happens.

23. **Q—B7** **R—B2**
24. **Q—Q8*ch*** **K—R2**
25. **P—B4** **Q—R4**

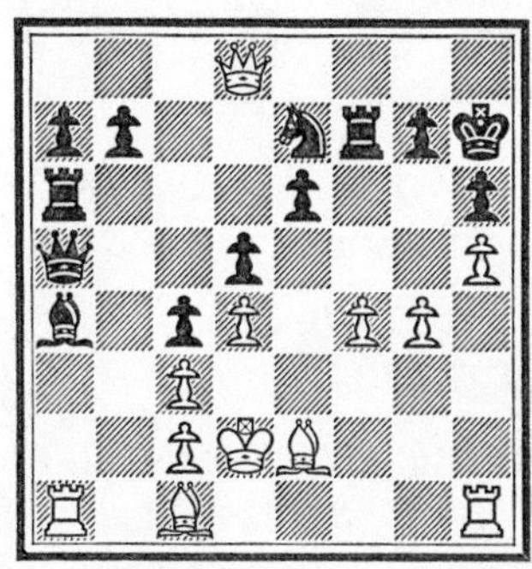

White fights on, and Black offers to exchange Queens before the White K-side Pawns become more dangerous.

26. **Q—QKt8** **Kt—B3**
27. **Q—K8** **R—K2**
28. **Q—K 6*ch*** **K—Kt1**
29. **B—R3**

White seems to be getting out of it, but is now met by a surprise. He may be attacking a Rook, but note that the Q on Kt6 has no place to go! So . . . .

29. . . . . **P—K4 !**

So that, if *30.* B × R, Kt × B wins the Q.

30. **BP × P** **Kt × QP !**

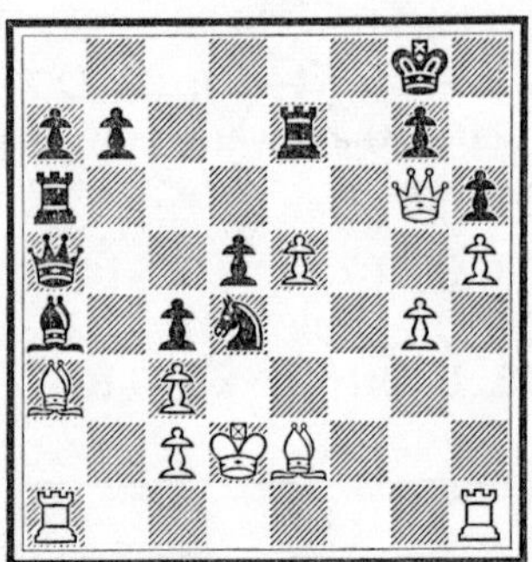

The White Q is trapped, but watch how much material White can get for it!

31. **B—Kt4**

If *31.* B × R, R × Q; *32.* P × R, Kt × B; *33.* K × Kt, Q × P, and more White Pawns will fall.

31.	**Q—Q1**
32. **Q × R**	**P × Q**
33. **P × Kt**	**R—Kt2** *!*
34. **R × B**	

White has a R and two B's for the Queen—but Black had seen far ahead when he made his 29th move.

RULE TO REMEMBER

Do not place your Queen in the enemy position unless you have an open road for its escape.

---

34.	**Q—Kt4***ch*
35. **K—Q1**	

For . . . . K—K1 loses a R after *36.* Q—B8*ch.*

35.	**P—R4** *!*
36. **B—KB3**	

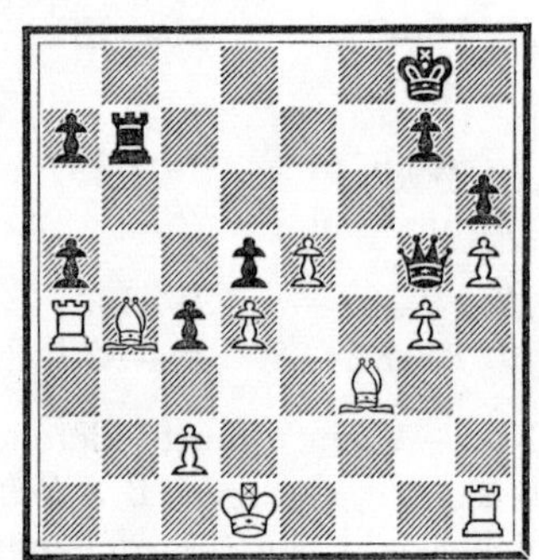

Any move by the B on Kt4 would lose after *36.* . . . . R—Kt8*ch*.

36.	**R × B**
37. **B × P***ch*	**K—B1**
38. **R—B1***ch*	**K—K1**
39. **B—B6***ch*	**K—K2**
40. **R × R**	**Q × P***ch*
41. ***Resigns***	

White can do nothing with his Pawns on K5 and Q4, while Black can easily force through another Queen. The resignation was in order.

16 Alekhine's Defense

Moscow, 1951

White	*Black*
L. Aronin	V. Mikenas

The Opening

Alekhine's introduction of Black's reply to *1.* P—K4, *1.* . . . . Kt—KB3, was part of the reaction to the power of the Ruy Lopez which occurred in the 1920's and 1930's. This defense is most powerful when White pushes his Pawns forward, only to find them under later attack. But games such as the one you will now examine show that White can beat back a hasty Black attack. There is still much to be learned about this opening. Avoid Alekhine's Defense as Black until you have studied dozens of games in which it was successful. As White, play for development and control of the center—as White does in this game.

White's Plan

The Russian master Aronin castles as soon as he can and then invites Black to attack the castled King position. When Black accepts the invitation, White is able to hit at a bare Black King. The game is over in 17 moves!

Black's Plan

Mikenas hardly has time to prepare a defense. Instead, he leaps at what seems to be a forced mate. Then he is hit by chess lightning!

Comment

Replay the game to Move 15 after you have studied it. Can you remember the attacking line that then wins for White? This is one of the most instructive games in chess literature.

1.	**P—K4**	**Kt—KB3**
2.	**P—K5**	**Kt—Q4**
3.	**P—Q4**	**P—Q3**
4.	**Kt—KB3**	

Black would prefer moves like *4.* P—QB4, Kt—Kt3; *5.* P—KB4, when White's advanced Pawns will be a target for Black later in the game. But Aronin prefers to develop, leaving the Black Kt on Q5 for some future P—B4 or B—B4.

If Black now plays *4.* . . . . P × P *?*, *5.* P × P and the White KP helps White keep a grip on the center.

4.	**B—Kt5**
5. **B—K2**	**P—K3**
6. **O—O**	**Kt—QB3**
7. **P—B4**	**Kt(Q4)—K2** *?*

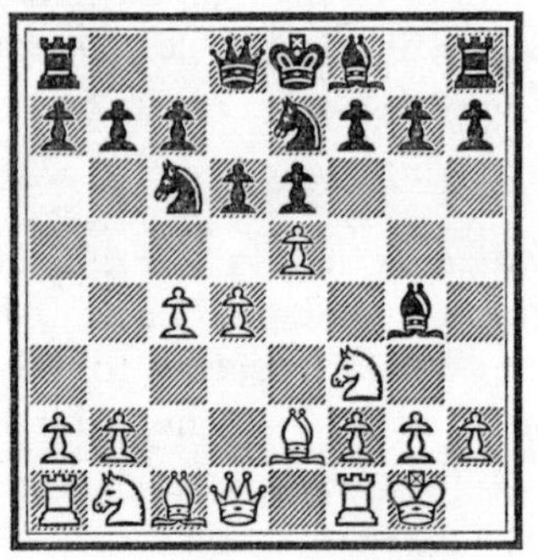

Black wants to avoid 7. . . . . Kt—Kt3; *8.* P × P, P × P (if *8.* . . . . Q × P; *9.* P—B5 wins a piece); *9.* P—QKt3, B—K2; *10.* Kt—B3, O—O; *11.* B—K3, P—Q4; *12.* P—B5, Kt—Q2; *13.* P—QKt4 *!*, and White has the better game. Black's major problem in the Alekhine Defense is to find good places for his pieces.

8. **P × P**	**Q × P**
9. **Kt—B3**	

Black cannot, here, try to win a Pawn, for *9.* . . . . B × Kt; *10.* B × B, Kt × P; *11.* B × KtP, R—QKt1; *12.* B—K4 is to White's advantage. And, if *9.* . . . . O—O—O, White has *10.* Kt—KKt5 to win the KBP and perhaps the exchange as well.

9.	**Kt—Kt3**

The fruits of the opening for Black—this Kt has made 4 moves, and is now on a square like KKt3!

10. **P—Q5**	**P × P**
11. **P × P**	**B × Kt**
12. **P × B** *!*	

This move is contrary to the usual principles of chess. You should not open your K position. You should not willingly double your Pawns. Aronin's plan is so deep and so perfect that we must conclude that he foresaw the rest of the game when he made his 12th move. Either that or the entire line is the result of midnight oil analysis!

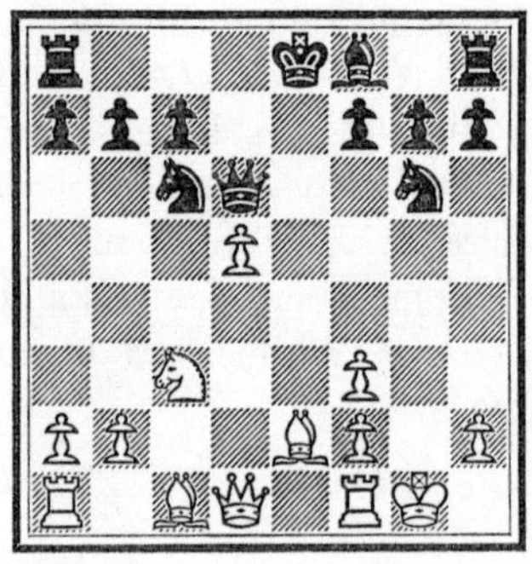

12.	**Kt(B3)—K4**

12. . . . . Kt—R5 would threaten *13.* . . . . Q—Kt3*ch* and *14.* . . . . Q—Kt7 mate, but White simply plays *13.* K—R1 and *14.* R—KKt1.

13. **Kt—Kt5** **Q—Q2**

Heading for KR6.

14. **P—B4** **Kt—R5**

The only other choice is to play *14.* . . . . Kt—B6ch; *15.* B × Kt, Q × Kt; *16.* R—K1*ch*, B—K2; *17.* P—Q6 and White's attack is strong.

15. **P × Kt** **Q—R6**

What is White to do? The threat is mate on KKt2, and nothing seems able to get in the way.

16. **Kt × P*ch*** **K—Q1**

That should do it. Now Black threatens the mate on Kt7 and this Kt as well. Will White resign? No! He plays his "bolt from the blue" instead!

17. **Kt—K6*ch* ! !** **Resigns**

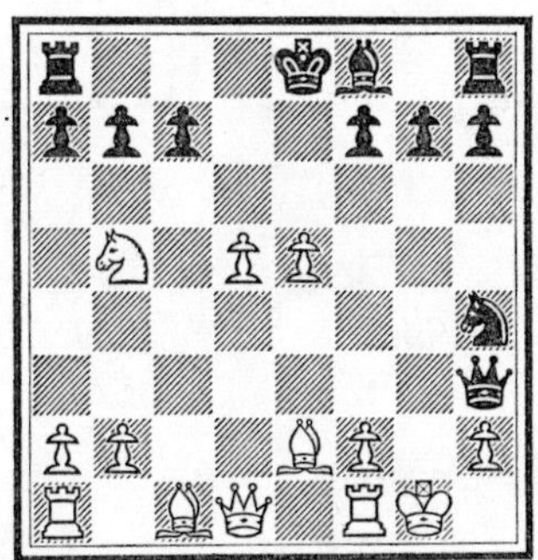

Magic indeed. Look at the possibilities:

a. *17.* . . . . P × Kt; *18.* P × P*ch* (by the Queen), K—K1 or K2; *19.* Q—Q7 mate!

b. *17.* . . . . P × Kt; *18.* P × P*ch*, K—B2; *19.* Q—Q7*ch*, K—Kt1; *20.* Q—Q8 mate.

c. *17.* . . . . K—K1; *18.* Q—R4*ch*; K—K2; *19.* P—Q6*ch*, K × Kt; *20.* B—Kt4*ch* wins the Queen.

d. *17.* . . . . K—K2; *18.* P—Q6*ch*, K—Q2; *19.* Q—R4*ch*, P—QKt4; *20.* Q × P(Kt5)*ch*, K × Kt; *21.* B—B4*ch*, K—B4; *22.* Q—Q7*ch* wins the Queen.

An incredible game!

RULE TO REMEMBER

When you play over a master game, try to work out possible continuations from the point at which one player resigned. For example, how does White win if Black plays *19.* . . . . K—Kt3 in variation *b* at the right?

---

17 Alekhine's Defense

Bled, 1931

White	*Black*
G. Stoltz	E. Colle

The Opening

Alekhine's Defense is best for Black when White's Pawns rush forward. These same Pawns later become targets for White's opponent. In the early days of this opening, games became so complicated that one would not know from move to move which player had the better game.

White's Plan

Stoltz, a Swedish master who had a fine tournament record, loved to attack and knew how to defend. In this game, he is given plenty of opportunity to do both. He wins an exchange, but is forced to defend himself afterwards.

Black's Plan

Edgar Colle, for years Belgium's greatest player, was a sick man for much of his chess career. His record in tournaments was therefore spotty. But when well, and inspired as he was in this game, he was as resourceful a player as ever lived. He gives up the exchange to gain control of one open line after another.

Comment

Both players make mistakes in this game, but White makes the last one—and it has been said that the winning chess player is he who makes the next to the last error!

1.	P—K4	Kt—KB3
2.	P—K5	Kt—Q4
3.	P—QB4	Kt—Kt3
4.	P—B5	Kt—Q4

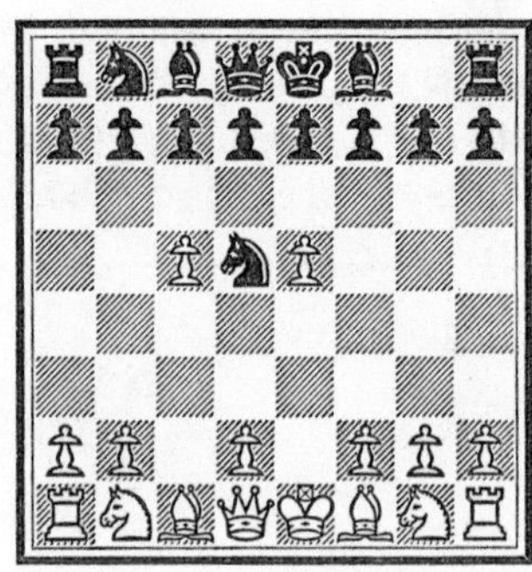

White's advanced Pawns will be a target. Black now threatens . . . . P—K3 and then . . . . P—Q3.

5. **Kt—QB3** **Kt × Kt**
6. **QP × Kt** **Kt—B3 ?**

Black adopts a second-best plan, to develop his KB on KKt2 and play against the KP. *6.* . . . . P—K3 and 7. . . . . P—Q3 are still in order, for the advanced White Pawns should be exchanged before they can be supported in force.

7. **Kt—B3** **P—KKt3**
8. **B—QB4** **B—Kt2**

RULE TO REMEMBER

The development of a Bishop at Kt2 is called a *fianchetto,* from the Italian word for *flank.*

---

9. **B—B4** **O—O**
10. **Q—Q2** **P—Kt3**

White's KP is solid. If *10.* . . . . P—Q3; *11.* O—O—O, P × KP; *12.* Q—K2, Q—K1; *13.* Kt × P and White has all the open lines. Black therefore tries to open up the Q side. And White's next move aims at the K side.

11. **P—KR4** **P—KR4**

Otherwise *12.* P—R5, with a strong attack.

12. **O—O—O** **P—K3**
13. **B—KKt5 !**

So that, if *13.* . . . . Q—K1; *14.* B—B6, and the White pieces will penetrate the K side via Q—Kt5, QR—Kt1, P—KKt4.

13. . . . . **P—B3**
14. **KP × P** **B × P**
15. **Q—B2**

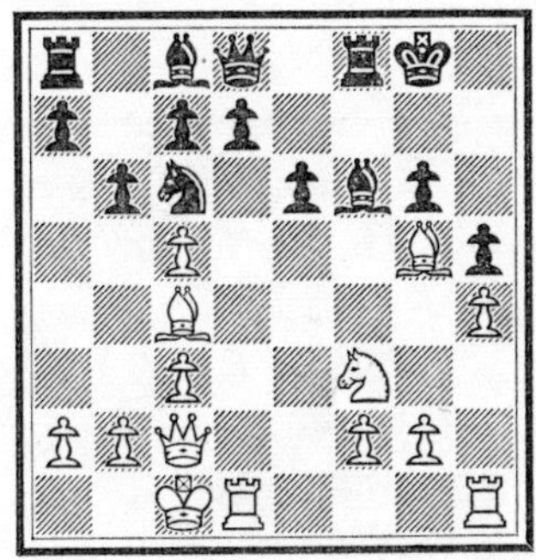

Threatening Q × P*ch.* For example: *15.* . . . . B × B; *16.* Q × P*ch,* K—R1; *17.* Q × P*ch,* K—Kt1; *18.* Q—Kt6*ch,* K—R1; *19.* P × B mate.

15. . . . . **Q—K1**
16. **B—Q3** **K—Kt2**
17. **P—KKt4 !** **RP × P**
18. **R(Q1)—KKt1 !**

18. P—R5 looks promising, because of *18.* . . . . P × Kt ?; *19.* B—R6*ch,* K × B; *20.* P × P*ch,* K—Kt2; *21.* R—R7*ch,* K—Kt1; *22.* P—Kt7, B × P; *23.* QR—Kt1, R—B2; *24.* B—Kt6, Kt—Q1; *25.* B × R*ch,* Q × B; *26.* Q—K4, B—Kt2; *27.* Q—KR4 and wins. But Black might not cooperate, and *18.* P—R5, B × B*ch;* *19.*

Kt × B, P × P would put a halt to the attack.

18.		**B × B*ch!***
19. **Kt × B**		**Kt—K4*!***

Black fights back. Exchanges will weaken White's attack.

20. **B—K4**	**B—R3**
21. **B × R*?***	

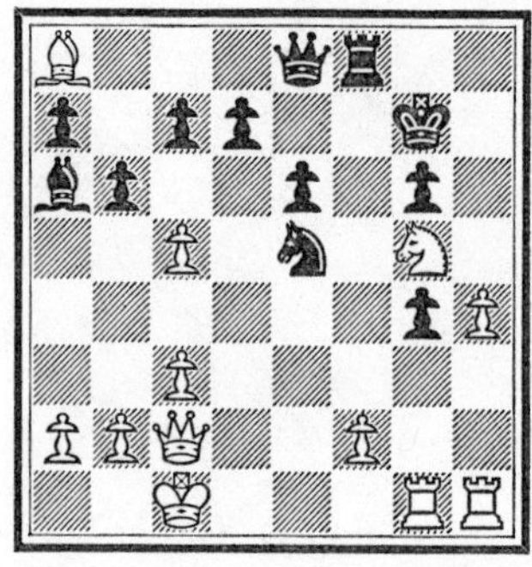

The exchange is not worth the counterattack which Black now develops. Better *21.* R—Kt3.

21.	**Kt—Q6*ch***
22. **K—Kt1**	**Q × B**

Threatening *23.* . . . . Kt × P(B4) and *24.* . . . . B—Q6. White's attack has been slowed, and is further slowed by the necessity of meeting this threat.

23. **P—QB4**	**Kt—K4**
24. **Q—B3**	**R—B4**

Still threatening . . . . B × P and . . . . B—Q6.

25. **P—B4*?***

White slips; *25.* P—Kt3 was better.

25.	**P × P e.p.**
26. **R—K1**	

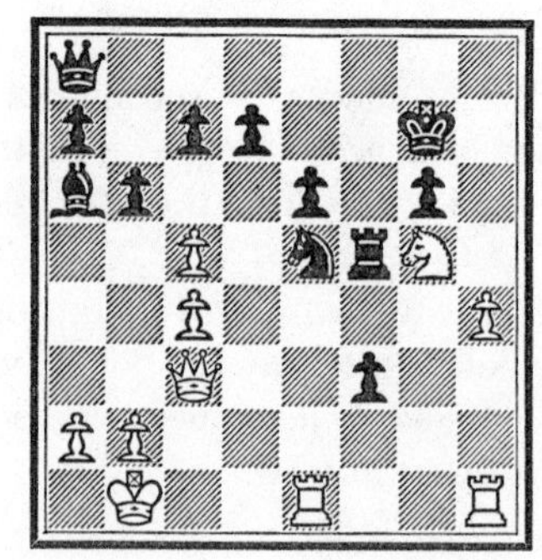

RULE TO REMEMBER

Check your position. Did you make the *en passant* capture correctly? Is the Black Pawn at KB6?

And now the passed Pawn explodes, and White never recovers.

26.	**P—B7*!***
27. **R × Kt**	

Hoping for *27.* . . . . P—B8(Q); *28.* R × Q, R × R*ch*; *29.* R—K1*ch*, R—B3; *30.* Kt—K4.

White would also win after *27.* R × Kt, Q × R*ch*; *28.* R—K1*dis. ch*, K—Kt1; *29.* R × Q, P—B8(=Q); *30.* R × Q, R × R*ch*; *31.* K—B2.

But Black will not cooperate. He moves his K out of the pin.

RULE TO REMEMBER

A supported passed Pawn can be blocked by placing a piece in front of it.

When you have a supported passed Pawn, try to attack the pieces which block it.

When a passed Pawn reaches the 7th rank, watch for Rook moves which check and also attack the blocking piece.

Why does White resign in this game? Because he will be a Queen behind after *32.* Q × Q, R—K8*ch*; *33.* Q × R, P × Q (=Q)*ch*; *34.* K—B2, Q × P and the capture of White's Knight in a move or two.

27.	K—Kt1 !
28. R—KB1	Q—Kt7 !
29. Q—Q3	

White's last chance. If *29.* . . . . R × R, then *30.* Q × KtP*ch* is followed by mate at B7 or R7.

29.	**B × P !**
30. **Q × B**	**R × R**

And now it is over. The Black Rook comes to the 8th rank no matter what White does.

31. **Q—Q3**	**Q × R*ch* !**
32. **Resigns**	

Because of *32.* Q × Q, R—K8*ch*. Colle played with determination and an extended series of brilliant moves. Once begun, the pressure he applied was never relaxed.

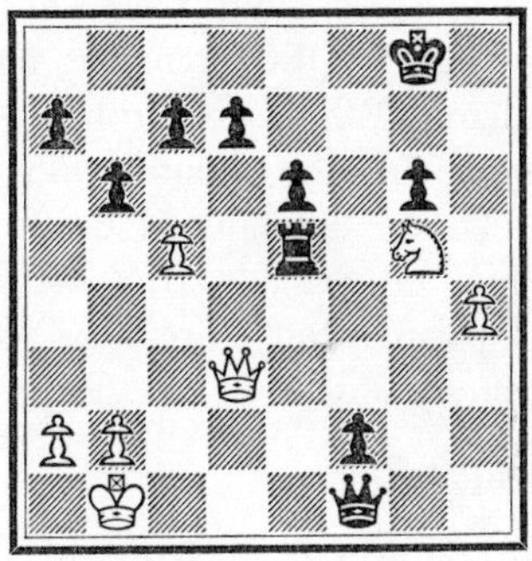

18 Caro-Kann Defense

U.S.A.–U.S.S.R. Radio Match, 1945

White	*Black*
I. A. Horowitz (U.S.A.)	S. Flohr (U.S.S.R.)

The Opening

The Caro-Kann Defense (*1.* P—K4, P—QB3) aims at neutralizing White's control of the center of the board. Played safely, the opening is drawish. When either side tries to develop an attack, fireworks can occur.

White's Plan

Al Horowitz was one of the world's finest attacking players. A chess writer and editor, he was too busy to play often. He was at his prime in the 1930s and 1940s, traveling widely to build chess interest. In this game, he gains an open file and attacks by placing his Rooks on it.

Black's Plan

Salo Flohr, one of Russia's leading players, is a former Czech who was once considered a near-challenger for the world's championship. In this game, he makes the error of opening up the game while behind in development.

The Outcome

Horowitz's ability to combine the action of his Rooks and Bishop turns a difficult position into an easy win built on a passed Pawn.

1. **P—K4** **P—QB3**
2. **P—Q4** **P—Q4**

Now, if 3. P × P, P × P Black has a half-open QB file opposed to White's half-open K file.

3. **Kt—QB3** **P × P**
4. **Kt × P** **Kt—B3**

Black can also play *4.* . . . . B—B4 or *4.* . . . . QKt—Q2. But he is willing to open things up at once.

5. **Kt × Kt*ch*** **KtP × Kt**

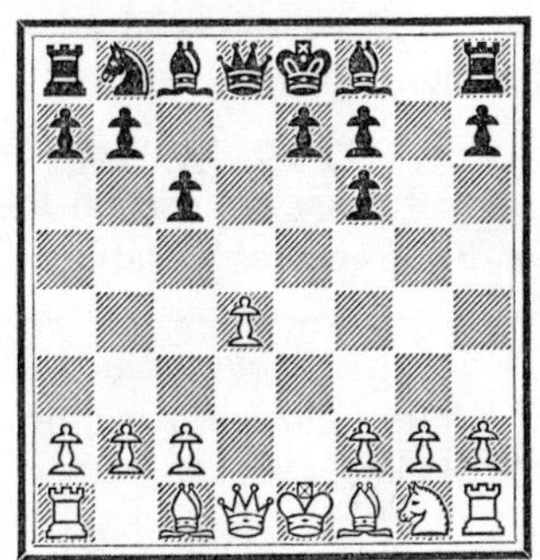

RULE TO REMEMBER

When you have a chance to capture a piece or Pawn with either one of two Pawns, it is usually better to capture *toward* the center of the chess board.

---

6. **Kt—K2*!***

6. B—QB4 or *6.* Kt—B3 are more usual, but Horowitz prefers to play Kt—K2 so that he can later place the Kt where it will be most effective.

6\. . . . . **B—B4**
7\. **Kt—Kt3**

And the Kt has found a good square.

7\. . . . . **B—Kt3**
8\. **P—KR4**

White wants to exchange the Kt for Black's B on Kt3. Thus, 9. P—R5, B—B4; *10.* Kt × B, Q—R4*ch*; *11.* B—Q2, Q × Kt; *12.* B—Q3 is in White's favor.

8. . . . . **P—KR3**
9. **P—R5** **B—R2**
10. **P—QB3**

This frees the Q from the defense of the QP.

10. . . . . **Q—Kt3**

To prevent White from moving his QB.

11. **B—QB4**

So that Black will not be able to play O—O—O without losing his KBP.

11. . . . . **Kt—Q2**
12. **P—QR4**

Giving Black another reason for avoiding O—O—O, when *13.* P—R5 and *14.* P—R6 would follow.

12. . . . . **P—R4**
13. **Q—B3** **P—K3**
14. **O—O** **B—B7**

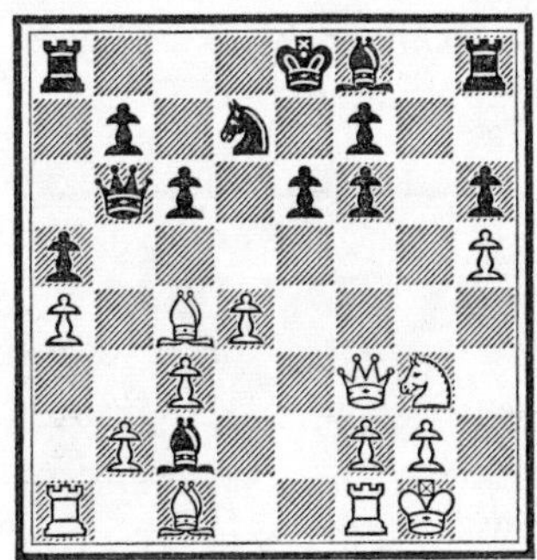

Black wants to play . . . . B—Kt6, to follow it with the exchange of B's or . . . . B—Q4.

15. **B—B4** **B—Kt6**

Not . . . . Q × KtP because of *16.* R—R2 and Black loses a B.

16. **B—Q3** **P—K4 ?**

An error, for it offers to open up the position of the uncastled King, and also makes White a present of the B5 square, to which a Kt or B can move.

17. **B—K3** **B—Q4**
18. **B—K4**

White is willing to exchange B's, after which he will have his Q on the same file as Black's K.

18. **. . . .** **Q—Kt6**
19. **P × P** **P × P**
20. **QR—Q1** **B × B**
21. **Q × B** **Q—K3**

Black does not have time to take the QKtP. If *21.* . . . . Q × KtP; *22.* R × Kt *!*, K × B; *23.* R—Q1*ch*, and Black's King is in a mating attack.

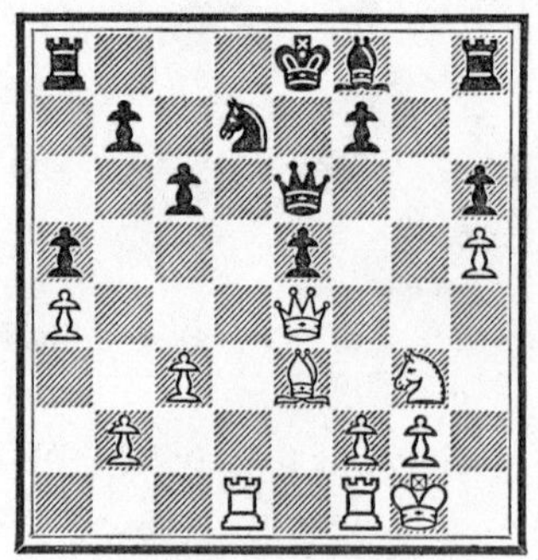

22. **R—Q2 *!***

RULE TO REMEMBER

Do not try to open up the game until you are certain that your King position is safe.

Double the Rooks on the open file! White follows a basic principle of chess.

22. **. . . .** **Kt—B3**
23. **Q—B3** **KR—Kt1**

Black seeks attacking lines.

24. **R(B1)—Q1** **R—Kt5 ?**

Horowitz described this as a blunder, for it allows the brilliancy which follows. *24.* . . . . Kt—Q4 was better.

25. **Kt—B5 *!***

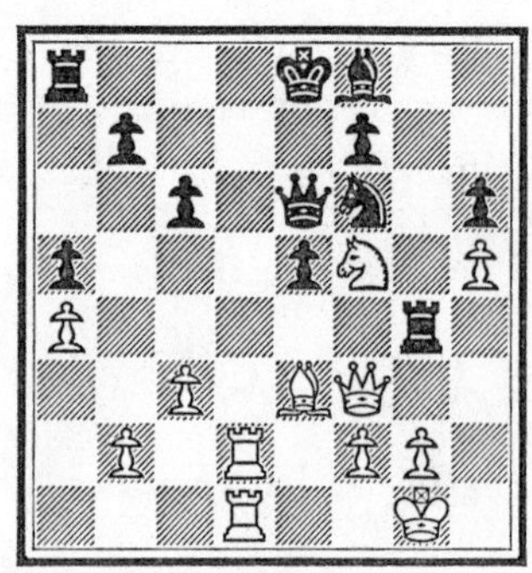

25. **. . . .** **P—K5**

To prevent *26.* R—Q6, B × R; *27.* R × B, Q—B5; *28.* R × Kt.

26. **B—Kt6 *!***

So that, if *26.* . . . P × Q; *27.* R—Q8*ch*, R × R; *28.* R × R mate.

26. . . . . R × P*ch*

The loss of the exchange is forced, for *26.* . . . . B—K2 allows *27.* Q × R, Kt × Q; *28.* Kt—Kt7*ch* and *29.* Kt × Q.

27. Q × R	Q × Kt
28. R—Q8*ch*	R × R
29. R × R*ch*	K—K2
30. Q—Kt3	

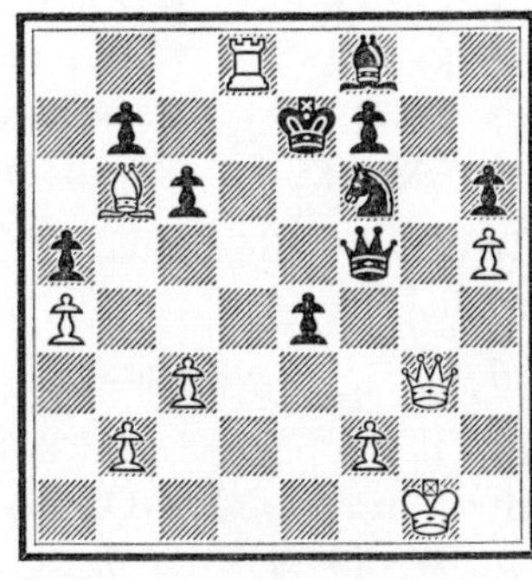

And now Black must do something about *31.* Q—Q6 mate.

30.	Kt—Q2
31. B—B7	

Still aiming for Q—Q6 mate.

31.	Q—Q4
32. P—QB4	Q—KKt4

White would force this anyway after *32.* . . . . Q—QB4; *33.* Q—R4*ch*.

33. Q × Q*ch*	P × Q
34. R—R8	K—K3

Black's QRP must fall, and then White will have another potential passed Pawn.

35. B × P P—KB4

Black also hopes for a passed Pawn, but his hope is in vain.

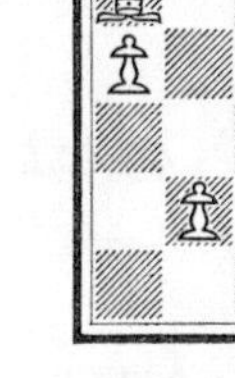

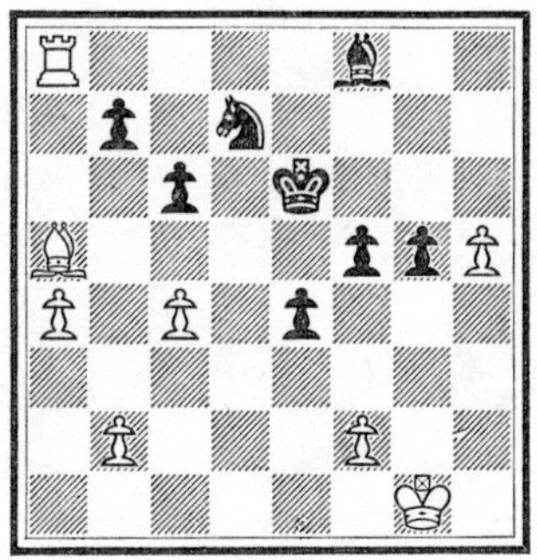

36. B—B3	P—B5
37. P—R5	P—Kt5
38. P—Kt4	P—B6
39. B—Q2	

Effectively blocking the Black Pawns. Now White will establish another passed Pawn.

39.	K—B2
40. R—R7	P—Kt6
41. R × P	Resigns

The QRP cannot be stopped.

RULE TO REMEMBER

This game contains three important keys to the improvement of your game:

1. **Doubled Rooks on an open file help you to invade the enemy position.**
2. **A Rook on the 7th or 8th rank in the endgame should be used to win one or more Pawns—especially to establish a passed Pawn.**
3. **Play to protect your passed Pawn as it advances to become a Queen.**

---

19 Caro-Kann Defense

World Championship Match, 1960

White	*Black*
M. Tal	M. Botvinnik

The Opening

Botvinnik played the Caro-Kann Defense repeatedly in the match which saw Tal emerge as the new world champion. Tal plays aggressively—a valuable style, but not always called for against a solid defense.

White's Plan

Tal sacrifices a piece for three Pawns, but fails to gain any advantage for the ending.

Black's Plan

Botvinnik reaches an ending in which a Knight proves more than enough to stop two Pawns.

What to Watch for

The game illustrates how important it is to keep your Pawns on the board in an ending in which you are a piece ahead.

1.	**P—K4**	**P—QB3**
2.	**P—Q4**	**P—Q4**
3.	**Kt—QB3**	**P × P**
4.	**Kt × P**	**B—B4**
5.	**Kt—Kt3**	**B—Kt3**
6.	**KKt—K2**	

To play Kt—B4, attacking the B again.

6. . . . . **Kt—B3**

Any developing move will do, such as *6.* . . . . Kt—Q2 or *6.* . . . . P—K3 or even *6.* . . . . Q—Kt3.

7.	**P—KR4**	**P—KR3**
8.	**Kt—B4**	**B—R2**
9.	**B—B4**	**P—K3**
10.	**O—O**	

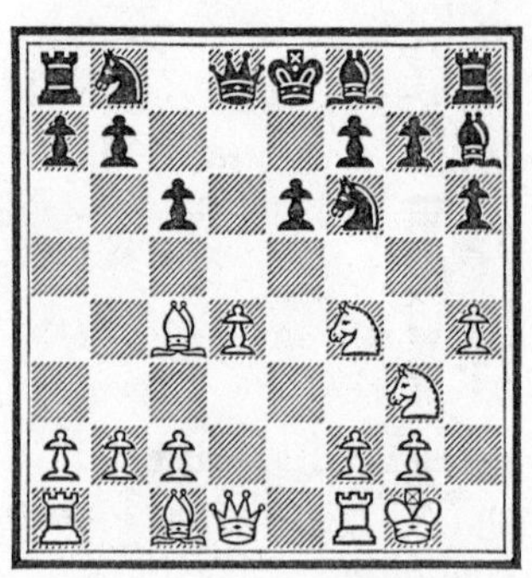

White's development is superior, but he really has no target

—one of the advantages of the Caro-Kann.

10. . . . . B—Q3
11. Kt × P ?!

A poor move against Botvinnik, but it might have worked out against some lesser master.

11. . . . . P × Kt
12. B × P(K6) Q—B2
13. R—K1 Kt(Kt1)—Q2

Now White must move the B on K6, for *14.* . . . . O—O—O will leave Black with a far superior game. The B move which follows at least prevents Black from castling.

14. B—Kt8*ch* K—B1
15. B × B R × B
16. Kt—B5 P—KKt3 *!*

Black gives up another Pawn to open the KR file and to free the R on R2.

17. B × P*ch* K—Kt1
18. Kt × B Q × Kt

Better than *18.* . . . . R × B; *19.* R—K6. Black wants as much room as possible for his pieces.

19. B—Kt5 R—K2
20. Q—Q3 K—Kt2

Now the R on R1 can move to wherever it will be needed, to K1 or KR1 or Q1.

21. Q—KKt3

White decides to exchange Queens before Black's pieces combine to develop an attack. Tal hopes to develop a passed Pawn on the K-side.

21. . . . . R × R*ch*
22. R × R Q × Q
23. P × Q R—KB1 *!*

It is too early to simplify by *23.* . . . . R—K1; *24.* B × Kt*ch*, Kt × B; *25.* R × R, Kt × R, for White may then break through with a passed Pawn on one side or the other.

24. P—B4 Kt—Kt5
25. P—Q5

White pushes this Pawn in order to force Black's pieces to occupy themselves in stopping it; the White K needs air!

25. . . . . P × P
26. P × P Kt(Q2)—B3

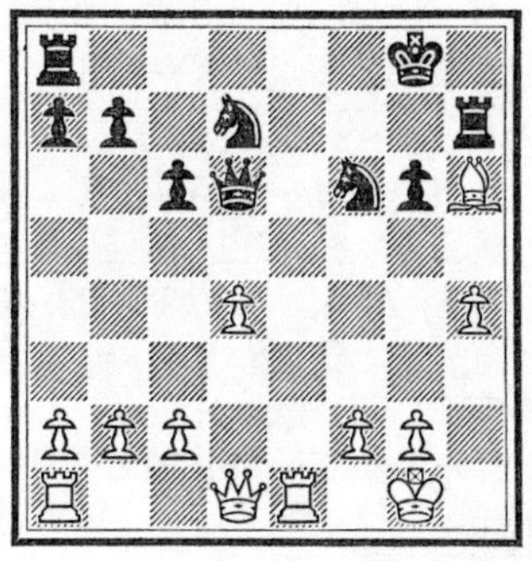

27. **P—Q6** **R—B2**
28. **R—QB1** **R—Q2**
29. **R—B7**

Black's pieces are tied down, but the K can still move. Black will pick off the QP by K—B2 and K—K3 if permitted to do so.

29. . . . . **K—B2**
30. **B × Kt** **Kt × B**

If *30.* B—B4, K—K3; *31.* K—B1, Kt—K4 and the QP still falls.

31. **K—B2** **K—K3**
32. **R × R** **K × R**
33. **K—B3** **K × P**
34. **K—B4** **K—K3**

White's K-side Pawns assure him a passed Pawn, but Black's King can block it.

35. **P—KKt4**

Better than K—Kt5, when . . . . K—B2 holds everything.

35. . . . . **Kt—Q4*ch***
36. **K—K4** **Kt—B3*ch***
37. **K—B4** **Kt—Q4*ch***
38. **K—K4** **Kt—Kt5**

Black's Kt maneuver forces White to play P—R3. This, in turn, will make the QKtP a target. As White's Q-side Pawns move, they become easier targets.

39. **P—R3** **Kt—B3**
40. **P—R5***?*

Better P—Kt5 and then P—KKt4 and finally P—R5. Now the Pawns will be blocked.

40. . . . . **P—KKt4***!*
41. **P—R6** **K—B3**
42. **K—Q5**

If *42.* P—R7, K—Kt2; *43.* K—B5, Kt—R4 and then *44.* . . . . Kt—B5.

42. . . . . **K—Kt3**
43. **K—K6**

Because if *43.* K—Q6, Kt—R4; *44.* K—B7, P—Kt3; *45.* P—Kt4, Kt—B5; *46.* K—Kt7, P—R4; *47.* P × P, P × P; *48.* K—R6, Kt × P; *49.* K × P, Kt—B7 and Black wins by picking off the White Pawns.

43.	Kt—R4
44. P—R4	Kt—Kt6
45. K—Q6	P—R4
46. K—Q5	K × P
47. K—B4	Kt—B8
48. K—Kt5	Kt—Q6
49. P—QKt3	Kt—B8
50. K × P	

An unfortunate necessity. If *50.* K—B4, K—Kt3, and the return of the Black King via B3, K4, B5 will mean the end for White.

50.	Kt × P*ch*
51. K—Kt4	Kt—B8
52. K—B3	

RULE TO REMEMBER

An extra Pawn or piece in the ending should be enough to win. When you are a Pawn or more ahead, try to keep one or more Pawns on the board. You will later force the win by Queening one of your Pawns.

If White goes after the QKtP, then Black's King picks up the K side Pawns while the Kt moves to Kt6 and stops the White QRP.

52.	K—Kt3
53. K—B2	Kt—K7

54. K—Q3	Kt—B8*ch*
55. K—B2	Kt—K7
56. K—Q3	Kt—B5*ch*
57. K—B4	K—B3
58. P—Kt3	Kt—K7
59. Resigns	

Because of *59.* K—Kt5, Kt × P; *60.* K—Kt6, Kt—K5; *61.* P—R5, Kt—Q3*!* A very instructive ending.

20 Sicilian Defense

Mar del Plata, 1955

White	*Black*
L. Pachman	M. Naidorf

The Opening

The Sicilian Defense (*1.* P—K4, P—QB4) is today the most popular defense to *1.* P—K4. In it, Black tries to develop pressure along the QB file, and White aims for P—KB4 and a K-side attack. White usually plays an early P—Q4, which, after Black plays . . . . P × P, makes White's P—KB4 possible. At the same time, it also opens the QB file and a positional struggle results.

White's Plan

Pachman, Czechoslovakia's leading master, plays cautiously in this game. He avoids P—Q4, and develops slowly.

Black's Plan

Black, a Polish master who settled in Argentina and became that country's leading chessmaster, has made great contributions to the theory of the Sicilian Defense. He seeks moves that contain small threats. These moves slowly weaken White's position. Then, as in this game, an attack can be directed against White's K position.

Comment

The game illustrates the attack on the KR file after P—KR4 and P—KR5 against a castled position.

1. **P—K4**	**P—QB4**
2. **Kt—QB3**	**P—Q3**
3. **P—Q3**	

A rarely played line. White avoids the opening of the QB file which would have occurred after *1.* P—K4, P—QB4; 2. Kt—KB3, P—Q3; 3. P—Q4, P × P; *4.* Kt × P—the most usual line of play against the Sicilian Defense.

3.	**Kt—QB3**
4. **P—KKt3**	**Kt—B3**
5. **B—Kt2**	**B—Kt5**

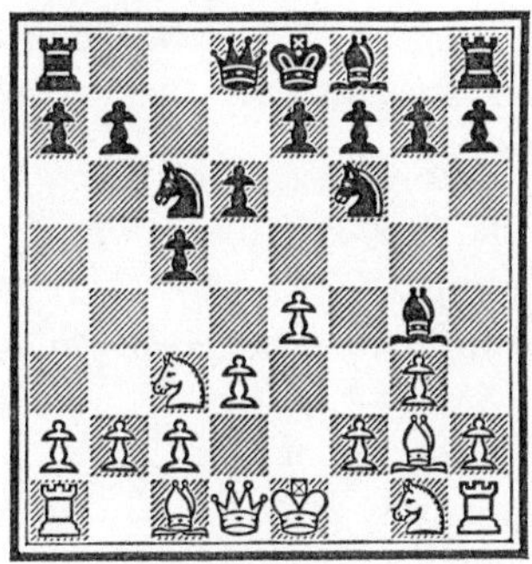

The Bishop attacks the White Queen. If *6.* P—B3 to block the attack, then White's K position is weakened and his pieces are cramped by the P on B3. But *6.* P—B3 was best.

6.	**Kt(Kt1)—K2**	**Kt—Q5 *!***
7.	**O—O**	

Too passive. *7.* P—KR3 was better, with the probable continuation 7. . . . . B—B6; 8. B × B, Kt × B*ch*; 9. K—B1 and *10.* K—Kt2.

7.	**. . . .**	**Kt—B6*ch* *!***
8.	**K—R1**	**P—KR4 *!***
9.	**P—KR3**	**P—K4**

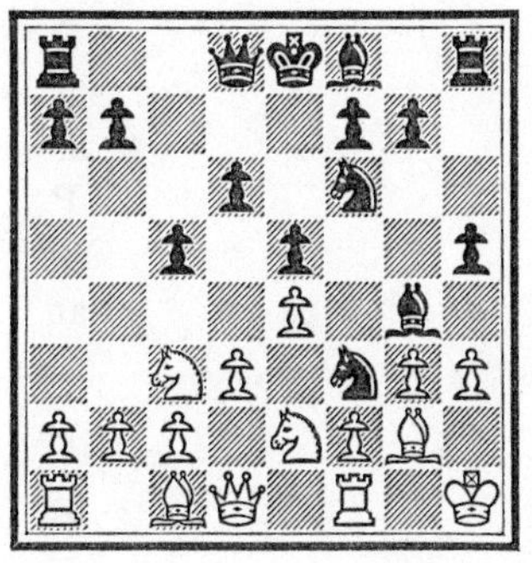

White cannot now play *10.* P × B, P × P*ch*; *11.* B—R3, R × B*ch*; *12.* K—Kt2, R—R7 mate. But Black could have played 9. . . . . P—R5; *10.* P × B, P × P*ch*; *11.* B—R3, R × B*ch*; *12.* K —Kt2, Q—Q2; *13.* Kt × P, Q × P; *14.* Q × Kt, R—R7*ch*; *15.* K × R, Q × Q, or 9. . . . . P—R5; *10.* P × B, P × P*ch*; *11.* B—R3, R × B*ch*; *12.* K—Kt2, Q—Q2; *13.* P × P, R—R7*ch*; *14.* K × Kt, P—KKt3; *15.* B—B4, Q × P*ch*; *16.* K—K3, P—K4 and Black regains his piece with a strong attack.

10. **Kt—Q5 *?***	

10. B—K3 was essential, to be followed by *11.* Kt—B1 and *12.* D × Kt.

10.	**. . . .**	**Kt × Kt**
11.	**P × Kt**	**Q—Q2**
12.	**Kt—B3**	

If *12.* Kt—Kt1, Kt—R7 *!*; *13.* P × B, P × P, and the attack on the KR file follows by . . . . Q —B4 and . . . . Q—R4.

12.	**. . . .**	**Q—B4**
13.	**B—K3**	**P—R5 *!***
14.	**Kt—K4**	**B—K2 *!***

So that, if *15.* P × B, P × P*ch*; *16.* B—R3, R × B*ch*; *17.* K—Kt2, R—R7*ch*; *18.* K × P, B—R5 mate!

15.	**P—B4**	**P × P**
16.	**P × P**	**R × P*ch* *!***

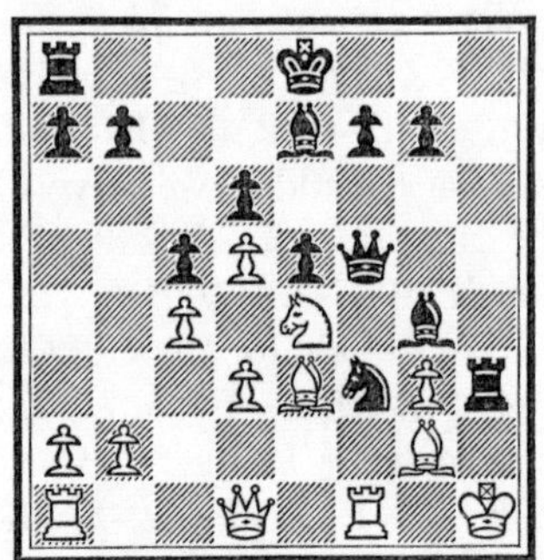

White's position crumbles. His next move is forced.

17. **B × R** **Q—R4**

There is no way to avoid . . . . Q × B*ch.*

18. **Q—R4*ch*** **K—B1**
19. **R × Kt**

19. K—Kt2 would not do, for Black would play *19.* . . . . Q × B*ch*; *20.* K—B2, Q—R7 mate.

19. . . . . **Q × B*ch***
20. **Resigns**

White wins a Queen by *20.* K—Kt1, B × R (threatening Q—Kt7 mate); *21.* Q—B2, Q—R8*ch*; *22.* K—B2, Q—Kt7*ch*; *23.* K—K1, Q × Q.

White cannot play the Sicilian as passively as he did this game!

RULE TO REMEMBER

You should not play passive moves in the opening! Do not permit your opponent to take control of the center without opposing such control!

If your opponent makes passive opening moves, try to take control of the center squares.

---

21 Sicilian Defense

World Championship
Challengers Tournament, 1959

White	*Black*
R. Fischer	M. Tal

The Opening

Fischer and Tal were matched four times in this tournament—and Tal, who was to be the next world champion, won all four games. He did this by playing lines which gave him chances for attack, even at the cost of weaknesses in his position.

White's Plan

Fischer plays for a K-side attack, while Tal counters on the Q-side. In the resulting complications, White's Kt and B are stranded on the Q-side.

Black's Plan

Tal develops a strong bind on the center, combining it with the opening of the K-side.

Comment

The open line of play in this game is one of the most popular in the Sicilian today.

1.	**P—K4**	**P—QB4**
2.	**Kt—KB3**	**P—Q3**
3.	**P—Q4**	**P × P**
4.	**Kt × P**	**Kt—KB3**
5.	**Kt—QB3**	**P—QR3**
6.	**B—QB4**	

6. B—K2 is also played at this point.

6.	. . . .	**P—K3**
7.	**B—Kt3**	**B—K2**
8.	**P—B4**	

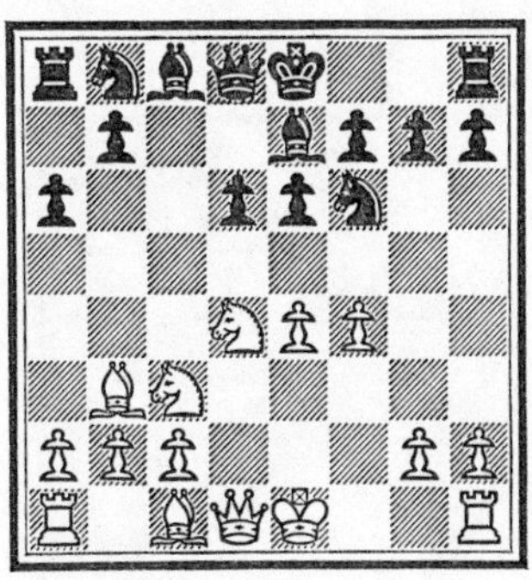

White prepares for the attack on the K-side, to come after preparations via P—K5 or P—B5.

8.	. . . .	**O—O**
9.	**Q—B3**	**Q—B2**
10.	**O—O**	**P—QKt4**

Inviting *11.* P—K5, P × P; *12.* Q × R, B—Kt2; *13.* Q—R7, B—B4, and the Q is trapped!

11.	**P—B5**	**P—Kt5!**
12.	**Kt—R4**	

Holding the QB5 square and threatening a later Kt—Kt6, but as things work out, the Kt is left stranded on QR4. Perhaps Kt—Q1—B2 would have been better.

12.	. . . .	**P—K4**

Black locks up the center. *12.* . . . . P × P; *13.* Kt × P would invite a White attack against KKt7.

13.	**Kt—K2**	**B—Kt2**
14.	**Kt—Kt3**	**Kt(Kt1)—Q2**
15.	**B—K3**	**B—B3**
16.	**B—B2**	

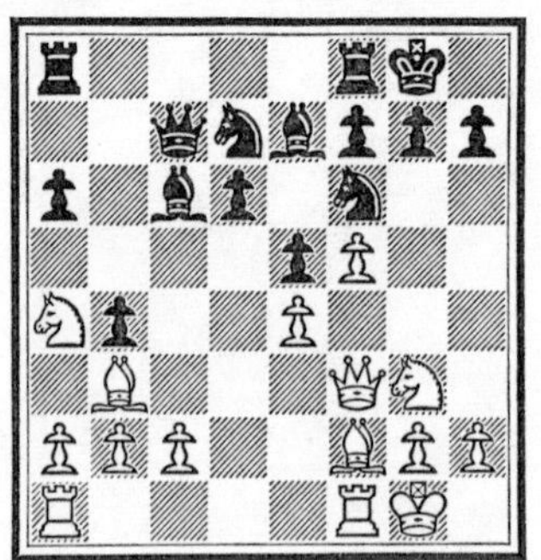

Now, if Black tries to win a piece by *16.* . . . . Q—R4; *17.* P—QR3!, B × Kt; *18.* P × P and *19.* R × B. Black threatens White's KP instead.

16.	. . . .	**Q—Kt2**
17.	**R(B1)—K1**	**P—Q4!**

This is often the freeing move in the Sicilian Defense. White must capture on Q5, to avoid *18.* . . . . P × P.

18.	**P × P**	**Kt × P**
19.	**Kt—K4**	**Kt—B5**
20.	**P—B4?**	

20. B—Kt3 is better. Now the B on QKt3 is out of play.

20.	. . . .	**P—Kt3**

To play *21.* . . . . P × P, and the Black Pawns march on.

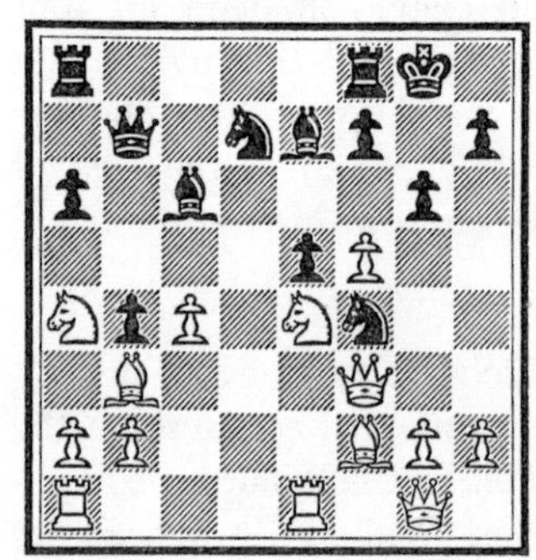

21.	**P × P**	**P—B4!**
22.	**P—Kt7**	

If *22.* P—B5*ch*, K—Kt2.

22.	. . . .	**K × P**
23.	**Q—Kt3*ch***	**K—R1**
24.	**Kt(K4)—B5**	

White seeks exchanges. If *24.* Kt—Q2, Black has *24.* . . . . Kt × P and *25.* . . . . B—R5!

24.	Kt × Kt
25. **B × Kt**	**B × B*ch***
26. **Kt × B**	**Q—QB2**
27. **Q—K3 ?**	

Giving up the exchange. Better, but still giving Black a better game, was *27.* Kt—Q3, Kt × P; *28.* Q × P*ch*, Q × Q; *29.* R × Q, P—B5.

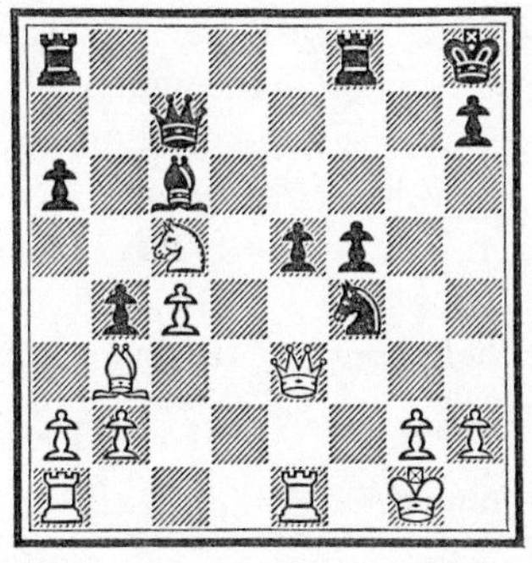

27.	**QR—K1**
28. **R—K2**	**Kt × R*ch***
29. **Q × Kt**	**B × P**

White cannot take the Bishop. If *30.* Q × B, R—KKt1 wins the Queen. If *30.* K × B, Q × Kt.

30. **Kt × P**	**Q—R2*ch***
31. **K × B**	

Because if *31.* P—B5, R—B3; *32.* B—B4, R—KKt3; *33.* K—B2, P—B5 and Black's Pawns march on.

31.	**R—Kt1*ch***
32. **K—R3**	

On *32.* K—B1, Q—Kt8 mate.

On 32. K—R1, Q—R1*ch*; 33. Any Q move to block the check, Q × Q mate.

RULE TO REMEMBER

Black has two winning advantages in this position: the protected passed Pawns and the open KKt file.

Place a Rook behind a passed Pawn to protect it as it advances.

Be ready to place a Rook on an open file. Combine its action with that of another piece—as Black does with his Queen in this game.

---

32.	**Q—KKt2**

Better the threat of . . . . Q—R3*ch* than . . . . Q × Kt.

33. **B—Q1**

Hoping for defense by *33.* . . . . Q—R3*ch*; *34.* Q—R5. But Black has another threat!

33.	**R—K3**
34. ***Resigns***	

Mate cannot be prevented after *34.* . . . . R—R3*ch* and *35.* . . . . Q—Kt7 and *36.* . . . . Q × RP mate.

White never recovered from *20.* P—B4 ?

RULE TO REMEMBER

Do not make Pawn moves which block your developed pieces—like P—B4 by White in this game.

---

22 Sicilian Defense

Warsaw, 1935

White	*Black*
P. Keres	W. Winter

The Opening

There are a number of openings in which White gives up several Pawns in the search for better development. Paul Keres, whose talent for attack is legendary, has played many brilliant games featuring opening sacrifices. In this game, he proves that Black cannot go Pawn-hunting in the Sicilian Defense.

White's Plan

Keres sacrifices three Pawns for development, and then gives up a Knight to set Black's King up for a quick finish.

Black's Plan

Winter was one of England's best players. In this game he makes the mistake of underestimating his teen-age opponent—the same mistake dozens of masters later made when playing Bobby Fischer. Winter fails to develop his pieces, goes pawn-hunting, and finds himself mated while his QR and QKt sit helplessly on their original squares.

Comment

The game illustrates again the importance of developing your pieces before attempting aggressive play.

1. **P—K4** **P—QB4**
2. **Kt—KB3** **Kt—KB3**

Black invites 3. P—K5, hoping to be able to attack it later on.

3. **P—K5** **Kt—Q4**
4. **Kt—B3 *!***

White does not fear 4. . . . . Kt × Kt; 5. QP × Kt, when his lines of play would be open.

4. . . . . **P—K3**
5. **Kt × Kt** **P × Kt**
6. **P—Q4** **P—Q3**

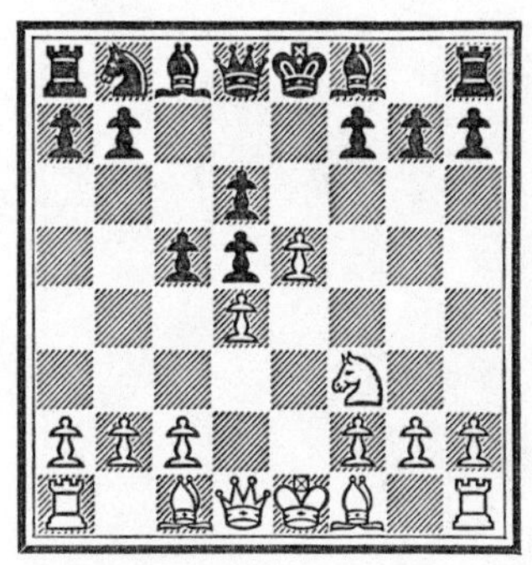

7. **B—KKt5** **Q—R4*ch*?**

There are two better moves, 7. . . . . B—K2 and 7. . . . . Q—Kt3. The latter gives Black a good game if White tries to win a Pawn by 7. . . . . Q—Kt3; 8. QP × P, P × P(B4); 9. Q × P, B—K3; *10.* B—Kt5*ch,* Kt—B3 (*10.* . . . . Q × B would allow *11.* Q—Q8 mate); *11.* B × Kt*ch,* P × B; *12.* Q—Q2, P—KR3; *13.* B—R4, P—Kt4; *14.* B—Kt3, R—Q1.

8. **P—B3** **P × P(Q5)**
9. **B—Q3!**

Keres offers the QBP and QKtP to gain a lead in development.

9. . . . . **P × BP**

And Black goes a-hunting, not realizing that he may soon step into a bear trap!

10. **O—O** **P × KtP?**

A losing idea. Development is essential, by *10.* . . . . Kt—B3 or *10.* . . . . B—K3.

11. **R—Kt1** **P × P**
12. **Kt × P** **B—Q3**
13. **Kt × P!** **K × Kt**
14. **Q—R5*ch*** **P—KKt3**

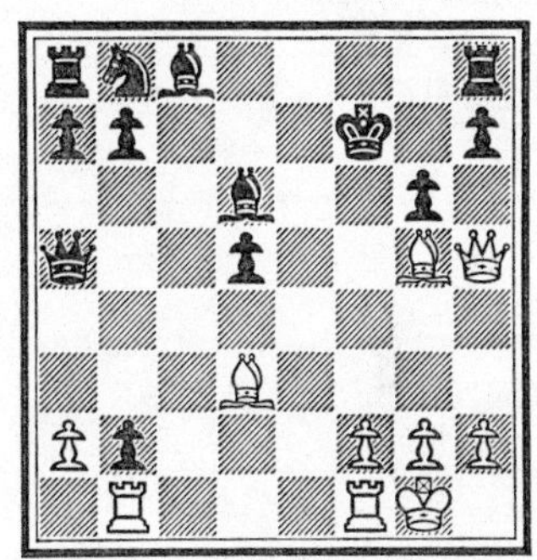

Black has no defense.

a. If *14.* . . . . K—K3; *15.* B—B5*ch,* K × B; *16.* B—Q8*ch* wins the Queen.

b. If *14.* . . . . K—K3; *15.* B—B5*ch,* K—K4; *16.* R(B1)—K1*ch,* K—Q5; *17.* B—K3*ch,* K—B6; *18.* Q—Q1! and mate on Q4, Q3, or QKt3 next move.

c. If *14.* . . . . K—Kt1; *15.* Q—K8*ch,* B—B1; *16.* B—K7, Kt—Q2; *17.* B—KB5, P—KR3; *18.* B—Kt6 and mate follows on B7 or B8.

d. If *14.* . . . . K—B1; *15.* R(B1)—K1, B—Q2; *16.* Q—B3*ch,* K—Kt1; *17.* B—K7!, B × B; *18.* R × B and mate follows on B7 or K8.

15. **B × Pch!** **P × B**
16. **Q × R** **B—KB4**

16. . . . . Kt—Q2 would not stop the attack, for White can play *17.* Q—R7*ch*, K—B1; *18.* B—R6*ch*, K—K1; *19.* Q × P*ch*, K—Q1; *20.* Q × B and White wins after *20.* . . . . P—Q5; *21.* P—KR4, Q—K4; *22.* B—Kt5*ch*, K—K1; *23.* R(B1)—K1.

RULE TO REMEMBER

Beware of Queen moves early in the game!

---

17. **R(B1)—K1**

White threatens *18.* Q—B6*ch*, K—Kt1; *19.* R—K8*ch*, B—KB1; *20.* R × B*ch*, K—R2; *21.* R—R8 mate. Black blocks the Rook.

17. . . . . **B—K5**
18. **R × B!** **P × R**
19. **Q—B6*ch*** **Resigns**

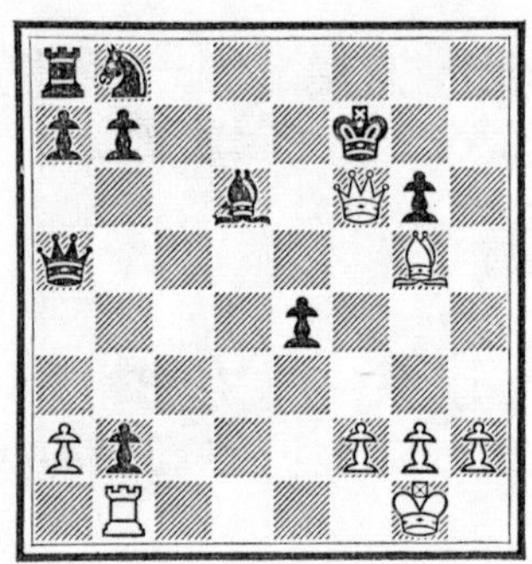

The win is forced.

a. If *19.* . . . . K—Kt1; *20.* Q × P*ch*, K—B1; *21.* Q × B*ch*, K—Kt1; *22.* Q—K6*ch*, K—Kt2; *23.* Q—K7*ch*, K—Kt1; *24.* B—B6 and mate on KKt7 follows.

b. If *23.* . . . . K—Kt3 in line *a* above, then *24.* Q—B6*ch*, K—R4; *25.* Q—R6*ch*, K—Kt5; *26.* P—KR3*ch*, K—B4; *27.* Q—B6 mate.

c. If *19.* . . . . K—K1; *20.* Q—K6*ch*, K—B1; *21.* B—R6 mate.

The game points its own moral—do not go Pawn-hunting in the opening!

23 Sicilian Defense

Nottingham, 1936

White	*Black*
A. Alekhine	M. Botvinnik

The Opening

This game was the first meeting between Alekhine, then world champion, and Botvinnik, the Russian champion and future world titleholder. The line they play is important, for it leads to a draw by perpetual check as Black gets in P—Q4 and then invades on the K-side.

White's Plan

White pushes his Pawns through on the K-side after developing his pieces to support them.

Black's Plan

Black counters in the center, finding the best moves, but not able to do more than equalize.

What to Watch for

The perpetual check in this game had to be planned for. It involves two piece sacrifices. Very often, masters play for and are satisfied with such quick draws.

1.	P—K4	P—QB4
2.	Kt—KB3	P—Q3
3.	P—Q4	P × P
4.	Kt × P	Kt—KB3
5.	Kt—QB3	P—KKt3
6.	B—K2	B—Kt2
7.	B—K3	

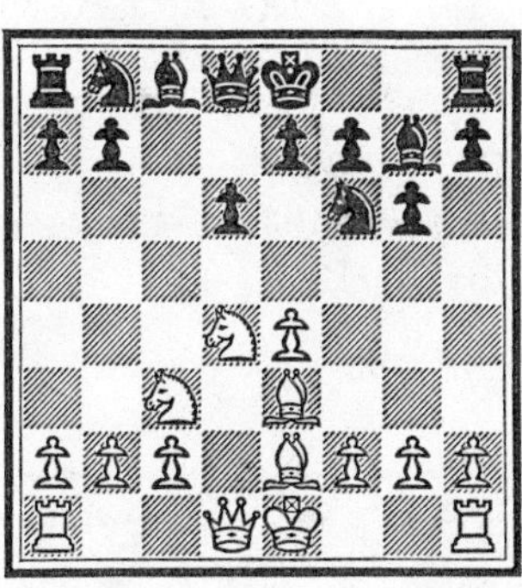

This order of moves leads to the Dragon Variation of the Sicilian Defense. Black will castle, complete his development, and then play for . . . . P—Q4. White will counter by pushing K-side Pawns. First he supports his Knight with this Bishop move.

7. . . . . **Kt—B3**
8. **Kt—Kt3**

White avoids exchanges.

8. . . . . **B—K3**
9. **P—B4**

Threatening *10.* P—K5 if 9. . . . . P—Q4.

9. . . . . **O—O**
10. **P—Kt4**

A King-side attack without castling. White wants to play *11.* P—B5 and *12.* P—Kt5.

10. . . . . **P—Q4!**

To answer *11.* P—K5 with *11.* . . . . P—Q5; *12.* Kt × P, Kt × Kt; *13.* B × Kt, Kt × P and White cannot play *14.* B × Kt, B × B; *15.* Q × B, Q × B; *16.* R—Q1, Q—B5 because the K position would be open for attack by Black.

11. **P—B5**

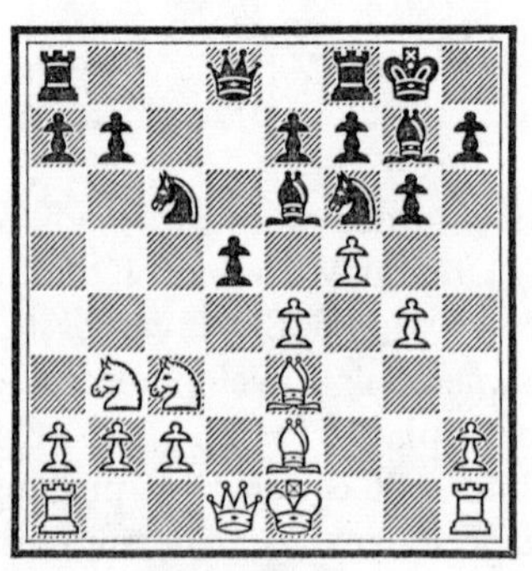

White pushes on, and Black places the B on its only square.

11. . . . . **B—B1**
12. **P × QP**

If *12.* B—B3?, P × KP; *13.* Kt × P, Kt × Kt; *14.* B × Kt, B × KtP and Black has won a Pawn.

12. . . . . **Kt—Kt5!**

Now Black can regain the Pawn, either by . . . . Kt(Kt5) × P or by . . . . P × P.

13. **P—Q6**

White rejects *13.* P × P, RP × P; *14.* B—B3, Kt × KtP; *15.* B × Kt, B × B; *16.* Q × B, Kt × P*ch; 17.* K—K2, Kt × R; *18.* R × Kt, B × Kt; *19.* P × B, Q × P and Black has a R and 3 Pawns for a Kt and B. Alekhine felt that this position would then be in Black's favor, and pushes the QP on instead.

On *13.* B—B3, P × P; *14.* P—Kt5, Kt—K1; *15.* P—QR3! White should stand better.

13. . . . . **Q × P**

13. . . . . P × QP? would fail because of *14.* P—Kt5; *15.* P—B6, and the Black B is locked in.

14. **B—B5**

If *14.* Q × Q, P × Q; *15.* O—O—O, then Black has *15.* . . . . P × P or *15.* . . . . R—K1.

14. . . . . **Q—B5**

Alekhine felt this was the saving move for Black. White cannot now play *15.* B × P because of *15.* . . . . Kt—K5; *16.* Kt × Kt, Q × Kt and Black threatens . . . . Q × R*ch*, ... Q × B, and . . . . Kt × P*ch*. White therefore accepts the sacrificed Kt.

15. **R—KB1** **Q × RP**

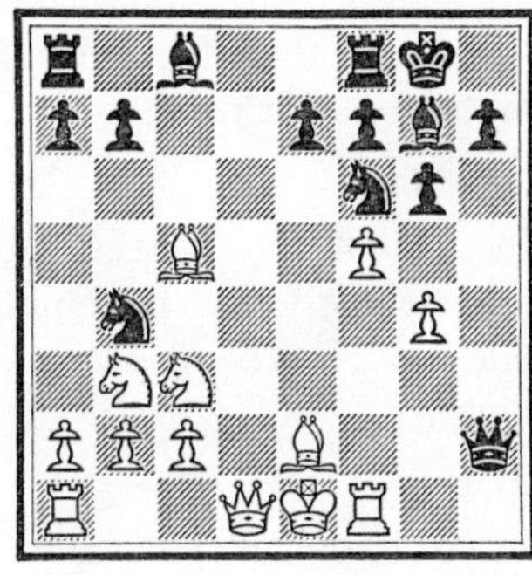

16. **B × Kt** **Kt × P** ***!***

Another sacrifice, intended to leave the White K bare for the checks by the Queen. The Kt must be taken, for Black threatens *17.* . . . . Q—Kt6*ch*; *18.* K—Q2, R—Q1*ch*; *19.* B—Q3, B—R3*ch*; *20.* K—K2, Q—K6 mate.

17. **B × Kt** **Q—Kt6*ch***
18. **R—B2**

a. If *18.* K—K2, Q × B*ch*.
b. If *18.* K—Q2, B—R3*ch*; *19.* K—K2, Q—K6 mate!

18. **. . . .** **Q—Kt8*ch***
19. **R—B1** **Q—Kt6*ch***
20. **R—B2** **Q—Kt8*ch***

Drawn

Drawn by perpetual check. Although White is two Knights ahead, he has no way to escape the checks without also losing his two Bishops. Thus, if *21.* K—K2, Q × B*ch* and *22.* . . . . Q × B is to Black's clear advantage.

RULE TO REMEMBER

Beginners should avoid such complicated lines of play as the one in Game 23. White can avoid the tension of the Dragon Variation by seeking a simplifying line, such as:

(*a*) *1.* P—K4, P—QB4; 2. Kt—KB3, P—Q3; 3. B—Kt5*ch*.

(*b*) *1.* P—K4, P—QB4; 2. Kt—KB3, P—Q3; *3.* P—Q4, P × P; *4.* Kt × P, Kt—KB3; 5. B—Kt5*ch*.

---

24 Sicilian Defense

Yugoslavia, 1972
(Chess Olympics)

White	*Black*
A. Karpov	E. Ungureanu

The Opening

Black success with the Sicilian Defense usually depends on counterplay in the center or on the Q-side. The Rauzer Attack is a method of preventing such counterplay. White develops his pieces, opens the center by exchanges, and then tries to control the center while pressing on the K-side.

White's Plan

Anatoly Karpov is the fastest-rising young chessmaster in the Soviet Union. In this game he plays to obtain two Bishops against a Bishop and a Knight. This gives him greater mobility when he opens lines. He concludes with a carefully calculated attack involving his two Bishops and a K-side invasion.

Black's Plan

Black usually gains a half-open QB-file in the Sicilian Defense. Ungureanu concentrates his pieces on the Q-side to take advantage of that file. He fails to protect his K-side.

Comment

Note how Karpov's pieces protect his King while remaining mobile enough to be used for the final attack.

1.	P—K4	P—QB4
2.	Kt—KB3	Kt—QB3
3.	P—Q4	P × P
4.	Kt × P	Kt—B3
5.	Kt—QB3	P—Q3
6.	B—KKt5	P—K3
7.	Q—Q2	

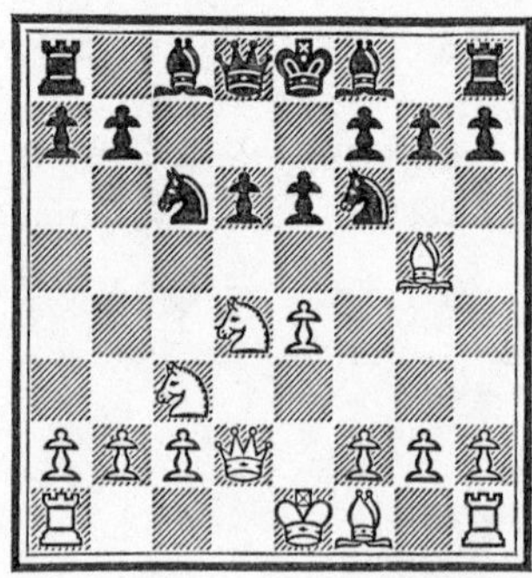

White will castle, complete his development, and begin to clear the center. Black needs time to complete his development, and is blocked by his KP and QP. However, there are as yet no weak points in Black's position.

7. . . . . **B—K2**

Black must develop his pieces. If *7.* . . . . P—KR3; *8.* B × Kt, P × B; *9.* O—O—O permits White to remain far ahead in development.

8. **O—O—O** **O—O**

RULE TO REMEMBER

When you and your opponent have castled on opposite sides of the board, try to gain control of the center before you attack his King position. Play for open lines for your pieces.

9.	**P—B4**	**Kt × Kt**
10.	**Q × Kt**	**Q—R4**
11.	**B—B4**	**B—Q2**

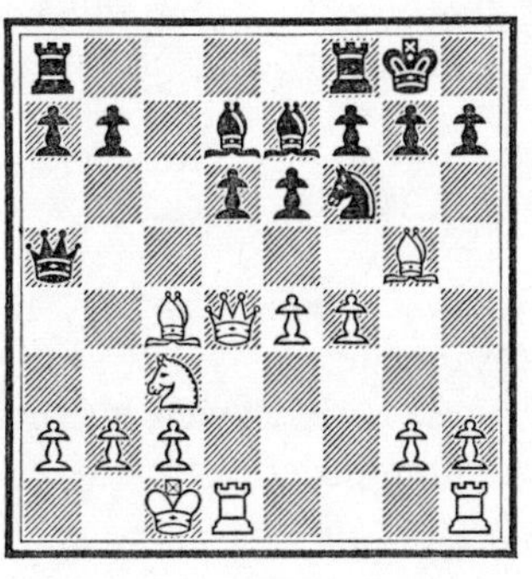

What is White's plan? He has completed his development and controls the center. Black is not yet fully developed (both Bishops lack scope). White must now seek moves that prevent Black from getting open lines.

12. **P—K5**

White opens the center while he still controls it. *12.* P—K5 forces Black to delay any efforts to improve the position of his pieces.

RULE TO REMEMBER

Make moves that force your opponent to move pieces he has already developed—especially when his development is still incomplete!

12.	. . . .	**P × P**
13.	**P × P**	**B—B3 *!***

13. . . . . Kt—Q4 would lose a piece after *14.* B × B, Kt × B; *15.* Q × B. *13.* . . . . B—B3 really defends the attacked Knight, for if White now plays *14.* P × Kt, Q × B*ch* leaves Black a Pawn ahead.

14. **B—Q2 *!*** **Kt—Q2**

If Black played *14.* . . . . either Rook to Q1, White would win material by *15.* Kt—Q5.

RULE TO REMEMBER

As a general rule, do not attack enemy pieces while your own pieces are under attack. After *15.* Kt—Q5, White would be attacking Black's Q, B, and Kt.

15. Kt—Q5	Q—Q1
16. Kt × B*ch*	Q × Kt

RULE TO REMEMBER

Two Bishops are usually better than a Knight and a Bishop or two Knights—especially when the center is open.

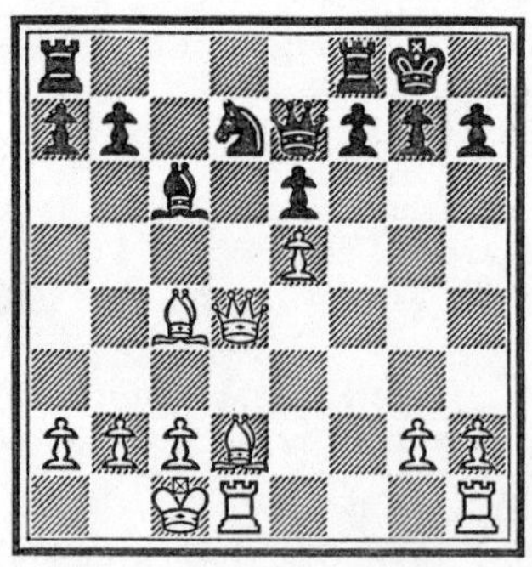

Black threatens to capture White's KKtP. Should White protect it?

17. KR—K1 *!*	KR—B1

17. . . . . B × P would be a mistake. White would reply *18.* R—Kt1, B—B3; *19.* Q—Kt4 threatening mate and a pileup against Black's K-side.

RULE TO REMEMBER

Do not capture Pawns when doing so opens attacking lines for your opponent!

18. Q—B4	P—QR4

Black prepares a counterattack with the Q-side Pawns.

19. K—Kt1

RULE TO REMEMBER

Make certain your King is safe before your pull your pieces away for an attack.

19.	Kt—Kt3 *?*

Black suddenly changes plans. He should have played *19.* . . . . P—QKt4; *20.* B—Q3, Kt—B4, threatening to exchange pieces and then continue the advance of his Q-side Pawns.

20. B—Q3	Kt—Q4
21. Q—KKt4	Q—B4

Black is concentrating his pieces against White's King. However, he is leaving his own King unprotected.

22. R—K4 *!*

The Rook moves to the center, where it has greater mobility. It can later move to the KR or KKt file, or go to QB4 to drive back the Black Queen.

22. . . . . P—QKt4
23. **Q—R3 !**

This is a hidden attack on the Black KRP. The Bishop on Q3 and the Queen on R3 both bear down on that Pawn. *24.* R—KR4 is also threatened.

23. . . . . **Kt—Kt5**
24. **B—K3 !**

This move sacrifices material for a few moves, but opens the key Q-file to prevent the later escape of Black's King.

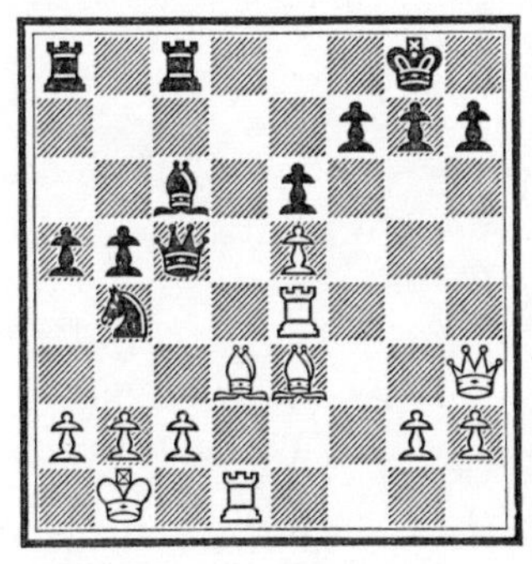

24. . . . . **B × R**

Any Queen move by Black loses!

a. 24. . . . . Q—Q4; *25.* R × Kt, P × R; *26.* B × P*ch,* K—B1; *27.* R × Q

RULE TO REMEMBER

Do not sacrifice material unless you see how to regain it or gain a drawing or mating attack. In this game Karpov had seen six moves ahead in the main line and eight moves in one of the possible lines.

b. 24. . . . . Q—K2 (or B1); *25.* R × Kt, Q × R; *26.* P—R3, Q—R5; *27.* Q × RP*ch,* K—B1; *28.* B—B5*ch,* K—K1; *29.* Q—Kt8*ch,* K—Q2; *30.* Q × BP*ch,* K—Q1; *31.* Q—K7 mate

25. **B × B !**

White plays for a quick win, and decides not to take Black's Queen. He sees he would have only a small advantage in the end-game after *25.* B × Q, B × B; *26.* P × B, R × B. Instead, Karpov will win a piece.

25. . . . . **Q × P**
26. **Q × P*ch*** **K—B1**
27. **B × R** **K—K2**

Black cannot play *27.* . . . R × B; *28.* Q—R8*ch,* K—K2; *29.* Q × R, Q × B; *30.* Q—Q8 mate.

28. **Q—K4 !**

Protecting both Bishops.

28. . . . . **Q—B2**
29. **Q—Kt7 !** **Resigns**

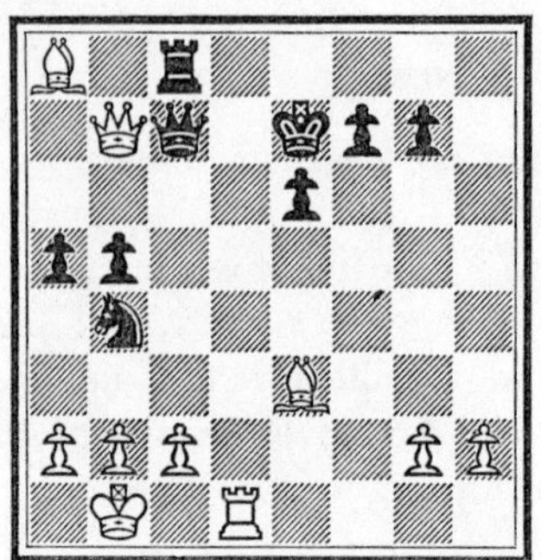

Why does Black resign? He cannot play his planned counter-attack, *29.* . . . . Q × P*ch,* with mate to follow, because his Queen is pinned! He must exchange Queens, *29.* . . . . Q × Q; *30.* B × Q, when White remains a piece ahead with an easy win.

25 Sicilian Defense

Reykjavik, Iceland, 1972

White	*Black*
Boris Spassky	Robert J. Fischer

The Opening

The Najdorf System is a counterattacking line of play in the Sicilian Defense. Black blocks the center and seeks play on the Q-side. In this game, Black then tries to win a Pawn at the cost of several Queen moves. In return, White gains better development. He uses this development to trap Black's Queen—which explains why this line is called the "Poisoned Pawn Variation."

White's Plan

Boris Spassky lost the world's championship to Bobby Fischer in 1972. This is one of the two games he won. He permits the Poisoned Pawn Variation, plays to develop quickly, and then wins Black's Queen.

Black's Plan

Fischer, one of the deepest thinkers in chess history, did not plan far enough ahead in this game. He was certain he could win a Pawn and then retreat his Queen or begin an attack while White was trying to trap the Queen.

Comment

The general rule "Do not waste time trying to win a Pawn unless you have first developed your pieces!" is again illustrated by this game between two giants of the chess world.

1.	**P—K4**	**P—QB4**
2.	**Kt—KB3**	**P—Q3**
3.	**P—Q4**	**P × P**
4.	**Kt × P**	**Kt—KB3**
5.	**Kt—QB3**	**P—QR3**
6.	**B—KKt5**	**P—K3**
7.	**P—B4**	**Q—Kt3**

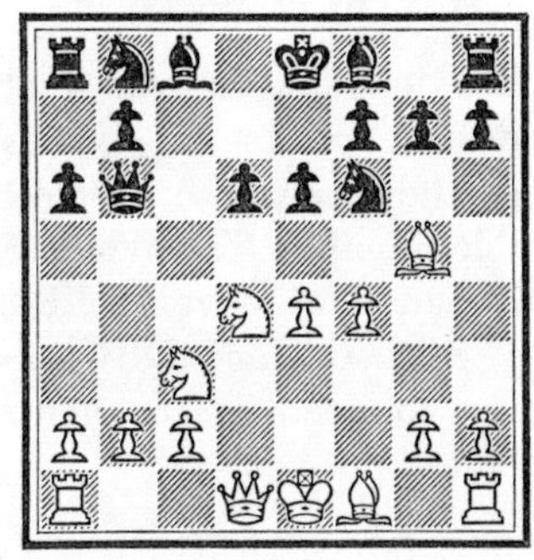

Black's 7. . . . . Q—Kt3 is the key move of the Poisoned Pawn Variation. White decides to continue his development and sacrifices the QKtP.

8. **Q—Q2** *!* **Q × P**
9. **Kt—Kt3** *!*

This limits the escape route for the Black Queen. *9.* R—QKt1, Q—R6; *10.* R—Kt3, Q—R4 would bring White's Rook into play, but would also permit the Black Queen to flee.

9. . . . . **Q—R6**

Black must play this move at once. Otherwise, White will play *10.* P—QR4 and *11.* R—R2, when the Black Queen is trapped!

10. **B × Kt** *!*

White removes the only developed piece on Black's K-side.

10. . . . . **P × B**
11. **B—K2** *!*

RULE TO REMEMBER

Make opening moves that place your pieces on squares where they have the greatest possible mobility. The White B at K2 can now move to KB3, KKt4, KR5, Q3, and QB4—according to need as the game continues.

White prepares to castle, and also threatens *12.* B—R5, with pressure against the Black King.

11. . . . . **P—KR4**

Black prevents *12.* B—R5. But he is still undeveloped. With his next move, White completes his development—well worth a Pawn, since five Black pieces remain on their original squares!

12. **O—O** **Kt—B3**

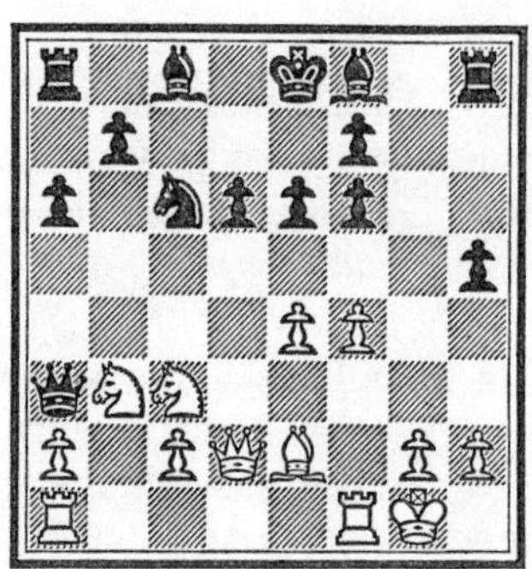

13. **K—R1**

White avoids a possible check on the KKt1—QR7 diagonal. He can also play Kt—Kt1 at once.

13. . . . . **B—Q2** *?*

Fischer hopes to play O—O—O on his next move. He fails to see the threat against his Queen.

14. **Kt—Kt1** *!*

How can a move that *un*develops a piece be praised? For the next six moves, this Knight will be part of a plan to trap Black's Queen.

14. . . . . **Q—Kt5**

14. . . . . Q—Kt7 ? would be a blunder, losing the Queen after *15.* P—QR4, *16.* Kt—R3, and *17.* Kt—B4 or KR—QKt1.

15. **Q—K3** **P—Q4 ?**

Fischer weakens. He should have tried to free his Queen by *15.* . . . . P—B4; *16.* P × P, P—Q4. Instead, the move *15.* . . . . P—Q4 returns the Pawn and still leaves the Queen in danger.

16. **P × P** **Kt—K2**

RULE TO REMEMBER

Seek moves that slow down your opponent's development!

Avoid moves that free your opponent's cramped position!

---

17. **P—B4 !** **Kt—B4**

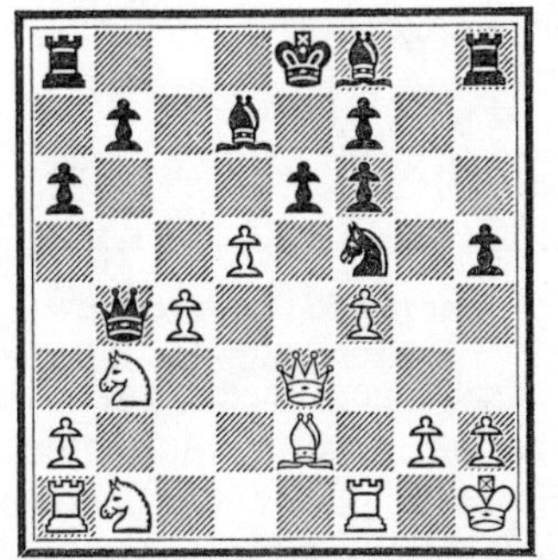

Black wants to free his pieces. He does not play *17.* . . . . O—O because White can then attack along the QKt file. *17.* . . . . Q—Q3 would be weak because of *18.* Kt—B3 threatening *19.* P—B5.

18. **Q—Q3** **P—R5 ?**

This is an error, even though it seems to threaten mate by *19.* . . . . Kt—Kt6*ch*; *20.* P × Kt, P × P *discovered ch;* *21.* K—Kt1, B—B4*ch;* *22.* Kt × B, Q × Kt*ch;* *23.* R—B2, Q × R mate. White's nineteenth move answers this threat, for the move B—R3 would block the attack after the discovered check.

19. **B—Kt4 !** **Kt—Q3**
20. **Kt(1)—Q2** **P—B4 ?**

Even though he is undeveloped and under attack, Fischer wastes a move in this attack against the White Bishop. *20.* . . . . O—O—O would have been a little better, although White's attack would still be successful.

RULE TO REMEMBER

You should not try to counterattack until your pieces have been developed. If your opponent is more fully developed, it is easy for him to defend—for he can bring more pieces to whatever point you place under attack.

---

21. **P—QR3 *!*** **Q—Kt3**

If *21.* . . . . . Q—R5; *22.* Kt—B5, Q—R4; and White can force the position open. For example, *23.* Kt × B, K × Kt; *24.* Kt—Kt3, Q—B2; *25.* P—B5, Kt—Kt4; *26.* P × P double check, K—B1; *27.* B × P wins quickly.

22. **P—B5** **Q—Kt4**
23. **Q—QB3 *!***

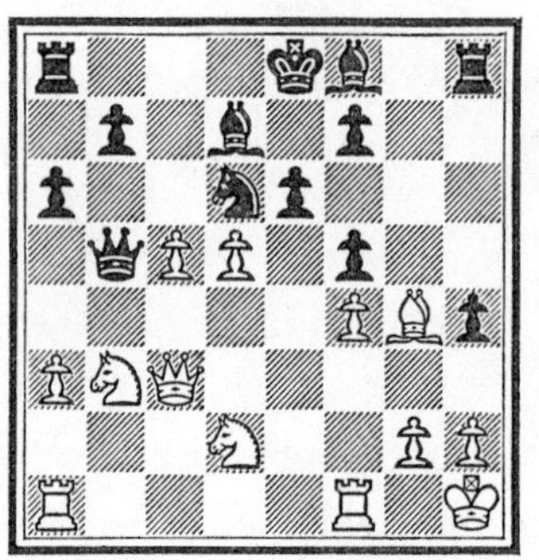

Black is lost. There are too many threats. For example:

a. P × Kt
b. P—QR4 (winning the Black Queen)
c. Q × R

23. . . . . **P × B**

Although *23.* . . . . . R—KKt1 looks like a way out, it fails after *24.* P—R4, B—Kt2; *25.* Kt—Q4, B × Kt; *26.* Q × B, Q—R4; *27.* Kt—Kt3, Q—Q1; *28.* P × Kt, P × B; *29.* P × P, B × P; *30.* Kt—B5, Q—B1; *31.* Kt × B*ch*, P × Kt; *32.* QR—B1, Q—Q1; *33.* KR—K1, K—B2; *34.* R—B7*ch* and mate soon follows.

24. **P—R4** **P—R6**

If *24.* . . . . . Q—K7; *25.* QR—K1 locks all doors for the Black Queen.

25. **P × Q** **P × P*ch***
26. **K × P** **R—R6**

Black plays on for a few more moves, but has no hope with only a Bishop against a Queen.

27. **Q—B6** **Kt—B4**
28. **P—B6** **B—B1**

28. . . . . . Kt—K6*ch* fails against *29.* K—Kt1, Kt × R; *30.* P × B*ch*, and *31.* R × Kt or *31.* Q × BP*ch*.

29. **P × KP** **P × KP**
30. **KR—K1**

Threats: *a.* Q × Kt; *b.* R × P*ch*; *c.* Q—Kt6*ch*; etc. Black could have resigned several moves ago.

30. . . . . **B—K2**
31. **R × P** Resigns

RULE TO REMEMBER

Exchange pieces when you have an advantage in material. The fewer pieces your opponent has, the greater your advantage becomes.

26 Queen's Gambit

Kemeri, 1937

White	*Black*
A. Alekhine	R. Fine

The Opening

All of the games we have thus far examined began with *1.* P—K4. But there are other possible opening moves—19 others, and every one of them has been played at some time. *1.* P—Q4 usually results in a kind of game quite different from the KP opening. In QP games, White tries to play P—QB4 and P—K4, while Black aims for the same moves.

White's Plan

Alekhine offers the QBP and, when Black takes it, is playing a Queen's Gambit. He gains time (develops faster than his opponent), grips the center, and then succeeds in forcing through a passed Pawn.

Black's Plan

Fine is outplayed after the opening, and finally permits a quick mate in a lost position. His plan—to force an early draw by exchanging pieces—fails because he loses too much time.

Comment

The game is a good introduction to the QP openings.

1. **P—Q4**	**P—Q4**
2. **P—QB4**	**P × P**
3. **Kt—KB3**	

If 3. Kt—QB3, Black can play 3. . . . . P—K4 and free his game. 3. Kt—KB3 prevents 3. . . . . P—K4.

3.	**Kt—KB3**
4. **Q—R4*ch***	**Q—Q2**

RULE TO REMEMBER

A beginning player who tries the Queen's Gambit should play it as Alekhine does here. Get the Pawn back by Q—R4*ch* early in the game. Then you have the QB file available for applying pressure on the Black position.

Black can also play *4*. . . . . P—QB3, *4*. . . . . B—Q2, and even *4*. . . . . Kt—Q2. He prefers to play for the quick exchange of Queens.

5. **Q × BP**	**Q—B3**
6. **Kt—R3**	

Alekhine is willing to exchange Queens, but wants to gain a move in doing so. He now threatens *7*. Q × Q*ch*, Kt × Q; *8*. Kt—Kt5.

6.	**Q × Q**
7. **Kt × Q**	**P—K3**
8. **P—QR3**	

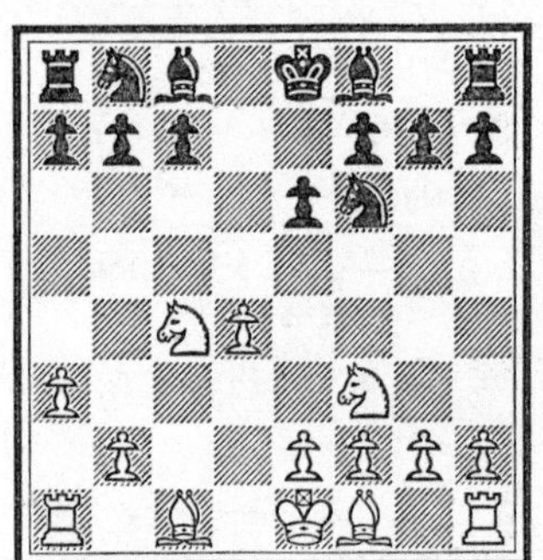

White has gained two moves, and Black should keep the game closed by *8*. . . . . P—B3 or *8*. . . . . B—K2. Instead, he opens it up and plays on with inferior development.

8.	**P—B4 ?**
9. **B—B4**	**Kt—B3**
10. **P × P**	**B × P**
11. **P—QKt4**	

Gaining more time, as the Black B must return to K2. If *11*. . . . . B—Q5; *12*. Kt × B, Kt × Kt; *13*. O—O—O and Black loses another move in retreating his Kt.

11.	**B—K2**
12. **P—Kt5**	**Kt—QKt1**
13. **Kt—Q6*ch***	**B × Kt**

Forced, as *13*. . . . . K—Q1 or *13*. . . . . K—Q2 (to protect the B at QB1) loses after *14*. Kt × BP.

14. **B × B**	**Kt—K5**
15. **B—B7**	**Kt—Q2 ?**

15. . . . . O—O is preferable, to be followed by *16*. . . . . P—QR3. Black is cramped by the P on White's Kt5, and should play to remove or exchange it as soon as possible. *15*. . . . . Kt—Q2 does nothing in that direction.

16. **Kt—Q4 !**

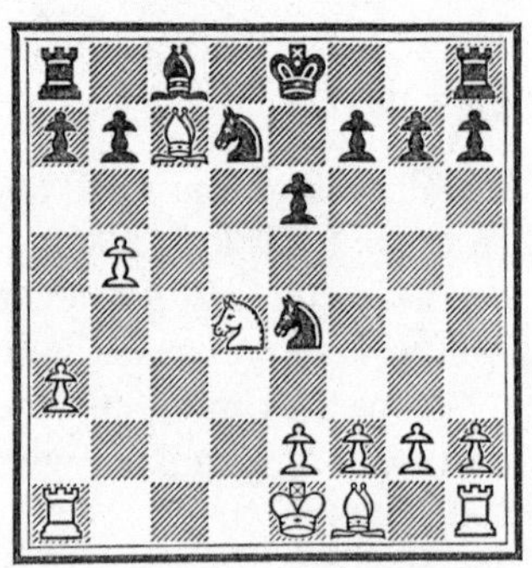

White is not afraid of *16*. . . . . P—K4, for he would then play *17*. Kt—B5.

16.	....	Kt—Kt3
17.	P—B3	Kt—Q4

RULE TO REMEMBER

Check to see if you can attack a piece before you retreat your own attacked piece. Now Black threatens Kt × B if White takes the Kt on his K4.

You will see the same tactic on Black's 20th move.

---

18. **B—R5*!***

The B is best placed here. If *18.* B—K5, P—B3*!*

18.	....	Kt(K5)—B3
19.	Kt—B2	

If *19.* P—K4, Kt—K6 would result in the exchange of White's KB.

19.	....	B—Q2
20.	P—K4	R—QB1
21.	K—Q2	

The King is better placed here than it would be after a later O—O. With the Queens off the board, an uncastled King can become an active piece.

21.	....	Kt—Kt3
22.	Kt—K3	

To prevent *22.* .... Kt—B5*ch* (fork of K and B).

22.	....	O—O
23.	P—QR4	R(KBI)—Q1 (threat—discovered attack!)

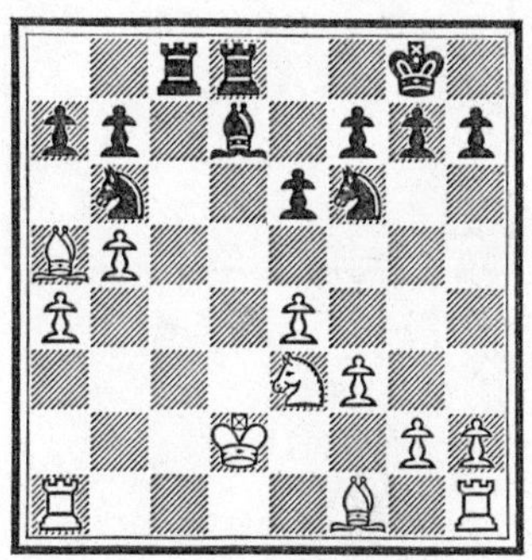

24.	B—Q3	P—K4

Black has developed his pieces, and now makes plans for his counter-attack. Given time, he would play Kt—R4, P—Kt3, Kt—Kt2 and P—B4. White, however, doesn't give him the time.

25.	R(KR1)—QB1	B—K3
26.	R × R	P × R
27.	B—Kt4	Kt—K1
28.	P—R5	Kt—Q2
29.	Kt—Q5	

White forces the exchange of the Black B for this Kt, gaining a passed Pawn as a result. If Black does not take the Kt, then he faces the threat of Kt—K7.

29.	....	B × Kt
30.	P × B	

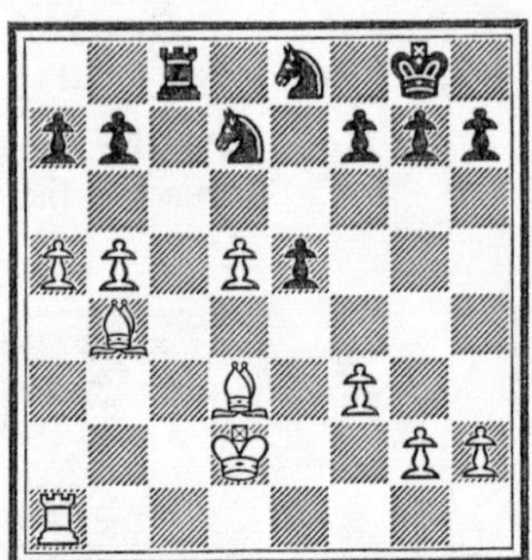

30. . . . . **Kt—B4**
31. **B—B5!**

Inviting *31.* . . . . Kt—Kt6*ch*; *32.* K—Q3! Kt × R; *33.* B × R, P—QKt3; *34.* P—Q6 and wins.

31. . . . . **R—Q1**

So, that, on *32.* B × Kt, R × P*ch* and *33.* . . . . R × B.

32. **K—B3**

Now *32.* . . . . R × P loses to *33.* K—B4.

32. . . . . **P—QKt3**
33. **P × P** **P × P**
34. **B × Kt** **P × B**
35. **P—Kt6**

Black is hopelessly lost. White now threatens P—Kt7 and R—R8.

If *35.* . . . . R—Kt1; *36.* P—Kt7, R × P; *37.* R—R8, K—B1; *38.* B—Q7 wins the Kt. Black decides to welcome a quick finish.

35. . . . . **Kt—Q3**
36. **B—Q7!!** **R × B**

If *36.* . . . . Kt—Kt2; *37.* B—B6, R—Kt1; *38.* B × Kt, R × B; *39.* R—R8*ch*.

37. **R—R8*ch***

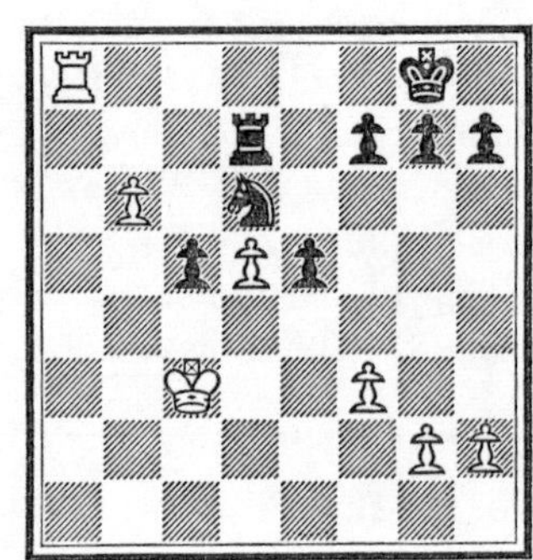

White here announced mate in two, by:

37. . . . . **R—Q1**
38. **R × R*ch*** **Kt—K1**
39. **R × Kt** **mate**

or

37. . . . . **Kt—B1**
38. **R × Kt*ch*** **R—Q1**
39. **R × R mate**

and so,

37. . . . . **Resigns**

RULE TO REMEMBER

The most usual way in which chess games are won is by the creation of passed Pawns. Try to set up a passed Pawn!

---

27 Queen's Gambit

Semmering, 1926

White	*Black*
R. P. Michel	A. Rubinstein

The Opening

White must play very sharply in the Queen's Gambit Accepted. Otherwise Black counters quickly on the Q-side and forces White to lose time in defending or rearranging his pieces.

White's Plan

Michel here plays the early part of the game passively, and permits his opponent to take the initiative. In the middle game play, Michel holds his own, later missing a chance for a draw.

Black's Plan

Akiba Rubinstein was one of the world's finest players in the 1920's and 1930s. His play was marked by a search for complications in which his superior ability to produce combinations often led to surprising victories. In this game he applies pressure on the Q-side and then offers a Pawn in a deep combination. The final dozen moves illustrate a mating attack with Queen and Bishop against an exposed King.

Comment

This game shows how to maintain pressure in the center while attacking on the Q-side. White is unable to prepare an attack because he must make one defensive move after another.

1.	P—Q4	P—Q4
2.	P—QB4	P—K3
3.	Kt—KB3	P × P
4.	P—K3	Kt—KB3
5.	B × P	P—B4
6.	Kt—B3	P—QR3

RULE TO REMEMBER

Black, when playing against the Queen's Gambit, should try to play . . . . P—QB4 as soon as possible. However, it should be prepared for by moves which will prevent White from answering . . . . P—QB4 with P—Q5.

Black has achieved one objective—the move . . . . P—B4. Now he aims at the advance of his Q-side Pawns. White should play 7. P—QR4, but makes an inferior move instead.

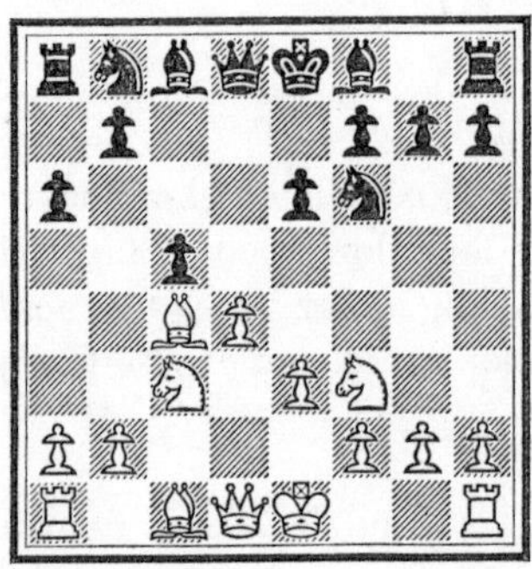

7. **O—O?** **P—QKt4**
8. **B—Q3** **B—Kt2**

White must now be concerned about two Black threats, to advance the Q-side Pawns and to open up the K side by a later . . . . B × Kt.

RULE TO REMEMBER

Avoid positions in which your Queen is on the same file as a supported enemy Rook. A discovered attack may cost you material.

Try to place your Rook or Bishop on the same line as your opponent's Queen. Then look for a discovered attack. (*See move 10.*)

---

9. **Q—K2** **Kt(Kt1—Q2)**
10. **R—Q1** **Q—Kt3 !**

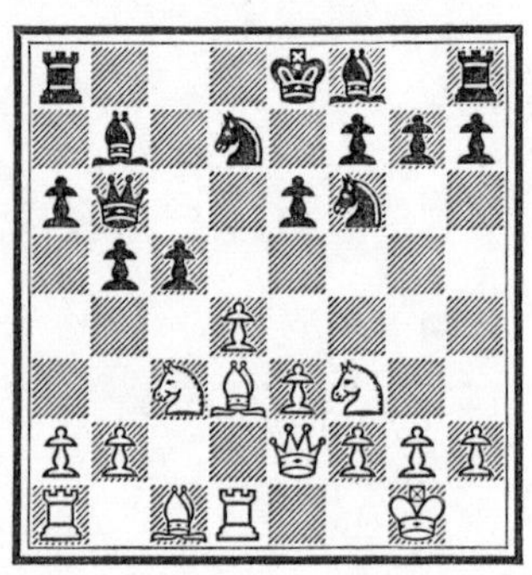

The Queen is best placed here, where it aims at White's Q4 and also supports the Q-side Pawns.

11. **P—QR4** **P—Kt5**
12. **P—R5?**

White cannot afford the time for this maneuver. The P on R5 will be a target for Black, and this will pin down the White Rook in defending it. *12.* Kt—Kt1 was better.

12. **. . . .** **Q—B2**
13. **Kt—Kt1** **B—K2**
14. **Kt(Kt1) —Q2** **O—O**
15. **Kt—B4** **R(B1)—Q1**
16. **B—Q2** **Kt—K5**

Each side has completed its development, but Black's counter comes first.

17. **Kt(B3) —K5** **Kt × Kt**

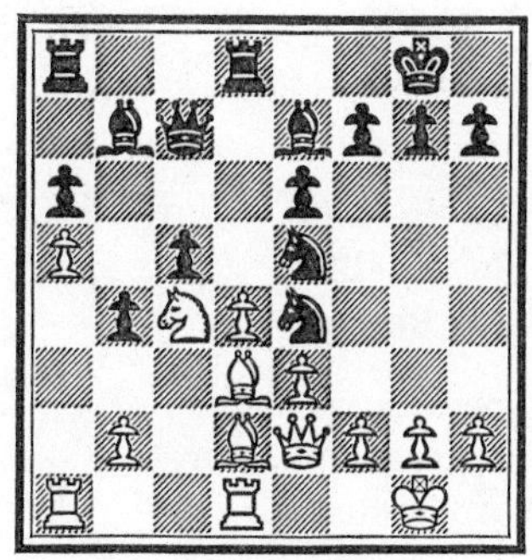

18. **P × Kt**

If *18.* Kt × Kt, P × P wins a Pawn for Black.

18.	**Kt × B**
19. **R × Kt**	**B—QB3**
20. **Kt—Kt6**	**R—R2**

White is faced by the inability to mount an attack, for he must defend the Pawn at K5. For example:

a. 21. Q—R5 (double attack on Black's KRP), P—Kt3; and White cannot defend the Pawn on K5.

b. 21. QR—Q1, Q × P; 22. B × RP*ch*, K × B; 23. R × R, B × R; *24.* R × B would be to White's advantage, but Black could play:

c. 21. QR—Q1, P—Kt3; 22. P—B4, as in the game.

21. **P—B4**	**B—K1**
22. **R(R1)—Q1**	**P—Kt3**

The Black K-side is now secure, and White, lacking any targets, permits Black to relieve the pressure on the Q file.

23. **B—B4**	**R × R**
24. **R × R**	**K—Kt2**
25. **P—QKt3**	**P—R4**
26. **B × P (R6)**	

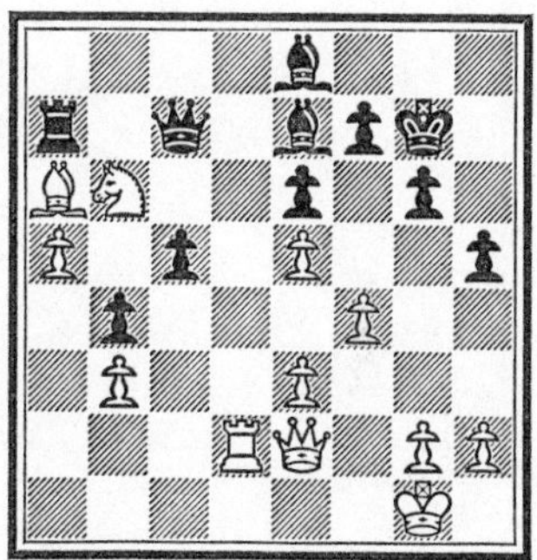

White takes the RP, and Black surprises him with a deep combination.

26.	**P—B5** *!*
27. **Q × P**	

Best. If *27.* B × P, R × P; *28.* Kt—R4, B × Kt; *29.* P × B, R × P establishes a passed Pawn for Black!

27.	**Q—B4** *!*

White cannot play *28.* Q × Q, B × Q; when the P on K3, the B and the Kt would all be under attack.

28. **K—B2**	**Q × RP**
29. **Kt—B8**	**B—R5***ch*
30. **P—Kt3**	**R × B**
31. **Kt—Q6**	

On *31.* P × B, R—B3 would win the Kt.

31.	R × Kt*!*
32. P × R	B—QKt4
33. Q—B7*?*	

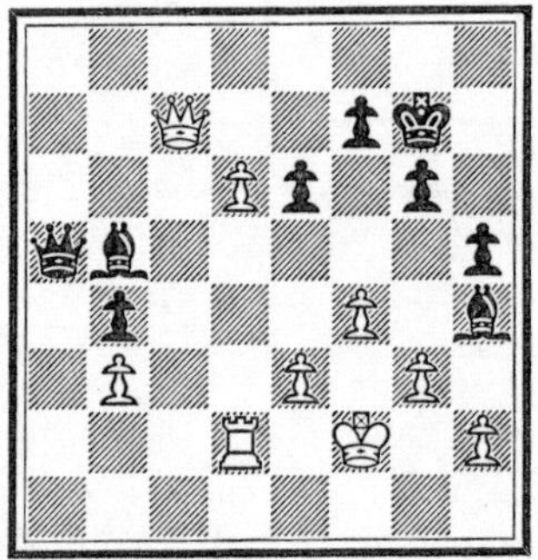

An error, but one not recognized until months after the game, when analysis indicated a probable draw after 33. Q—B5, B—Q1; *34. P*—Q7.

33.	Q—R8*!*
34. P × B	Q—B8*ch*
35. K—Kt3	Q—K8*ch*
36. R—B2	Q—Kt8*ch*
37. K—B3	Q—R8*ch*
38. R—Kt2	

Forced, for White would lose after 38. K—Kt3, B—B3; 39. P—Q7, Q—Kt8*ch; 40.* K—R3, Q—Kt5 mate.

38.	Q—Q8*ch*
39. K—Kt3	Q—Kt5*ch*
40. K—B2	Q—K7*ch*
41. Resigns	

Because of mate after *41.* K—Kt1, Q—B8 mate or *41.* K—Kt3, Q × P mate.

RULE TO REMEMBER

Do not sacrifice in the ending unless you clearly see how the sacrifice will give you a won game. It is not enough just to get an attack. The attack must win!

---

28 Queen's Gambit Declined

Reykjavik, Iceland, 1972

White	*Black*
Robert J. Fischer	Boris Spassky

The Opening

In the Queen's Gambit (*1.* P—Q4, P—Q4; 2. P—QB4, P × P) White usually gains control of the center and regains the gambit Pawn. Black therefore usually avoids the gambit (chessplayers say Black plays the Queen's Gambit Declined) by playing 2. . . . . P—K3. Black tries to keep a Pawn on Q4, and must solve the problem of finding a way to develop his QB.

White's Plan

Fischer rarely plays *1.* P—Q4. In this game he tries to shock and surprise his opponent by developing a Queen's Gambit type of position. He expects Spassky to use a defense that had until then proven successful. But Fischer had prepared a new way to slow down Black's development. He then uses his own better development to open the position and attack on the K-side.

Black's Plan

Black is concerned about the development of his Q-side pieces. He plans to place his Bishop on QKt2, his Knight on Q2, and then advance his QBP to gain control of center squares. He discovers that his method is too slow.

Comment

The game illustrates the value of open lines when you are better developed than your opponent. Observe how White builds up pressure on the Q-side and then rushes his pieces to the K-side for a crushing attack.

1.	**P—QB4**	**P—K3**
2.	**Kt—KB3**	**P—Q4**
3.	**P—Q4**	**Kt—KB3**
4.	**Kt—B3**	**B—K2**

Black can take the QBP at any time, but to do so would make

RULE TO REMEMBER

This is now a Queen's Gambit Declined. It has been reached by *transposition*—playing the moves of an opening in some different order.

When you know an opening well, you can often reach a desired position or variation of the opening by *transposing* moves.

the game a Queen's Gambit—the very opening Black has decided *not* to play.

5. **B—Kt5**	**O—O**
6. **P—K3**	**P—KR3**

Modern chessmasters seek *elastic* positions—those in which they can decide the direction of play themselves rather than just answer the opponent's threats. *6.* . . . . P—KR3 is played to force White to make a decision—to take the Knight or to retreat.

7. **B—R4**	**P—QKt3**

This attempt to develop the hemmed-in Bishop proves to be a waste of time.

8. **P × P**

Black has declared his plan—to develop a Bishop on QKt2. White therefore tries to force Black to keep a Pawn on Q4, where it will block the movement of the Bishop.

RULE TO REMEMBER

A Bishop played to Kt2 is on a *long diagonal.* If you have a Bishop on a long diagonal, try to keep that diagonal free of your own Pawns. This gives the Bishop scope for future activity.

When your opponent has a Bishop on a long diagonal, try to force him to keep his own Pawns on that diagonal.

8.	**Kt × P**
9. **B × B**	**Q × B**
10. **Kt × Kt**	**P × Kt**

Examine the position. The Pawn on Q4 would block the Bishop if Black played B—Kt2. Spassky will play the Bishop to K3 instead. Then 7. . . . . P—QKt3 was a wasted move.

11. **R—B1**	**B—K3**
12. **Q—R4**	**P—QB4**

Otherwise White can play *13.* P—QKt4. This would hold back the Black QBP and permit White to attack along the QB file.

RULE TO REMEMBER

A file is *half open* when only one player has a Pawn on it. The other player is then said to have a half-open file.

Place a Rook or a Queen on a half-open file to threaten the capture of the enemy Pawn on that file.

---

13. **Q—R3** **R—B1**

13. . . . . P × P was impossible because of *14.* Q × Q. Meanwhile, White attacks the QBP three times. Black has to play *13.* . . . . R—B1 to bring a third piece to the defense of that Pawn.

14. **B—Kt5** *!*

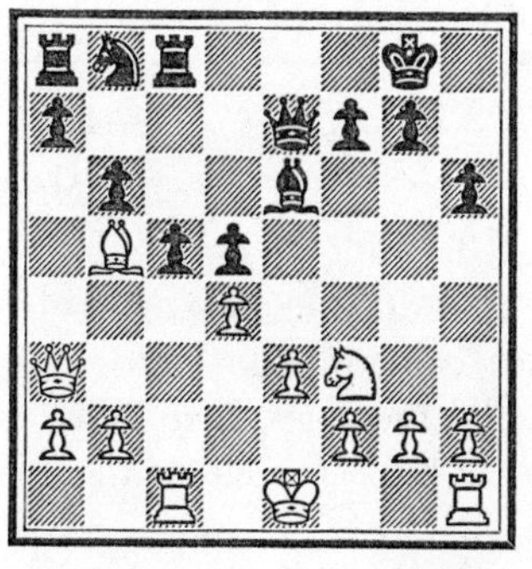

This is Fischer's new move—perhaps the critical move of the game. Suddenly Black is unable to complete his development. *14.* . . . . Kt—Q2 loses a Pawn after *15.* B × Kt, Q (or B) × B; *16.* P × P, P × P; *17.* R × P.

14. . . . . **P—R3**

Black must waste time as he tries to complete his development. He now hopes to play *15.* . . . . Q—Kt2 and *16.* . . . . P × P.

15. **P × P** **P × P**

Black cannot play *15.* . . . . P × B because White would then win the exchange with *16.* Q × R.

RULE TO REMEMBER

The two Black Pawns on Q4 and QB4 are called *hanging Pawns.* Such Pawns are easily attacked, and can be defended only by pieces.

***Avoid hanging Pawns!* They are usually a weakness.**

Accept hanging pawns only when they can easily be advanced, to threaten the making of a new Queen.

---

16. **O—O**

White has completed his development. Black cannot get his pieces into play except by placing them clumsily—where they block one another's activity.

16. . . . . **R—R2**
17. **B—K2**

Since Black's Queen now protects the Rook, White must retreat the Bishop.

17. . . . . **Kt—Q2**
18. **Kt—Q4** *!*

Black cannot take this Knight, for his Pawn on B4 is still pinned. If *18.* . . . . P × Kt; *19.* Q × Q. The Black Knight on Q2 blocks the contact between Black's Rook and Queen.

18. . . . . **Q—B1** *?*

Either *18.* . . . . Kt—B1 or *18.* . . . . Kt—B3 is better. Black's pieces still block one another.

RULE TO REMEMBER

Do not leave your pieces on squares where they block the action of your other pieces!

---

19. **Kt × B** **P × Kt**
20. **P—K4** *!*

Should Black take this Pawn? If he does, White can play *21.* R—B4 and soon pick off the disconnected Black Pawns.

20. . . . . **P—Q5** *?*

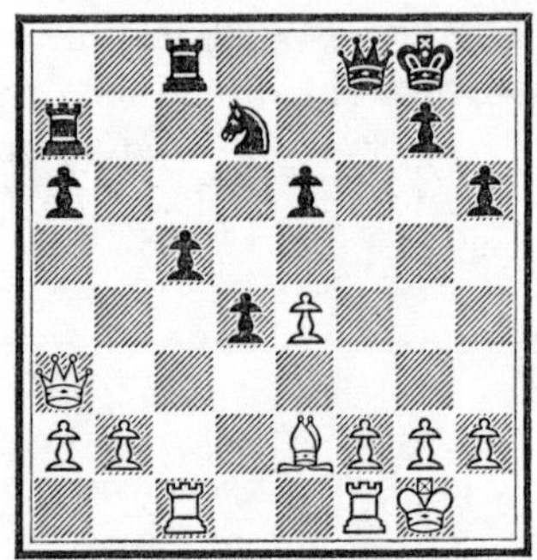

Suddenly White's Bishop can become active. *20.* . . . . P—B5 was better.

21. **P—B4** **Q—K2**
22. **P—K5**

RULE TO REMEMBER

A Pawn that cannot be defended by other Pawns is called an *isolated* Pawn. A Pawn that is on the second or third rank is called a *backward* Pawn. The Black Pawn on K3 is an isolated backward Pawn. It can be defended only by pieces.

Avoid *isolated* Pawns.

Avoid *backward* Pawns.

---

22. . . . . **R—Kt1**
23. **B—B4** **K—R1**
24. **Q—R3**

A sudden change. The Queen has come to the K-side. It attacks the backward Pawn and is on the same file as the Black King.

RULE TO REMEMBER

Do not leave your King on a rank, file, or diagonal along which your opponent is attacking.

23. . . . . K—R1 takes the Black King off the diagonal along which the White Bishop is attacking.

24.	Kt—B1
25. P—QKt3	P—QR4
26. P—B5 *!*	

Black is lost. Every White piece can bear down on the K-side, while Black's pieces remain tied down in defensive roles.

26.	P × P
27. R × P	Kt—R2
28. QR—KB1	

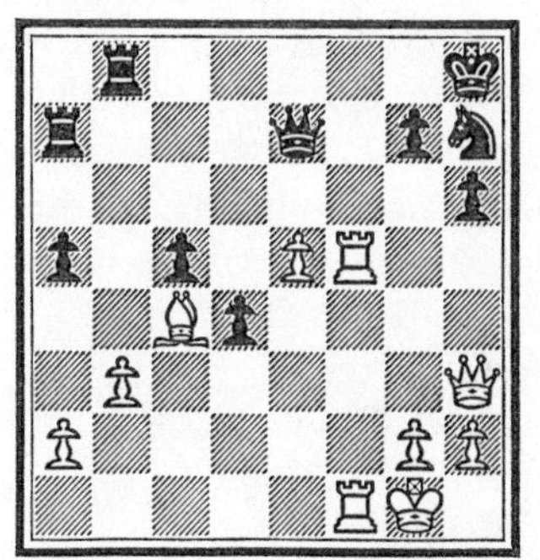

28.	Q—Q1
29. Q—Kt3	R—K2
30. P—KR4	

White's pressure on the K-side is so great that he has time to play this move, blocking any future Black defense of the K-position by . . . . Kt—Kt4.

RULE TO REMEMBER

Try to double your Rooks on an open file. One Rook can then advance to any desired square on the file, remaining protected by the other Rook.

30.	R(1)—Kt2
31. P—K6	R(Kt2)—B2

Black protects the QBP. He does not have the countermove *31.* . . . . P—Q6 because White would win the QP after *32.* R—Q5.

32. Q—K5 *!*

RULE TO REMEMBER

A piece is *centralized* when it occupies one of the four center squares. It can then attack in any direction.

A centralized piece has the greatest possible mobility. Try to centralize your pieces in the middle game or end game!

32.	Q—K1
33. P—R4 *!*	

White delays his attack until all possible Black counters have been prevented. 33. P—R4 locks up the Q-side.

33. . . . . **Q—Q1**
34. **R(1)—B2**

White makes a few quiet moves while he completes his thinking about the coming K-side attack. Black can only mark time with Queen moves.

34. . . . . **Q—K1**
35. **R(2)—B3** **Q—Q1**
36. **B—Q3 *!***

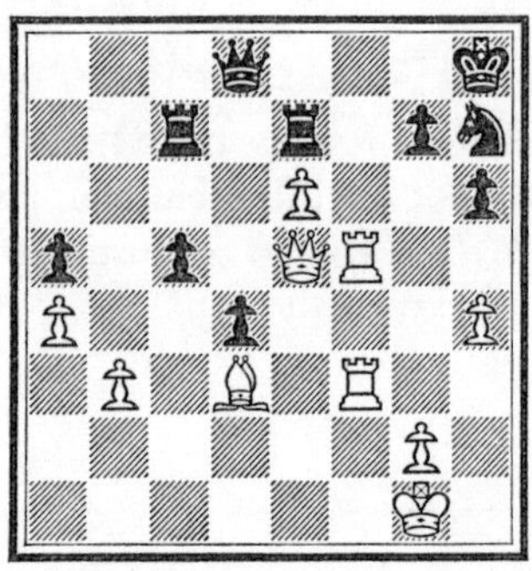

A quietly murderous move. White will place his Queen on K4, and then threaten mate on KR7. For example, *36.* . . . . Q—K1; *37.* Q—K4, Q—Q1; *38.* R—B8*ch !,* Kt × R; *39.* R × Kt*ch,* Q × R; *40.* Q—R7 mate.

36. . . . . **Q—K1**
37. **Q—K4 *!*** **Kt—B3**

This is the only move to avoid the threatened mating attack beginning with *38.* R—B8*ch.*

38. **R × Kt *!***

RULE TO REMEMBER

Do not sacrifice material unless you can see the attack that follows to its conclusion—mate, a forced draw, or the gain of material.

---

38. . . . . **P × R**
39. **R × P** **K—Kt1**

Black can do nothing to prevent the winning attack on his King.

a. If *39.* . . . . Q—R4 (to protect the RP); *40.* R—B8*ch,* K—Kt2; *41.* Q—R7*ch,* K × R; *42.* Q—R8 mate!

b. If *39.* . . . . K—Kt2; *40.* R—Kt6*ch,* K—B1; *41.* Q—B5*ch,* R—B2; *42.* P × R, R × P; *43.* Q × P*ch,* Q—K2; *44.* Q—B8*ch,* Q—K1; *45.* R—Kt8*ch,* K × R; *46.* Q × Q*ch.*

c. If *39.* . . . . K—Kt2; *40.* R—Kt6*ch,* K—R1; *41.* Q—K5*ch,* R—Kt2; *42.* R × P*ch,* K—Kt1; *43.* B—Kt6, Q—K2; *44.* B—B7*ch,* R × B; *45.* P × R*ch,* Q × P; *46.* R—R8 mate.

40. **B—B4 *!***

Threatening *41.* R—B7 and then either mate or the win of Black's Queen (*41.* R—B7, R × R; *42.* P × R*ch,* R × P; *43.* Q × Q*ch*).

40.	K—R1
41. Q—B4	Resigns

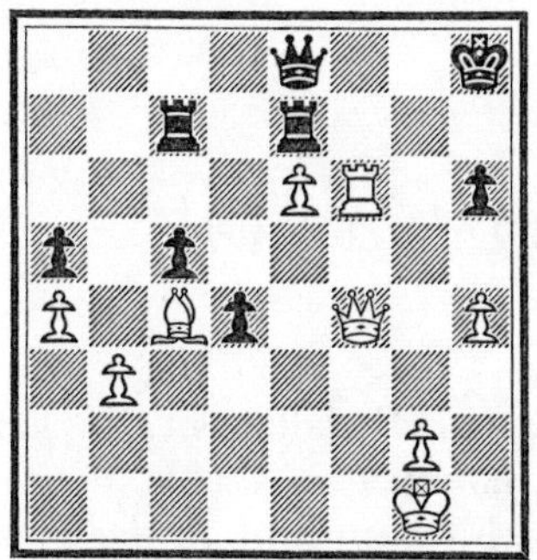

Why must Black resign? He has no answer to the threats of R—B8*ch* or Q × P*ch*. If he tries *41.* . . . . . R—B1, then *42.* R × P*ch*, R—R2; *43.* Q—B6*ch*, K—Kt1; *44.* P—K7 *dis. ch.*, R—B2; *45.* R—R8 mate.

RULE TO REMEMBER

This game teaches three important lessons:

1. **Seek opening moves that cramp your opponent's development.**
2. **Seek an attacking move in the center to open the game.**
3. **Once the position is open, try to centralize your pieces.**

---

29 Albin Counter-Gambit

Berlin, 1920

White	*Black*
S. Tarrasch	S. Tartakower

The Opening

Black can treat the Queen's Gambit in a manner analogous to the Falksbeer Counter-Gambit (See Game 2.) After *1.* P—Q4, P—Q4; 2. P—QB4, P—K4; 3. P × KP, P—Q5 Black s advanced QP restricts White's development, while the White P on K5 remains a target.

White's Plan

Dr. Tarrasch, in his long career, won many prizes for brilliant chess play. This game is considered one of his best efforts, made especially notable by the way he smashes open Black's castled K position.

Black's Plan

Dr. Tartakower was an eccentric among chessmasters, ever experimenting, ever playing the innovator—and usually winning with new ideas and smooth techniques. His failure in this game is, however, excusable, for Tarrasch turns genius in the course of the encounter!

Comment

The game illustrates the type of play which can occur in the Albin Counter-Gambit.

RULE TO REMEMBER

A counter-gambit occurs when Black replies to White's offer of a Pawn in the opening with a counter-offer of a Pawn.

---

1. P—Q4	P—Q4
2. P—QB4	P—K4
3. P × KP	P—Q5
4. Kt—KB3	P—QB4

4. . . . . Kt—QB3 is more usual, for it protects the QP and also attacks the P on White's K5.

5. P—K3	Kt—QB3
6. P × P	P × P

Black keeps the P on Q5, with resulting control of QB6, and always the threat of a future . . . . P—Q6.

7. **B—Q3** **Kt(Kt1)—K2**

Black cannot regain his Pawn by 7. . . . . Kt × P, for White would not play 8. Kt × Kt? Q—R4*ch*; 9. B—Q2, Q × Kt; but would instead have 8. Q—K2, P—B3; 9. Kt × Kt, P × Kt; *10.* Q × P*ch*, or 8. Q—K2, P—B3; 9. Kt × Kt, Q—R4*ch*; 10. K—Q1, Q × Kt; *11.* Q × Q*ch*, P × Q; *12.* R—K1.

8. **Kt(Kt1)—Q2** **B—Kt5**
9. **Q—Kt3** **Q—B2**
10. **O—O** **O—O—O**
11. **R—K1**

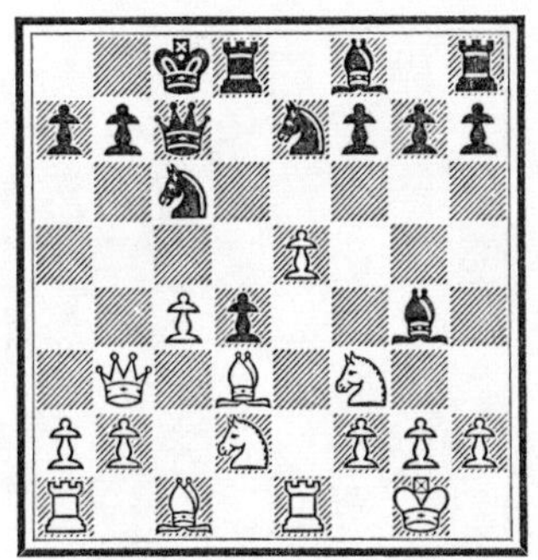

The White and Black plans of play are now set. White will apply pressure on the Q-side, while Black will try to control the center and perhaps manage to advance his passed Pawn.

11. . . . . **Kt—Kt3**
12. **P—KR3**

12. B × Kt would be a poor move, even though it holds the KP, for Black would answer *12.* . . . . RP × B, opening the KR file for attack against White's King.

RULE TO REMEMBER

Avoid moves which open lines of attack against your castled King position.

---

12. . . . . **B—K3**
13. **B—K4** **Kt(Kt3) × P**
14. **Kt × Kt** **Q × Kt**

Because *14.* . . . . Kt × Kt is followed by 15. B × P*ch*, Q × B; *16.* R × Kt.

15. **Kt—B3**

Possible, but not good, was *15.* Q × P*ch*, K × Q; *16.* B × Kt*ch*, K × B; *17.* R × Q, B—QKt5*!*; *18.* P—QKt3, B—B6; *19.* R—Kt1, P—Q6 and the strength of the QP is worth the Pawn.

15. . . . . **Q—QB4**
16. **B—B4*!***

Inviting *16.* . . . . B × P (B5)*?*, *17.* Q × B*!* Q × Q; *18.* B—B5*ch*, R—Q2; *19.* R—K8*ch*, Kt—Q1; *20.* Kt—K5*!*

16. . . . . **B—Q3**
17. **B × Kt** **P × B**

17. . . . . Q × B would permit *18.* Kt × P.

18. **B × B** **R × B**
19. **Kt—K5**

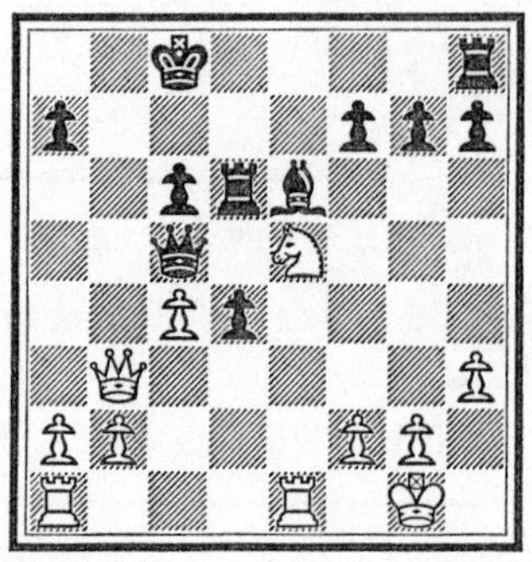

Defending the P on B4 and also threatening R(R1)—B1 and then Kt—Q3. Black cannot play *19.* . . . . . P—B3 because of *20.* Kt—Q3, Q × P; *21.* Q—R3 *!* R—Q2; *22.* R(R1)—B1, Q—Q4; *23.* Kt—B4, winning the B.

19. . . . . **R(R1)—Q1**
20. **Q—R4** *!*

White frees the road for P—QKt4 and P—B5 or P—Kt5.

20. . . . . **P—Q6** *!*

RULE TO REMEMBER

A supported passed Pawn should be advanced. This ties down enemy pieces to stop the Pawn from Queening.

---

21. **P—QKt4** **Q—Q5**
22. **Kt × P(B6)** **R × Kt**

Black here gives up the exchange instead of trying *22.* . . . . B—Q2 *?* which fails after *23.* Q—R6*ch,* K—B2; *24.* Kt × Q.

23. **Q × R*ch*** **K—Kt1**
24. **P—B5** **P—Q7**
25. **R(K1)—Q1** **B—B4**

Given the time, Black would continue with *26.* . . . . . B—B7, regaining the exchange and threatening to win by playing *27.* . . . . . B × R; *28.* R × B, Q—QB5 and *29.* . . . . . Q—B8.

26. **Q—Kt5*ch*** **K—B2**
27. **Q—R5*ch*** **K—Kt1**
28. **P—Kt5**

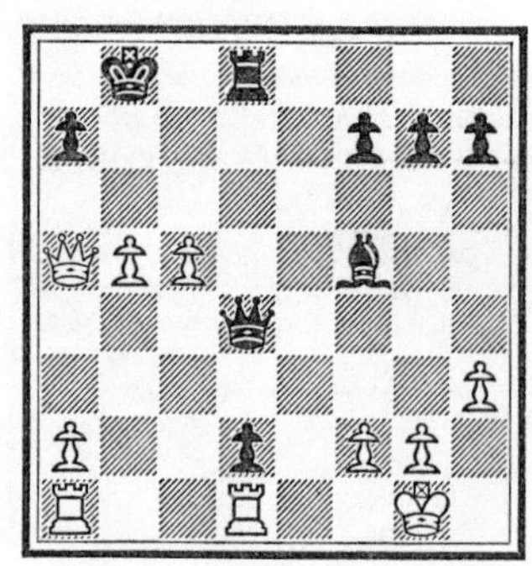

Well calculated. Tarrasch sees that his opponent will not have time to play B—B7 and B × R.

28. . . . . **B—B7** *?*

A pity, for *28.* . . . . R—Q4 would have held the position.

29. **P—Kt6**

Threatening, on *29.* . . . . B × R ?; *30.* Q × P*ch,* K—B1; *31.* Q—B7 mate.

29. . . . . **R—Q2**
30. **P × P*ch*** **K—R1**

Black cannot play . . . . R × P because of Q × P, and White has an easy win.

31. **P—B6** **R—Q4**
32. **P—B7 ! !**

Now *32.* . . . . . R × Q loses a piece after *33.* P—B8(Q)*ch,* K × P; *34.* Q × B.

32. . . . . **B—B4**
33. **P—B8(Q)ch** **B × Q**
34. **Q—B7 !** **R—QKt4**

RULE TO REMEMBER

Your opponent plays a gambit in order to gain time or space. Be ready to return the Pawn when doing so will allow you to regain time or space.

To stop *35.* Q—Kt8 mate. Black could have resigned here, for the ending is hopeless a Rook down.

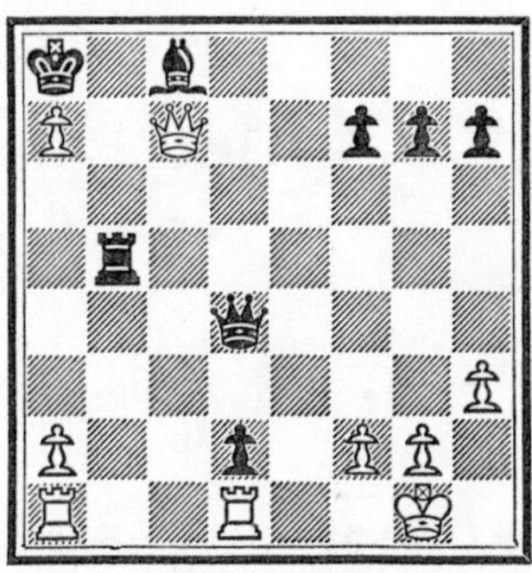

35. **Q × B*ch*** **K × P**
36. **P—QR4** **R—QB4**
37. **Q—Kt4 !** **Q × R**
38. **R × Q** **R—B8*ch***
39. **Q—Q1** **Resigns**

Black achieved his major objective in the Albin Counter-Gambit—a free QP, but it proved insufficient. The Albin is rarely played, for, as games like this one demonstrate, aggressive play by White is hard to meet.

30 Queen's Pawn Opening

Moscow, 1945

White	*Black*
A. Kotov	I. Boleslavsky

The Opening

Russia's world chess supremacy became evident in 1945, when that country's players began a series of matches with the leading masters of other countries. They had, for years, been analyzing and experimenting with the many openings which can arise after *1.* P—Q4 other than the Queen's Gambit. The next five games, all won by Russian masters, will illustrate some of these other defenses to *1.* P—Q4, as well as some of the ways they can be handled by White.

White's Plan

Alexander Kotov is a leading Russian politician, chess player and chess author. In this game, he brings a Bishop out at once, and, in the play which follows, discovers why the idea is a poor one.

Black's Plan

Issac Boleslavsky was at his best form when this game was played. He here demonstrates that concern with development which is essential to sound chess.

Comment

The game was played in the 14th Russian championship, in which Botvinnik finished first and Boleslavsky second.

1. P—Q4 Kt—KB3

Black delays . . . . P—Q4 to avoid the Q Gambit. The Kt move is best for this purpose, since KB3 is the normal square for the piece anyway.

2. B—Kt5

This move has been most actively played by the American master Bill Ruth, and is often called Ruth's Opening. Its chief value is its novelty.

2. . . . . Kt—K5
3. B—B4 P—Q3

Black has several other good moves here, such as *3.* . . . . P—QB4 and *3.* . . . . P—Q4. Amusing would be *3.* . . . . P—KKt4 ?; *4.* B—K5, P—B3 ?; *5.* P—K3, P × B??; *6.* Q—R5 mate.

4. **P—KB3**	**Kt—KB3**
5. **P—K4**	**P—KKt3**

Black has allowed White to gain control of the center. Slow development could have given White a better game, but he tries for a quick attack instead.

6. **Q—Q2 ?**	**Kt(Kt1)—Q2**
7. **B—KR6 ?**	**B × B**
8. **Q × B**	

White has managed to prevent Black from castling K-side —but has wasted valuable time. Black quickly attacks on the Q-side.

8.	**P—B4**
9. **P—B3**	**Q—Kt3 !**

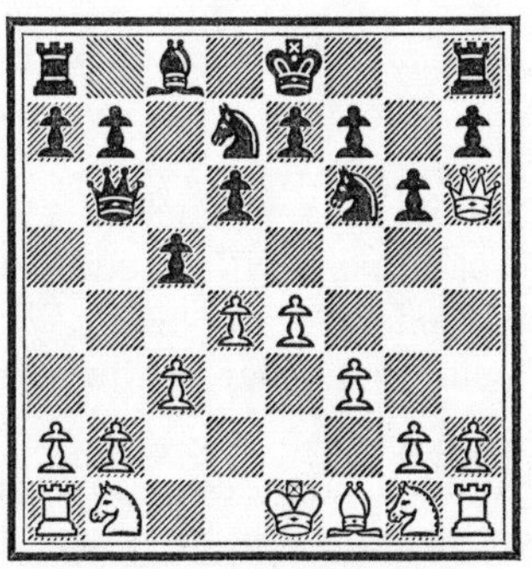

Black now threatens *10.* . . . . P × P or *10.* . . . . Q × P. White's reply is forced.

10. **Q—Q2**	**P × P**
11. **P × P**	**P—K4**
12. **Kt—QR3 ?**	

Kotov must have been ill—or tired—or chess-blind. QR3 is rarely a healthy square for a Kt. *12.* P—Q5 was best.

12.	**P—Q4**

Black realizes that the capture of the P on Q5 would lose valuable time. He plays to open up the game.

13. **P(Q4) × P**	**Kt(Q2) × P**
14. **B—Kt5*ch***	

For *14.* P × P, O—O would result in a gift of an open K file to Black.

14.	**K—B1**

The King takes the slow road to castling. He here invites *15.* Q—R6*ch*, K—K2*!*

15. **P × P**	**K—Kt2**
16. **Kt—K2**	**P—QR3**

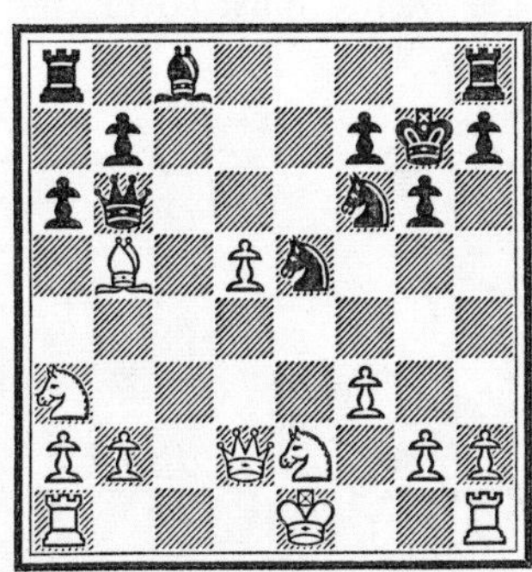

Where is White's B to go? If *17.* B—R4, B—B4 threatens

. . . . Kt—Q6*ch* and then . . . Kt—B7*ch* to win a Rook. *17.* B—Q3 permits *17.* . . . . Kt × QP or *17.* . . . . Kt × B*ch*; *18.* Q × Kt, B—B4 and the Black R's come into play.

17. **B—B4** **R—K1**
18. **R—Q1**

If *18.* O—O—O, Kt × B; *19.* Kt × Kt, Q—B2; *20.* P—QKt3, P—QKt4 wins a piece.

18. . . . . **B—R6**

Simple, once you see it. If *19.* P × B, Kt × BP*ch* wins the Queen. Meanwhile, the KKtP must be defended. If *19.* R—KKt1, Kt × BP*ch*; *20.* P × Kt, Q × R mate.

19. **K—B1** **Kt × BP** *!*

Neither the Kt nor the B can be taken.

20. **Q—B4** **Kt—Kt5** *! !*

Too many threats at once. Now, on *21.* P × B, Q—B7 mate. White must cover the B2 square.

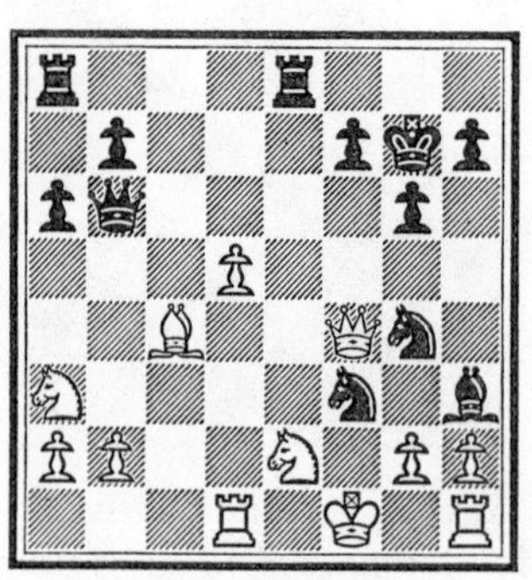

21. **Q × Kt(B3** **Kt—K6*ch***
22. **K—K1** **B × P**
23. **Q—B2** **B × R**
24. **R—Q3** **Q—Kt5*ch***
25. **R—Q2** **R(R1)—B1**

Better than *25.* . . . . Kt × B; *26.* Q—Q4*ch,* K—Kt1; *27.* Kt × Kt.

26. **B—Kt3** **B × P**
27. **B × B** **Kt × B**
28. **Q—Q4*ch*** **Q × Q**
29. **R × Q** **Kt—B3**
30. **Resigns**

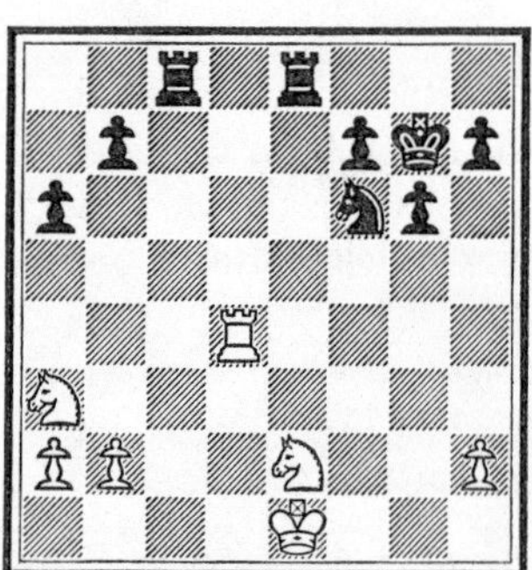

White has no better move. Black's Rooks will penetrate and pick off one or more White Pawns. Note that White's Kt is still at QR3 !

In the final position, a possible continuation could be:

30. **Kt—B4** **P—QKt4**
31. **Kt—Q6** **R × Kt*ch !***

32.	K × R	R—B7*ch*
33.	R—Q2	R × R*ch*
34.	K × R	

Now Black will win easily by forcing through a passed Pawn on the K side.

RULE TO REMEMBER

When you go into the ending with extra material, it is possible to give back some of it to obtain an easily won position.

---

31 Slav Defense

Moscow, 1949

White	*Black*
P. Dubinin	N. Novotelnov

The Opening

A group of defenses to the QP opening, called the Slav Defenses, are built around the moves. *1.* P—Q4, P—Q4; 2. P—QB4, P—QB3. Black's idea is to keep the center closed during the opening stages, and to be able to recapture with the QBP or KP if White should play QBP × QP. Black usually gets an even game with the Slav defense, but finds it difficult to get much counterplay.

White's Plan

The games of Pyotr Dubinin reveal great knowledge of the openings. A great chess teacher, he specialized in lines that permitted quick attacks. In this game he invites Black to castle into what seems a safe K position. He then attacks Black on the Q-side.

Black's Plan

Nikolai Novotelnov was long one of Russia's leading masters. However, Dubinin beat him frequently—what chess players call a "cousin" relationship! In this game he tries to open up the game before he has developed his pieces.

Comment

White's opening uses the Catalan formation in which the KB is developed on KKt2.

1. **P—Q4**	**P—Q4**
2. **P—QB4**	**P—QB3**
3. **Kt—KB3**	**P—K3**
4. **Q—B2**	

White plans P—KKt3 and B—Kt2, and places his Q on B2 to be able to recapture if Black takes the BP.

4.	**Kt—KB3**
5. **P—KKt3**	

The White B at Kt2 will aim at the Black P on Q5.

5.	Kt(Kt1)—Q2
6. B—Kt2	B—Q3
7. O—O	Kt—K5 ?

Black declares his intentions too soon. Better is *7.* . . . . . O—O first, instead of trying to set up an outpost on K5 while still undeveloped.

RULE TO REMEMBER

Do not move the same pieces too often in the opening. You need your opening moves to develop as many pieces as possible. When you move the same piece twice, you have lost time.

---

8. Kt—B3	P—KB4
9. R—Kt1 !	O—O ?

Another weak move. White is threatening to advance the Q side Pawns, and Black should prevent this by *9.* . . . . . P—QR4.

10. P—QKt4 !	P—QR3
11. P—QR4	Q—B3

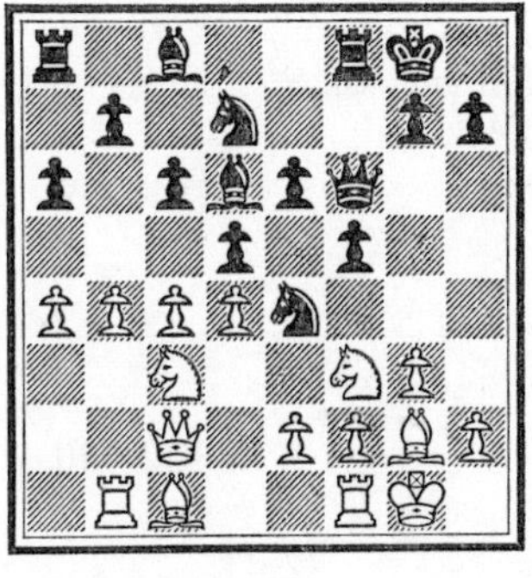

Black hopes to develop a K side attack—but he is still undeveloped. Better was *11.* . . . . . Kt × Kt; *12.* Q × Kt, Kt—B3, or the immediate *11.* . . . . . Kt (Q2)—B3.

12. P—Kt5	RP × P
13. RP × P	P—K4 ?

A doubtful plan to open up the center, for White can now invade on the Q side. Best for Black was *13.* . . . . . Q—B2 and *14.* . . . . . Kt × Kt or *14.* . . . . . Kt(Q2)—B3. One should not attack while still undeveloped!

14. KtP × P	KtP × P
15. P × QP	

So that *15.* . . . . . BP × P; *16.* Kt × P leaves White a valuable P ahead.

15.	Kt × Kt
16. Q × Kt	P—K5

If *16.* . . . . . BP × P; *17.* Q—B6 wins the QP, or *17.* Kt × P and *18.* B × P*ch.*

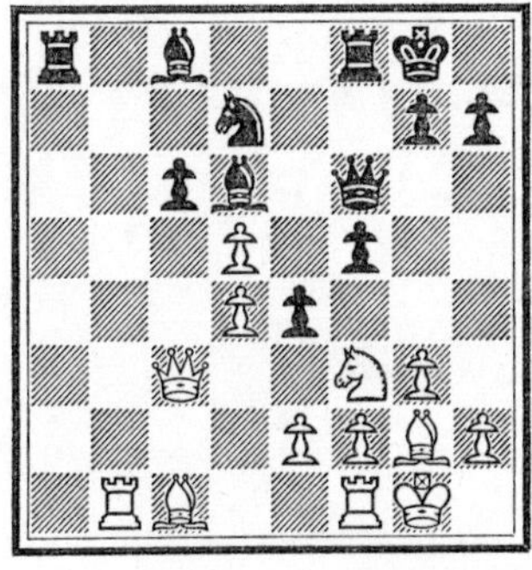

17. **P × P *!*** **P × Kt**
18. **Q × P *!***

A temporary sacrifice, for the Black Kt really has nowhere to go!

RULE TO REMEMBER

Watch for possible discovered attacks. If Black here played *18.* . . . . Kt—Kt1; *19.* P—B7 *!* attacks the Kt with the BP. At the same time, White has the discovered attack Q × R. Thus, Black would lose if he played *18.* . . . . Kt—Kt1.

---

18. . . . . **R—Kt1**
19. **B—Kt5 *!***

Now, if *19.* . . . . Q × B *?*; *20.* Q—Q5*ch* and *21.* Q × B (double attack!).

19. . . . . **R × R**

Hoping for *20.* B × Q *?*, R × R*ch*; *21.* K × R; Kt × B; and Black can hold the game.

20. **R × R** **Q × P**
21. **P × Kt** **B × P(Q2)**

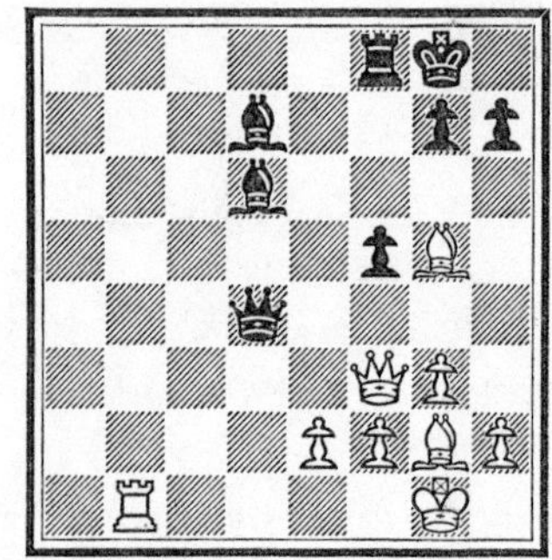

Not too bad, one might imagine, for Black has escaped with only one Pawn minus. True, but he also has too many pieces on the Q file, and White moves right in!

22. **Q—Kt3*ch !*** **K—R1**
23. **R—Q1** **Q—B4**

a. *23.* . . . . B—R5; *24.* R × Q, B × Q; *25.* R × B.
b. *23.* . . . . Q—K4; *24.* B—B4 and *25.* R or B × B.
c. *23.* . . . . Q—KKt5; *24.* R × B, B—R5; *25.* Q—B7.

24. **Q—Q3** **Resigns**

Black loses a piece. The game illustrates again the first principle of opening play—*Develop your pieces!*

32 Slav Defense

Moscow, 1950

White	*Black*
T. Petrosian	A. Tolush

The Opening

Many a game has been lost as the result of an early opening up of a castled K position by the move B × Kt. When a player is forced to reply P × B, leaving the Kt file open, a crushing attack can soon follow. Then a closed QP game quickly becomes a wide open game reminiscent of a King's Gambit!

White's Plan

The play of Tigran Petrosian has been compared to the movements of the tiger after which he is named. He stalks his opponent, keeping his ideas well hidden behind a series of quiet moves. He tries to limit the other player's available moves. In this game he gains a winning attack after ten moves when his opponent permits the opening of the King-side.

Black's Plan

Black's basic errors in this game are to allow the K-side to be opened, and to attempt to counterattack before completing his development.

Comment

The game shows how even the great masters can be punished for neglecting the basic principles of correct chess play.

1. **Kt—KB3**	**Kt—KB3**
2. **P—B4**	**P—K3**
3. **Kt—B3**	**P—Q4**
4. **P—Q4**	**P—B3**

A Slav Defense after all, although the order of moves differs from that in Game 31. White now exchanges Pawns in order to fix Black's Pawns on Q4 and QB3. Such exchanges are intended to limit Black's future options. For example, one result of the exchange is that Black cannot later counter in the center by . . . . P—K4.

5. **P × P**	**KP × P**
6. **Q—B2**	**B—Q3**

A move of dubious value. The B may be needed elsewhere—on K2 or QKt5. *6.* . . . . Kt—QR3 and 7. . . . . Kt—B2 may be better, or even *6.* . . . . B—K2. Now White pins the Kt at once.

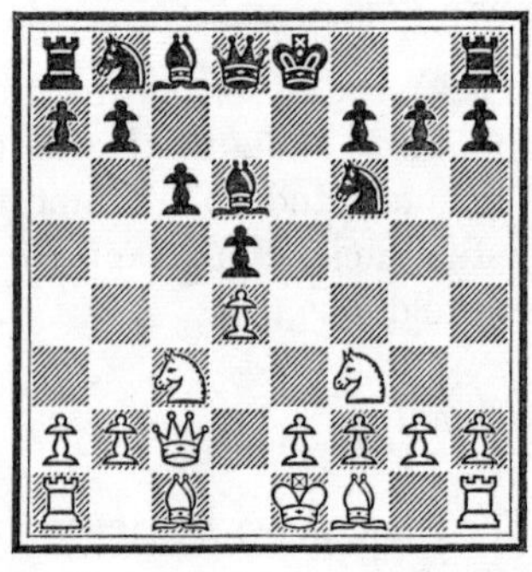

7. **B—Kt5**	**O—O**
8. **P—K3**	**B—KKt5**
9. **Kt—K5 *!***	

White moves right in. If 9. . . . . B × Kt; *10.* P × B, P—KR3; *11.* B—R4, P—KKt4; *12.* B—Kt3, Kt R4; *13.* P—B4*!*

9.	**B—R4**
10. **P—B4**	**Q—R4*?***

10. . . . . Q—K1 gives some hope, for *11.* B × Kt, P × B; *12.* Kt—B3, Q × P*ch* is in Black's favor.

11. **B—Q3**	**P—KR3 *?***

Better to lose a P by . . . . Kt(Kt1)—Q2 or . . . . Kt—K5. Now White smashes through.

12. **B × Kt**	**P × B**
13. **P—KKt4 *!***	

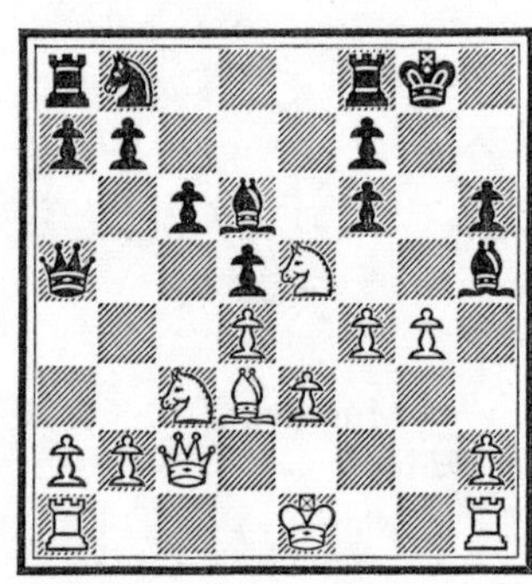

13.	**P × Kt**
14. **BP × P**	**B—K2**
15. **O-O-O *!***	

Surprise! White could have played *15.* P × B, when Black would have scrambled for safety by *15.* . . . . R—Q1; *16.* . . . . K—B1, or have tried *15.* . . . . Kt—Q2 and *16.* . . . . K—R1.

15.	**B—Kt4**

On *15.* . . . . B—Kt3; *16.* P—KR4*!*, B × B; *17.* Q × B, and Black cannot defend against White's R(Q1)—B1—B5—R5.

16. **P × B**	**K—R1**

If *16.* . . . . B × P*ch*; *17.* K—Kt1, K—R1; *18.* Q—K2, B × P; *19.* Q—Q2, B × P; *20.* Q × P wins.

17. **Q—B2**	

Threatening *18.* Q—B5 and *19.* Q—R7 mate.

17. . . . . . **P—KB4**
18. **P—KR4**

The B is driven away so that White's Q can enter.

18. . . . . . **B—K2**
19. **Q—B4** **Resigns**

Black realizes that his game is hopeless. Let's see why:

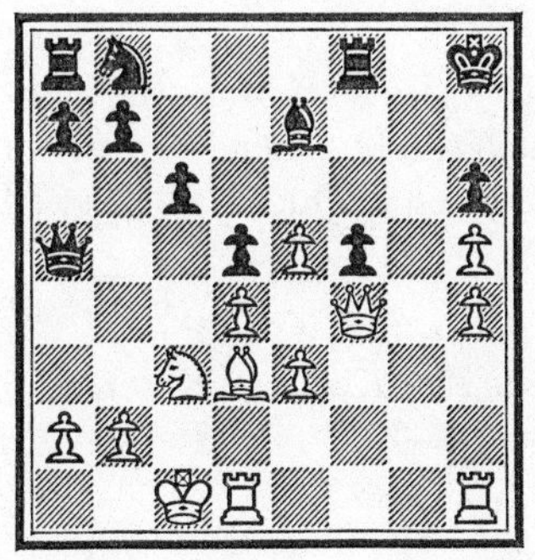

White threatens *20.* R(R1)—Kt1 and *21.* Q × P(R6).

a. If *19.* . . . . . R—B2; *20.* R(R1)—Kt1, B—B1; *21.* P—K6, R—K2; *22.* Q—K5*ch,* B—Kt2, *23.* R × B*!,* R × R; *24.* P—K7 and Black has no defense against P—K8(Q).

b. If *19.* . . . . . K—R2; *20.* B × P*ch,* R × B; *21.* Q × R*ch,* K—R1; *22.* Q—Kt6, B—B1; *23.* R(R1)—Kt1, and Black has no defense against mate.

c. If *19.* . . . . . K—Kt2; *20.* Q—Kt3*ch,* K—R1; *21.* Q—Kt6, R—Q1; *22.* R(R1)—Kt1 and mate follows.

RULE TO REMEMBER

One of the weakest of all Pawn formations (hardest to defend) is a single Pawn on KR2 or KR3 and isolated doubled Pawns on KB2 and KB3.

Be ready to play B × Kt against a castled position when you can force your opponent to have such weak Pawns.

---

33 Slav Defense

Moscow, 1947

White	*Black*
D. Bronstein	G. Levenfish

The Opening

The Slav Defense, as we have seen, permits a quick White attack if Black neglects development. Another pitfall for Black in this opening is the wasting of time by a hasty attack on the Q-side. One such attack is the Meran Variation, as in this game.

White's Plan

Bronstein, one of the world's great attacking players, is a David in search of Goliaths. He seeks complications and finds in them positions which permit decisive assaults.

Black's Plan

Grigori Levenfish was a leading master for 50 years. He was also an attacking player who sought complications. In this game his failure to prepare for castling leaves his King in a hopeless position.

Comment

The game illustrates the havoc which can be wrought by the invasion of a Queen on the 7th rank.

1. **P—Q4**	**P—Q4**
2. **Kt—KB3**	**Kt—KB3**
3. **P—B4**	**P—B3**
4. **P—K3**	

This move is less sharp than a move like *4.* Q—B2. Black could now play *4.* . . . . . B—B4, solving the problem of developing the QB.

4.	**P—K3**
5. **B—Q3**	**P × P**

Black takes the P, turning the game into a Q Gambit—with the important difference that White has used two moves to play his B from KB1 to QB4.

6. **B × P(B4)**	**Kt(Kt1)—Q2**
7. **Kt—B3**	**P—QKt4**

Now follows a series of P moves in which White tries to take a grip on the center while Black works on the Q-side.

8. B—Q3	P—QR3
9. P—K4	P—B4
10. P—K5	P × P

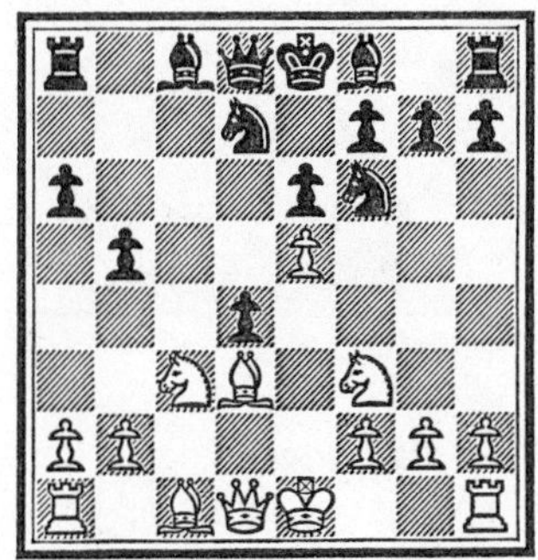

The Meran Variation. Consider some of the alternatives for White:

a. 11. P × Kt, P × Kt; *12.* O—O, Q × P, and Black holds.

b. 11. Kt × P(Q4), Kt × P and Black stands better.

c. 11. Kt × KtP, P × Kt; *12.* P × Kt, Q—Kt3 and the Black QP holds after *13.* P × P, B × P.

d. 11. Kt × KtP, Kt × P; *12.* Kt × Kt, P × Kt; *13.* Q—B3, B—Kt5*ch*; *14.* K—K2, R—QKt1; *15.* Q—Kt3, Q—Q3; *16.* Kt—B3, Q × Q; *17.* RP × Q, B—B4 and White will have a better ending. But Black can avoid this line by playing *11.* . . . . P × Kt as in variation *c* above.

White therefore tries another move.

11. Kt—K4	Kt—Q4
12. O—O	B—Kt2 ?

Black would have done better to play *12.* . . . . B—K2, which would permit castling or . . . . K—B1 when necessary.

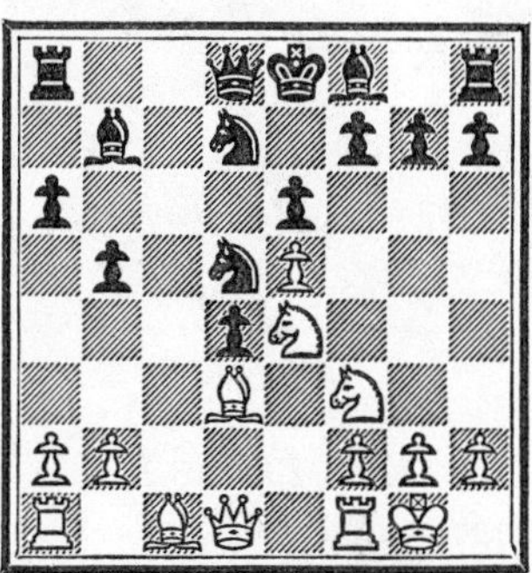

13. B—Kt5	Q—Kt1

To cover the Q3 and K4 squares.

14. P—QR4	Kt × P ?

This permits White to open up the Q-side. *14.* . . . . P—Kt5 was better. Keep the lines closed when you are behind in development.

15. Kt × Kt	Q × Kt
16. P × P	P—QR4
17. P—B4	Q—Kt1
18. P—B5	

RULE TO REMEMBER

Try to open the KB file when your opponent has not yet castled. In this game, Black's Q-side is open, and he must either leave his King where it is or castle while White has open lines of attack on the castled position.

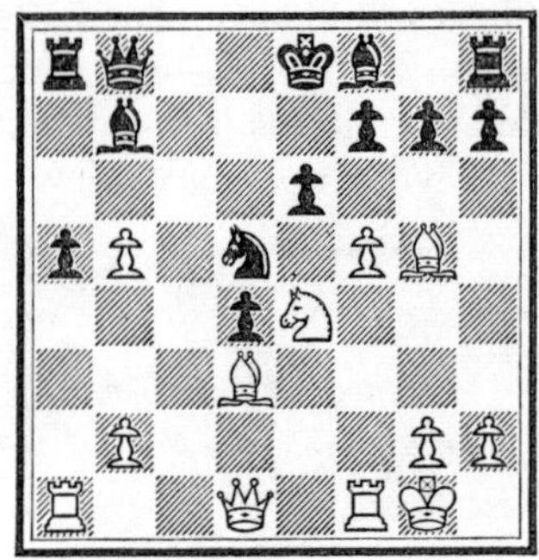

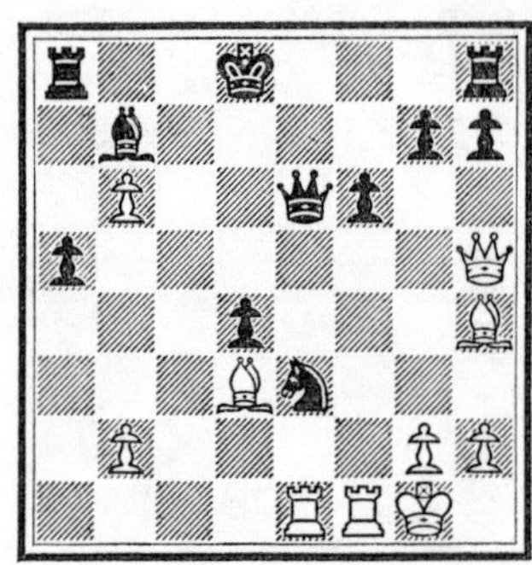

Now the Black K-side is opened up. If *18.* . . . . P × P; *19.* R × P (B5) and then Q—Kt3 and B—QB4 or R to Q1 or KB1 will apply more pressure than Black can stand.

18. . . . . **Q—K4**
19. **P—Kt6** **B—Q3**

Black had to move the B to make room for the K on KB1, since White threatened B—Kt5*ch !*

20. **Kt × B*ch*** **Q × Kt**
21. **P × P** **P—B3**

21. . . . . Q × KP was impossible in view of *22.* R—K1, Kt—K6; *23.* Q—R4*ch,* K—B1; *24.* Q × QP.

22. **Q—R5*ch*** **K—Q1**

Not *22.* . . . . P—Kt3; because of *23.* B × KtP*ch !*

23. **B—R4** **Q × KP**
24. **R(R1)—K1** **Kt—K6**

Black is undeveloped (R's at R1) and has weaknesses (K exposed, P on Q5, pin of Kt). White needs only a move which takes advantage of all of this. He finds it.

25. **Q—QB5 *!*** **Q—Q4**
26. **Q—B7*ch*** **K—K1**
27. **Q × P**

Defending the mate threatened by Black on Kt7 and also hitting the R at KR1.

27. . . . . **R—KB1**

Not *27.* . . . . R—KKt1; *28.* B—Kt5*ch,* Q × B; *29.* Q × R*ch,* K—Q2; *30.* Q—B7*ch.*

28. **B—Kt5*ch*** **B—B3**
29. **B × B*ch*** **Q × B**
30. **B × P**

Black is lost, as the threat of *31.* B × P and the loss of the Kt cannot be met.

30. . . . . **R—B2**
31. **Q—Kt8*ch*** **R—B1**

32. Q—Kt5	K—Q2
33. R—B2 ?	

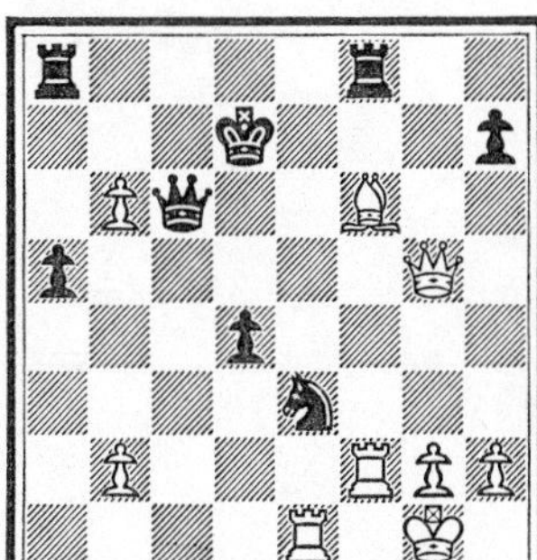

33. Q—Kt7*ch*, K—K3; *34.* Q—K7*ch*, K—Q4; *35.* Q—K5*ch*, K—B5; *36.* R—B1*ch* would win immediately. But White's position is so superior that he can win with second-best moves.

33.	Q × P(Kt3)
34. Q—Kt7*ch*	K—B3
35. B × P	R × R
36. B × Kt	

White avoids the trap *36.* B × Q, R × P*ch*; *37.* Q × R, Kt × Q, when Black would draw.

RULE TO REMEMBER

A *King hunt* is the chasing of your opponent's King about an open board until it has been forced into a square where:

1. It is mated by the combined action of two or more of your pieces;
2. Its exposed position forces your opponent to give up material to prevent a mate;
3. A pin or double attack wins enemy material. The final position of this game demonstrates such a pin.

---

36.	Q × P
37. R—B1*ch*	K—Kt4
38. Q—Kt7*ch*	K—R5
39. R—B4*ch*	K—R6
40. B—B1	Resigns

There is no longer any hope, as the Q must fall. This game reinforces the significance of being concerned for the safety of your King before attempting aggressive action.

34 Slav Defense

U.S.A.–U.S.S.R. Radio Match, 1945

White	*Black*
A. S. Denker	M. Botvinnik

The Opening

Opening analysis by masters is so thorough that it permits them to turn a small error by an opponent into the basis for a winning attack. The Slav Defense seems deceptively easy for both sides, with the locked Pawn structure caused by the opening moves. But either side can explode into action, as this celebrated victory by Botvinnik demonstrates.

White's Play

Arnold Denker was U.S. champion when this game was played. He plays aggressively, but not as accurately as he should.

Black's Play

Botvinnik surprises his opponent with a line of play that had been the subject of extensive Russian analysis.

Comment

The game ends with proper fireworks as Black gives up two Rooks for a Queen, and then picks off a piece.

1. **P—Q4**	**P—Q4**
2. **P—QB4**	**P—K3**
3. **Kt—QB3**	**P—QB3**
4. **Kt—B3**	**Kt—B3**
5. **B—Kt5**	**P × P**
6. **P—K4**	

White aims for a K-side attack in exchange for the Pawn.

6.	**P—Kt4**
7. **P—K5**	**P—KR3**
8. **B—R4**	

If 8. P × Kt, P × B; 9. Kt × P, P × P; and Black will have all the open lines he needs for attack on either wing.

8.	**P—Kt4**
9. **Kt × KKtP**	

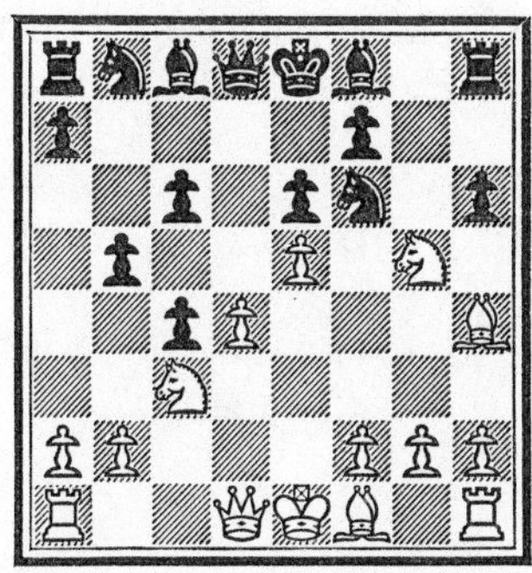

White makes a temporary sacrifice of this Kt, for he will later be able to capture the pinned Kt on Black's KB3.

9.	P × Kt
10. B × KtP	Kt(Kt1)—Q2

White should now play *11.* P—KKt3 and *12.* B—Kt2. The Kt on Black's KB3 can be taken at the moment Black breaks the pin by a Q move, ... B—K2, or . . . . R—KKt1. But White takes the Kt at once and permits Black to block P—KKt3.

11. P × Kt ?	B—QKt2 !
12. B—K2	Q—Kt3

Every Black move increases the pressure. *12.* . . . . Q—Kt3 prepares for . . . . P—B4; . . . . O—O—O; . . . . P—QR4; any one of which would create problems for White.

13. O—O	O—O—O
14. P—QR4	

Little can be done about the threatened invasion of the Q-side Pawns. White should have tried *14.* B—B3, Kt—K4; *15.* B—K3, although Black's attack would still be strong.

14.	P—Kt5
15. Kt—K4	P—B4 !

If *16.* P × P, Kt × P(B4) wins a piece.

16. Q—Kt1

The Kt at K4 must be protected. *16.* Q—B2, P—Kt6; *17.* Q—Kt1, B—Q4 would leave Black in control of the board.

16.	Q—B2

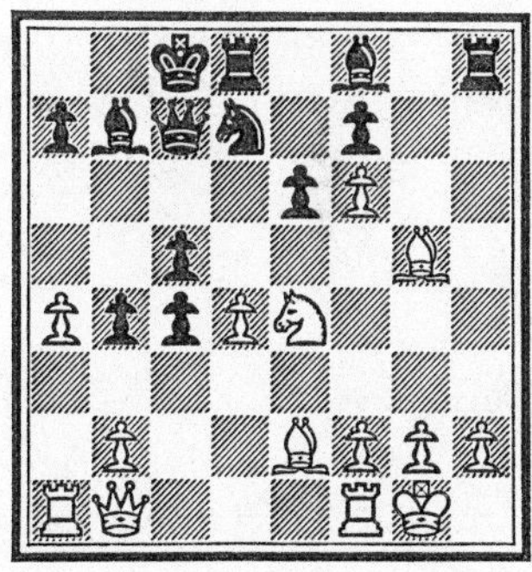

How is White to meet the threat of mate on KR2 ? *17.* P—R3 invites a future sacrifice on KR3 or KKt2. Best would be P—KKt3. The move Denker selects puts his Kt out of play.

RULE TO REMEMBER

You are playing through a perfect example of a cramped position, and will see how it limits the movements of a player's pieces. White cannot move the Bishop on Kt5; White's castled position invites a check; the Pawn on Q4 must be defended; there is no point in the Black position against which to mount an attack.

Play against cramped positions by piling up threats against its weak points—such as the White Pawn on Q4.

---

17. **Kt—Kt3**	**P × P**
18. **B × P**	**Q—B3 !**

Another mate threat, on KKt7. Of course, Black could not have played *18.* Q × B? because of *18.* . . . . R—B1.

19. **P—B3**	**P—Q6**

This move really attacks the White B on Kt5, via the threat of *20.* . . . . Q—B4*ch* and *21.* . . . . Q × B. More important, it opens a line for Black's KB.

RULE TO REMEMBER

***Beware of double attacks!* If White here plays *20.* Q × P, Kt —K4 will win White's B on QB4.**

---

20. **Q—B1**	**B—B4*ch***
21. **K—R1**	

If *21.* B—K3, P—Q7; *22.* Q × P, Kt—K4 wins a piece.

21.	**Q—Q3**

The threats are too numerous for White to meet. The most immediate is *22.* . . . . Q × Kt, when the Q cannot be recaptured.

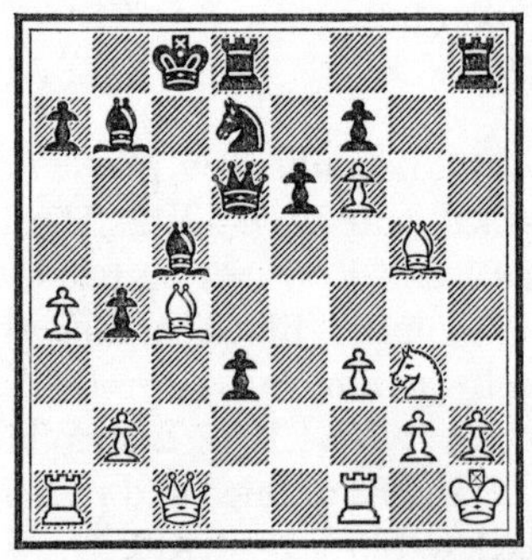

White is lost.

a. If *22.* any Kt move, Black mates or takes the Kt.

b. If *22.* B—KR6, P—Q7; *23.* Q × P, Q—K4; *24.* R(R1)—K1, Q × P(B3); *25.* B—KKt5, R × P*ch*; *26.* K × R, R—R1*ch*; *27.* B —R6, R × B*ch* wins.

c. If *22.* B—B4, R × P*ch*; *23.* K × R, R—R1*ch*; *24.* Kt—R5, R × Kt*ch*; *25.* K—Kt3, P—K4; *25.*

B—K3, Q × P; *26.* K—B2, R—R7; *27.* Q—Q1, Q—R5*ch*; *28.* K—Kt1, R—R8 mate.

d. If 22. P—B4, R × P*ch,* 23. K × R, R—R1*ch*; *24.* Kt—R5, R × Kt*ch;* 25. K—Kt3, R × B*ch*; *26.* K—R3, R × P wins quickly.

22. **Q—B4**	**R ×** ***Pch !***
23. **K × R**	**R—R1*ch***
24. **Q—R4**	**R × Q*ch***
25. **B × R**	**Q—B5**
26. **Resigns**	

Black attacks both Bishops, and must win one of them. There might follow *26.* K—R3, Q × B(B5); *27.* R(R1)—B1, Q—Q4; and Black will win by forcing the QP through.

35 Slav Defense

Moscow, 1967

White	*Black*
L. Portisch	T. Petrosian

The Opening

One reason for Black success with the Slav Defense is the absence of weak points in his position. When a position is closed (no open lines), the defender's task is always easier. The Exchange Variation of the Slav Defense is an attempt by White to open some lines as quickly as possible. Black should then try to develop quickly, so that his pieces can defend on whatever side White attacks.

White's Plan

Lajos Portisch, Hungary's best player, knows how to take quick advantage of open lines. He offers a Pawn to gain time to bring his pieces to better attacking positions on the K-side.

Black's Plan

Tigran Petrosian was world champion when this game was played. He decides he can win a Pawn. In so doing, he delays the building of proper defenses for his King.

Comment

The game illustrates how even a world champion can be punished when he fails to develop his pieces!

1. **P—Q4**	**P—Q4**
2. **P—QB4**	**P—QB3**
3. **P × P**	**P × P**

This is the Exchange Variation of the Slav Defense. White hopes to be first to make use of the open QB file.

4. **Kt—KB3**	**Kt—KB3**
5. **Kt—B3**	**Kt—B3**
6. **B—B4**	**P—K3**

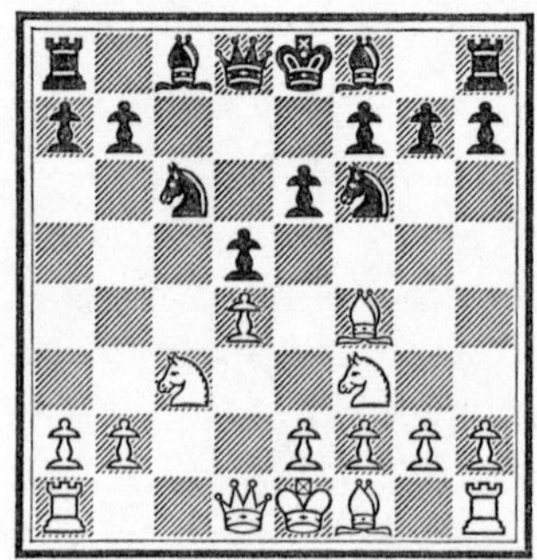

Why does Black lock in his QB with *6.* . . . . P—K3? He realizes that *6.* . . . . B—B4; *7.* P—K3, P—K3; *8.* Q—Kt3 or *8.* B—QKt5 lead to positions in which White has greater play on the Q-side. Petrosian wants to play . . . . B—Q3 to exchange Bishops and keep the position simple.

7.	**P—K3**	**B—Q3**
8.	**B—Kt3!**	

White retreats instead of exchanging. If Black now plays *8.* . . . . B × B; *9.* RP × B opens the KR file for a possible attack against Black's K-side.

RULE TO REMEMBER

It is dangerous to castle when your opponent has an open Rook file along which he can attack with Rooks or Queen and Rook.

8.	. . . .	**O—O**
9.	**B—Q3**	

RULE TO REMEMBER

Place a Bishop at Q3 to prepare an attack against the enemy castled King. The Bishop then bears on the center for greater mobility.

9.	. . . .	**R—K1**

Black would like to play *10.* . . . . P—K4, releasing his Bishop at QB1. White now prevents this freeing move.

10.	**Kt—K5**	**B × Kt**
11.	**P × B**	**Kt—Q2**
12.	**P—B4**	**Q—Kt3?**

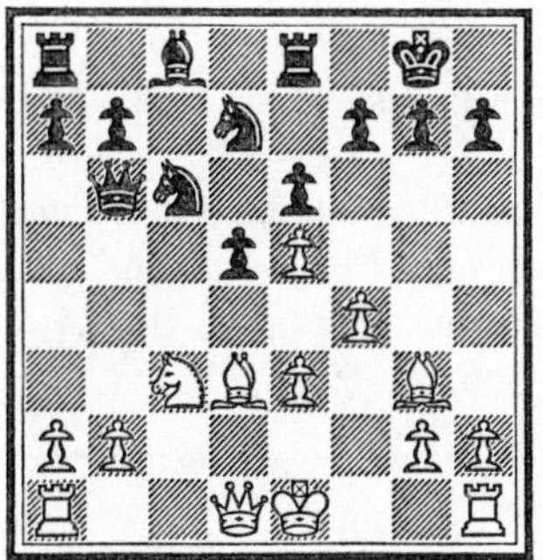

What makes *12.* . . . . Q—Kt3 a poor move?

a. The QB and QR remain undeveloped.

b. The Black Queen attacks two Pawns, and can win one of them. However, this will waste two more moves, as the Queen takes a Pawn and then retreats to avoid being trapped.

c. 12. . . . . Kt—B4 is better. White would play B—Kt1 to avoid the exchange of his well-placed Bishop. Black could then play . . . . P—QKt3 to develop his Bishop at R3.

13.	**O—O** *!*	**Q × KP***ch*
14.	**K—R1**	**Q—Kt3**

What was wrong with Black's play? He has wasted three

moves to gain a Pawn. White has gained time to begin a K-side attack.

15. **Q—R5** **Kt—B1**

RULE TO REMEMBER

Do not permit holes in your position (squares on which enemy pieces can be posted).

15. **. . . . . P—Kt3 would be a blunder here. White would then play *16.* Q—R6, and would threaten mate after B—R4 and B—B6.**

---

16. **R—B3*!***

The White Rook is heading for KKt3 or KR3, to increase the pressure against the Black King.

16. **. . . .** **Kt—Kt3**

If Black tries *16.* . . . . . Q × P (apparently winning another Pawn), White answers strongly with *17.* R—QKt1! This would win the Black Queen:

a. If *17.* . . . . . Q—R6; *18.* Kt × P, P × Kt; *19.* B × P*ch*, Kt × B; *20.* R × Q

b. If *17.* . . . . . Q × Kt; *18.* B × P*ch*, Kt × B; *19.* R × Q

c. If *17.* . . . . . Q—Q7; *18.* B—K1

17. **B—KB2*!***

White gains another move. Black still cannot take the Pawn at QKt7. If *17.* . . . . . Q × P; *18.* R—QKt1, Q × Kt; *19.* R—R3, P—KR3; *20.* B × Kt, P × B; *21.* Q × KtP and White wins the exchange.

17. **. . . .** **Q—Q1**
18. **Kt—Kt5** **Kt(B3)—K2**
19. **Kt—Q6**

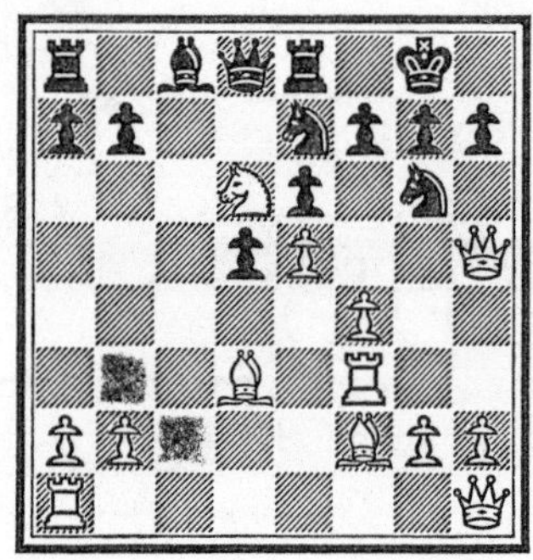

White has anchored the Knight at Q6, where it is protected by the Pawn at K5. The Knight attacks KB7 and QKt7 (so that Black cannot play . . . . B—Q2 without losing a Pawn).

19. **. . . .** **B—Q2**

White can win the exchange now by Kt × R. But he sees a winning attack, and plays for a mate instead of satisfying himself with a small material advantage.

20. **B—R4*!*** **Q—Kt3**

Black cannot play *20.* . . . . . Kt × B because of *21.* B × P*ch*, K—B1; *22.* Q × P mate, or, if

21. . . . . K—R1; *22.* Kt × P mate.

RULE TO REMEMBER

A mating attack is better than the win of material. Look for an attack on the enemy King when your development is better than that of your opponent.

---

21. **R—R3**	**P—KR3**
22. **B—B6 ! !**	

This sacrifice pries open the Black position. Black can take the Bishop, but would then be unable to prevent mate. For example: *22.* . . . . P × B; *23.* P × P, Q × Kt; *24.* Q × P(R6), Kt—B4; *25.* Q—R7*ch,* K—B1; *26.* Q—R8*ch,* Kt × Q; *27.* R × Kt mate.

22.	**Q × P**
23. **R—KB1**	

The final threat is *24.* B × P, followed by *25.* Q × P*ch,* *26.* Q—R7 and mate at KB7.

23.	**Kt—B4**
24. **B × Kt**	**Resigns**

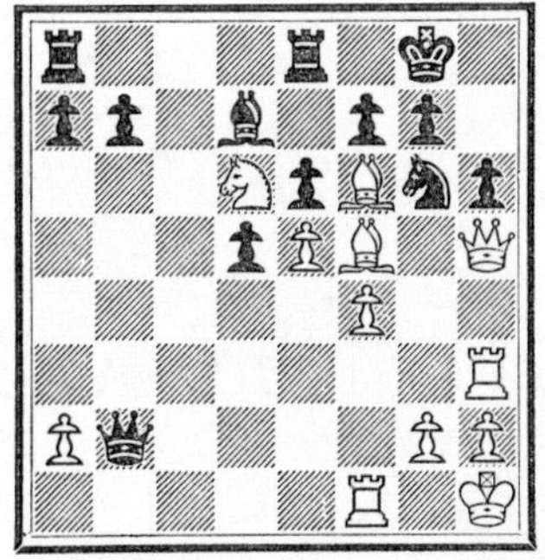

Black resigns because he cannot prevent mate.

a. If *24.* . . . . P × B(B3); *25.* Q × P, R—K2; *26.* B × Kt, and Black cannot answer the threat of Q—R8 mate.

b. If *24* . . . . P × B(B4); *25.* B × P, K × B; *26.* Q × P*ch,* and mate follows on KB7.

RULE TO REMEMBER

Do not waste several moves to gain a Pawn in the opening—especially when you are not yet fully developed!

Do not be afraid to offer a Pawn in the opening when you gain two or three developing moves for it—especially when you can then open the position to take advantage of your better development.

---

36 Nimzovich Defense

New York, 1948

White	*Black*
A. S. Denker	R. Fine

The Opening

The period between the World Wars saw the development of a new approach to the chess openings. This treatment, called the "hypermodern" theory, owed much to the ideas of Aron Nimzovich, whose name (with such variations in spelling as Niemczovicz and Niemzowitch) is associated with many of the basic chess ideas in use today. One of his ideas is that Black can defend against the Queen's Pawn openings by holding back the center Pawns until the game has taken a more definite form.

White's Plan

White plays aggressively, but allows his K-side to be opened up, with fatal results.

Black's Plan

Reuben Fine, until he retired from active play in the 1950s, was the traditional "second best" chess player in the United States. He often finished just behind Samuel Reshevsky in national chess events, but made one of the best international records in history during the 1930s and 1940s. In this game he wins by paying proper attention to the steady development of his pieces.

Comment

Observe how Black opens up the K-side. He does not challenge the center until he is fully developed.

1. **P—Q4**	**Kt—KB3**
2. **P—QB4**	**P—K3**
3. **Kt—QB3**	**B—Kt5**
4. **Q—B2**	

A popular line of play. White can also play *4.* P—QR3, *4.* P—K3, *4.* P— KKt3 and *4.* Kt—B3, each of which leads to a different kind of game.

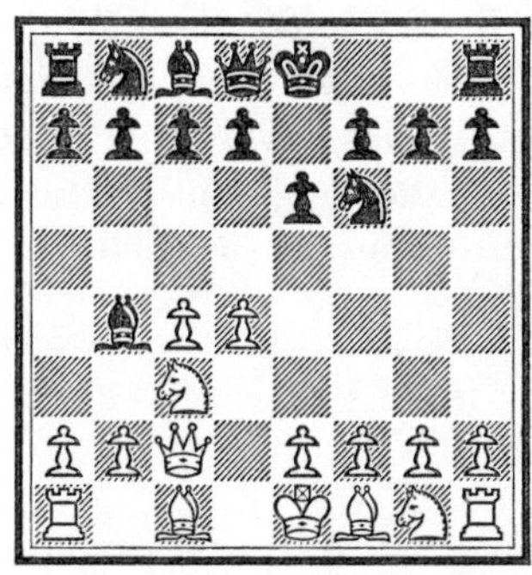

4. . . . . Kt—B3
5. P—K3 O—O

Black's objective is rapid development. White aims at control of the center—but the control he can achieve is without any pressure on Black.

6. Kt—K2 P—Q4
7. P × P P × P
8. P—QR3 B—Q3

White is playing without a plan. His last three moves have given Black an advantage in development.

9. Kt—Kt3 P—KKt3 *!*

The White Kt must be kept out of B5.

10. B—Q3 P—QR3

And the other Kt out of Kt5 *!*

11. B—Q2 B—K3

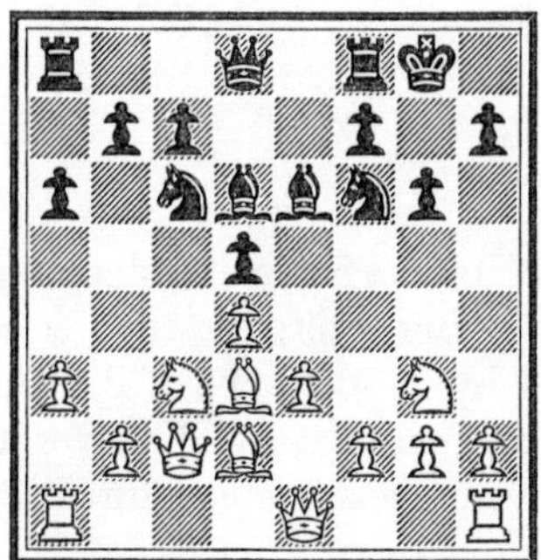

12. Kt(B3)—K2 Q—Q2
13. O—O Kt—K1

How is Black to attack? He plans to advance the KBP. White tries to prevent this advance, but creates other problems in the process.

14. P—B3 *?* P—B4
15. P—K4 *?*

White's idea was a poor one. He permits Black to hit at his K side, for the previous two White moves have opened holes in White's position.

15. . . . . B × Kt *!*
16. P × B

If *16.* Kt × B, Kt × P.

16.	QP × P
17. P × P	Kt × P
18. Kt × Kt	Q × Kt*ch*
19. K—R2	

Black is a Pawn ahead, temporarily. But White can counter-attack by B—B3 and P × P. Black must, and does, find moves to prevent these counter-thrusts.

19.	R—Q1*!*
20. R—B3	Kt—B3*!!*

The Kt returns to the scene of action with crushing effect.

21. P × P	B × P
22. Q—Kt3*ch*	R—B2
23. B—B3	

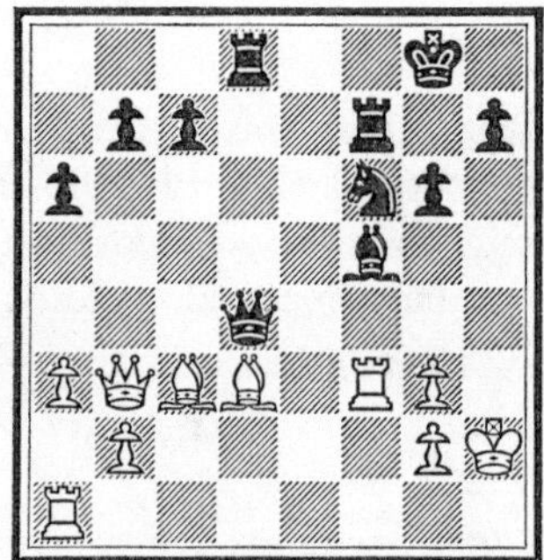

23. B—QB4, which appears to win material at B7, loses instead to 23. . . . . Kt—Kt5*ch*; 24. K—R1, Q × B(Q7); 25. B × R*ch*, K—Kt2; and White cannot defend against the threat of 26. . . . . Q—R3*ch*; 27. K—Kt1, Q—R7*ch*; 28. K—B1, Q—R8*ch*; 29. K—K2, Q × P*ch*; 30. K—K1, Q—Q7*ch*; 31. K—B1, Kt—K6*ch !*; 32. R × Kt, B—R6*ch;* 33. K—Kt1, Q—Kt7 mate. A ten-move combination like this, involving a direct single attacking line, is easily seen by a master like Fine.

23.	Kt—Kt5*ch*
24. K—R1	Q—B4*!*
25. B × B	

For now 25. B—B4 would be met by 25. . . . . B—K3, and the Black Q comes in at KR4!

RULE TO REMEMBER

Beware of open lines in a castled King position! Black's attacking moves in this game revolve around threats to use the open Rook file and the open diagonal QR2—KKt8.

---

25.	P × B
26. R—Q1	R—Q3
27. R × R	Q × R
28. K—Kt1	Q—R3

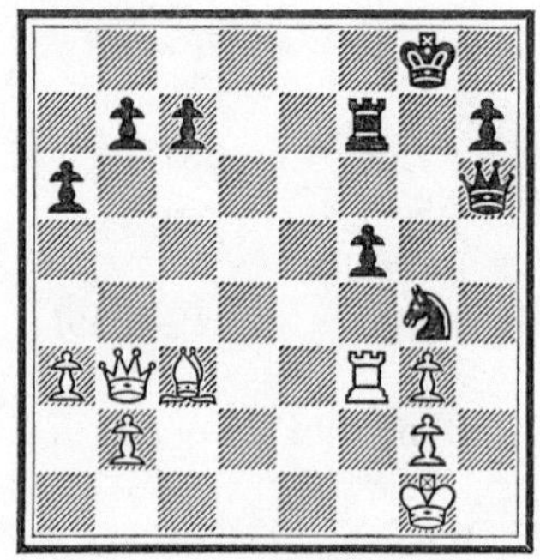

White here overstepped the time limit, and lost "on time." However, he was lost in any event, for he has no defense against Black's threats of . . . . Q—B8*ch* or . . . . Q—R7*ch*.

a. If 29. Q—B2 (to stop 29. . . . . Q—B8*ch*), Q—R7*ch*; *30.* K—B1, Q—R8*ch*; *31.* K—K2, Q × P*ch* wins at least a Rook.

b. If 29. R—Q3, Q—B8*ch*; *30.* Q—Q1, Q × Q*ch*; *31.* R × Q, K—B1; and Black's extra Pawn is a winning advantage.

Reuben Fine's retirement from active play removed one of the world's greatest players from the chess scene!

RULE TO REMEMBER

An open King position can be attacked in three ways: on the rank, along the file, and on the diagonal. The move Q—B8*ch* in the final position involves all three kinds of attack. Play these moves from that position.

***29.* P—R4 (which is the same as assuming that White does nothing), Q—B8*ch* (attack on the rank); *30.* R—B1, Q—K6*ch* (attack on the diagonal); *31.* K—R1, Q—R3*ch* (attack on the file!); *32.* K—Kt1, Q—R7 mate.**

---

37 Nimzovich Defense

New York, 1941

White	*Black*
Edward Lasker	F. J. Marshall

The Opening

The Nimzovich Defense can be played aggressively by both sides, and an open game can result. In this game, played in the annual tournament of New York's Marshall Chess Club, both players press on—but White breaks through.

White's Plan

Edward Lasker is one of the great chess teachers, a master whose books and articles have had a great influence on chess. He here takes his chances on attacking a former champion of the United States.

Black's Plan

Frank James Marshall held the championship of the United States for some 30 years, until his retirement in 1936. This game, played in his last years, still reflects his fighting spirit. He loses after snatching at a Pawn.

Comment

The ending illustrates the win with Queen and Rook when the King is exposed and on the run.

1. **P—Q4**	**Kt—KB3**
2. **P—QB4**	**P—K3**
3. **Kt—QB3**	**B—Kt5**
4. **P—KKt3**	**O—O**
5. **B—Kt2**	**P—Q4**

Black would like to play . . . . Kt(Kt1)—Q2 and . . . . P—B4, but White decides to open up the game.

6. **P × P**	**P × P**
7. **B—Kt5**	**P—B4**

Black would like to play *8.* P × P, P—Q5*!*; 9. P—QR3, P × Kt; *10.* P × B, P × P*!*

8. **P—QR3**	**B × Kt*ch***
9. **P × B**	**P × P**
10. **P × P**	**Kt—B3**

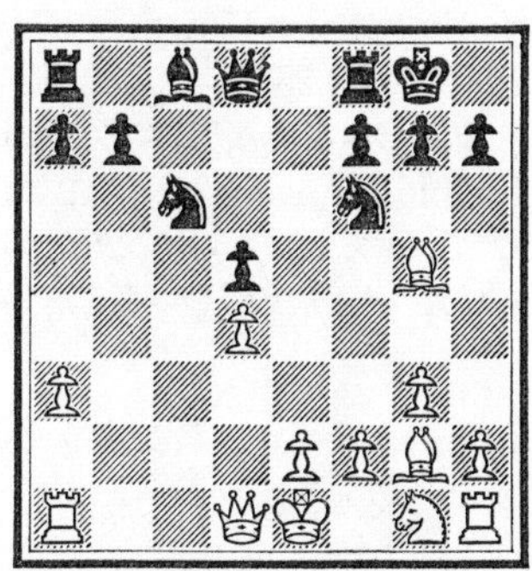

The Black P on Q4 is a target, and White goes after it at once. It would here be best to play *11.* Kt—B3, castle, and then attack the QP. As White plays it, Black gets an equal game.

11. **B × Kt** **Q × B**
12. **P—K3**

If *12.* B × P, Kt × P.

12. . . . . **R—K1 !**

So that *12.* B × P still is met by *12.* . . . . Kt × P*!*

13. **Kt—K2** **B—Kt5**
14. **O—O**

14. R—R2 would have held the QP, for *14.* . . . . B × Kt; *15.* R × B, and Black still must worry about his QP.

14. . . . . **B × Kt**
15. **Q × B** **Kt × P**
16. **Q—Q1*!*** **Kt—B3**
17. **Q × P**

If *17.* B × P, R(R1)—Q1; *18.* Q—Kt3, R—Q2 with equality.

17. . . . . **R(R1)—Q1**

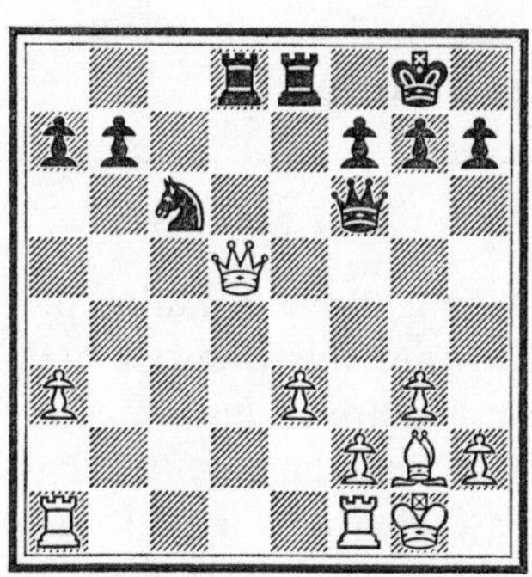

17. . . . . P—QR3 was better. Now White's Q begins to pick at the Black Pawns.

18. **Q—QKt5** **R—K2**
19. **R(R1)—B!** **R—B2**

If *19.* . . . . Kt—K4; *20.* B × P, R—Kt1; *21.* Q—R6*!* R(K2) × B; *22.* Q × R*!*, R × Q; *23.* R—B8*ch*, Q—Q1; *24.* R × Q mate.

20. **R—B4** **P—KKt3**

Black acts to provide an escape square for his King. *20.* . . . . P—KR3 might have been better.

21. **B—Q5*!***

A quiet but strong move. White keeps Black's R from going to the 7th rank.

21. . . . . **Q—Q3**
22. **R—Q1** **Q × RP?**

Black makes the slip which loses the game. On *22.* . . . . Q

—K2 he could have defended, but now, with the Q away from the scene of action, White can become brilliant!

RULE TO REMEMBER

Do not move a major piece away from the scene of action when you are under attack!

Offer your opponent a Pawn if his taking it will pull an important piece away from the squares where it is needed!

---

23. **R × Kt!**

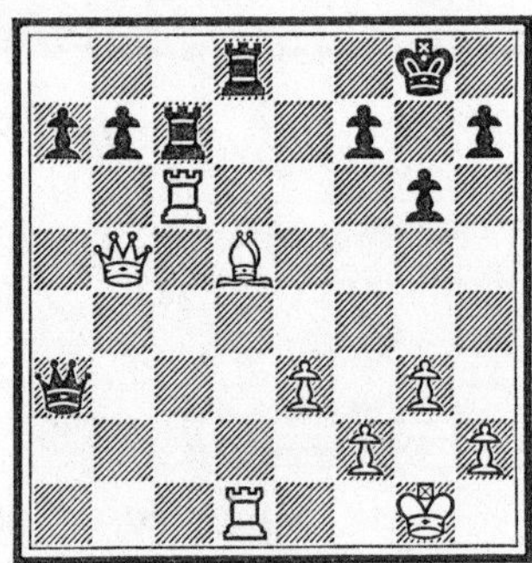

Black cannot now play *23.* . . . . P × R; *24.* B × P*ch,* K × B; *25.* Q—B4*ch,* K—K2; *26.* Q—K4*ch,* K—B2; *27.* R × R, and Black's King is exposed to further attack.

23.	**R × B**
24. **R(Q1) × R**	**Q—R8*ch*?**

Black hopes to keep White's Queen from attacking along the long diagonal. However, *24.* . . . . R × R; *25.* R—Q8*ch,* K—Kt2; *26.* Q—K5*ch,* R—B3 was preferable, or even *24.* . . . . R × R; *25.* Q × P, Q—R3; *26.* Q—Kt8*ch,* K—Kt2; *27.* Q—K5*ch,* R—B3.

25. **K—Kt2**	**R × R**
26. **R—Q8*ch***	**K—Kt2**
27. **Q—Kt4!**	

Threatening to win Black's Queen by *28.* Q—B8*ch,* K—B3; *29.* Q—R8*ch.*

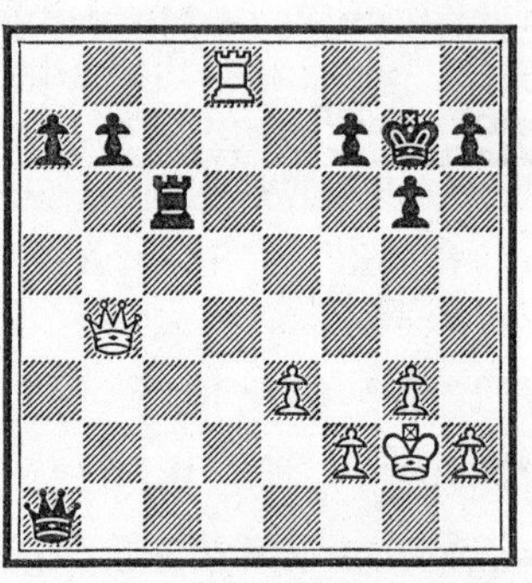

RULE TO REMEMBER

Always consider the several moves your opponent may make in reply to your attack. For example, can Black defend here by 27. . . . . P—KR4? Not really, for White would continue *28.* Q—B8*ch,* K—R2; *29.* Q × P*ch,* K—R3; *30.* Q—B8*ch,* Q—Kt2; *31.* Q × Q*ch,* K × Q; *32.* R—Q7*ch,* K—B3; *33.* R × P and White would win the ending.

---

27.	**Q—B6**
28. **Q—B8*ch***	**K—B3**
29. **R—Q6*ch***	**K—Kt4**

For *29.* . . . . R × R would lose the Q after *30.* Q—R8*ch.*

30. **P—R4*ch***	**K—R4**

Or *30.* . . . . K—Kt5; *31.* P—B3, K—R4; *32.* P—Kt4*ch,* K × P; *33.* Q—R6 mate.

31. **R—Q5*ch***	**Resigns**

Mate is forced.

a. *31.* . . . . K—Kt5; *32.* P—B3 or R—Kt5 mate.

b. *31.* . . . . P—B4; *32.* R × P*ch !,* R × R; *33.* Q × P*ch,* K—R3; *34.* Q—Kt5 mate.

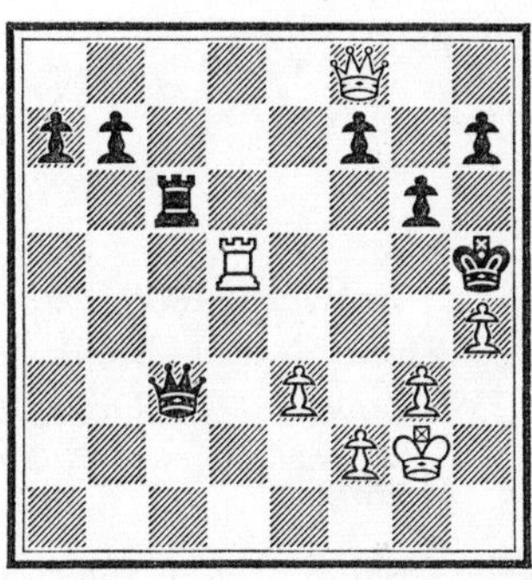

38 Colle System

Antwerp, 1936

White	*Black*
G. Koltanowski	M. Defosse

The Opening

The Colle System is the result of Edgar Colle's search for an opening that would give White a quiet closed game without weaknesses, and which, when opened up, would give attacking chances. The key moves, for White, are P—Q4, Kt—KB3, P—K3, B—Q3 and, after completing development, P—K4.

White's Plan

George Koltanowski, chess-master, organizer, and showman (and a leading chess journalist as well!), gained fame as a brilliant blindfold player. He once played 34 games simultaneously while blindfolded, keeping each position in his mind while hearing and answering one move at a time from each opponent. Impossible? He didn't lose a single game! In this game he bears steadily on his opponent's King position, lining up his Bishops for the sacrifices that follow.

Black's Plan

Black makes the mistake of exchanging or moving away the pieces that could defend his castled King position. He is then surprised, and defeated, by a double offer of Bishops—both of which he must accept. His King then stands alone—forced into the open and unable to prevent or defend an attack by White's Queen and Rook.

Comment

The game illustrates the power of two Bishops aimed at a castled King, and finally provides another demonstration of how to win with a Queen and Rook attacking an undefended King.

1.	**P—Q4**	**Kt—KB3**
2.	**Kt—KB3**	**P—K3**
3.	**P—K3**	

White holds back the QBP. He is aiming for the K side, and wants to keep a P on Q4.

3. . . . .
4. **B—Q3** **P—B4**
5. **P—B3**

A key move of the Colle System. If Black now plays *5.* . . . . P—B5; *6.* B—B2, and the KP will go to K4 when White is ready.

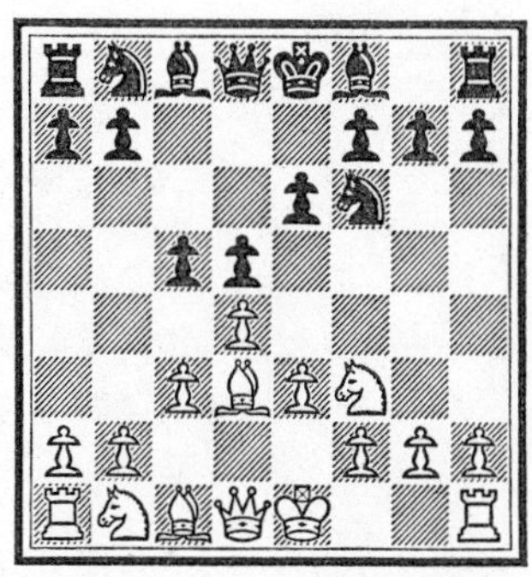

5. . . . . **Kt—B3**
6. **Kt(Kt1)—Q2** **B—K2**
7. **O—O** **O—O**
8. **P × P**

Now White is ready for P—K4, but first clears the Q file so that Black cannot isolate a White P by . . . . BP × QP.

8. . . . . **B × P**
9. **P—K4*!***

This move assures White of at least an equal game, and can lead to a better game against any but a perfect defense.

9. . . . . **Q—B2**
10. **Q—K2** **B—Q3**

To prevent *11.* P—K5.

11. **R—K1** **Kt—KKt5**

Still preventing P—K5, and also hitting at White's KRP.

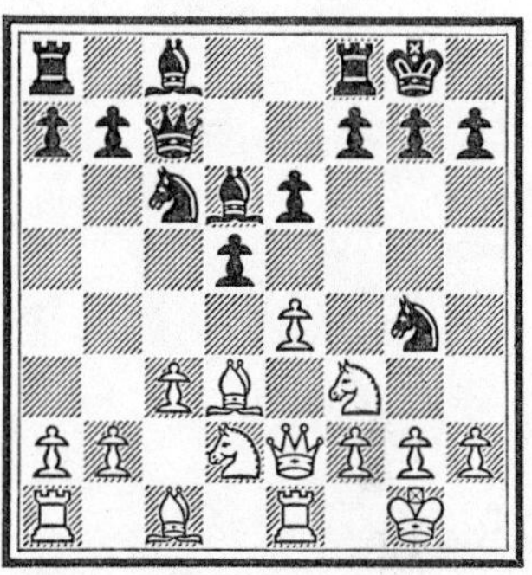

12. **P—KR3** **Kt(Kt5)—K4**
13. **Kt × Kt** **Kt × Kt**
14. **P × P** **P × P**
15. **Kt—B3** **Kt × Kt*ch ?***

Black fears *15.* . . . . Kt × B; *16.* Q × Kt because of a possible *17.* Kt—Kt5, but the line he selects is no better.

16. **Q × Kt**

White has achieved his opening objectives. The White pieces are easily developed; he has no weaknesses; the Black position is not well defended.

16. . . . . **B—K3**
17. **B—K3** **R(R1)—Q1**
18. **B—B2** **P—QKt4**

Black seeks counterplay by . . . . P—Kt5.

19.	**B—Q4**	**B—QB4**
20.	**R(R1)—Q1**	**P—Kt5**
21.	**B—K5**	**B—Q3**

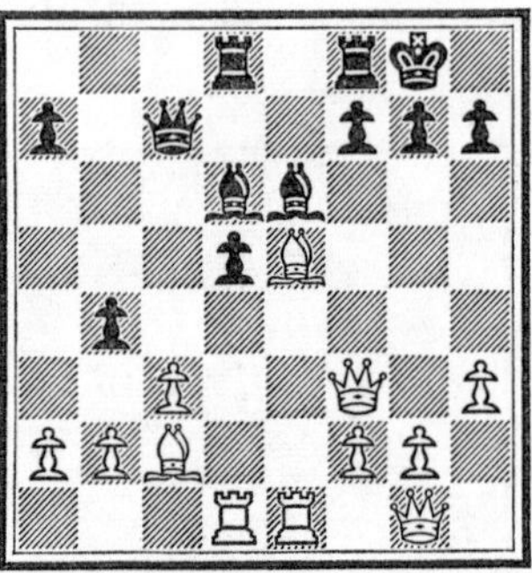

And now the big surprise—the penalty for leaving the K defense to Pawns alone!

RULE TO REMEMBER

Look for a chance to sacrifice against the enemy King position when there are no pieces defending it.

Do not leave the defense of your king to Pawns alone!

22.	**B × P*ch!***	**K × B**

For *22.* . . . . K—R1; *23.* Q—R5 will lead to a quick mate.

23.	**Q—R5*ch***	**K—Kt1**
24.	**B × P!**	**K × B**

If *24.* . . . . P—B3; *25.* B × R, R × B; *26.* R × B. Black must therefore take the B to avoid *25.* Q—R8 mate.

25.	**Q—Kt5*ch***	**K—R2**
26.	**R—Q4**	

How is Black to prevent *27.* R—R4 mate?

26.	. . . .	**B—R7*ch***
27.	**K—R1**	**Q—KB5**
28.	**R × Q**	**B × R**
29.	**Q × B**	**R—KKt1**
30.	**R—K5**	**Resigns**

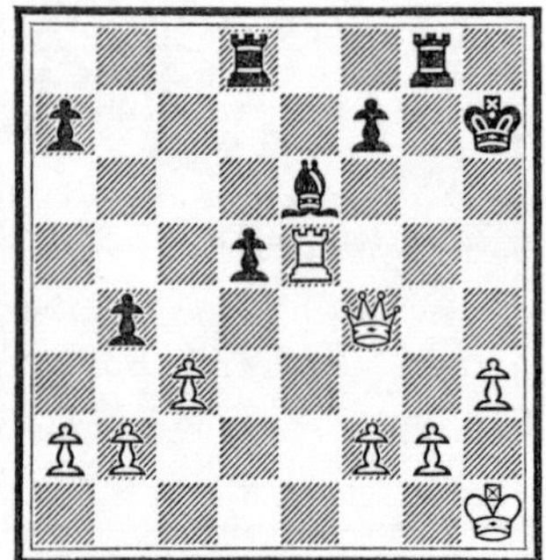

White threatens mate by *31.* R—R5*ch* and *32.* Q—R6 mate.

a. If *30.* . . . . K—Kt2; *31.* R—Kt5*ch,* K—B1; *32.* R × R*ch,* K × R; *33.* Q—Kt5*ch* and *34.* Q × R.

b. If *30.* . . . . R—Kt3; *31.* Q—R4*ch* and *32.* Q × R.

c. If *30.* . . . . K—Kt3; *31.* R—Kt5*ch* and *32.* Q—R4 mate.

RULE TO REMEMBER

Always check each possible enemy move. Find the White moves that mate after *30.* . . . . R—KR1; 31. R—R5*ch,* K—Kt1.

---

39 Colle System

Nice, 1930

White	*Black*
E. Colle	J. J. O'Hanlon

The Opening

The Colle System often leads to sparkling K-side attacks. World Champion Alexander Alekhine awarded the first brilliancy prize at the 1930 Nice tourney to Edgar Colle even though he chose a winning line which was less pretty than the best move available.

White's Plan

Colle takes advantage of O'Hanlon's disregard of development to shower his opponent with pieces, forcing the win when the opening is scarcely over!

Black's Plan

The Colle System was still new when this game was played, and its deceptive simplicity proved a trap to O'Hanlon. He makes the mistake of leaving his King position undefended.

Comment

The game is as interesting for what might have happened as for what actually occurred.

1.	**P—Q4**	**P—Q4**
2.	**Kt—KB3**	**Kt—KB3**
3.	**P—K3**	**P—B4**
4.	**P—B3**	**P—K3**
5.	**B—Q3**	**B—Q3**
6.	**Kt(Kt1)—Q2**	**Kt(Kt1)—Q2**

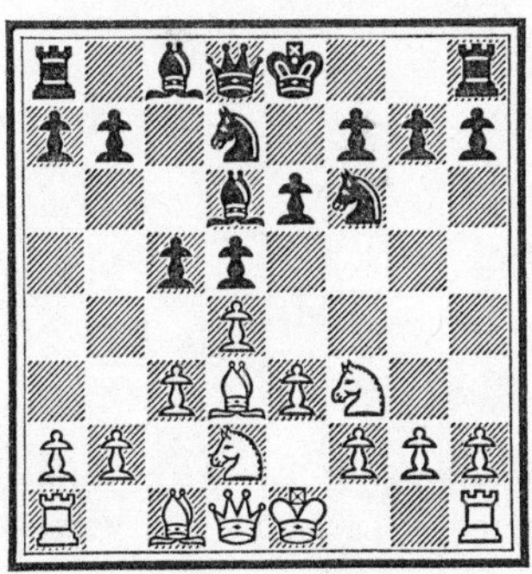

7.	**O—O**	**O—O**
8.	R—K1	**R—K1 ?**

Black is deceived into thinking that all he is faced with is a problem in symmetrical development. He should have played *8.* . . . . P—K4 to challenge the center. Now White does so instead.

9.	**P—K4**	**QP × P**
10.	**Kt × P**	**Kt × Kt**
11.	**B × Kt**	**P × P ?**
12.	**B × P*ch* !**	

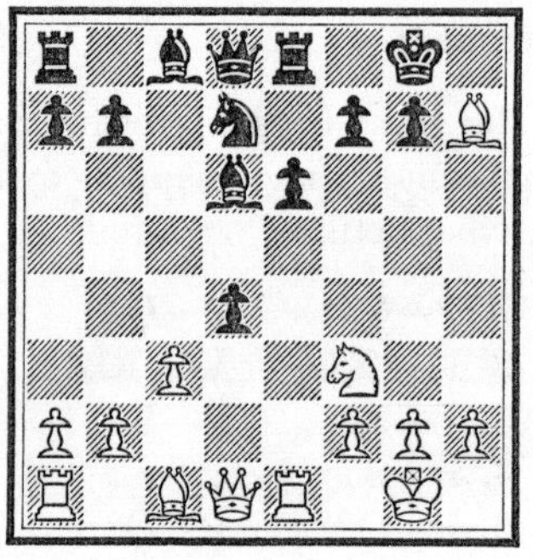

Black has invited a K-side attack. His best was *11.* . . . Kt—B3.

12. . . . . **K × B**

Had he sensed what was to come, Black would have played *12.* . . . . K—B1.

13. **Kt—Kt5*ch*** **K—Kt3**

Black is faced with difficult choices. If *13.* . . . . K—Kt1; *14.* Q—R5, Kt—B3; *15.* Q × BP*ch;* K—R1; *16.* R—K4 *!*, Kt × R; *17.* Q—R5*ch,* K—Kt1; *18.* Q—R7*ch,* K—B1; *19.* Q—R8*ch,* K—K2; *20.* Q × P mate.

14. **P—KR4 !** **R—R1**

On *14.* . . . . P—B4; *15.* P—R5*ch,* K—B3; *16.* Q × P*ch,* K—K2; *17.* Q × P mate!

15. **R × P*ch* ! !**

One blow after another. Now *15.* . . . . P × R would be met by *16.* Q—Q3*ch,* K—B3; *17.* Q—B3*ch,* K—Kt3, *18.* Q—B7*ch,* K—R3; *19.* Kt × P*ch,* K—R2; *20.* Q × P mate.

15. . . . . **Kt—B3**
16. **P—R5*ch* !** **K—R3**

There is no hope.
a. If *16.* . . . . R × P; *17.* Q—Q3*ch,* K—R3; *18.* Q—R7 mate.
b. If *16.* . . . . K—B4; *17.* Q—Q3*ch,* K—Kt5; *18.* Q—R3 mate.

17. **R × B ?**

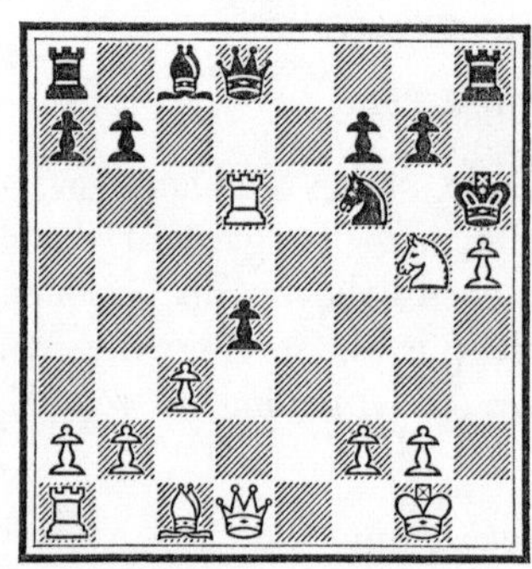

This move deserves a question mark only because White had much better. Simplest was *17.* Q—Q3, with these possibilities among others.

a. If *17.* . . . . P × R; *18.* Q—Kt6 mate.

b. If *17.* . . . . B × R; *18.* Kt × B (discovered check), K × P; *19.* Q—B5*ch*, K—R5; *20.* Q—Kt5 mate.

c. If *17.* . . . . Q—R4; *18.* Kt × P*ch*, K × P; *19.* Q—R3*ch*, K—Kt3; *20.* Kt × R mate.

17. . . . . **Q—R4**

Of course *17.* . . . . Q × R loses the Q after *18.* Kt × P*ch*.

18. **Kt × P*ch*** **K—R2**
19. **Kt—Kt5*ch*** **K—Kt1**

Or *19.* . . . . K—R3; *20.* Kt—K6*ch*, K—R2; *21.* Q—Q3*ch*, K—Kt1; *22.* R—Q8*ch*, K—B2; *23.* Kt—Kt5*ch*, K—K2; *24.* R × R wins.

20. **Q—Kt3*ch*** **Resigns**

Mate follows on *20.* . . . . K—B1; *21.* Q—B7 mate, or on *20.* . . . . Kt—Q4; *21.* R × Kt, B—K3; *22.* R—Q8*ch*, R × R; *23.* Q × B*ch*, K—B1; *24.* Q—B7 mate.

RULE TO REMEMBER

The Colle System is recommended as a good line of play for beginners who want to gain practice in QP openings.

---

40 Benoni Counter-Gambit

Budapest, 1948

White	*Black*
J. Foltys	E. Gereben

The Opening

Black can begin his counterplay against P—Q4 on his first move, by playing *1*. . . . . P—QB4. This opening, the Benoni Counter-Gambit, requires a tenacious mind which is willing to lock up a position, apply pressure, and wait for an opportunity to attack.

White's Plan

This is one of the best games played by a master who won few tournaments but always fought well against the strongest opposition. Early in the game, he sets two goals: to control the center and to make moves that delay Black's development. As part of his plan, he sacrifices Pawns to gain time to mobilize his forces against an uncastled King.

Black's Plan

Black plans to lock up the center, develop his pieces slowly, and then seek some attacking line. But he fails to seek moves that apply pressure—that is, that threaten something.

Comment

The game illustrates how an apparently blocked position can be opened up.

1. **P—Q4**	**P—QB4**
2. **P—Q5**	

If 2. P × P, Black can regain the P at once by 2. . . . . Q—R4*ch*.

2.	**P—K4**?

Once thought best, this move is now recognized to be inferior.

Today, 2. . . . . P—Q3 is the most used move, usually in combination with . . . . P—KKt3 and . . . . B—Kt2, with pressure along the long diagonal and a later counter by pushing Q-side Pawns or by playing . . . . P—K3 or . . . . P—K4.

However, 2. . . . . P—K4 does lock up the center at once. But Black's weakness is that he then has no way to build an attack or develop his pieces for a proper defense when White begins one.

3. **P—K4**	**P—Q3**
4. **B—Q3**	**Kt—K2?**

Black plays too passively. *4.* . . . . P—QR3 and . . . . P—KKt3 and . . . . P—B4 were called for.

5. **Kt—K2**	**P—B4**
6. **P—KB4!**	

Countering in the center.

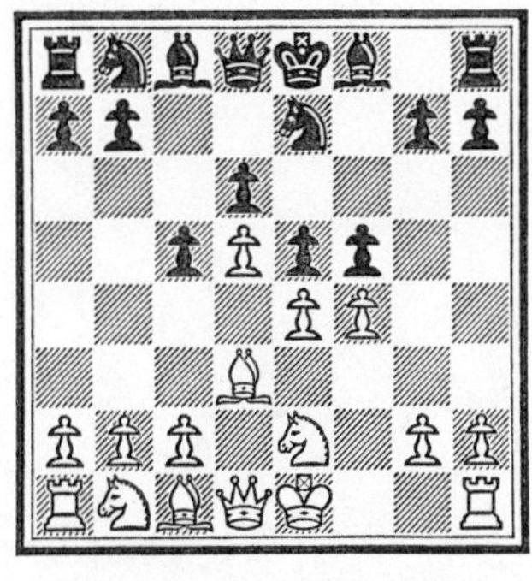

6.	**P × KP**
7. **B × P**	**Kt—Q2**
8. **O—O**	**Kt(Q2)—B3**
9. **Kt(Kt1)—B3**	

White develops easily, while Black's pieces stumble about without any sense of direction.

9.	**B—Kt5**
10. **P—KR3**	**B—R4**
11. **K—R2**	**B—Kt3**

Black hopes for *12.* B × B, Kt × B, with an equal game.

12. **Kt—Kt3**

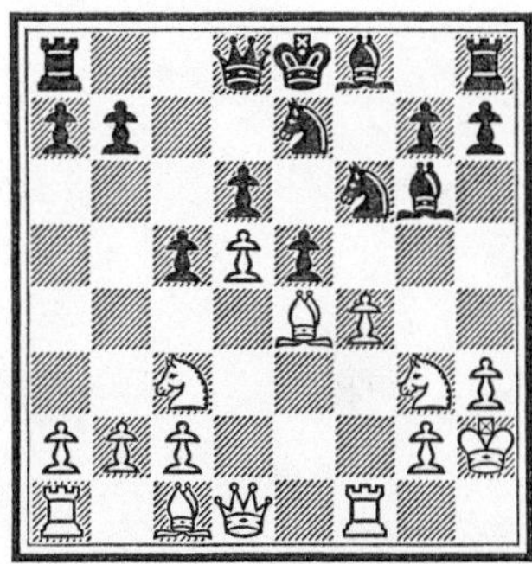

How is Black to proceed? Exchanging on the K side will leave him exposed to attack. Best is *12.* . . . . Q—Q2 and *13.* . . . . O—O—O. Instead, he takes his Queen away from the scene of action.

12.	**Q—Kt3?**
13. **P × P**	**P × P**
14. **P—Q6!**	

Very strong. If *14.* . . . . Kt—B1; *15.* R × Kt*!*, P × R; *16.* P—Q7*ch* wins. If *14.* . . . . Kt—B3; *15.* R × Kt*!*, P × R; *16.* Kt—Q5, Q—Q1; *17.* Kt—B7*ch*, K—Q2; *18.* Kt × R, Q × Kt; *19.* B × B, P × B; *20.* Q—Kt4*ch*, K × P; *21.* Kt—K4*ch*, K—K2; *22.* Q × P wins.

14. . . . . Kt(K2)—Kt1
15. **P—Q7*ch*!** **Kt × P**

The sacrifice permits a Kt to come in.

16. **Kt—Q5** **Q—Q3**
17. **B × B*ch*** **P × B**
18. **Kt—K4**

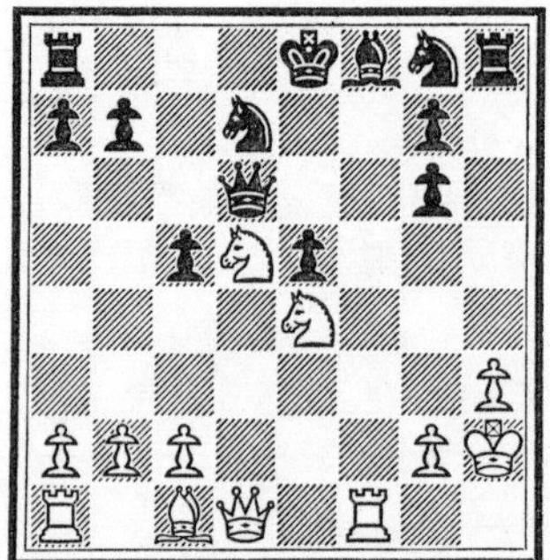

Black's opening strategy has clearly been refuted. Now he is subject to a crushing attack.

18. . . . . **Q—QB3**
19. **B—Kt5**

White prevents *19.* . . . . O—O—O and is ready to bring his QR into play.

19. . . . . **Kt—R3**

19. . . . . B—K2 or *19.* . . . . Kt—K2 would lose.

a. *19.* . . . . B—K2; *20.* Kt × B, Kt × Kt; *21.* Kt—Q6*ch*, K—Q1; *22.* Kt—B7*ch* and *23.* Kt × R.

b. *19.* . . . . Kt—K2; *20.* R × B*ch*, R × R; *21.* B × Kt.

20. **P—B4** **Kt—Kt3**

If *20.* . . . . Kt—B2; *21.* Q—B3.

21. **Q—B3** **Kt × P**

On *21.* . . . . Kt × Kt; *22.* P × Kt, Q × P; *23.* Kt—B6*ch* wins the Queen. (Discovered attack!) Similarly, *21.* . . . . Kt × Kt; *22.* P × Kt, Q—B2; *23.* P—Q6, B × P; *24.* Kt × B*ch*, Q × Kt; *25.* B × Kt, P × B; *26.* Q—B7*ch*, K—Q1; *27.* R(R1)—Q1 wins the Queen. (Pin!)

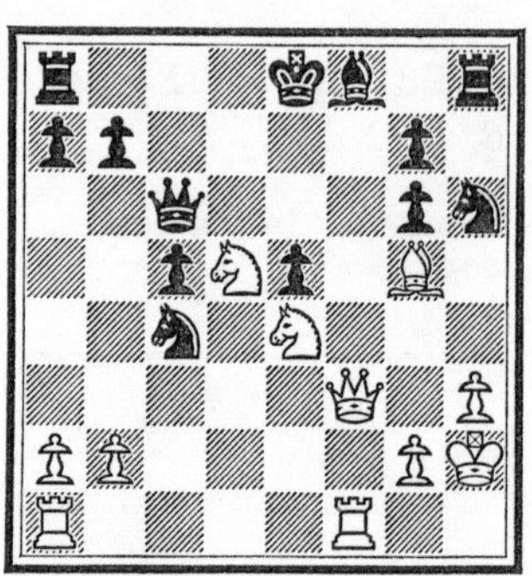

22. **B × Kt!**

Now Black cannot take this B because of *22.* . . . . P × B; *23.* Q—B7*ch*, K—Q1; *24.* R—B6, Q—Q2; *25.* Q × B*ch*!, R × Q; *26.* R × R*ch*, Q—K1; *27.* R × Q*ch*, K × R; *28.* Kt—B7*ch*!, K—Q2; *29.* Kt × R and White wins easily.

22. . . . . **O—O—O**
23. **B × P!** **Resigns**

A fitting conclusion to a well-played game by White. Black

cannot play *23.* . . . . B × B because of *24.* Kt—K7*ch,* winning the Queen. On *23.* . . . . R—Kt1; *24.* B × B*!* and Black still cannot take the Bishop. White thus remains a piece ahead after *24.* . . . . Q × Kt; B × R.

RULE TO REMEMBER

Placing a Knight on Q5 when your opponent has not yet castled carries the threat of Kt—QB7*ch* and the win of a Rook. In this game, Black could not play *17.* . . . . Q × B (to avoid the weak doubled Pawns on his KKt file) because the Queen had to remain on Q3 to prevent White's threatened Kt—B7*ch.*

When you control the center, you can move one piece away from it and replace it with another. Note how White used the square K4, first for a Bishop, then for a Knight!

---

41 Benoni Counter-Gambit

World Championship Match, Moscow, 1960

White	*Black*
M. Botvinnik	M. Tal

The Opening

This game can teach two lessons. It demonstrates the modern treatment of the Benoni. It also proves that even the two best players in the world can make mistakes.

White's Plan

The 1960 match, won easily by Tal, saw Botvinnik uncertain for the first time in a decade of world mastery. He weakens, but later finds a win. (He lost the championship in 1960, but regained it in 1961.) He tries to keep Black's position locked up, while keeping lines open on his own half of the board.

Black's Plan

Tal gives up a Pawn to gain time for an attack. Although he is able to combine pressure in the center with a strong K-side attack, he makes a second-best move under time pressure, which permits White to sacrifice material to force through a dangerous passed Pawn.

Comment

The ending has a Rook hopping about trying in vain to stop three passed Pawns.

1.	**P—Q4**	**Kt—KB3**
2.	**P—QB4**	**P—K3**
3.	**Kt—KB3**	**P—B4**
4.	**P—Q5**	**P × P**
5.	**P × P**	**P—KKt3**

White has a strong QP, made stronger by the fact that no Black Pawn can attack it. Black places his B on the long diagonal to apply pressure himself on K4, Q5 and QB6.

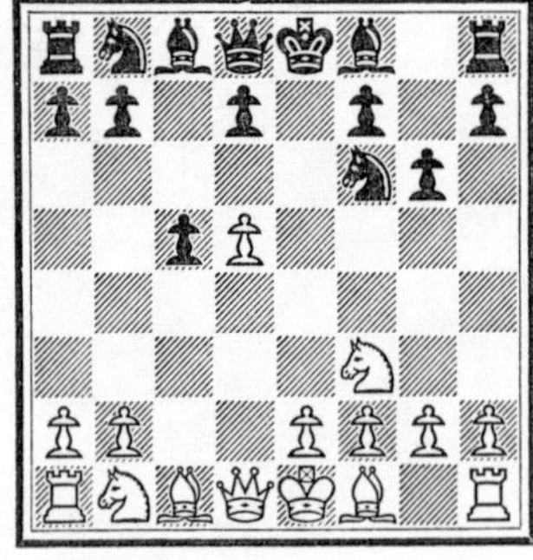

6. Kt—B3 B—Kt2
7. B—Kt5 O—O

Black is in no hurry to play . . . . P—Q3, and castles first to get his KR into play.

8. P—K3 R—K1
9. Kt—Q2 P—Q3
10. B—K2 P—QR3

Black prepares to advance on the Q-side, and White realizes that he must prevent this. White's general plan seems to be to limit Black's movement.

11. P—QR4 *!* Kt(Kt1)—Q2
12. O—O Q—B2

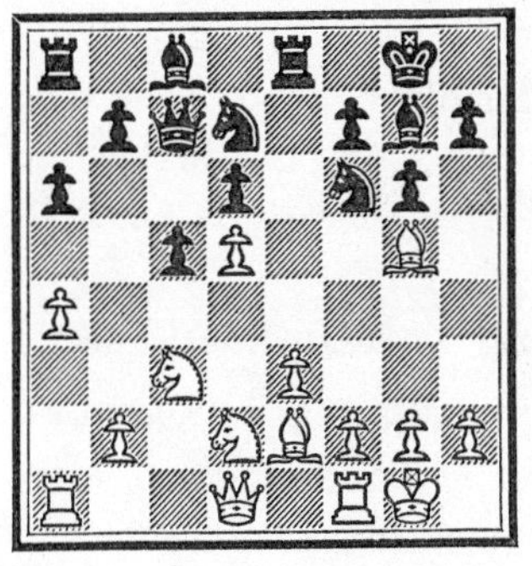

13. Q—B2 Kt—Kt3

Black wants White to close up the game by protecting the QP with *14.* P—K4, but Botvinnik prefers to keep the KP where it is.

14. B—B3 P—B5 *?*

Tal slips, for this advanced

RULE TO REMEMBER

In a closed position, like the one in this game, develop your pieces behind your Pawns to the squares where they will be most useful once the position is opened. Black's Q on B2 can support an advance on the Q side, supports the K4 square, and can protect KB2 if White attacks.

Pawn cannot long be held. *14.* . . . B—B4 was better.

15. B × Kt B × B
16. P—R5 *!*

The Kt is driven back, and will temporarily block the Black B on B1.

16. . . . . Kt—Q2
17. Kt(B3)—K4 *!*

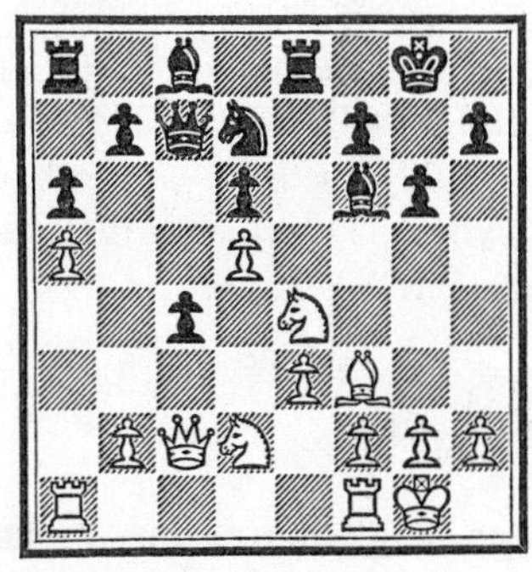

Attacking the B and also opening a second attack on Black's advanced Pawn.

17.	B—K4
18. Q × P	Q—Q1
19. Q—R2	

Freeing the QR to go to B1.

19.	P—B4
20. Kt—B3	P—KKt4

Tal prefers to attack, even though he is a Pawn down and has not completed his development.

21. Kt—B4	P—Kt5
22. B—K2	Q—B3

White really has little more than the fact he is a Pawn ahead to keep him happy. Black is building something on the K side, and White decides to distract him by action on the Q side.

23. Kt—R4	K—R1
24. P—KKt3 *?*	

And now he changes his mind. *24.* R(R1)—B1 or *24.* Kt(R4)—Kt6 would have been better than this attempt to block the advancing Black Pawns.

24.	P—R4 *!*
25. P—B4 *?*	

Two weak moves in a row! This move opens up play against the K position. *25.* R(R1)—B1 was still called for, to be followed by *26.* Kt(B4)—Kt6.

RULE TO REMEMBER

Do not open up your King position when you are under attack!

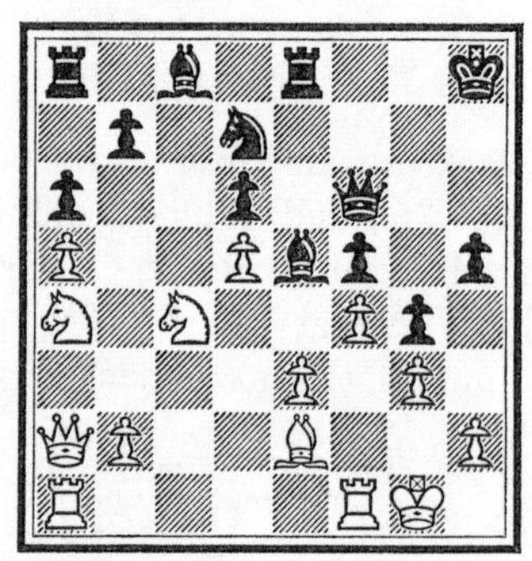

25.	B—Q5

Simple and good. White cannot play *26.* P × B, Q × P*ch;* followed by *27.* . . . . R × B.

26. Q—R3	R—QKt1
27. Kt(R4)—Kt6	P—R5 *!*

Now White has achieved Kt—Kt6, but has given Black time to prepare for this move. Black now threatens P × P, Q—R3, and Q—R6.

28. R(R1)—Q1	B × Kt
29. P × B	Kt—B4

Black brings more force to bear against the K-side, now threatening *30.* . . . . Kt—K5 to attack the P on Kt3 again.

30. P × P	B—Q2 *!*

Preparing to pin the Kt on B4.

31. **Q—B3** **Q × Q**
32. **P × Q** **B—Kt4**

Black is two Pawns down, but really has a better game. He can regain the Pawns easily by . . . . B × Kt and . . . . R × P, which White now blocks.

33. **R(B1)—K1** **Kt—K5** *!*

Black ties up the other White R to the defense of the QBP.

34. **R(Q1)—B1** **R(Kt1)—B1** *?*

The wrong Rook, as White now demonstrates.

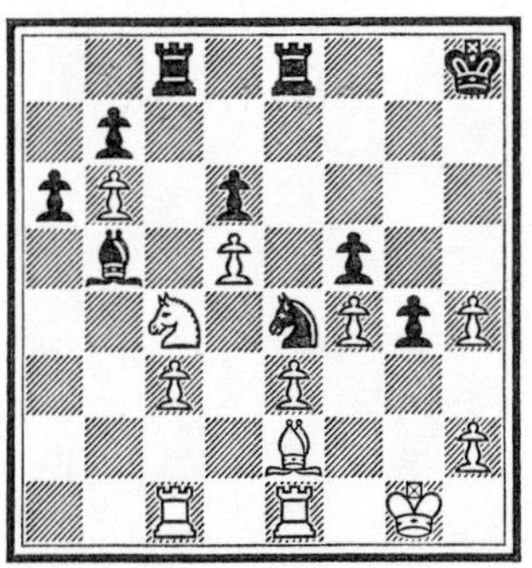

35. **Kt—R5** *!*

Botvinnik saves the game with a beautiful combination.

35. **. . . .** **B × B**
36. **R × B** **Kt × P**
37. **R × Kt** *!* **R × R**
38. **Kt × P**

White will have three passed Pawns—more than Black can handle. If Black had played the other R to QB1 on his 34th move, then White would not have *38.* Kt × P now.

38. **. . . .** **R(K1) × P**
39. **R × R** **R × R**
40. **Kt × P** **R—Q6**
41. **Kt—B7*ch*** *!* **Resigns**

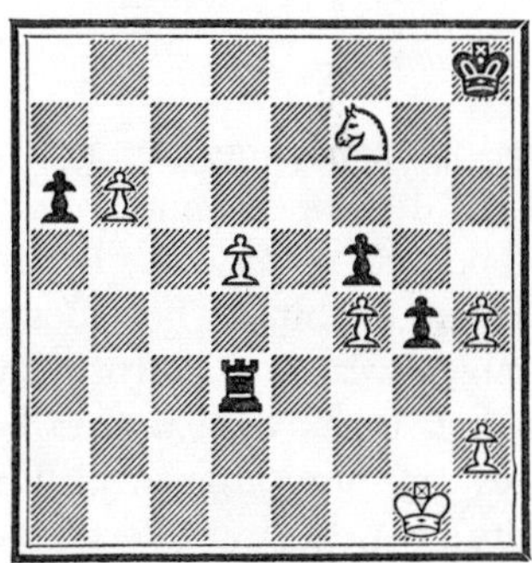

Black has no defense.

a. 41. . . . . K—Kt1; *42.* P—Kt7, R—QKt6, *43.* Kt—Q8 and White pushes on the QP and KRP while the Black R watches the QKtP.

b. 41. . . . . K—Kt2; *42.* P—Kt7, R—QKt6; *43.* Kt—Q8, K—B3; *44.* P—Q6, P—R4; *45.* P—R5*!*, P—R5; *46.* P—Q7, P—R6; *47.* Kt—B6, P—R7; *48.* P—Q8(Q)*ch*, and wins.

42 Benko Gambit

Spain, 1970

White	*Black*
A. O'Kelly	R. Toran

The Opening

Pal Benko, American grandmaster, developed an aggressive method of using the Benoni Counter-Gambit. The Benko Gambit gives up a Pawn in the opening. Black then masses his forces in an attack against White's Q-side.

White's Plan

When faced with a counter-gambit, White should keep his pieces in the center, ready to attack. O'Kelly waits until most of Black's pieces are on the Q-side. He then hits at the Black K-position.

Black's Plan

Toran tries to regain his sacrificed Pawn. He hopes to be able to switch his pieces to the K-side in time to stop any White attack.

Comment

Watch White's Queen Rook. O'Kelly's success depends upon getting this piece into play at the right time!

1.	**P—Q4**	**Kt—KB3**
2.	**P—QB4**	**P—B4**
3.	**P—Q5**	**P—QKt4**

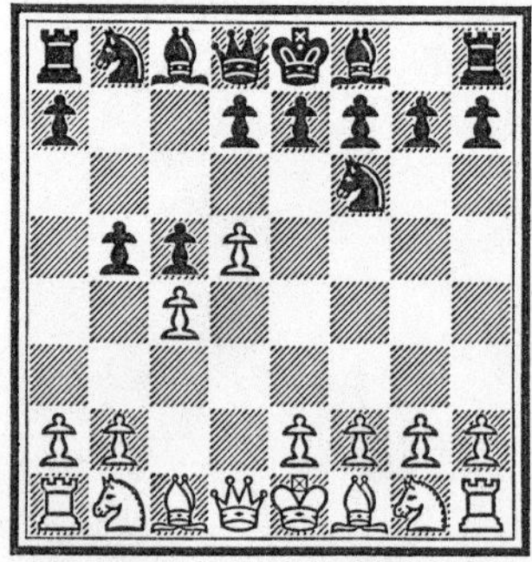

This is the key position of the Benko Gambit. White can take the Pawn and hold it for a long time. In exchange, Black gains much faster development and open lines on the Q-side.

4.	**P × P**	**P—QR3**
5.	**P × P**	**B × P**

6. Kt—QB3	P—Q3
7. Kt—KB3	P—Kt3

Black will place his B on KKt2, castle, develop the QKt at Q2, and move the Q and the KR to the half-open files. White cannot develop as quickly.

8. **Kt—Q2 !**

This Knight is ready to defend on the Q-side and can also move toward the center.

8.	B—KKt2
9. P—K4	O—O
10. B × B !	Kt × B
11. O—O	Kt—Q2

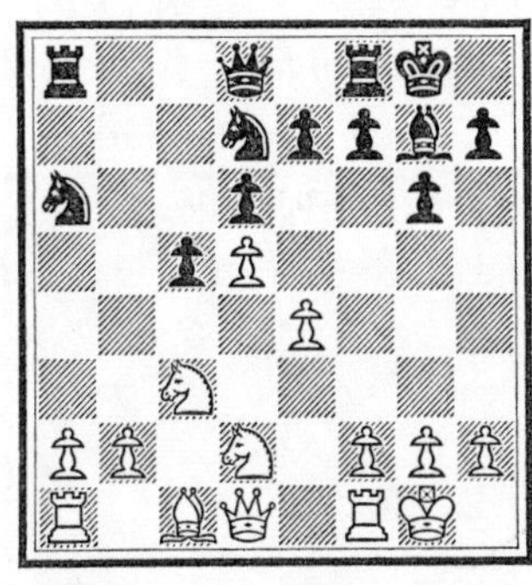

Black is carrying out his plan to attack on the Q-side. White prepares for a counter-thrust in the center.

12. Kt—B4	Kt—Kt3
13. Kt—K3	Q—Q2
14. P—QR4 !	

White prepares an exit route for his QR.

RULE TO REMEMBER

When your opponent attacks on the flank, look for a way to counter-attack in the center. When you control the center, you can block your opponent's lines of attack.

---

14.	Q—Kt2
15. R—R3	R(B1)—Kt1

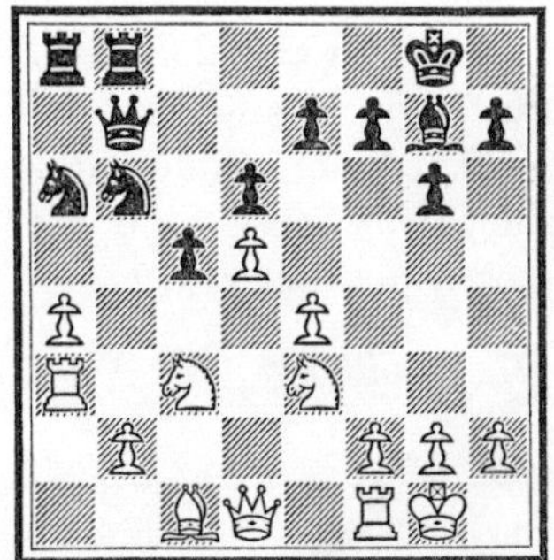

Black has massed his forces on the Q-side. But this means the K-side is undefended. White hits it at once.

16. P—R4 !	Kt—Q2
17. P—R5	Kt—B3
18. P × P	RP × P
19. P—B4 !	

White threatens P—K5 and then P—K6, which would leave Black's K-position open to attack.

19.	Q—Kt5
20. P—K5 !	Kt—R4

RULE TO REMEMBER

Advance your center Pawns to open the position when your opponent's pieces are unable to block them.

Do not advance center Pawns unless you can defend them.

If Black plays *20.* . . . . Kt—K5, White gains a quick attack with *21.* Q—B3, Kt × Kt; *22.* P × Kt, Q—Kt2; *23.* P—B5*!*, threatening P × KtP as well as P—B6. White would quickly achieve his goal—to open the Black K-position.

21. **Q—B3** *!*

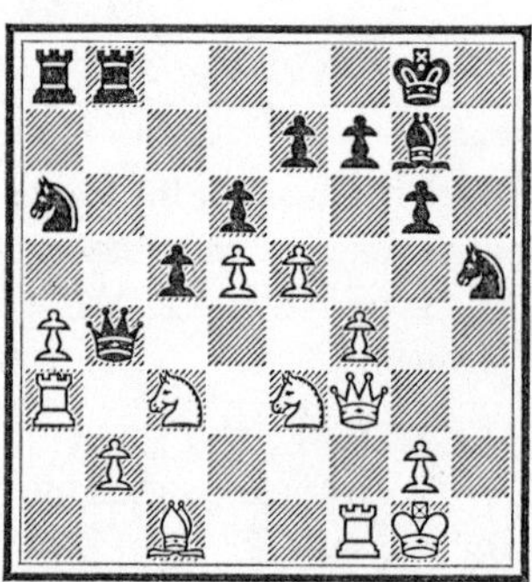

Black is lost. White now threatens P—Kt4, winning the Black Knight. The White Queen and Rook also bear down on KB7.

21.	**P × P**
22. **P × P**	**Q—R5**

The only way to save the Knight. If White now plays *23.* P—Kt4, Black would reply with *23.* . . . . . B × P, threatening mate by *24.* . . . . . Q—R7.

23. **Q × P*ch***	**K—R2**

How can White continue the attack? The Rook at R3 must be brought to the K-side.

24. **Kt—B5** *!*	**P × Kt**
25. **Q × P*ch***	**K—R1**
26. **Kt—K4**	

Now the road is clear! Will Black be able to bring his Rooks to the defense of his King?

26.	**R—KB1**
27. **Kt—B6** *!*	

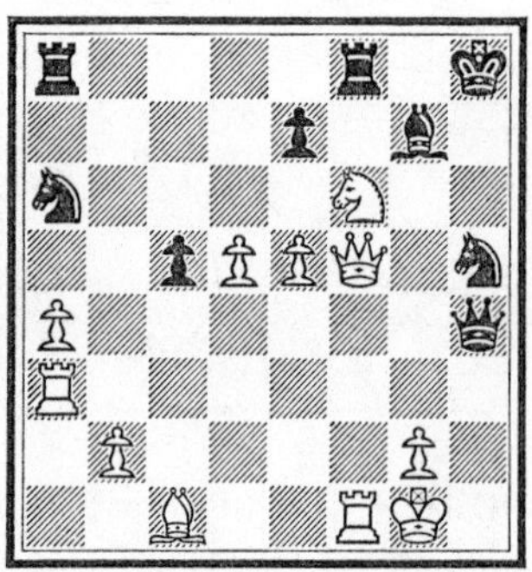

This final sacrifice closes all doors for Black. The White Knight can be captured in five ways, but none can halt the attack!

a. *27.* . . . . . P × Kt; *28.* R—R3, Q—Q5*ch*; *29.* B—K3, and White threatens mate by *30.* Q

RULE TO REMEMBER

Note Black's inactive pieces on the Q-side.

Make certain your King is safe before moving its defenders away.

Do not plan an attack unless you can defend your King at the same time.

× Kt*ch*, K—Kt1; *31.* P—K6 and 32. Q—R7 mate. If Black moves the Rook at KB1, then 32. Q—B7 mate.

b. 27. . . . . B × Kt; 28. R—R3, Q—Q5*ch*; 29. B—K3, and the Black King is again without defense.

c. 27. . . . . R × Kt; 28. P × R, and White threatens R—R3 as well as Q × Kt.

d. 27. . . . . Q × Kt; 28. P × Q, Kt × P; 29. Q—K6 and the threat of R—R3*ch* wins quickly.

27.	**Kt × Kt**

Black tries the fifth way to capture.

28. **P × Kt**	**B—R3**

If 28. . . . . R × P, then 29. R—R3!, R × Q; *30.* R × Q*ch* and *31.* R × R leaves White an exchange and two Pawns ahead.

29. **R—R3**	**Q—Q5*ch***
30. **K—R2**	**R × P**
31. **Q—Kt5!**	**Resigns**

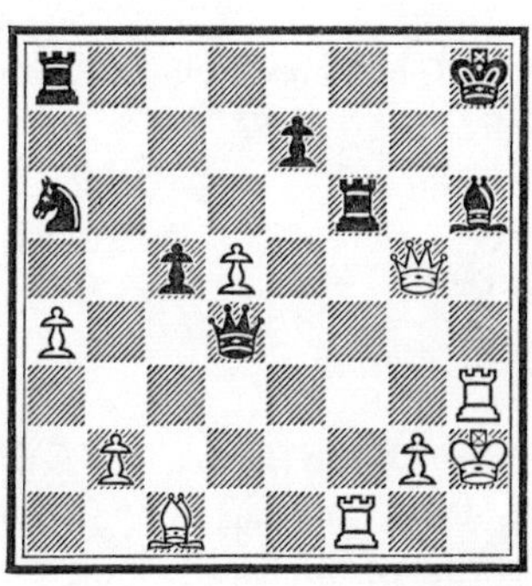

White's threat of 32. R × B*ch*, R × R; 33. Q × R*ch*, K—Kt1; *34.* Q—K6*ch*, K—R1; 35. R—B4 forces mate or the win of Black's Queen. For example, 35. . . . . Q—Q6; *36.* R—R4*ch*, K—Kt2; 37. B—R6*ch*, K—R1; 38. B—B8*ch*, Q—R2; 39. R × Q*ch*, K × R; *40.* Q—R6*ch*, K—Kt1; *41.* Q—Kt7 mate.

43 Dutch Defense

Match, Yugoslavia–Russia, 1957

White	*Black*
V. Pirc	A. Tolush

The Opening

The Dutch Defense (*1.* P—Q4, P—KB4) has long been a favorite of such attacking players as Keres and Botvinnik. It permits easy development for Black, and frequently results in a K-side attack that is hard to meet.

White's Plan

White opens with *1.* P—QB4 in this game, but the next moves soon set up the Dutch Defense position in which Black's Pawn on KB4 prevents White from making the freeing move P—K4.

Black's Plan

Black gets the better game, as he often does in this opening, when he is able to advance his KBP to open the KB file.

What to Watch for

Note how White concentrates his efforts on the Q-side, only to find that the real scene of action is on the other wing.

1. **P—QB4**	**P—KB4**
2. **Kt—KB3**	**Kt—KB3**
3. **P—KKt3**	

White will make good use of the long diagonal.

3.	**P—K3**
4. **B—Kt2**	**B—K2**
5. **O—O**	**O—O**
6. **P—Q3**	**P—Q4**
7. **P—QKt3**	

It is never easy to control both wings through developing Bishops on Kt2. The Bishops are immobilized by the need to place Knights on B3. White does better here with the immediate 7. P × P, and play on the QB file.

7.	**P—B4*!***

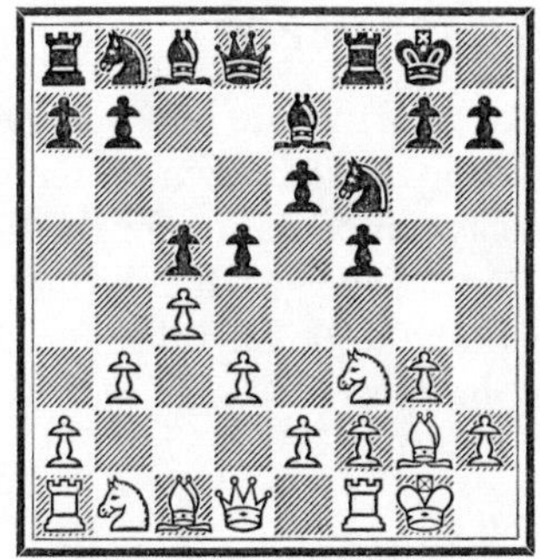

Black aims for an eventual . . . . P—Q5, and prepares for that move now.

8. **P × P** **P × P**
9. **B—Kt2** **Kt—B3**
10. **P—Q4**

Played to prevent *10.* . . . . P—Q5, and in hopes of isolating Black's QP after *11.* P × P.

10. . . . . **P—QKt3!**

Black is determined to keep a Pawn on QB4, still planning to play a later . . . . P—Q5.

11. **P × P** **P × P**
12. **Kt—B3** **B—R3!**

The alternative, *12.* . . . . B—K3; *13.* Kt—KKt5 would lose the QP for Black. Now he adds the threat of a future . . . . B × KP.

13. **R—B1** **R—B1**
14. **Kt—K1**

The Black P on Q4 is attacked three times, and defended twice. It must now move to Q5. Since this was Black's plan right along, White has helped rather than hindered it.

14. . . . . **P—Q5**

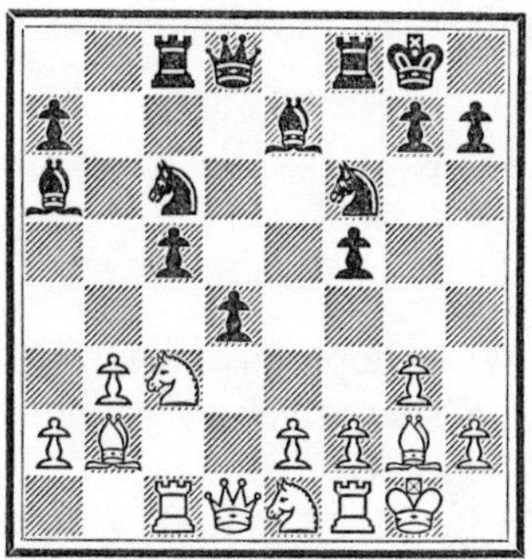

15. **Kt—R4** **Kt—K4**

With the threat of pushing the QP after preparing for it by

RULE TO REMEMBER

A supported Pawn on K5 or Q5 cramps your opponent's position and limits his moves because the Pawn may advance at any time. If your pieces are developed, try to obtain such an advanced Pawn.

An advanced Pawn in the center can be exchanged to remove its threat to advance. If such an exchange is not possible, try to exchange or attack the Pawn's defenders. In this position, those defenders include the Black Pawn on QB4.

. . . . Q—Q3 and . . . . R(B1) —Q1.

16. **Kt—Q3**	**Kt × Kt**
17. **P × Kt**	**Kt—Q2** *!*

This fine move gives further support to the P on QB4 and prepares for . . . . P—KB5.

18. **R—K1**	**Kt—Kt3**
19. **Kt × Kt**	**P × Kt**
20. **P—QKt4**	

White hopes to delay the coming K-side attack by countering on the Q-side. If *20.* . . . . P × P; *21.* R × R, B × R; *22.* B × P*!*

20.	**K—R1**
21. **Q—Kt3**	**QR—B2**

To protect the QB after *22.* P—Kt5, B—Kt2.

22. **P—QR4**	**P—KB5** *!*

The breakthrough which is characteristic of the Dutch Defense. *23.* P × P, R × P leaves White's K side too open.

23. **R—K6**	**B—KKt4**

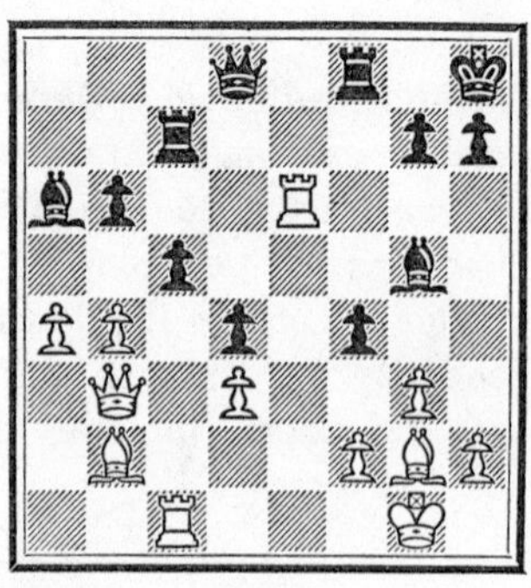

24. **P × QBP** *?*

An error. White hopes to gain a strong passed Pawn on the Q-side as compensation for the loss of the exchange—but he never gets time to do anything further on the Q-side. Better here was *24.* R—B2.

24.	**P × KKtP**
25. **RP × P**	**B × R**
26. **B × B**	**R × P(B4)**
27. **B—Q2**	

Hoping for *28.* B—Kt4 or *28.* R × P.

27.	**Q—QB1**
28. **R × P**	**Q—B4** *!*

Black suddenly threatens to come in with . . . . Q × P*ch* and . . . . R—R4*ch.*

29. **B—B4**

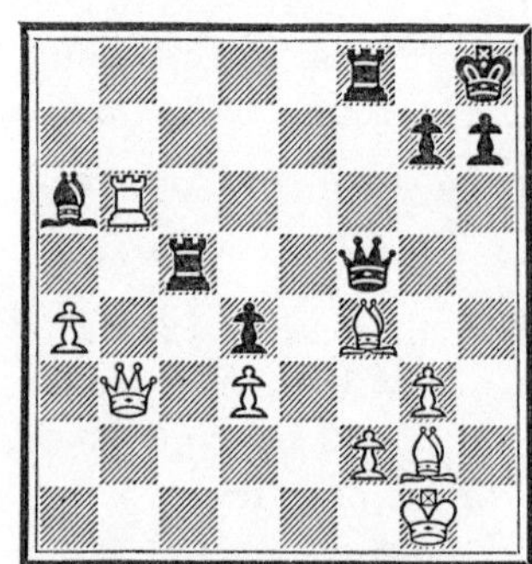

29.	**B × P**
30. **R—Kt8**	**B—B5** *!*

This move cuts off White's chance of invading on the K-side with his Q.

31. Q—Kt4	R × R*!*
32. Q × R*ch*	B—Kt1*!!*

Everything is now safe, and White must worry about the Black QP as well as the combined assault of Q and R against the King.

33. K—R2*?*

This makes it easy. A longer but still inadequate defense would follow *33.* Q—Kt2, P—Q6; *34.* B—K3, R—B7.

33.	Q—R4*ch*
34. B—R3	Q—B6*!*
35. Resigns	

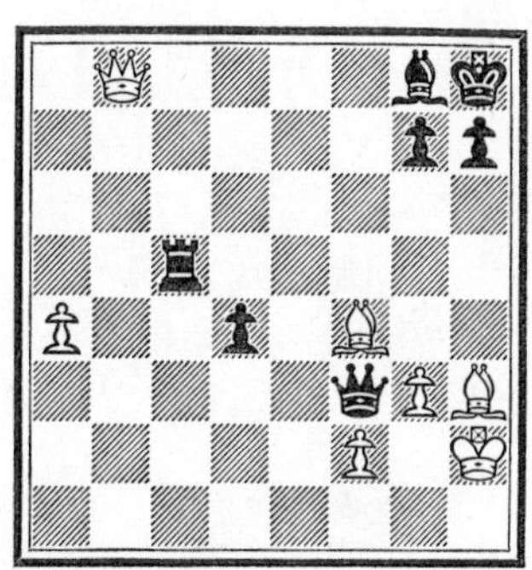

There is no defense.

a. If *35.* K—Kt1, R—B7; *36.* B—K6, Q × BP*ch*; *37.* K—R1, Q—Kt7 mate.

b. If *35.* Q—Kt2, R—KR4; *36.* Q × P, Q—Kt5.

c. If *35.* B—Kt2, Q × P.

RULE TO REMEMBER

Plan for a possible P—KB5 against a position in which your opponent has P's on KB2, KKt3, KR2. This will open an attacking line of play along your KB file.

---

44 Dutch Defense

Dortmund, 1951

White	*Black*
N. Rossolimo	H. Grob

The Opening

The Dutch Defense is one of the strongest replies to *1.* P—Q4. Black plays *1.* . . . . P—KB4, or *1.* . . . . P—K3 and *2.* . . . . P—KB4. He hopes to gain a grip on his K5 square as a counter to White's hold on other center squares. The game then takes its course because of such key squares as White's Q5 and Black's K5. They become pivot points about which the play revolves. The control of one central square, and the squares near it, can bring a quick, clear victory.

White's Plan

White, the French champion several times, obtains such a pivot point at Q5 in this game. With it, he crushes his opponent —for he brings every piece to or near it, and pivots them against the K position.

Black's Plan

Black, many times champion of Switzerland, leaves his Q in the mountains this time, and plays the critical part of the game in effect a Queen down.

Comment

The game illustrates what happens when one player has a clear plan and the other does not.

1. P—Q4	P—K3
2. P—QB4	P—KB4
3. P—KKt3	

White is going to concentrate on control of Q5.

3.	Kt—KB3
4. B—Kt2	P—B4
5. Kt—KB3	P × P
6. O—O !	

The QP will not run away. Development comes first.

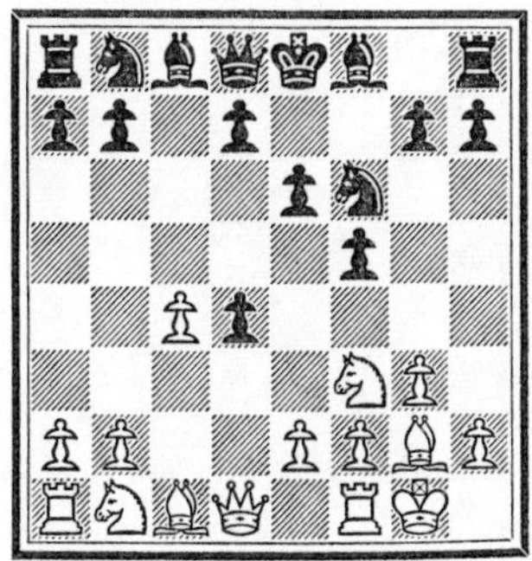

6. . . . .   **Q—B2**

To force *7.* Q × P. If *7.* Kt × P, then . . . . Q × BP wins a P for Black.

7. **Q × P**   **Kt—B3**
8. **Q—Q1**   **P—Q3**
9. **Kt—B3**   **P—QR3**
10. **P—Kt3**

While the Q5 square remains under control, the QB will bear on K5.

10. . . . .   **B—K2**
11. **B—Kt2**   **O—O**
12. **R—B1**

This Rook also helps control Q5, for White is already threatening *13.* Kt—Q5 *!*, P × Kt; *14.* P × P and the R holds the Kt on Black's QB3 where it must remain for *15.* P × Kt.

12. . . . .   **Kt—Q1**
13. **Kt—K1**

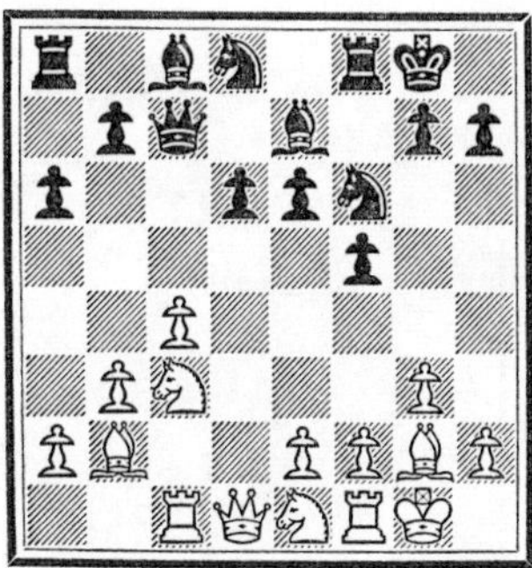

The Kt aims for more control of Q5 via Q3 and KB4, and opens the diagonal for the KB.

13. . . . .   **P—K4**

Black gives up the fight for White's Q5, and plays for a possible K-side counterattack.

14. **Kt—Q3**   **P—QR4** *?*

Probably played to prevent Kt—Kt4 and then Kt(Kt4)—Q5. But White has other entries to his pivot square.

15. **P—B5** *!*   **P × P**
16. **Kt—Q5**   **Kt × Kt**
17. **B × Kt*ch***   **B—K3**

The Q5 square will mean little if enough pieces can be exchanged.

18. **B × KP**   **Q—Kt3**

Holding the QKtP and protecting the B at K3.

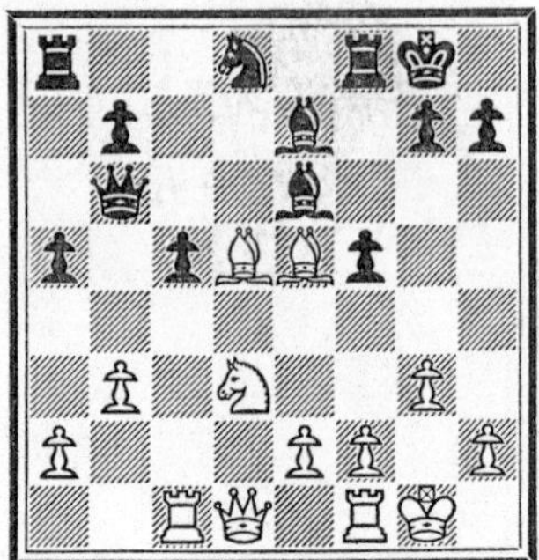

Black seems to have worked out a good defense. He now threatens . . . . B × B. What is White to do to keep up the pressure?

19. **Kt—B4**

Now *19.* . . . . B × B ?; *20.* Kt × B and Black loses material. If *20.* . . . . Q—K3 (to protect the B) *21.* Kt × B*ch,* Q × Kt; *22.* B—Q6 and *23.* B × R.

19.	**B—B2**
20. **P—K4**	**Kt—K3**
21. **B × Kt**	**B × B**
22. **Kt—Q5 !**	

Back to the pivot square, again threatening Kt × B*ch* and B-Q6.

RULE TO REMEMBER

Look for a key center square that you can control. If you control it, try to bring many pieces to bear on it. If possible, use it as a pivot square for attack.

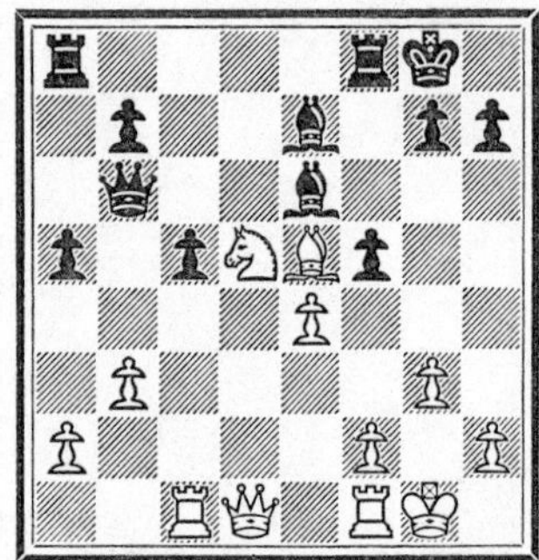

22.	**B × Kt**
23. **Q × B*ch***	**K—R1**
24. **P × P**	

And White has won a Pawn. If now *24.* . . . . R × P; *25.* B × P*ch,* K × B; *26.* Q × R (Discovered attack!).

24.	**R(R1)—Q1**
25. **Q—K4**	

Again threatening B × P*ch* because of the then exposed Black B.

25.	**R(Q1)—K1**

Black wants to play . . . . B—B3, and therefore keeps a R on KB1 for an eventual recapture on KB3 if White should take the B.

26. **K—Kt2**

Long-range planning. White wants to play P—KB4 to support his B, and moves the K to Kt2 first, so as not to be subject to a check on . . . . P—B5 by Black.

26.	**B—B3**
27. **P—B4**	**Q—Kt4**

So that the Q will aim at K5 on . . . . P—B5; thus *28.* . . . . B × B; *29.* P × B, P—B5 would be good for Black.

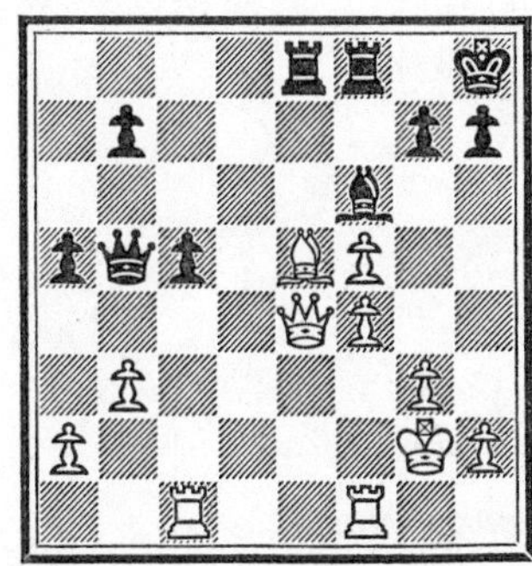

28. R(KB1)—Q1 !

Aiming at the pivot square again. Now *28.* . . . . B × B; *29.* P × B, P—B5; *30.* R—Q5 and *31.* P × P leaves White another Pawn ahead.

28. . . . . **P—QKt3**

To permit the Q to leave without having to worry about the Q-side Pawns. The move really is not a good one, but what is Black to do? *28.* . . . . R—Q1; *29.* P—KKt4 would create new dangers.

29. **R—Q6** **P—KR3**
30. **R(B1)—Q1** **Q—R3**

Black has no moves that can save the position. If *30.* . . . . R—K2 (hoping to double Rooks on the K-file); *31.* R—K6, R—Q2; *32.* R × R, Q × R; *33.* B × B !, R × B; *34.* P—KKt4, and White's K-side Pawns will force the win.

31. **R—K6** **R—Q1**
32. **R × B !** **Resigns**

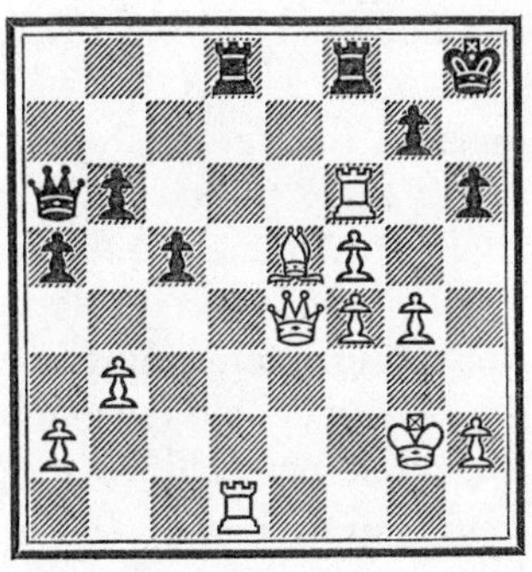

Black must lose a piece. If *32.* R × R(Q8); *33.* R × R*ch*, K—R2; *34.* Q—B4 !, Q × Q; *35.* P × Q, R—Q7*ch*; *36.* K—B3, R × QRP; *37.* R—B7, P—KR4; *38.* P—B6, and Black cannot avoid R × P*ch*, P—B7 and P—B8 (Q). The pivot square won the day!

45 Budapest Defense

Syracuse, 1934

White	*Black*
S. Reshevsky	A. S. Denker

The Opening

The Budapest Defense (*1.* P—Q4, Kt—KB3; 2. P—Q4, P—K4) is another counter-gambit, one in which Black places White on the defensive at once, at the cost of a Pawn. It is rarely played, but produces interesting games. If White tries to hold the gambit Pawn, Black soon achieves a significant lead in development.

White's Plan

Samuel Reshevsky, the leading player in the United States for some 20 years (until the advent of that chess phenomenon called Bobby Fischer) was in top form in this game. He develops his pieces as rapidly as possible, and then attacks in the center.

Black's Plan

Black makes the mistake of trying to force White to take a second Pawn, and finds himself swamped by invading Pawns and pieces when White decides to develop soundly instead.

What to Watch for

The final attack shows Q and Kt hitting at an uncastled King.

1. **P—Q4**	**Kt—KB3**
2. **P—QB4**	**P—K4**
3. **P × P**	

There is no reason why White should not take the Pawn.

3.	**Kt—Kt5**

3. . . . . Kt—K5 has also been played. Black then threatens . . . . B—Kt5*ch,* and forces White to lose time with *4.* P—QR3, when *4.* . . . . B—B4; 5. P—K3 leaves White somewhat cramped—but still a Pawn ahead.

4. **P—K4*!***

A key move for White. He opens lines for his pieces, and invites *4.* . . . . Kt × KP; *5.* P—B4, with control of the center.

Black has nothing better, but tries another Pawn offer in hopes of gaining in development.

4. . . . . P—Q3 ?
5. B—K2 !

White refuses *5.* P × P, B × P and goes after the Kt instead.

5. . . . . Kt × KP
6. P—B4

White has obtained the position discussed in the note to his 4th move, but with the additional advantage of a KB in action.

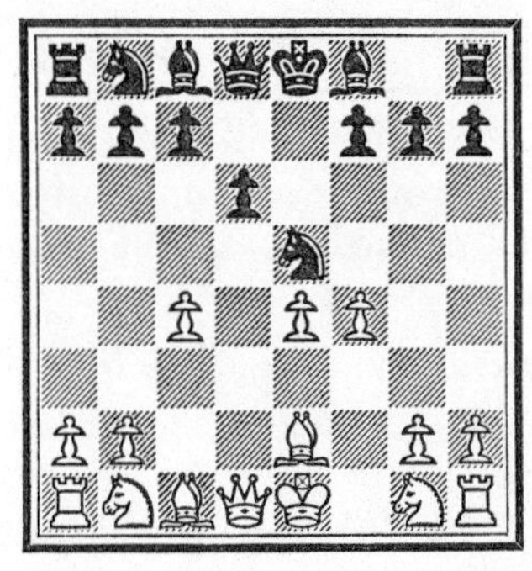

6. . . . . Kt—Kt5

Chess players call moves like this one "Coffee House moves," a reference to the trappy and unsound chess played in some European coffee-houses. If White takes the Kt, Black will play . . . . Q—R5*ch* to recover the piece. *6.* . . . . Kt—Kt3 was better.

7. Kt—KB3 Kt—QB3
8. O—O B—Q2
9. Kt—B3 B—K2

White develops steadily, and Black, belatedly, does the same. But he has made too many Kt moves, and will now have to make a few more!

10. P—KR3 Kt—B3

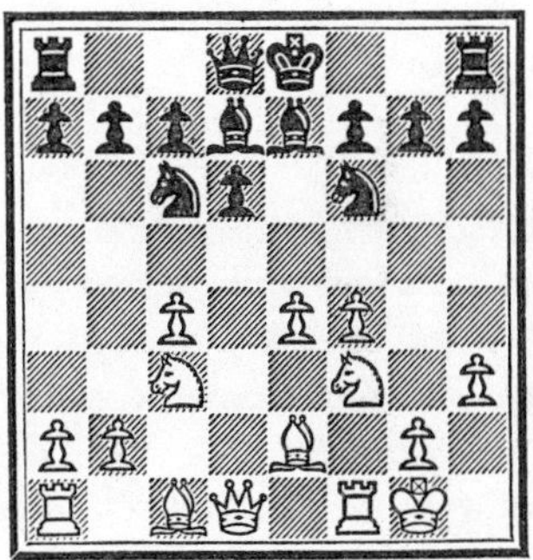

White is ready, and finds his target—the Kt at Black's KB3.

11. P—K5 ! P × P
12. P × P Kt(KB3)—Kt1

A sad choice. Black did not like *12.* . . . . Kt—KR4; *13.* Kt—K4, O—O; *14.* Kt(B3)—Kt5, B × Kt; *15.* B × B, P—B3; *16.* B × Kt, P × B; *17.* R × R*ch*, K × R; *18.* Q—B3*ch*, K—Kt1; *19.* Q—B7*ch*, K—R1; *20.* P—K6 !, B—B1; *21.* R—KB1 and wins.

Play through this possible line. Why can't Black hold the position with the move *20.* . . . . Kt

—K4? You should see the answer at once. White would play *21.* Q—B5, when *two* Black pieces would be attacked. In the final position, why can't Black defend with *21.* . . . . P—KKt3? This would permit White to play *22.* Kt—B6, and Black cannot prevent the mate on White's KR7 or (if Black defends the KRP by . . . . Q—Kt1) on KKt8.

RULE TO REMEMBER

Avoid moves that open your King position and permit the posting of enemy pieces in the holes you have created—especially by moves like P—KKt3 when you do not yourself control your KB3 square!

---

13. **B—K3** **P—B3**

Black tries to break out by getting rid of the White KP—more loss of time.

14. **B—Q3 !** **P × P**
15. **Kt—Kt5 !**

White threatens *16.* Kt—B7 to win a Rook. At the same time, the lines are open for action by the Q and the R(B1).

15. . . . . **Kt—B3**

It appears that Black has closed the lines, but White has a sledgehammer!

16. **R × Kt !**

And now there are no good moves for Black. White's sacrifice of the exchange, like all sound sacrifices, is justified by the result—an entry into the enemy position.

16. . . . . **B × R**
17. **Q—R5*ch*** **P—KKt3**
18. **B × P*ch* !**

The principle is unchanged. Sacrifice whatever you must to break through to a vulnerable King.

18. . . . . **P × B**

White announced mate in two moves:

a. *19.* Q × P*ch*, K—B1; *20.* Q—B7 mate.

b. *19.* Q × P*ch*, K—K2; *20.* B—B5 mate.

RULE TO REMEMBER

Avoid opening ideas which involve wasting time. Every move should help develop your position. The Budapest defense is too difficult a game for inexperienced players.

---

46 Gruenfeld Defense

Match, Switzerland-Italy,
Venice, 1951

White	*Black*
E. Strehle	V.Nestler

The Opening

The Gruenfeld Defense is one of the most interesting of the hypermodern openings. It is here presented in a game which shows its original form. Black invites a number of exchanges in the center in order to establish a strong Bishop on the long diagonal. In many cases, this Bishop throws White on the defensive.

White's Plan

White is a Swiss master who plays in few tournaments, but whose tactical ability is high—as he demonstrates in this game. He gains quick control of the center, and makes it the base for his attack.

Black's Plan

Black, one of Italy's best players, becomes timid in the course of this game, plays a few indifferent moves, and finds himself caught up in a mating attack.

What to Watch for

Observe especially how White uses his advanced Pawns as part of his attacking force.

1. **P—Q4**	**Kt—KB3**
2. **P—QB4**	**P—KKt3**

Defenses to *1.* P—Q4 in which Black develops a Bishop at Kt2 are often called Indian Defenses. The Gruenfeld Defense uses 3. . . . . P—Q4; other Indian Defenses use 3. . . . . B—Kt2; 4. . . . . P—Q3; and other moves which wait for White to declare his intentions.

3. **Kt—QB3**	**P—Q4**
4. **P × P**	**Kt × P**
5. **P—K4**	**Kt × Kt**
6. **P × Kt**	**B—Kt2**
7. **B—QB4**	**P—QB4**

Black follows through with his opening plan—to apply pressure on the long diagonal.

8. **Kt—K2**	**P × P?**

Pressure applied should not be relaxed so suddenly. *8.* . . . . Kt—B3 was better.

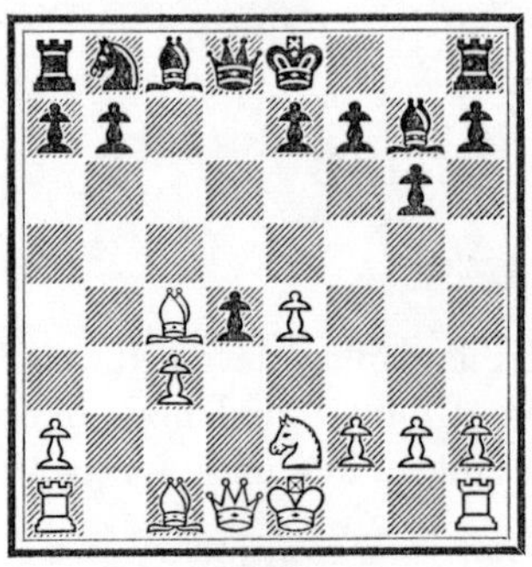

RULE TO REMEMBER

Black's Q5 square is the pivot point about which he should plan his play. He should have tried to bring more pieces to bear on this square before making any exchanges.

When you have created tension in the center, do not release that tension unless you are fully developed or can gain material or a better position through exchanges. As Black plays this game, it is White who makes the central squares strong points.

9.	**P × P**	**Kt—B3**
10.	**B—K3**	**Q—R4*ch* ?**

Black wants to exchange Queens, hoping to place a R on Q1 after *11.* Q—Q2, Q × Q*ch*; *12.* K × Q, O—O. But White does not oblige.

11.	**B—Q2 !**	**Q—Q1**
12.	**B—B3**	**O—O**
13.	**O—O**	**B—Q2**

The Bishop is weak on this square, blocking the Q as it does. Better was *13.* . . . . P—Kt3 and *14.* . . . . B—Kt2, to add to the pressure on White's center Pawns.

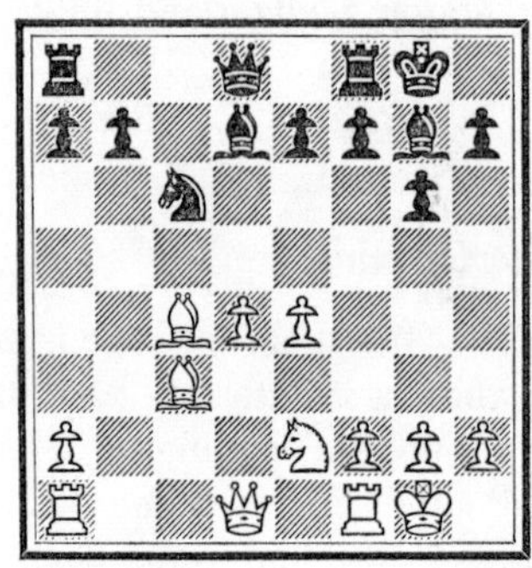

14.	**Q—Q2**	**R—B1**
15.	**B—Kt3**	

Otherwise *15.* . . . . Kt × P; *16.* B × Kt, R × B loses a Pawn.

15.	. . . .	**R—B2 ?**

A move without purpose. Black could have tried *15.* . . . . P—QR4; *16.* P—QR4 or *15.* . . . . Q—K1.

16.	**R(R1)—B1**	**B—Kt5**
17.	**P—B3**	**B—B1**
18.	**R(KB1)—Q1**	

White strengthens his center.

18. . . . . P—Kt3
19. P—Q5 *!* Kt—Kt1

Or *19.* . . . . Kt—K4; *20.* Kt—Q4, and the Kt will come in at Kt5 or B6 after the Black Kt is driven away from K4.

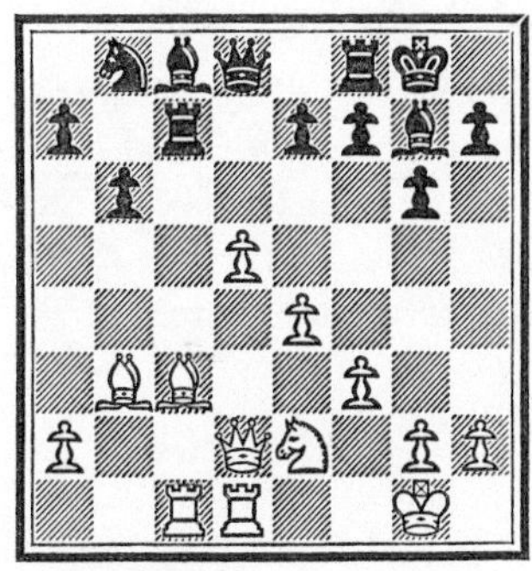

20. B × B K × B
21. Q—Q4*ch* K—Kt1
22. R × R Q × R
23. R—QB1 Q—Q1

RULE TO REMEMBER

Try to gain control of an open file. Very often, it is possible to do this by first exchanging, as in this game.

Exchanges usually lessen the force of an attack. In this game, however, the result of the exchanges is that Black is left completely undeveloped while White is ready for the action to follow.

24. P—B4 *!* B—R3
25. Kt—Kt3 Q—Q2

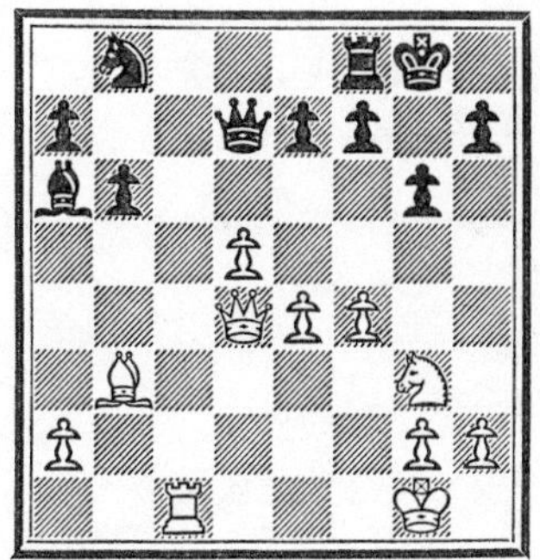

26. R—B3 *!*

Threatening *27.* Kt—B5, P × Kt; *28.* R—Kt3 mate.

26. . . . . Q—Kt4
27. P—QR4 Q—Q2
28. Kt—B5 *!*

Threat: *29.* Q—Kt7 mate.

RULE TO REMEMBER

Black lost this game because he ignored three important rules for chess success:

1. **He allowed White to gain control of the center.**
2. **He permitted White to gain control of an open file.**
3. **He did not co-ordinate the action of his pieces.**

Do not give up the center!
Contest open files!
Plan to place your pieces so that they fit into your over-all plan!

---

28.	**P—B3**
29. **P—Q6*ch***	**P—K3**
30. **R—B7**	

White comes in from all directions.

30.	**Q—K1**
31. **Kt—Kt7 *!***	

And the Black Q has no squares! If *31.* . . . . Q—Q1; *32.* Kt × P.

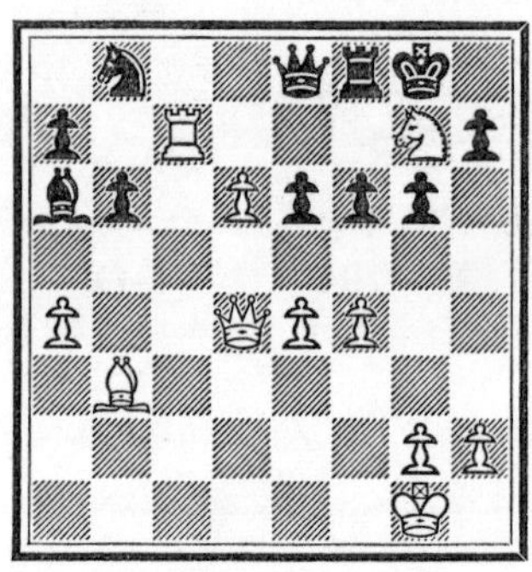

31.	**Kt—B3**
32. **Q—B3**	**Q—R1**

White cannot take the Kt because his own Kt would then be unprotected. Yet he has such a simple way out!

33. **Kt × P**	**Resigns**

The Kt will discover check on its next move, with fatal results. If *33.* . . . . Kt—R4; *34.* Kt—Kt5*ch*, Kt × B, *35.* Q × Kt*ch*, K—R1; *36.* R × *P* mate.

47 Gruenfeld Defense

Moscow, 1934

White	*Black*
V. Chekhover	V. Alatortsev

The Opening

The Gruenfeld Defense can be played positionally by White. Black's best chances come from the positions in which he can exert strong pressure along the diagonals. Well, then, why not keep the position blocked until White has developed? Black's normal position in this opening is not a free one, and it can become poor if Black makes premature efforts to open it up. This game is a model of proper tactics for White in the quiet treatment of the Gruenfeld Defense.

White's Plan

White quickly decides to concentrate on the development of his pieces. He gains control of important central squares and uses them to apply pressure on Black's Queen side. Then he gains time by attacking Black's Queen and switches his attack to the King side.

Black's Plan

Black makes the opening error of creating holes in his position. He then brings his Queen out in an attempt to force exchanges and reach a simplified ending. When his opponent gains time by attacking that Queen again and again, Black finds himself faced with a quick loss. He finally permits a mate in one rather than continue in a lost position.

What to Watch for

Observe how wasted Pawn moves in the opening leave Black no time for proper developing moves. Instead, he must defend the weaknesses in his position from the tenth move until the end of the game. At the end, most of his pieces are useless and misplaced.

1.	**P—Q4**	**Kt—KB3**
2.	**P—QB4**	**P—KKt3**

3. **Kt—QB3** **P—Q4**
4. **P—K3**

4. B—Kt5 is sometimes played, as is *4.* Q—Kt3. The quiet *4.* P—K3, with its goal of concentration on development, is as good a treatment of the Gruenfeld as has been found.

4. . . . . **P—K3**

4. . . . . B—Kt2 was better. Why open up so many lines for possible future invasion?

5. **Kt—B3** **B—Kt2**
6. **B—Q3** **O—O**
7. **O—O** **P—Kt3**

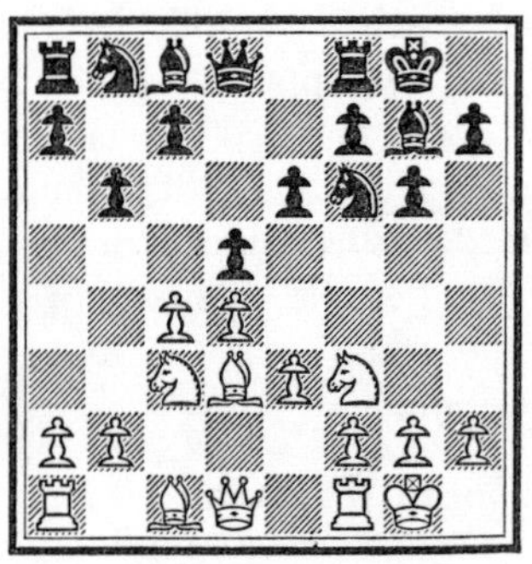

Black would like to play . . . . B—R3, to then exchange his restricted B for White's active one. White refuses to oblige, and clears the center first.

8. **P × P**

Otherwise Black plays *8.* . . . . P × P and *9.* . . . . B—R3.

8. . . . . **Kt × P**
9. **Kt × Kt**

To clear the QB file for Q or R.

9. . . . . **Q × Kt**

Black invites *10.* P—K4, when he can plan for a later attack on the then weak QP. As the game works out, 9. . . . . P × Kt would have been better. Black never gets his desired exchange of Bishops.

RULE TO REMEMBER

Occupy half-open files as soon as you can! From this move on, White will have the advantage —based on the fact that he is attacking along open lines and leaving Black no time to make normal developing moves.

---

10. **Q—B2** *!*

The QBP is threatened, as is the win of a R by *11.* B—K4. Black tries a counter attack instead of *10.* . . . . P—QB3 or *10.* . . . . P—KB4, either of which would leave weak Pawns.

10. . . . . **B—QR3**
11. **B—K4** **Q—QKt4**

The only move, threatening . . . . Q × R mate and giving Black time for . . . . P—QB3.

12. **R—K1**

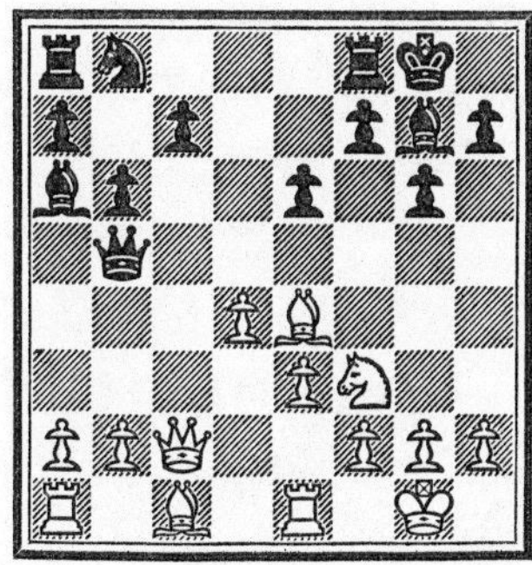

12. . . . . P—QB3
13. P—QR4 Q—KR4
14. P—R5

Black is tied up, but not yet lost. If *14.* B × P ?, R—B1 wins the B (Pin!). White plays to tie up more of Black's pieces on the Q side.

14. . . . . R—B1
15. Kt—Q2

The Kt will go to B4, from where it can hit Black at Q6, Kt6 or K5.

15. . . . . Q—QKt4
16. Kt—B4 *!*

White offers a piece by *16.* . . . . Q × Kt; *17.* Q × Q, B × Q; *18.* P × P and Black cannot prevent the threatened P—Kt7 *!* If *18.* . . . . B—QR3; *19.* R × B, Kt × R; *20.* P—Kt7, R—K1; *21.* P × R(Q)*ch*, R × Q; 22. R—R1 leaves White a Pawn ahead with a superior ending.

16. . . . . Kt—Q2
17. P—QKt3

17. Kt—Q6 would have lost the Kt after *17.* . . . . . Q—Kt5, threatening mate at K8 (Double attack!). After *17.* P—QKt3 White threatens *18.* Kt—Q6, for he will answer *18.* . . . . . Q—Kt5 by *19.* B—QR3.

17. . . . . . B—B1
18. B—Q3

Black must now worry about *19.* Kt—K5, which would win the Black B at QR3.

18. . . . . . Q—R4
19. B—K2 Q—KKt4

One of the rewards of a well-developed position is that it is so easy to develop it even further. Each White move creates new problems for Black.

20. P—K4 Q—Q1
21. B—Kt2 P—QKt4

21. . . . . B × Kt; *22.* Q × B, P—QB4; *23.* P—Q5 was not appetizing for Black, but was certainly better than the stranglehold which now comes.

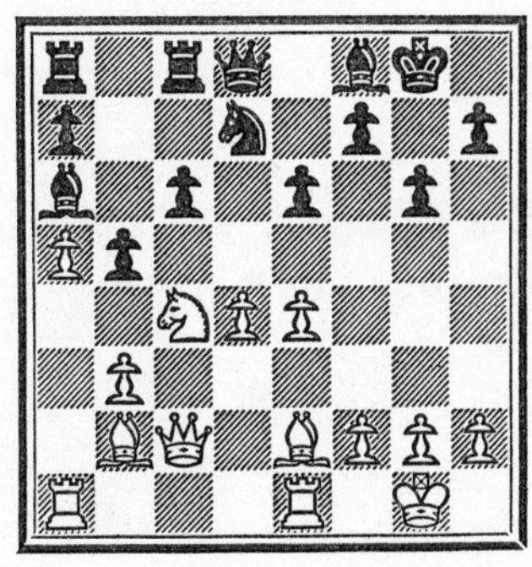

22. **Kt—K3** **P—QB4**
23. **P—Q5** **P—K4**

Black makes every effort to lock up the position so that he can then have time to rearrange his pieces.

24. **Kt—Kt4** **P—B3**
25. **Q—Q2**

While White brings his pieces to the K-side.

25. . . . . **P—R4 ?**

Black was unduly concerned about *26.* Kt—R6*ch*, for *26.* . . . . B × Kt; *27.* Q × B, Q—B1 would have held.

26. **Kt—K3** **B—Q3**
27. **B × RP !**

What thoughts impel such a sacrifice?

a. Black's pieces are tied up on the Q-side.

b. The Black King is exposed.

c. With Kt—B5, Q—R6, R—K3 at least three White pieces will be able to attack. Best of all, the Kt at B5 cannot be driven away.

27. . . . . **P × B**

If *27.* . . . . K—Kt2; *28.* B × P and the attack would be similar to that in the actual game. And, on *27.* . . . . Q—K1; *28.* Kt—B5 *!*, P × B; *29.* Kt × B wins.

28. **Kt—B5** **B—B1**

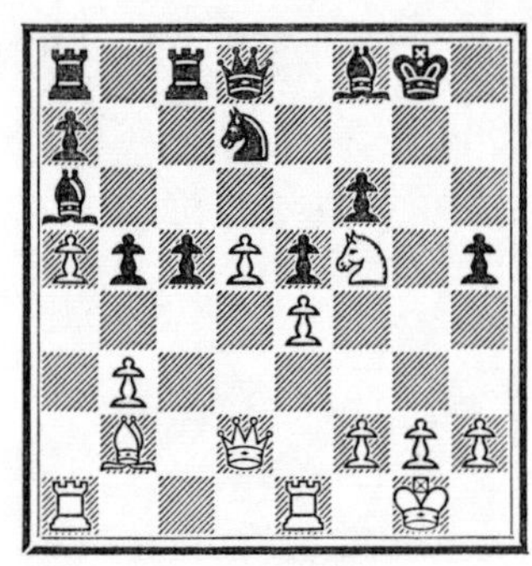

29. **R—K3**

White brings his third piece to the attack.

29. . . . . **K—R2**
30. **Q—K2**

The Black KRP cannot be saved. If *30.* . . . . K—Kt3; *31.* R—Kt3*ch*, K—B2; *32.* Q × P mate. Or *30.* . . . . K—Kt3; *31.* R—Kt3*ch*, K—R2; *32.* Q × P*ch*, B—R3; *33.* Q × B mate.

30. . . . . **Q—K1**
31. **R—KR3** **B—KKt2**

If *31.* . . . . Q—Kt3; *32.* R × P*ch*, K—Kt1; *33.* R—R6 *!*, B × R; *34.* Kt—K7*ch*, K—Kt2; *35.* Kt × Q, K × Kt; *36.* Q—Kt4*ch* and *37.* Q × Kt wins easily for White. (The attack succeeds because of a double attack at its end.)

32. **R × P*ch*** **K—Kt1**
33. **Q—Kt4** **Q × R ?**

What's the use? Or so Black must have thought. If *33.* . . . .

Q—B1 (to prevent the mate on Kt2); *34.* Kt—R6*ch*, K—R2; *35.* Q—B5*ch*, K—R1; *36.* Q—Kt6 and Black can do nothing while White continues with *37.* Kt—B5*ch*; *38.* R—R7 and *39.* Kt—R6 mate.

34. **Q × B mate.**

A game like this is a chess player's dream—Black was so tied up that it was as if White were two Rooks and a Bishop ahead!

RULE TO REMEMBER

Black's poor play in this game points up three important rules:

1. **Do not bring out your Queen early in the game!**
2. **Do not make Pawn moves that create holes in your position!**
3. **Do not waste time seeking exchanges in the opening when your pieces are not yet developed!**

---

48 Reti Opening

New York, 1924

White	*Black*
R. Reti	E. Bogoljubow

The Opening

Few men studied chess so thoroughly as did Richard Reti. This grandmaster-author enriched a generation of chess students by his writings and contributions. One of these, the opening named after him (*1.* Kt—KB3) was introduced in the strongest tournament Reti had yet entered—that of New York, 1924.

White's Plan

Reti's idea is to hold back the KP and QP, applying pressure along one of the long diagonals and then deciding where the later attack is to be. His game against Ewfim Bogoljubow saw his ideas work out well.

Black's Plan

Black makes only one weak move in this game, but never recovers from its effects.

Comment

The final moves, quiet and merciless, remind one of a biologist calmly pinning a live specimen to a board.

1. Kt—KB3 Kt—KB3

On *1.* . . . . P—Q4, Reti's method was to play *2.* P—B4 and, if *2.* . . . . P—Q5; *3.* P—K3, P—QB4; *4.* P—QKt4*!*

2. P—B4 P—K3
3. P—KKt3 P—Q4
4. B—Kt2

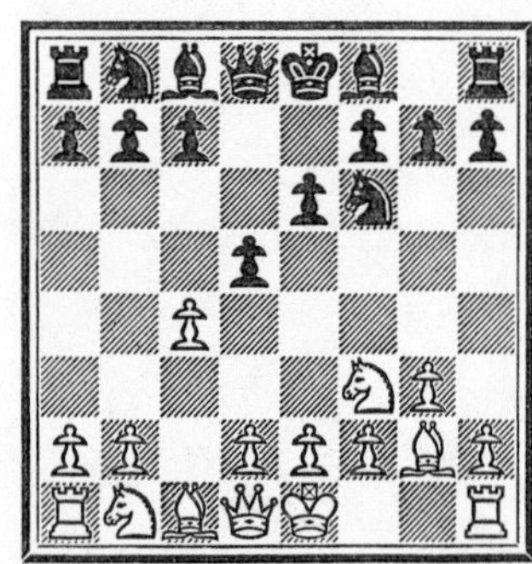

White need not fear *4.* . . . . P × P, when he can regain the

Pawn with *5.* Q—R4*ch* or play a gambit with 5. P—Kt3*!*

4. . . . . **B—Q3**
5. **O—O** **O—O**
6. **P—Kt3**

Reti plans to operate on both long diagonals.

6. . . . . **R—K1**
7. **B—Kt2** **Kt(Kt1)—Q2**
8. **P—Q4*!***

Played to prevent a Black counter by *8.* . . . . P × P and 9. . . . . P—K4. Now *8.* . . . . P × P; *9.* P × P, P—K4?; *10.* P × P, Kt × P; *11.* Kt × Kt, B × Kt; *12.* Q × Q*!*, R × Q; *13.* B × B and Black has lost a piece. On *8.* . . . . P—K4; *9.* P × KP, Kt × P; *10.* P × P loses a Pawn for Black.

8. . . . . **P—B3**

Still aiming at . . . . P—K4, Black first protects his QP.

9. **Kt(Kt1)—Q2** **Kt—K5?**

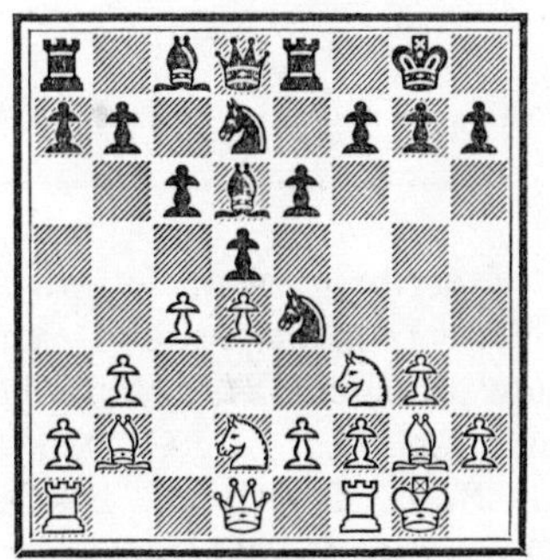

A weak move, leaving Black's Pawn position poor. *9.* . . . . P—K4 was better, although White would exchange on K4 and then play against Black's QP with a good chance of winning it.

10. **Kt × Kt** **P × Kt**
11. **Kt—K5** **P—KB4**

This move is forced if the KP is to be protected. If *11.* . . . . Kt—B3; *12.* Q—B2 and Black cannot defend a second time. To be considered was *11.* . . . . P—K6, when *12.* P × P, B × Kt; *13.* P × B would leave White's Pawns as targets on the K file. However, White would have answered *11.* . . . . P—K6 with *12.* P—B4, and the Black KP would later fall.

12. **P—B3*!***

Black must take the Pawn unless he wants to try *12.* . . . . Kt × Kt; *13.* P × Kt, B—B4*ch*; *14.* K—R1, P—K6; *15.* Q × Q, R × Q; *16.* R(R1)—Q1, when White will control the Q file and later pick off the Black P on K6.

12. . . . . **P × P**
13. **B × P**

Better than *13.* P × P, for White now has play along the KB file.

13. . . . . **Q—B2**
14. **Kt × Kt** **B × Kt**
15. **P—K4*!***

The KP hits at the center. *16.* P—K5 is not threatened, but instead White plays to maintain tension and to restrict Black's choice of squares.

15. . . . . **P—K4**

Black makes his best move, offering this Pawn in order to open up lines of play for his pieces.

16. **P—B5 !**

Preventing Black from getting his KB into play.

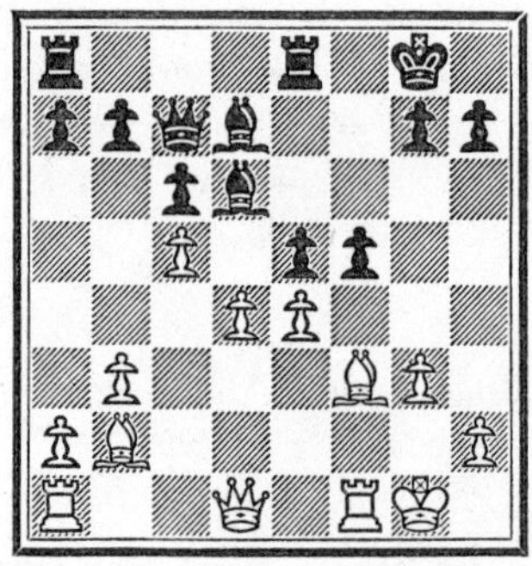

16. . . . . **B—KB1**

16. . . . . B—K2; *17.* P × BP, B × P; *18.* B—R5, P—KKt3; *19.* R × B *!*, P × R; *20.* B × R, R × B; *21.* Q—R5 wins a Pawn for White.

17. **Q—B2**

Now *17.* P × BP, etc., as in the previous note, would be met by an eventual *21.* . . . . Q—B2, holding everything.

17. . . . . **P × QP**
18. **P × BP** **R(R1)—Q1**

Black hopes to keep the QP, for *19.* B × P, B(Q2) × P; *20.* Q × B, R × B would ease matters for him.

19. **B—R5 !**

Apparently only a harmless poke at the Rook, but in reality the key to the play that follows.

19. . . . . **R—K4**
20. **B × P** **R × P(KB4)**

Black still imagines he has the variation he aimed for with his 18th move.

21. **R × R** **B × R**
22. **Q × B** **R × B**
23. **R—KB1 !**

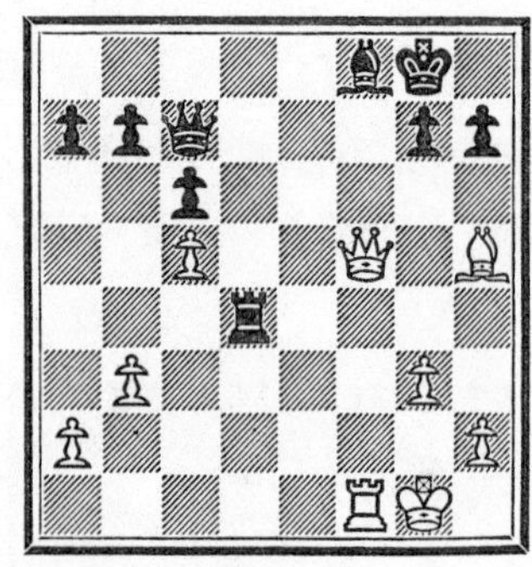

Everything even, but what a difference in the positions! White now threatens *24.* Q × B mate and, on *23.* . . . . Q—K2; *24.* B—B7*ch*, K—R1; *25.* B—Q5 *!*, Q—B3; *26.* Q—B8 *!* wins.

23. . . . . R—Q1
24. B—B7*ch* ! !

One of the most beautiful moves ever played, and made even more so by its sequel.

24. . . . . K—R1
25. B—K8 ! Resigns

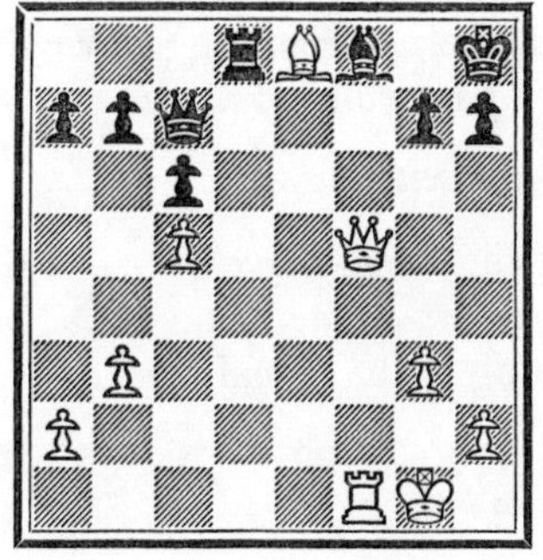

One can well imagine the feeling of amazement which gripped Bogoljubow at this point. The sword hangs suspended on its tearing hair, and nothing can keep it away.

a. If *25.* . . . . R × B; *26.* Q × B*ch*, R × Q; *27.* R × R mate.

b. If *25.* . . . . Q—K2; *26.* Q × B*ch*, etc., anyway.

c. If *25.* . . . . P—KR3; *26.* Q × B*ch*, K—R2; *27.* Q—B5*ch*, K—R1; *28.* B—Kt6 and White remains a piece ahead with mating threats.

RULE TO REMEMBER

Consider every possible defense! For example, how does White win if Black plays 25. . . . . B × P*ch* ? You will see the proper sequence after *26.* Q × B, R × B; if you note that White then has two pieces hitting at his KB8 square.

---

49 Reti Opening

Leningrad, 1934

White	*Black*
G. Lisitsyn	V. Ragozin

The Opening

One of the advantages of the Reti Opening is its very lack of an immediate demand upon Black. It permits the widest choice of defenses, and Reti Openings sometimes wind up as Sicilian Defenses, French Defenses, or Queen's Gambits.

White's Plan

Lisitsyn, a positional player who became a leading authority on the Reti Opening, often found himself playing against unusual defensive ideas attempted by opponents who feared his superior knowledge of the more commonly played lines. In this game he cracks one such defense by the sudden gift of a Bishop.

Black's Plan

Black is so intent on avoiding moves that Lisitsyn might know that he neglects the proper development of his pieces.

Comment

The "might have beens" in the last part of the game are as exciting as the actual finish.

1. Kt—KB3 **P—K3**
2. P—K4

Anything goes, such as 2. P—Q4, 2. P—B4, 2. P—QKt3, and even 2. P—K3.

2. . . . . **P—Q4**
3. Kt—B3

A curious kind of French Defense has been reached. Black should now play 3. . . . . P—QB4 or 3. . . . . Kt—KB3, but instead tries to establish a beachhead on Q5.

3. . . . . **P—Q5**
4. Kt—K2 **P—QB4**
5. P—B3 !

White strikes at the advanced Pawn before it can be further reinforced.

RULE TO REMEMBER

Try to occupy center squares with Pawns when those Pawns can be supported.

If your opponent advances a center Pawn, try to exchange it before it can be supported by other Pawns or pieces.

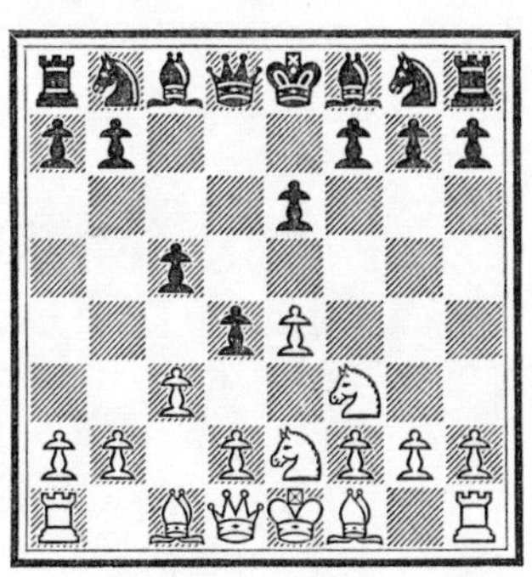

5. . . . . **P × P**

5. . . . . P—Q6 looks good at first sight, but loses two Pawns after 6. Kt—B4, P—B5; 7. Q—R4*ch* and 8. Q × BP.

6. **KtP × P** **Kt—KB3**
7. **Kt—Kt3** **Kt—B3**
8. **B—Kt5** **B—Q2**

Black does not like 9. Kt—K5 and *10.* Q—R4, and plays 8. . . . . B—Q2 to break the pin on the Kt at once.

9. **O—O** **P—QR3**
10. **B—K2**

RULE TO REMEMBER

Avoid exchanges which improve the mobility of your opponent's pieces!

The Black B at Q2 has little mobility. White does not wish to strengthen it by *10.* B × Kt, B × B.

10. . . . . **B—Q3**

Black invites the Pawn sacrifice which follows. *10.* . . . . B—K2 was better.

11. **P—Q4**

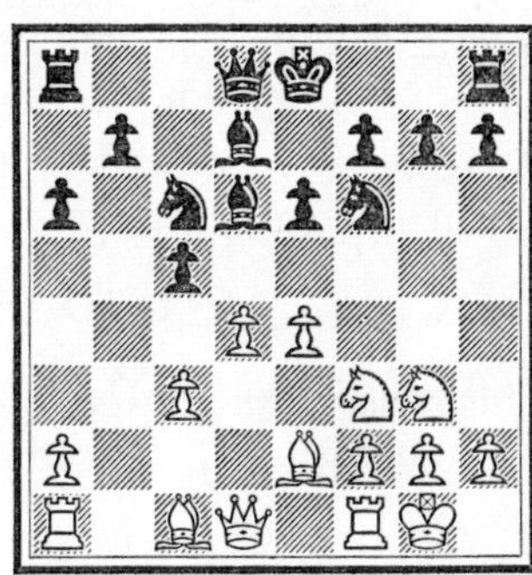

11. . . . . **B × Kt**
12. **BP × B**

The best rule is usually to recapture towards the center (RP tack using the open B file against × B), but White foresees an at- Black's castled K position.

12. . . . . **P × P**
13. **P × P** **Kt(KB3) × P**
14. **B—Q3**

White gains valuable attacking time by hitting at this Kt. Gain of time is a frequent and proper reason for a Pawn sacrifice.

14. . . . . Kt—Q3
15. B—R3 *!*

More gain of time—Black is temporarily prohibited from castling.

15. . . . . Kt—Kt4
16. B—Kt2

Not as good as *16.* B × Kt, but still good enough to keep the attack going. On *16.* B × Kt, P × B; *17.* B—B5, P—QKt3; *18.* B—Q6, B—B1; *19.* Kt—K5, Kt × Kt (if . . . . Q × B; *20.* Kt × BP *!*); *20.* P × Kt Black would remain intolerably cramped.

16. . . . . O—O

Black has castled at last, but is faced by a strong K side attack.

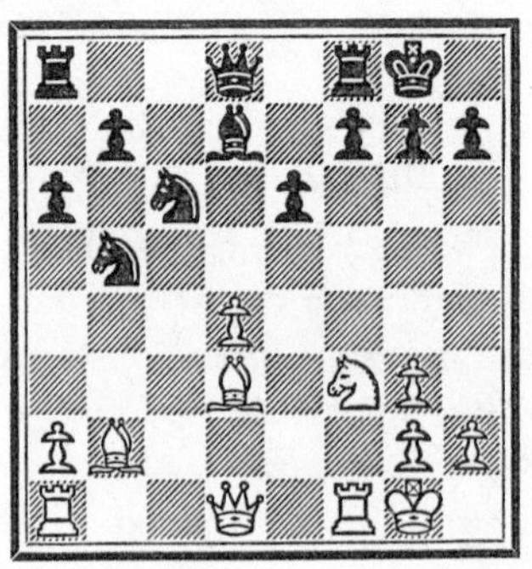

17. P—KR4 *!*

To support the Kt after *18.* B × P*ch!*, K × B; *18.* Kt—Kt5*ch* —the mating attack by Kt and Q.

17. . . . . P—R3
18. P—R4 Kt—B2
19. B—R3 R—K1 *?*

19. . . . . Kt—K2 and *20.* . . . . Kt(B2)—Q4 was a better defensive plan. Now White can make use of the open diagonal (QR3—KB8) as a key part of a brilliant winning attack.

20. B—R7*ch !*

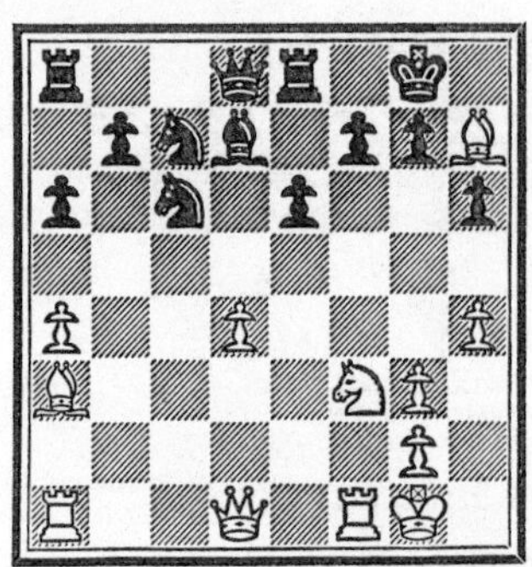

What can this mean? Suppose Black just refuses the gift by playing *20.* . . . . K—R1?

a. *20.* . . . . K—R1; *21.* Kt—Kt5, P × Kt; *22.* Q—R5, P—KKt3; *23.* B × P*ch*, K—Kt2; *24.* Q—R7, mate.

b. *20.* . . . . K—R1; *21.* Kt—Kt5, Q—Kt1 (White threatens *22.* Kt × BP*ch*); *22.* Kt × P*ch*, K × B; *23.* Q—Q3*ch*, K—Kt1; *24.* Kt × P*ch*, P × Kt; *25.* Q—Kt6*ch*, K—R1; *26.* R—B7 and *27.* Q—R7 mate.

c. *20.* . . . . K—R1; *21.* Kt—Kt5, Q—Kt1; *22.* Kt × P*ch,* K × B; *23.* Q—Q3*ch,* P—Kt3; *24.* Kt—Kt5*ch,* P × Kt; *25.* R—B7*ch,* K—R3; *26.* P × P*ch,* K × P (if *26.* . . . . K—R4; *27.* Q—B3*ch,* K × P; *28.* Q—B4*ch,* K—R4; *29.* R—R7 mate); *27.* Q—K3*ch,* K—R4; and mate follows by *28.* R—R7*ch,* K—Kt5; *29.* Q—B4 mate.

So Black must take the Bishop after all!

RULE TO REMEMBER

Take the time to play through the notes to chess games—so that you can better understand the reasons for the moves made by the players! As you play through the three lines described here, ask yourself why Black's moves are forced.

---

20.	**K × B**
21. **Kt—Kt5*ch*!**	**K—Kt1**

The Kt could not be taken. If *21.* . . . . P × Kt; *22.* Q—R5*ch,* K—Kt1; *23.* Q × P*ch,* K—R1; *24.* Q—R5*ch,* K—Kt1; *25.* P × P, Kt—K2; *26.* B × Kt, Q × B; *27.* P—Kt6*!* and mate follows on R7.

22. **Kt × BP**	**Q—Kt1**
23. **Kt × P*ch***	**P × Kt**

For *23.* . . . . K—R2 allows the mating attack after *24.* Q—R5, P × Kt; *25.* R—B7*ch*; K—Kt1; *26.* Q—Kt6*ch* and *27.* Q—R7 mate.

24. **Q—Kt4*ch***	**K—R1**
25. **R—B7**	**Resigns**

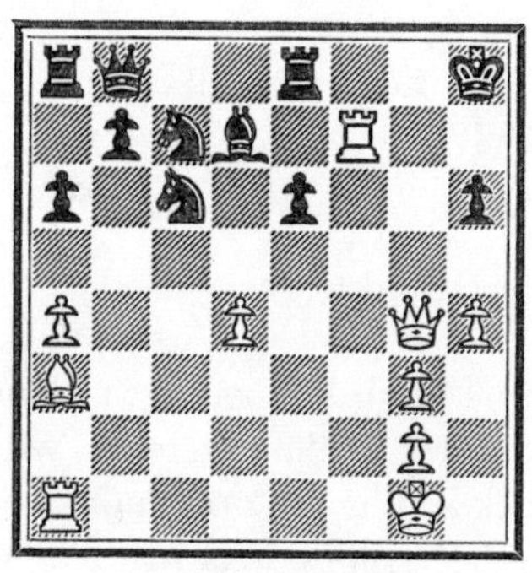

On *25.* . . . . R—Kt1; *26.* Q—R5, R—Kt2; *27.* Q × P*ch,* K—Kt1; *28.* Q × R mate.

RULE TO REMEMBER

This game illustrates how easy it is to win when you have:

1. Developed your pieces.

2. Obtained open lines for attack.

3. Lured your opponent's pieces away from his King position.

---

50 English Opening

Leningrad, 1934

White	*Black*
N. Riumin	M. Euwe

The Opening

The English Opening is a kind of reverse Sicilian Defense, with Black having the option of playing the White side of the Sicilian a move behind. This "missing" move gives White a relatively easy game.

White's Plan

Riumin's short life gave the chess world many brilliant and beautiful games. In this game he defeats the master who, a year later, became world champion. Watch how he successfully hits at an exposed King position.

Black's Plan

Euwe commits a basic error in his insistence on advancing his KBP until it is at KB6—by which time White's counterattack has built up full steam.

Comment

White's attack rolls on for some 15 moves before Black is forced to raise the white flag.

1. **P—QB4**	**P—K4**
2. **Kt—QB3**	**Kt—QB3**
3. **Kt—B3**	**Kt—B3**
4. **P—Q4**	

White plays P—Q4 before Black can.

4.	**P—K5**

Black plays for a win from the beginning. The alternative 4. . . . . P × P, 5. Kt × P, B—Kt5; 6. Kt × Kt, KtP × Kt; 7. B—Kt5 makes for an even game.

5. **Kt—Q2**

There was a time when White tried Kt—KKt5 here, but analysis has shown that Black gets the best of it after 5. . . . . P—KR3; 6. Kt(Kt5) × KP, Kt × Kt; 7. Kt × Kt, Q—R5*!* and the complications if White tries to remain a Pawn ahead with 8. Q—Q3 are not worth White's trouble.

5.	Kt × P
6. Kt(Q2) × P	Kt—K3

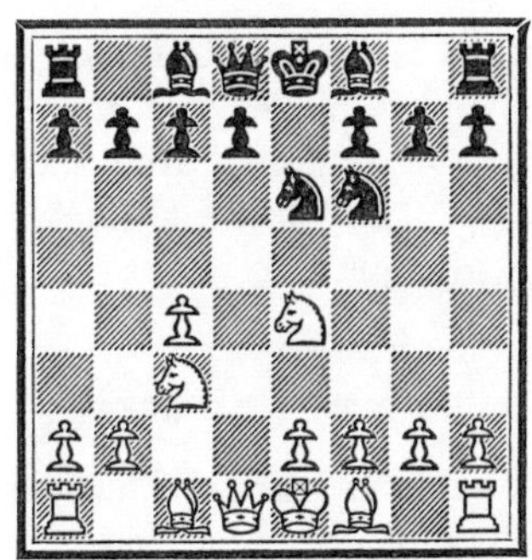

White has achieved a first goal of opening play: He has superior control of the center. Now he must decide on a plan for completing his development.

7. P—KKt3

The B is best developed at KKt2 because the P at QB4 would block its development on the diagonal KB1—QR6.

7.	Kt × Kt
8. Kt × Kt	P—KB4

Again Black declines a move which would result in an even game. Perhaps he expected to overwhelm his younger opponent, and so stayed away from the simplifying *8.* . . . . B—Kt5*ch; 9.* B—Q2, B × B*ch; 10.* Q × B.

9. Kt—B3	B—Kt5
10. B—Q2	O—O
11. B—Kt2	P—B5 ?

RULE TO REMEMBER

A move like P—KB5 by Black in this game is less effective if made before White has played O—O. P—KB5 can open up a castled King position—but is not really an attack otherwise.

This advance is good only if White takes the BP. As he doesn't, *11.* . . . . P—B5 remains a wasted move. Better were *11.* . . . . P—Q3 or *11.* . . . . P—QR4 (to impede Q side castling by White).

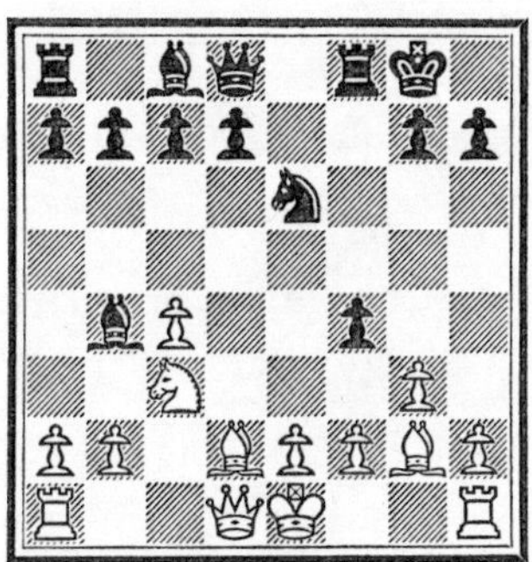

12. Kt—Q5	B—Q3 ?

Black expects the KBP to become the basis for an attack. But the B blocks his position at Q3. Better was . . . . B × B*ch.*

13. B—QB3

Now the White pieces begin to bear down on the Black K position.

13. . . . . R—Kt1

Necessary if the QB is to be developed.

14. Q—Q3 Q—Kt4
15. P—KR4 Q—R3
16. P—KKt4

Black's attack has now been stopped, for White's last 3 moves have opened up lines for counterplay on the K side. Meanwhile, Black's QR and QB remain undeveloped.

16. . . . . Kt—B4
17. Q—Q2 P—QKt3
18. O—O—O B—Kt2

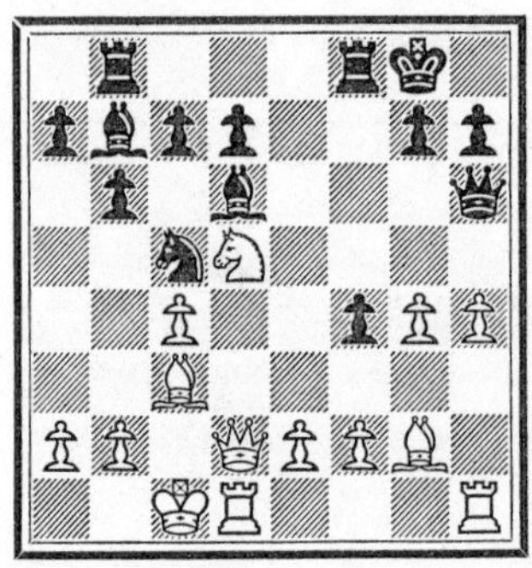

19. P—Kt5 *!*

This Pawn push gains time for another, as the Black Q must move away.

19. . . . . Q—K3
20. Q—Q4

White threatens mate on Kt7, which Black's next move easily prevents—but only by making the Q a target in return.

20. . . . . Q—B2
21. P—R5 *!* Kt—K3
22. Q—Q3 Kt—B4

Black is reduced to hoping he can repeat moves and thereby draw. On *22.* . . . . Kt × P; *23.* P—R6 *!*, and Black's K side will be wide open.

RULE TO REMEMBER

A game is a draw if the position is repeated three times with the same player to move.

---

23. Q—Q2 P—B6

Hoping for *24.* B × P(B3), B —B5; *25.* P—K3, B × KP; *26.* Q × B, Q × B.

24. P—Kt6 *!*

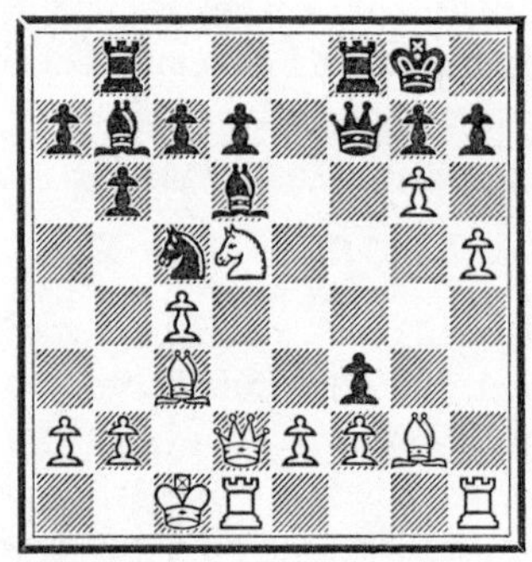

The winning move.

a. If *24.* . . . . RP × P; *25.* RP × P, Q × P; *26.* B × BP and *27.* R(Q1)—Kt1 will win.

b. If *24.* . . . . RP × P; *25.* RP × P, Q—B4; *26.* R—R8*ch !*,

K × R; *27.* Q—R6*ch,* K—Kt1 (the B on B3 prevents *27.* . . . . . P × Q); *28.* Q × P mate.

c. If *24.* . . . . . Q—B4; *25.* B × BP, B—B5; *26.* Kt—K7*ch,* K—R1; *27.* B × P*ch,* K × B; *28.* Kt × Q*ch,* R × Kt; *29.* P—K3.

Black must try to sell his Queen as dearly as possible instead.

24.	**Q—B5**
25. **Kt × Q**	**B × Kt**
26. **P—K3**	**P × B**
27. **R—R4**	**B—Kt4**

Black has two pieces for the Queen, and hopes to get more by . . . . Kt—K5 and . . . . R × P.

28. **P × P *ch***	**K × P**

28. . . . . . K—R1; *29.* P—R6, B × RP; *30.* R × B.

29. **Q—B2*ch***	**K—Kt1**
30. **R—Kt4**	**Kt—K3**
31. **P—B4 *!***	**B—B6**
32. **R × KtP**	**Resigns**

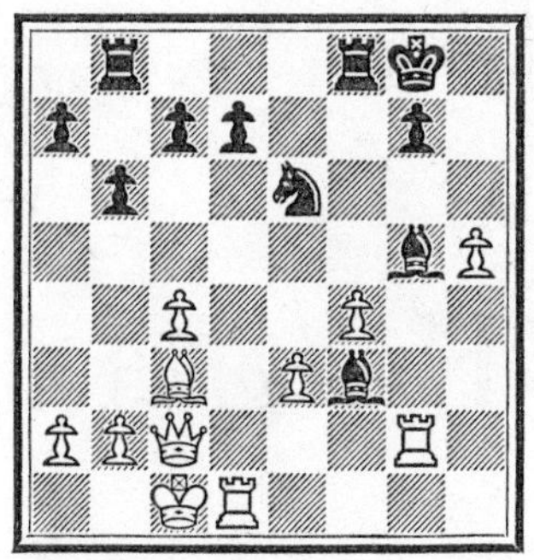

The game is lost.

a. *32.* . . . . . B × R(Kt7); *33.* Q × B, B—R3; *34.* R × P and White can force his KBP forward to drive away the Kt and then win by sacrificing on KKt7.

b. *32.* . . . . . B × R(Q1); *33.* Q × B, B—R3; *34.* R—Kt6 and White plays Q—Kt4, moves his K to B2, and advances his KBP to break through. Thus, *34.* R—Kt6, R—B2; *35.* Q—Kt4, K—B1; *36.* K—B2, R—K1; *37.* P—B5, Kt—B4; *38.* P—B6*!* and there might follow *38.* . . . . . R—K5; *39.* P × P*ch,* K—Kt1; *40.* R × B, R × Q; *41.* R—R8 mate.

51 English Opening

Dresden, 1926

White	*Black*
A. Nimzovich	A. Rubinstein

The Opening

Black has many replies to *1.* P—QB4, the best of which is probably the symmetrical *1.* . . . . P—QB4. Black can then play either for steady development or for the quick opening up of the game.

White's Plan

Aron Nimzovich was undoubtedly the most significant chess theorist of this century. Every modern chess master owes much to the concepts developed by Nimzovich in his play and in the several books he produced. In this game he locks up the center and attacks on the King side.

Black's Plan

Akiba Rubinstein, his opponent in this game, learned chess ideas rapidly, using new ideas as quickly as they appeared. He was renowned as the first end-game player of his era. He loses time in the opening of this game and remains on the defensive to the end.

Comment

The extensive notes to this game are intended to introduce some of Nimzovich's ideas.

1. **P—QB4**	**P—QB4**
2. **Kt—KB3**	**Kt—KB3**
3. **Kt—B3**	**P—Q4**

Black can very well continue with . . . . Kt—B3, but prefers to open up the game quickly. Most players today would play . . . . Kt—B3 and then aim for . . . . P—KKt3 and . . . . B—Kt2.

4. **P × P**	**Kt × P**
5. **P—K4**	

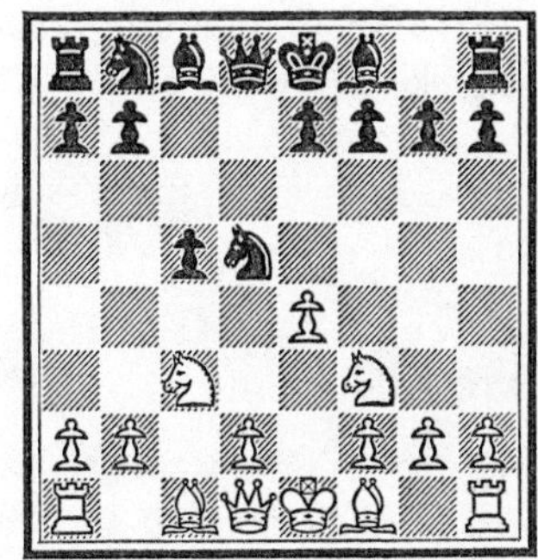

This move would be condemned when played by any other player but Nimzovich. It leaves White with a backward QP. When played in this game, the move caused great surprise. Yet Nimzovich defended it as gaining valuable time for the development of his KB.

5. . . . . Kt—Kt5

Black seeks to punish White at once, by playing *6.* . . . . Kt—Q6*ch*.

6. **B—B4**

The B will be blocked at once by Black's *6.* . . . . P—K3. Yet this is precisely what Nimzovich desired. On *6.* . . . . Kt—Q6*ch* he plays 7. K—K2 and the Black Kt must run away or exchange itself by 7. . . . . Kt × *Bch*; 8. R × Kt, when White will have four developed pieces to Black's none.

6.	**P—K3**
7. **O—O**	**Kt(Kt1)—B3?**

This appears to be a developing move, but really is not, for it leaves the Kt at Kt5 without a proper place to which to return. 7. . . . . P—QR3 was best, to threaten 8. . . . . P—QKt4 and 9. . . . . P—B5.

8. **P—Q3**

A quiet move with three aims:

1) To prevent . . . . Kt—Q6.

2) To open the line of the QB.

3) To threaten *9.* P—QR3, Kt—R3; *10.* B × Kt, P × B, when Black's doubled Pawns on the QR file would, in effect, leave White a Pawn ahead.

8. . . . . **Kt—Q5**

Black finds a way to avoid the exchange of his Kt(Kt5), and hopes to gain by the placement of his P on Q5 after the exchange. But Black welcomes this situation, for it erases the weakness of his own QP.

9. **Kt × Kt**	**P × Kt**
10. **Kt—K2**	

Now the Q-side is quiet and White can think of moves like P—B4 to gain a death grip on the center, or the invasion of the Black K-side by his Kt and Q.

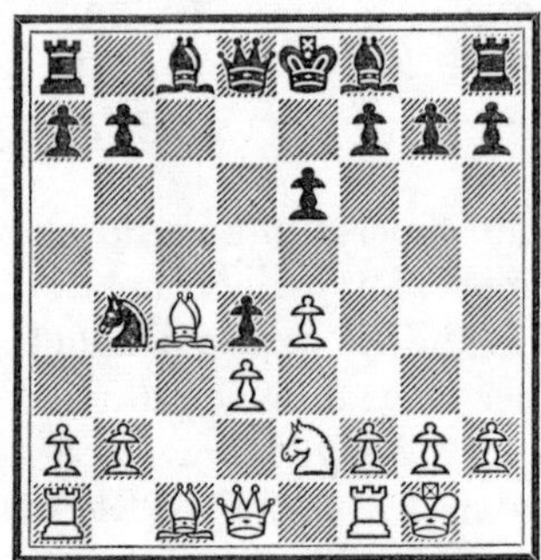

10. . . . . P—QR3

To meet the threat of *11.* B—Kt5*ch,* B—Q2; *12.* Kt × P*!,* to avoid which, he would be unable to play *11.* B—Kt5*ch,* Kt—B3; *12.* B × Kt*ch,* P × B; *13.* Q—R4*!,* still gaining a Pawn for White.

11. **Kt—Kt3*!***

A restraining move. Nimzovich felt that moves which limited the choices available to an opponent were best. Now the normal *11.* . . . . B—K2 would be met by *12.* Q—Kt4*!,* and the K-side is under attack. Black therefore plays to be able to answer *12.* Q—Kt4; *12.* . . . . O—O; *13.* B—R6 (threatening mate by *14.* Q × P mate), Q—B3. On *11.* . . . . B—K2; *12.* Q—Kt4, O—O; *13.* B—R6, B—B3; *14.* B × KtP*!,* B × B; *15.* Kt—R5*!,* and mate on Kt7 is forced.

11. . . . . **B—Q3**
12. **P—B4*!***

White's opening strategy has left Black without a target. He must now worry about White's further advance of the K-side Pawns.

12. . . . . **O—O**
13. **Q—B3**

White prefers not to declare himself, and to develop further instead of fixing the position by *13.* P—K5, B—B2; *14.* Q—Kt4, K—B1, when Black would be able to beat off any attack. With *13.* Q—B3 instead White still threatens the strong moves P—K5 or P—B5—but meanwhile Black must make a move, and whatever Black does will result in a target that White will then try to reach. Such "waiting" moves as *13.* Q—B3 are good when they add to one's development.

13. . . . . **K—R1*!***

Black is not one to await an attack. He moves the K to R1 to get away from any later checks by White's B and prepares to block White's Pawns by . . . . P—KB4.

14. **B—Q2** **P—B4**
15. **R(R1)—K1** **Kt—B3**
16. **R—K2**

White continues his development. *16.* R—K2 prepares for the doubling of the White Rooks on the K file or the KB file.

16. . . . . Q—B2?

This move really does not improve Black's position. *16.* . . . . B—Q2; *17.* . . . . R—B1, and then *18.* . . . . Kt—R4 should have been considered.

17. P × P P × P
18. Kt—R1!!

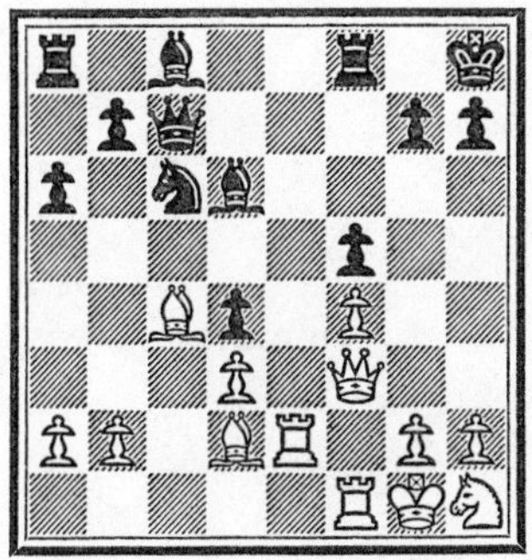

An incredible move! The Kt is pulled out of action in order to return via B2, R3 and Kt5. Nimzovich, secure in his superior development, realized that Black had no immediate counterattack in prospect, and decides to take the time to place his Kt in its best position. This move, Kt—R1, has been described as the most amazing attacking move in chess history!

18. . . . . B—Q2
19. Kt—B2 QR—K1
20. R(B1)—K1

White prefers to maintain control of the K file.

20. . . . . R × R
21. R × R

And now Black cannot play . . . . R—K1 because of *22.* Q—Q5!, Kt—K2; *23.* Q—B7, and Black's pieces are tied down while the White Kt can come up to aid in the attack.

21. . . . . Kt—Q1
22. Kt—R3

The Kt moves inexorably to Kt5.

22. . . . . B—B3

22. . . . . R—K1?; *23.* Q—R5!, R × R; *24.* Kt—Kt5!!, P—R3; *25.* Q—Kt6!!, P × Kt; *26.* Q—R5 mate is not inviting to Black.

23. Q—R5

The same attack is still possible on *23.* . . . . P—R3; *24.* Kt—Kt5! Black is therefore forced to open his K position further by . . . . P—Kt3. One might ask why Nimzovich played *23.* Q—R5 if it is to be driven back at once? The answer lies in his belief that one must make moves which induce enemy weaknesses, even if these moves lose some time.

23. . . . . P—KKt3
24. Q—R4 K—Kt2!

Necessary and strong. Otherwise the Black R must remain at

KB1 to prevent White's Q—B6 mate.

25. **Q—B2 !**

The weakness created on the K-side, White now turns his attention to the center. He hits at the P on Q4, not because he can take it, but because he wants the Black B removed from its control of K5.

25. . . . . **B—B4**
26. **P—QKt4**

He wants the B as much out of play as possible.

26. . . . . **B—Kt3**

The effect of White's last two moves has been to weaken Black's K-side. Now he returns there for further action.

27. **Q—R4** **R—K1**

27. . . . . R—B3 would lead to an amusing win by *28.* Kt—Kt5, P—R3; *29.* Kt—R7 !, R—Q3; *30.* R—K7*ch*, or *29.* . . . . R—B2; *30.* B × R, Kt × B; *31.* Q—B6*ch*, K × Kt; *32.* R—K7 !

28. **R—K5** **Kt—B2**

28. . . . . R × R; *29.* P × R, Q × P is too dangerous, for White will then play *30.* B—B4, Q—K1; *31.* Kt—Kt5, P—R3; *32.* Kt—K6*ch*, Kt × Kt; *33.* Q × P*ch*, K—Kt1; *34.* B—K5 !, Q—Q2; *35.* B × Kt*ch*, Q × B; *36.* Q—Kt7 mate.

29. **B × Kt !** **Q × B**
30. **Kt—Kt5 !**

The Kt enters the arena at last!

30. . . . . **Q—Kt1**

Forced to prevent *31.* Q × P*ch*.

31. **R × R** **B × R**
32. **Q—K1 !**

The much-traveled Queen comes in from the other side.

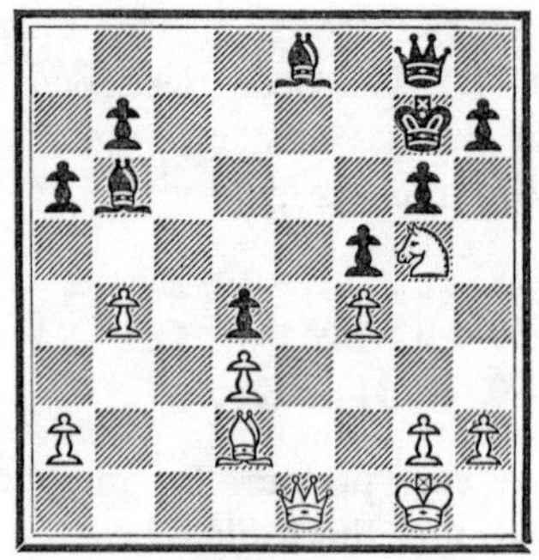

32. . . . . **B—B3**

Black had a last chance with 32. . . . . K—B1, but it fails after 33. Q—K5, B—Q1; *34.* Kt—K6*ch,* K—K2; 35. Q—B5*ch !*, and White wins the Q (after 35. . . . . K × Kt; *36.* Q—B4*ch,* or after 35. . . . . K—Q2; *36.* Kt—B8*ch*).

33. **Q—K7*ch*** **K—R1**

Black teeters on the edge. If 33. . . . . K—R3; *34.* Kt—K6 will force mate by 35. Q—Kt5 unless Black gives up his Q by . . . . Q × Kt.

34. **P—Kt5 *!***

The move which finally breaks through.

a. If *34.* . . . . . B × P; 35. Q—B6*ch* wins the B at Black's QKt3.

b. If *34.* . . . . . P × P; 35. Kt—K6 (threatening *36.* Q—B6*ch;* Q—Kt2; *37.* Q × Q mate), P—R4; *36.* Q—B6*ch,* K—R2; *37.* Kt—Kt5*ch,* K—R3; *38.* B—Kt4 *!* and 39. B—B8*ch* will force mate or win the Queen!

34.	**Q—Kt2**
35. **Q × Q*ch***	**K × Q**
36. **P × B**	**P × P**
37. **Kt—B3**	

The ending is easy. White can win the QRP and then push his own QRP through to Queen.

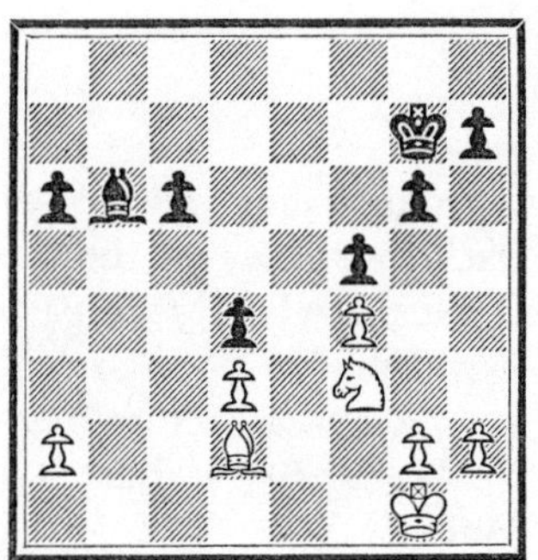

37.	**P—B4**
38. **Kt—K5**	**B—B2**
39. **Kt—B4**	**K—B2**
40. **P—Kt3**	**B—Q1**
41. **B—R5**	

If Black exchanges, then White will pick off the QRP with his remaining Kt.

41.	**B—K2**
42. **B—B7**	**K—K3**
43. **Kt—Kt6**	**P—KR3**
44. **P—KR4**	**P—Kt4**
45. **P—R5**	**P—Kt5**

Black has run out of moves. With everything blocked, all that would remain is for White's K to come to the Q-side.

46. **B—K5** **Resigns**

Few masters play on a piece behind. We can only assume that Rubinstein was still in a state of shock after the tremendous efforts required by this game.

RULE TO REMEMBER

Learn the many ideas of Aron Nimzovich—such as those so well illustrated by this game:

1. Develop your pieces, even if your Pawn structure seems weakened for a time (see Move 5).
2. Blockade the side of the board on which your opponent is strongest (see Moves 10–13).
3. Develop before attacking (see Moves 12–17).
4. Make moves that lead your opponent to weaken his position (see Move 23).
5. Use control of an open file to place a Queen or Rook on the seventh rank (see Move 33).

52 King's Indian Defense

Zurich, 1959

White	*Black*
F. Olafsson	R. Fischer

The Opening

The King's Indian Defense is an octopus-like affair in which Black develops carefully without attempting a break in the center. It is not the type of opening beginners should attempt, but it does repay study—if only to learn that there are many ways of suddenly exploding a position.

White's Plan

White plays the opening carefully, preparing for a King-side attack. Just as he is ready to begin this attack, he pauses to defend against some imagined threats. This loss of time permits his opponent to counterattack. White then enters into a long series of exchanges in search of an even ending.

Black's Plan

Bobby Fischer's great talent is the ability to judge a position quickly, and to make the best attacking moves in rapid order. In this game he is able to attack on both wings and the center at the same time. He finally gains a passed Pawn and forces it through. The game is a true champion's performance!

Comment

Observe how a passed Pawn supported by a Rook wins again.

1.	P—QB4	Kt—KB3
2.	Kt—QB3	P—KKt3
3.	P—Q4	B—Kt2

3. . . . . P—Q4 would be a Gruenfeld Defense—not elastic enough for Fischer.

4.	P—K4	P—Q3
5.	B—K2	O—O
6.	Kt—B3	P—K4

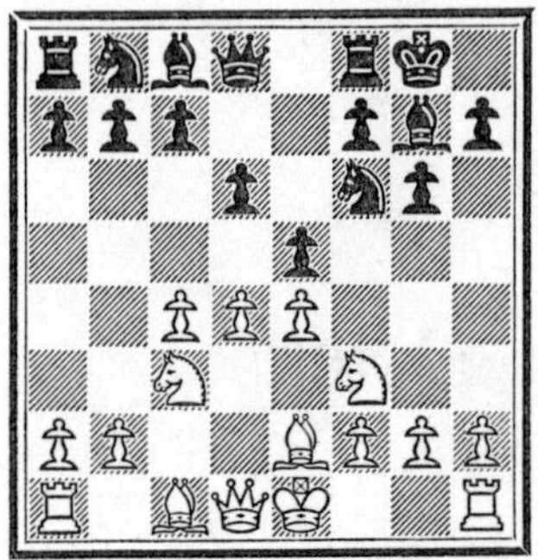

Black advances at last. White cannot win the KP. If *7.* P × P, P × P; *8.* Q × Q, R × Q; *9.* Kt × P, Black can play *9.* . . . . . Kt × P; *10.* Kt × Kt, B × Kt with easy equality.

7. **P—Q5**	**Kt(Kt1)—Q2**
8. **B—Kt5**	**P—KR3**
9. **B—R4**	**P—R3**

Black wants to play his Q to K1 to assist in action on the K side, and plays . . . . P—QR3 first to prevent *10.* Kt—QKt5.

10. **Kt—Q2**	**Q—K1**
11. **P—KKt4 !**	

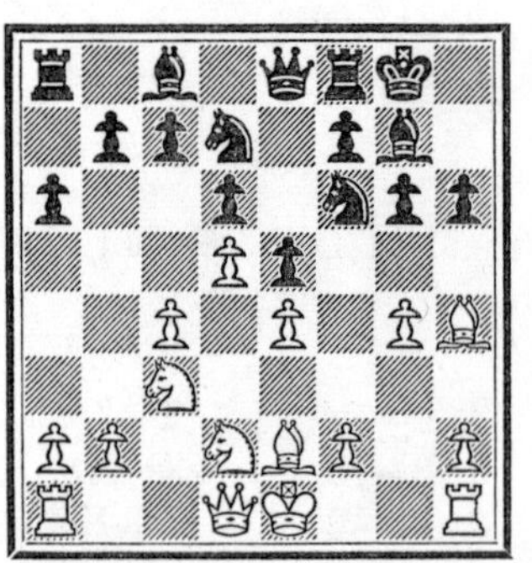

A true grandmaster move. The P stands at KKt4 threatening P—Kt5 and also impeding Black's possible later counter by P—KB4.

11.	**Kt—R2**
12. **Q—B2**	

Now that the Kt is gone from Black's KB3, White would do well to play B—Kt3 and P—KR4 as quickly as possible. He prepares to castle first.

12.	**Kt—Kt4 !**

Black invites *13.* B × Kt, P × B; *14.* P—KR4, P × P because he would then have enough time to organize a defense before Black could get his pieces to the K-side.

13. **P—KR3 !**

The best reply, to forestall Black's . . . . Kt—R6 and then . . . . Kt—B5.

13.	**Kt—B4**
14. **O—O—O**	**B—Q2**
15. **P—B3**	

White prepares his attack too deliberately. He wants this Pawn at KB3 to defend the Pawn on Kt4 when he plays P—KR4. R(Q1)—Kt1 was better.

15.	**Kt—R5**
16. **Kt × Kt**	**B × Kt**
17. **P—Kt3**	**B—Q2**

RULE TO REMEMBER

When you and your opponent have castled on opposite sides of the board, try to begin your attack on his King position as soon as possible. Begin by placing your Rooks on the files along which you plan to attack.

Black has induced White's P—Kt3 to create a target for his own Pawns later on.

18. **B—B2** **P—QB4*!***

This move sets up the action against White's Q-side Pawns.

RULE TO REMEMBER

Plan counterplay in the center when your opponent is preparing an attack against your castled position.

If you are planning an attack on the wing, try to blockade the center first. Fischer's move *18.* . . . . P—QB4 locks up the center and prepares . . . . P—QKt4.

---

19. **P—KR4** **Kt—R2**
20. **B—K3** **P—QKt4**
21. **Kt—Kt1*?***

A waste of time, aimed, perhaps, against an imagined invasion on QR6. Best, and strong, was R(Q1)—Kt1.

21. **. . . .** **P—B4*!***

Black loses no time in counterattacking. The absence of the Kt makes White's K4 square a proper target.

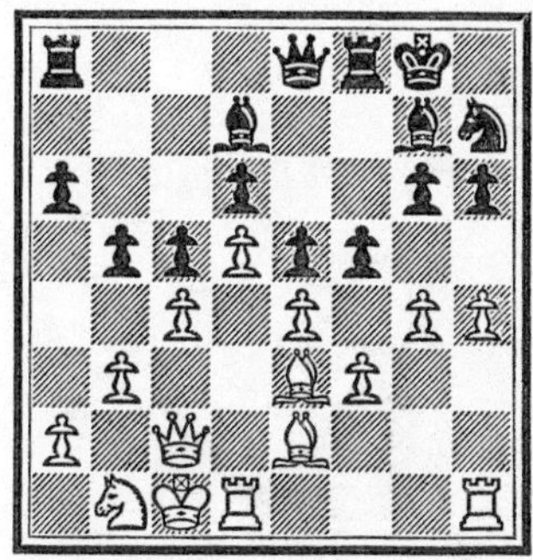

22. **KtP × P** **P(Kt3) × P**
23. **KP × P** **B × P**
24. **Q—Q2**

White hits at the KRP, but meets a move which opens every line for Black while permitting the KRP to go.

24. **. . . .** **P—K5*!***

For *25.* B × P, P—K6; *26.* B × P, Q—K4 would permit Black's entry.

25. **R(Q1)—Kt1**

Many moves too late.

25. **. . . .** **P × KBP**

Now *26.* B × BP would lose to . . . . B × Kt, and the White B on B3 is loose.

26. **B × RP** **R—R2**

The defense comes from way out in left field—yet Black had to know this move was there before he made his 21st move.

27. **B × B**	**R × B**
28. **R × R*ch***	**K × R**
29. **B—Q3**	

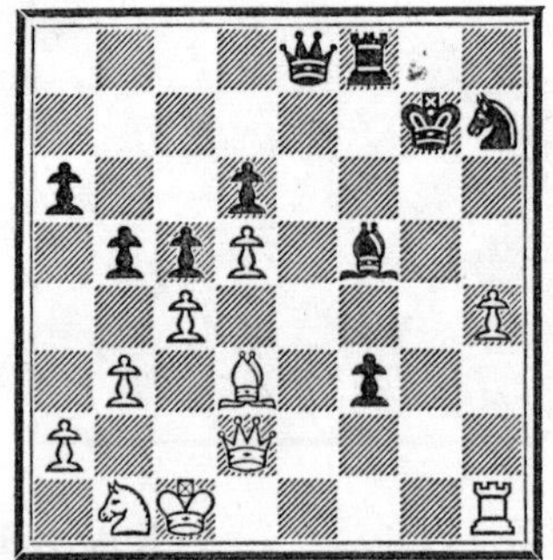

The Black P is still untouchable! *29.* Q—B3*ch*, Q—K4; *30.* Q × P, B × Kt; *31.* Q—Kt4*ch*, B—Kt3; *32.* P—R5, Q—R8*ch !*

29.	**P × P**
30. **R—Kt1*ch***	**K—R1**
31. **Q—B3*ch***	**Q—K4**
32. **Q× Q*ch***	**P × Q**

White is counting Pawns, and imagines the position will be even after the exchanges—but he is wrong! The Black KBP is too strong.

33. **B × B**	**R × B**
34. **P × P**	**Kt—B3**

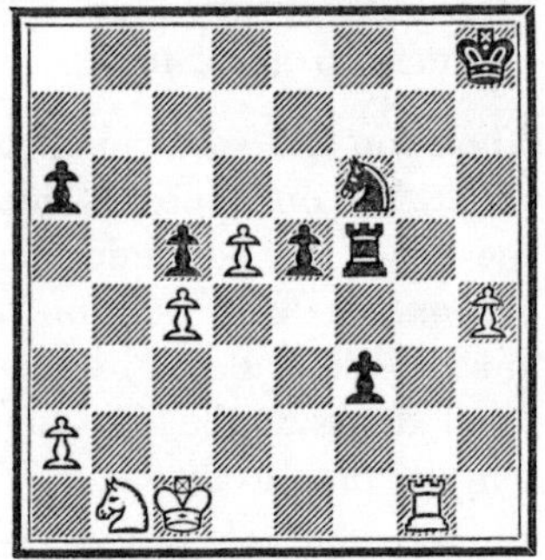

35. **Kt—Q2**	**P—B7 *!***
36. **R—R1**	

For *36.* R—B1, P—K5; *37.* K—Q1, P—K6; *38.* Kt—Kt3, Kt—K5 and *39.* . . . . Kt—Kt6 wins.

36.	**P—K5**
37. **K—Q1**	

37. Kt—B1 doesn't stop the KP because of *37.* . . . . Kt—Kt5 and, if *38.* K—Q2, R—B6 leaves White without a playable move.

37.	**P—K6**
38. **Kt—B1**	**R—K4**
39. **K—K2**	**Kt—R4**

Forcing the KP through, via . . . . Kt—B5*ch*.

40. **K—B3**	**P—K7**
41. **Resigns**	

Black must Queen a Pawn.

Part Three

Quiz Section

Quiz 1

White can win material or mate in each of these positions. Write the move or moves in the spaces provided (or use a separate sheet of paper if you plan to use these quiz sections as an occasional test of your chess skill). The answers are on page 263.

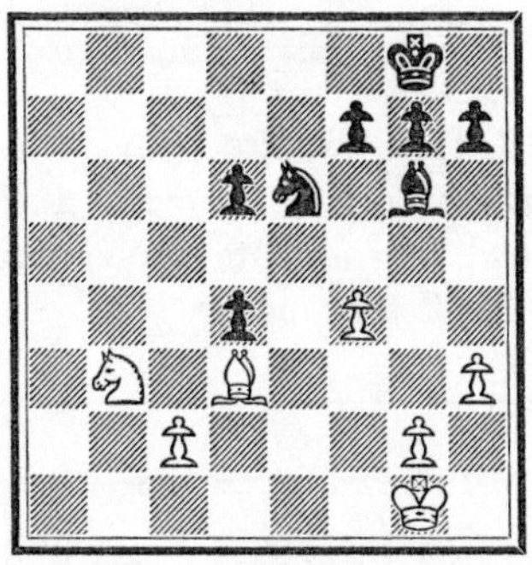

1. With what move does White win a piece by *forking* Black's Kt and B?

2. White would like to play P—B5, forking Black's Rook and Knight. However, he sees that Black could then escape by exchanging Rooks or checking by . . . . R—R3. What move can White play so that he can win by P—B5 on his following move?

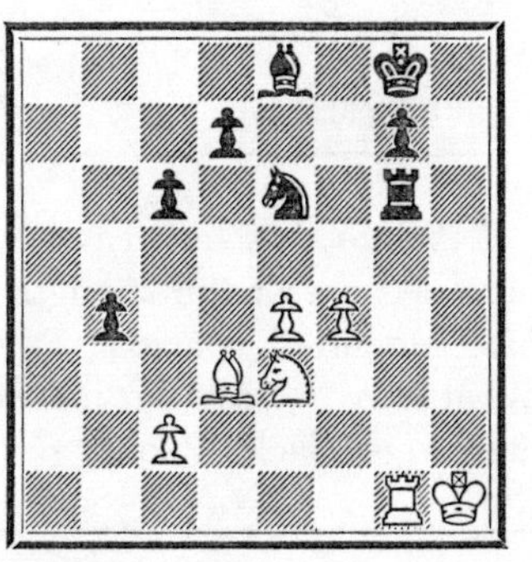

3. White's Pawn on *QB6* would win if it could be advanced to B7 while still pro-

tected. White's winning move is therefore the one that permits this Pawn advance. What is the surprise that defeats Black?

4. The material is even, but White sees that a Knight fork may be possible at QKt6, winning the Black Bishop at Q7. What White move therefore forces the gain of a piece?

5. White's Knight and Bishop are on the same diagonal as Black's King. Any Knight move will mean a discovered check. How does White now win a Bishop?

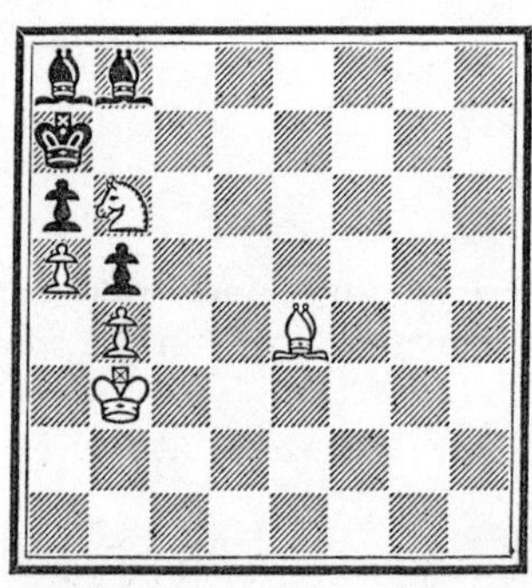

6. Here White can win a Bishop by Kt × B or B × B. Instead, he can mate in one move. What is that move?

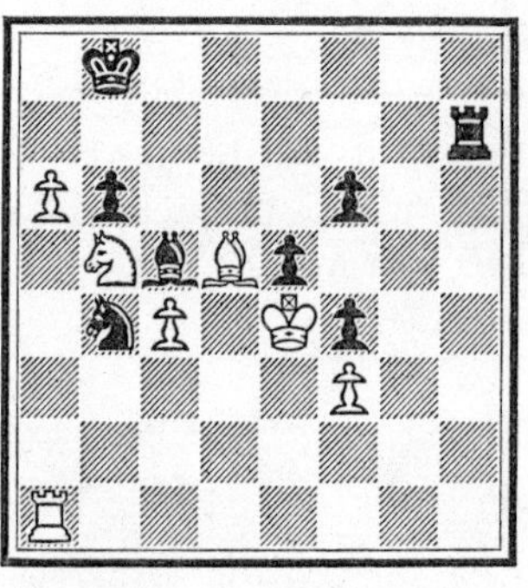

7. White has an easy win here because of the strength of his supported passed Pawn. What move forces the immediate win of Black's Rook?

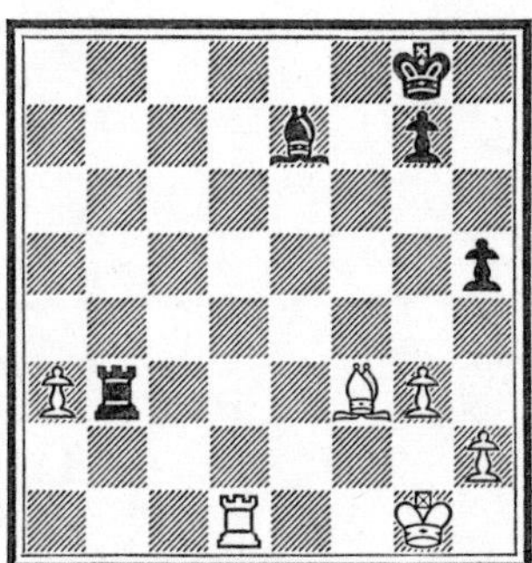

8. Black has just played . . . . R—Kt6, thinking he can win a Pawn because he is forking Pawn and Bishop. White's reply wins that Rook. What is the winning move?

____

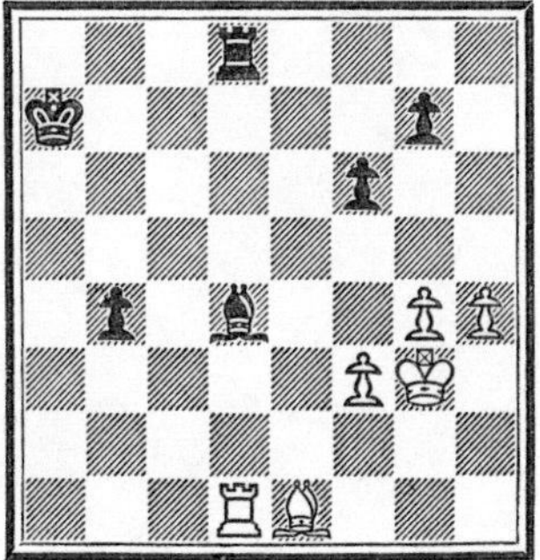

9. Note that Black's King is on the same diagonal as his Bishop. White would like to play B—B2, pinning whatever piece is at his Q4 square. Suppose a Rook were on that square instead of the Bishop? What is White's natural move in this position? ______

____

followed by ______________

____

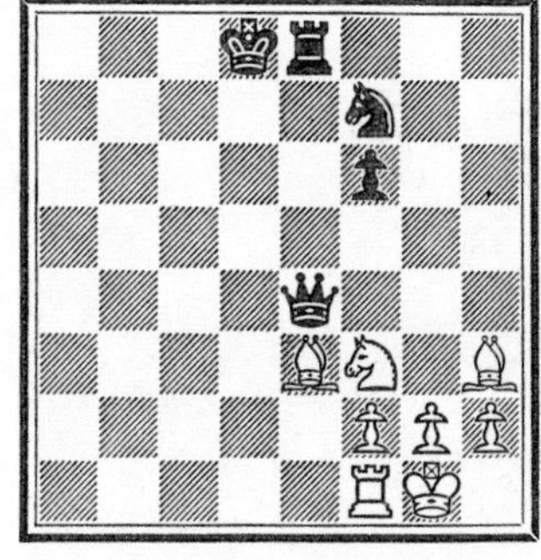

10. White can win this game if he can force Black's King to the King file. R—K1 would then pin and win Black's Queen, leaving White with a winning advantage in material. What move forces the King to the King file?

____

____

Quiz 2

You cannot win chess games unless you can recognize basic mating positions. Here are ten of them. In each case White mates in one move. The answers are on page 263.

1. ____________________ mate!

3. ____________________ mate!

2. ____________________ mate!

4. ____________________ mate!

5. ________________ mate!

8. ________________ mate!

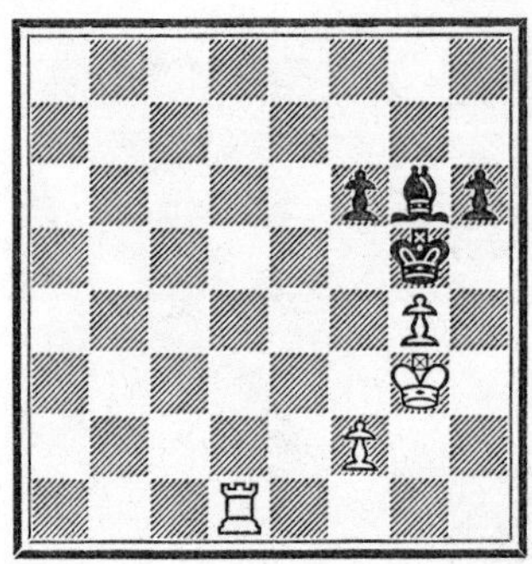

6. ________________ mate!

9. ________________ mate!

7. ________________ mate!

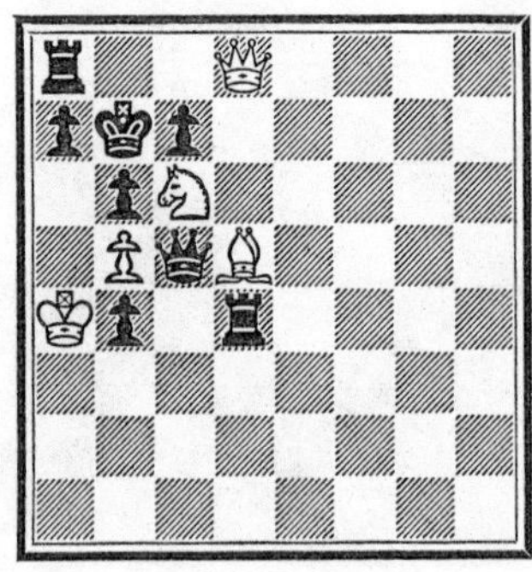

10. ________________ mate!

Quiz 3

The key to winning chess games is the ability to plan an attack and then carry it through to a successful conclusion. To do this, you must see more than one move ahead at a time. In each of these positions White can mate in two moves. Black's reply is forced in each case. All you have to do, then, is recognize the mating position, and make the two moves that lead to that mate. The answers are on page 263.

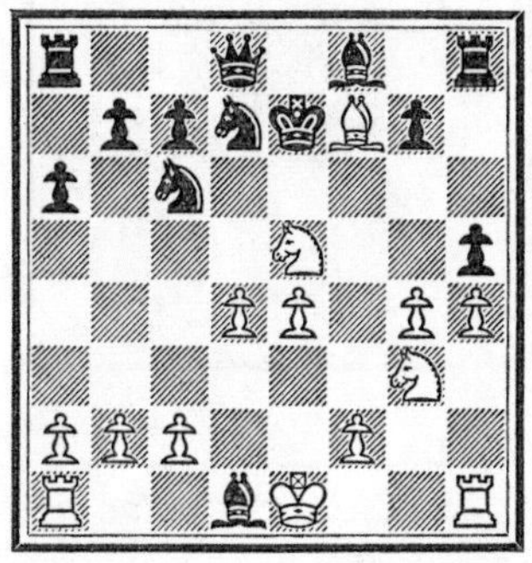

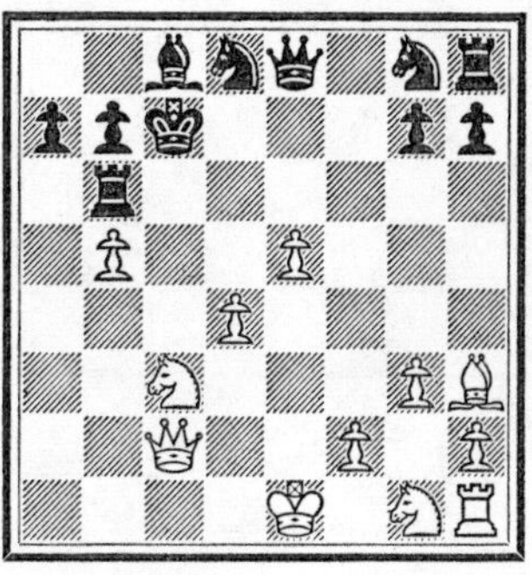

(1) 1. ________ ________
2. ________ mate!

(2) 1. ________ ________
2. ________ mate!

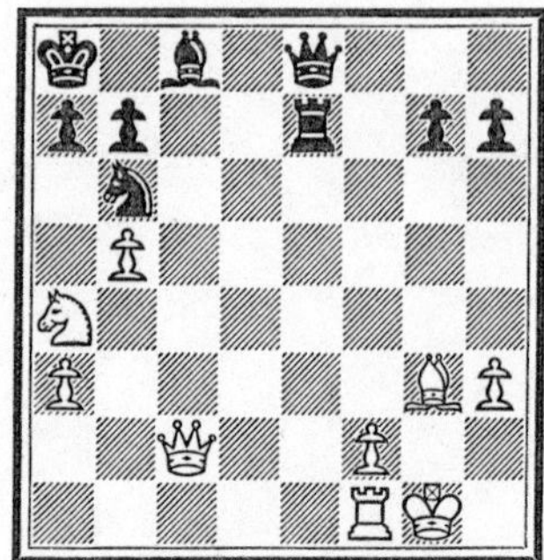

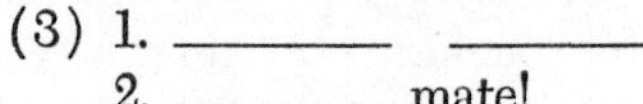

(3) 1. ________ ________
2. ________ mate!

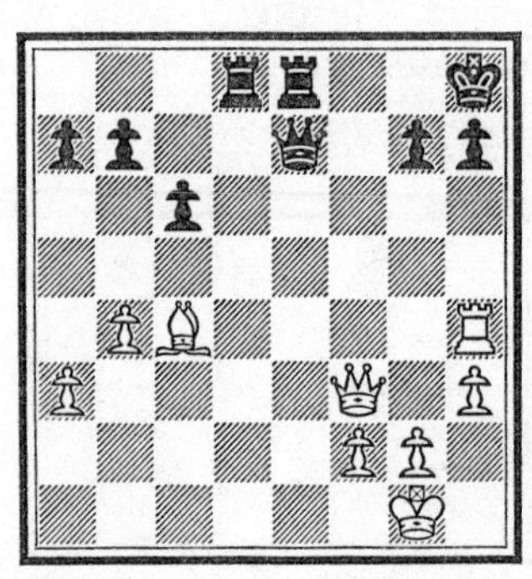

(4) 1. ________ ________
2. ________ mate!

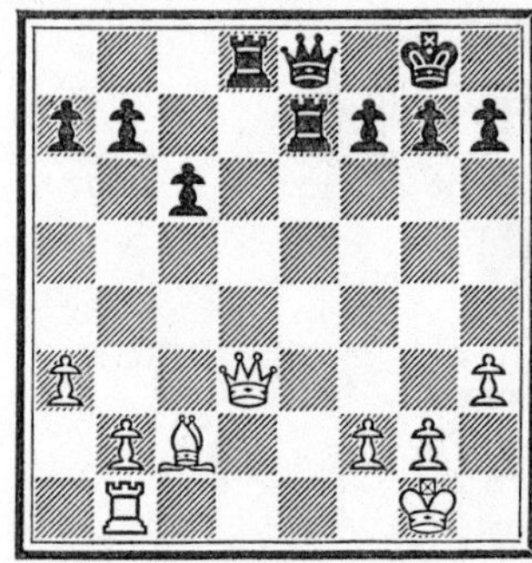

(5) 1. ________ ________
2. ________ mate!

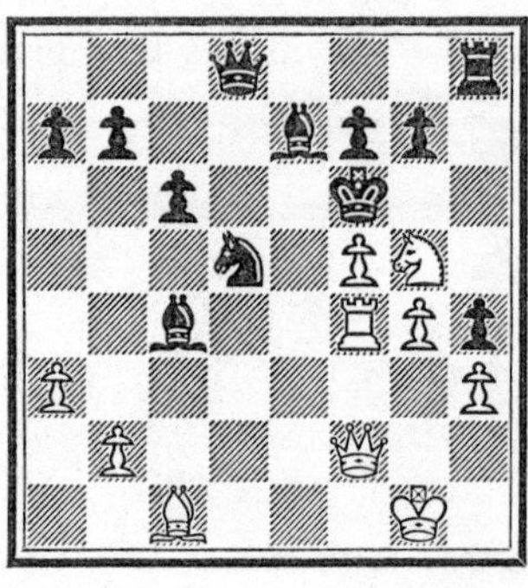

(6) 1. ________ ________
2. ________ mate!

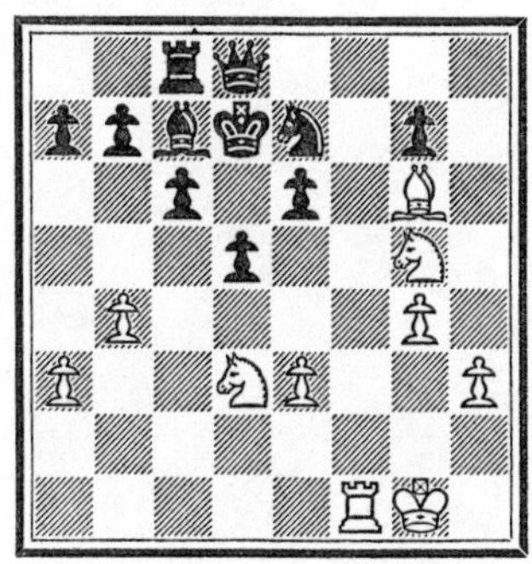

(7) 1. ________ ________
2. ________ mate!

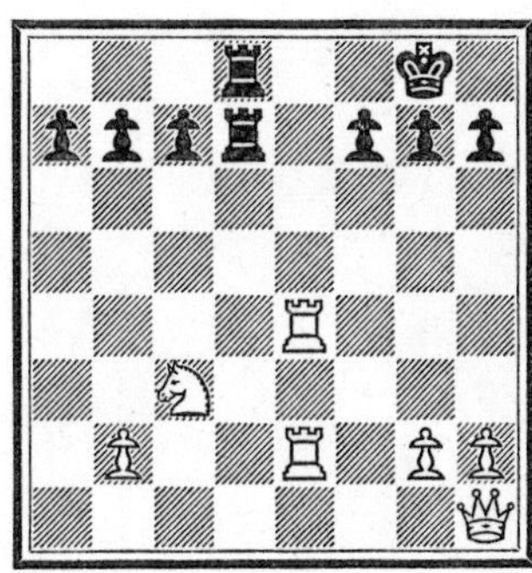

(9) 1. ________ ________
2. ________ mate!

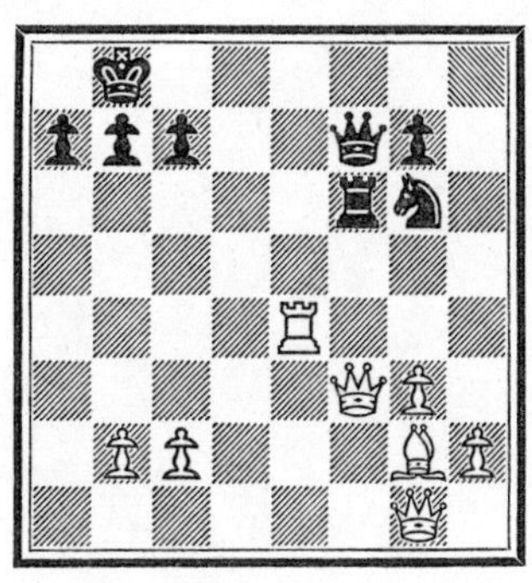

(8) 1. ________ ________
2. ________ mate!

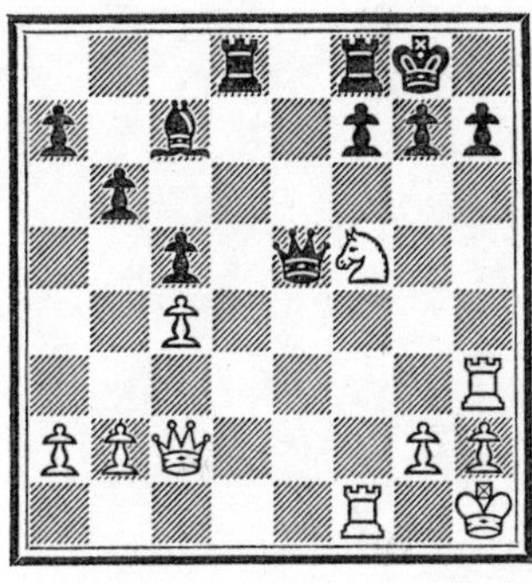

(10) 1. ________ ________
2. ________ mate!

Quiz 4

A Final Test of Your Chess Knowledge

How well have you grasped the chess ideas in this book? This final quiz contains a number of chess positions. Each position is followed by a group of questions with three possible answers. Select the best of these answers. A correct answer is worth two points.

There are fifty questions in all. The answers, plus a review of the chess RULE TO REMEMBER illustrated by each position, are on page 264. Consider yourself a

—Class A Chessplayer if you score 80 or better.
—Class B Chessplayer if you score 60 to 78 points.
—Class C Chessplayer if you score 40 to 58 points.

If you score 38 or less, you should study the RULES TO REMEMBER. You have not yet mastered these basic ideas of winning chess.

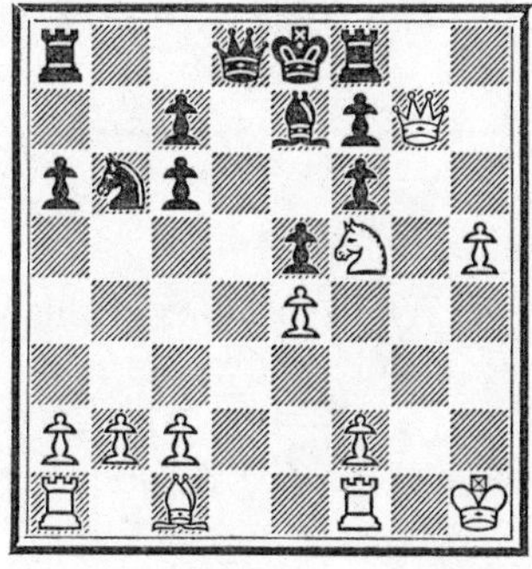

1. White's game is better because:
   (*a*) His Queen is well placed
   (*b*) He has an open diagonal for his Bishop.
   (*c*) He has a passed Pawn.

2. If Black is to move in this position, and plays . . . . Kt—Q2, White's best move is to:
   (*a*) Pin the Kt by R—Q1.
   (*b*) Play P—R6.
   (*c*) Develop his Bishop to K3.

3. If Black is to move in this position, and plays . . . .

K—Q2, White's best move would be:
(*a*) P—R6 (*b*) Q—Kt4 (*c*) R—Q1*ch*

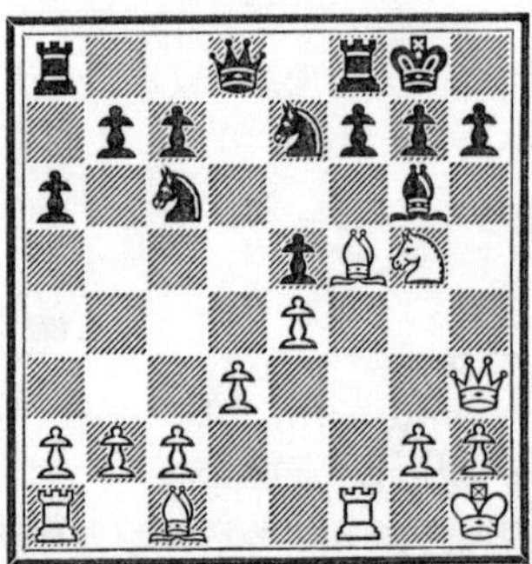

4. If White is to move in this position, his best move is:
(*a*) Kt × P (*b*) B × B (*c*) B—K3

5. If Black is to move in this position, his best move is:
(*a*) Q—Q3 (2) Kt—Q5 (*c*) B × B

6. If Black plays . . . . P—R3 in this position, White's best move would be Kt—B3, with the threat of:
(*a*) Kt—R4 (*b*) B × B (*c*) B × P

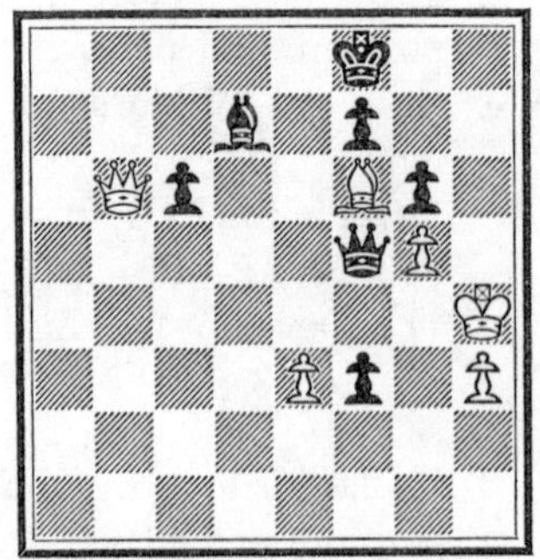

7. Black to move in this position could mate in one move by:
(*a*) Q—K5 (*b*) Q × RP (*c*) Q—Kt5

8. White to move in this position has a mate in four moves. His first move should be:
(*a*) Q—Kt4*ch*
(*b*) Q—Kt8*ch*
(*c*) Q—Q8*ch*

9. White to move in this position will win after:
(*a*) P—R6 (*b*) P—Kt6 (*c*) K—B8

10. Black to move in this position will win after:
(*a*) P—R7 (*b*) P—R3 (*c*) P—B6

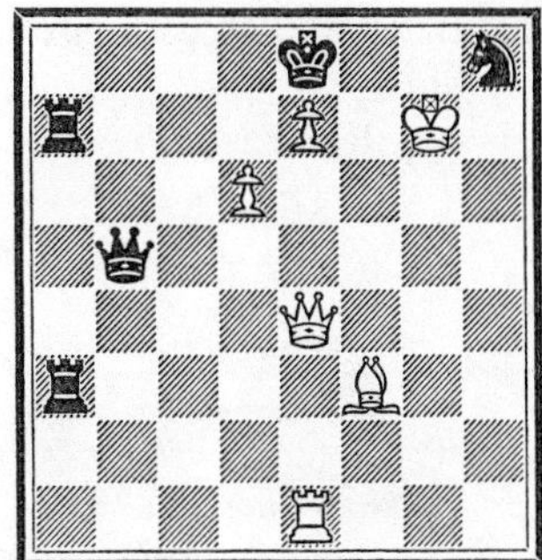

11. White's advanced Pawns have Black in a mating net. Q—B6*ch* followed by Q—B8 will win at once if Black's Queen can be decoyed away. White should therefore play:
    (*a*) R—QKt1
    (*b*) P—Q7*ch*
    (*c*) B—R5*ch*

12. White can also win by Q—B6*ch*. This wins because;
    (*a*) Black must lose his Queen without compensation.
    (*b*) White plays K × Kt after the exchange of Queens.
    (*c*) White Queens a Pawn after exchanges at B6 and Q7.

13. Make these moves from the given position: *1.* . . . . Kt—B2; *2.* Q—Kt6, Q—Kt7*ch !*; *3.* K—R7. Black now wins with:
    (*a*) Q—KR7 (*b*) Q—R1 (*c*) R × B

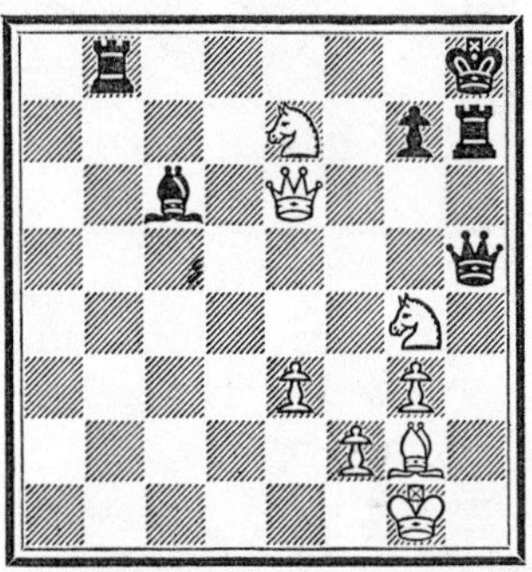

14. White to move in this position wins quickly after:
    (*a*) Kt × B
    (*b*) Kt—Kt6*ch*
    (*c*) B × B

15. Black to move can win by either of two of these moves.
    (*a*) R—Kt8*ch*
    (*b*) Q—R8*ch*
    (*c*) B × B

16. Suppose Black is to move in the above position. Which of these Black moves would permit White to mate in one move?
    (*a*) P—Kt4? (*b*) P—Kt3? (*c*) B—K1?

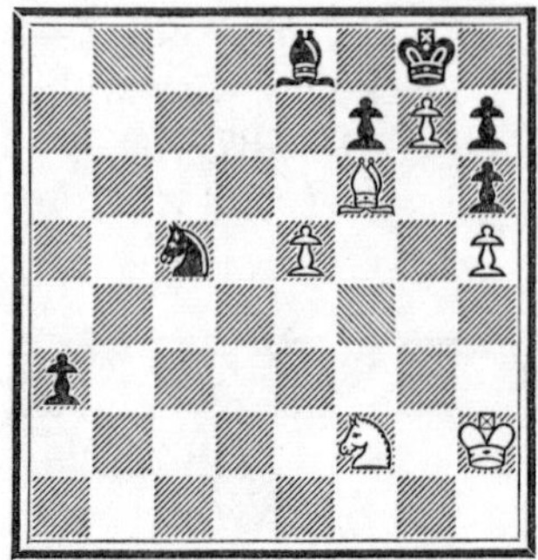

17. If it is White's turn to move in this position, he wins by:
(*a*) B—K7 (*b*) K—Kt3
(*c*) Kt—Kt4

18. Black to move in this position can defend by:
(*a*) P—R7 (*b*) B—Kt4
(*c*) Kt—K3

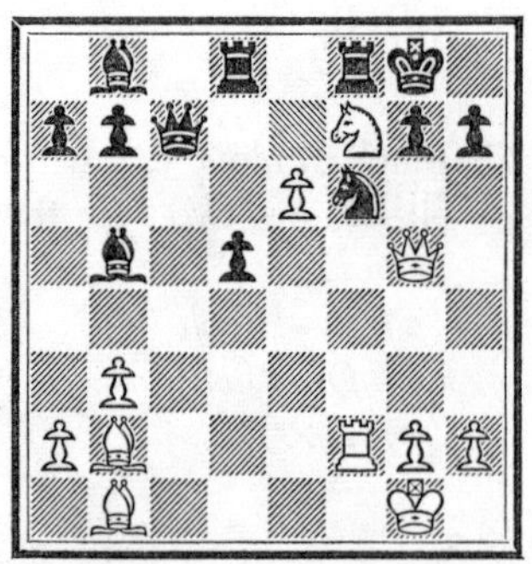

19. Black is subject to a mating attack after White plays:
(*a*) Kt × R
(*b*) Kt—R6*ch*
(*c*) Q × P*ch*

20. Black to play wins at once by:
(*a*) R × Kt (*b*) Q × P
(*c*) P—Q5

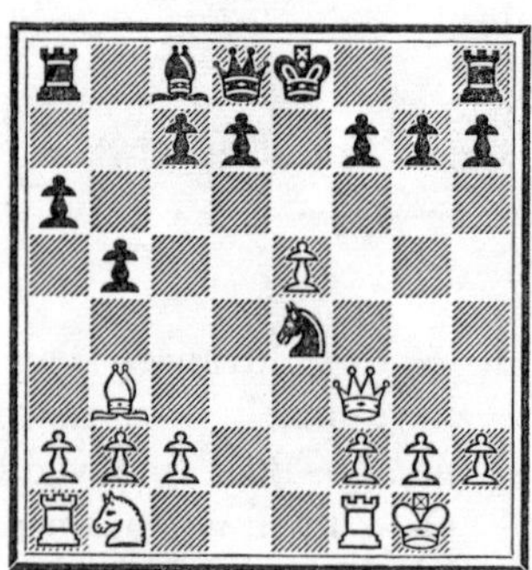

21. White threatens Q × P mate as well as Q × Kt. Black cannot defend by . . . . Kt—Kt4 because of:
(*a*) Q—Q5 (*b*) Q × R
(*c*) B × P*ch*

22. In the position above, Black cannot defend by . . . . P—Q4 because White will play:
(*a*) R—Q1 (*b*) B × P
(*c*) P ×P *e.p.*

23. The position illustrates:
(*a*) a forced mate
(*b*) a discovered attack
(*c*) a discovered check

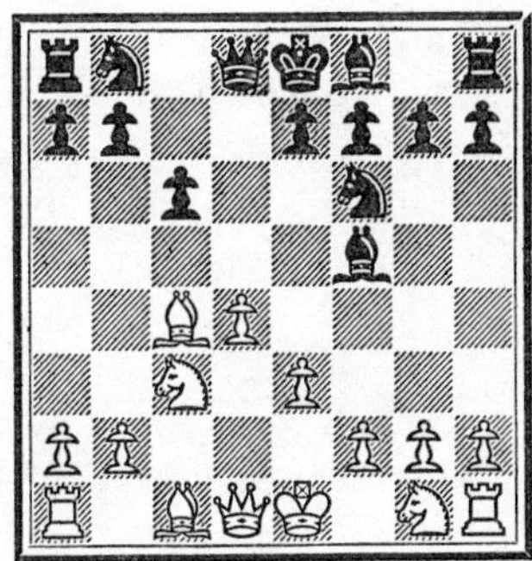

24. This position arises from a:
    (*a*) King's Gambit
    (*b*) Queen's Gambit
    (*c*) Ruy Lopez

25. White's winning move in this position is:
    (*a*) P—K4 (*b*) Kt—B3 (*c*) Q—Kt3

26. Black's error in the opening was to play:
    (*a*) B—B4 (*b*) Kt—B3 (*c*) P—B3

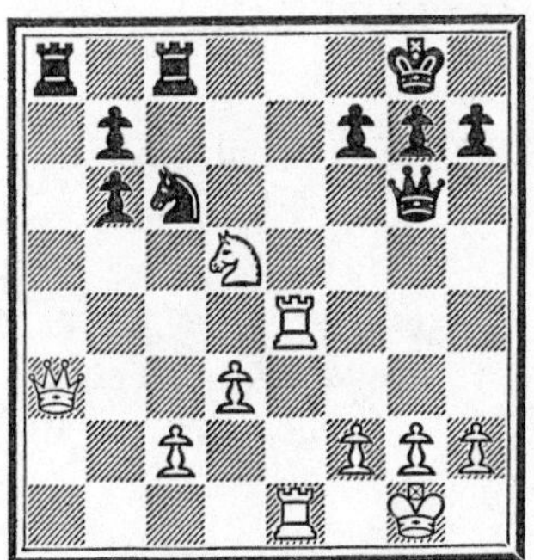

27. If Black plays . . . . R × Q? in this position, White wins by:
    (*a*) Kt—B4
    (*b*) Kt—K7*ch*
    (*c*) R—K8*ch*

28. Black to move gains an advantage by:
    (*a*) P—B4 (*b*) Q × R (*c*) Kt—R4

29. White to move in the above position wins by:
    (*a*) Q × R (*b*) R—K8*ch* (*c*) Kt—K7*ch*

30. From the above position, a possible line of play could be: *1.* . . . . P—B4?; 2. Q—Kt3, Kt—R4? White would then win by playing:
    (*a*) R—K6
    (*b*) Kt—B6 double check
    (*c*) Kt—K7 double check

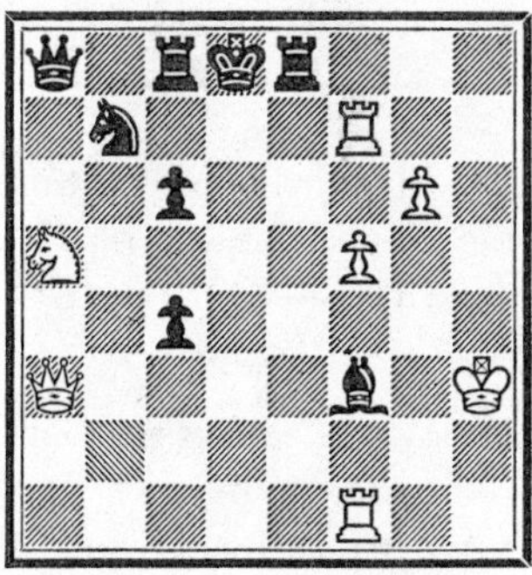

31. White mates in three moves, beginning with:
    (*a*) Q × B
    (*b*) Kt × Kt*ch*
    (*c*) R—Q1*ch*

32. Black to move can defend with:
 (*a*) Kt × Kt
 (*b*) Q × Kt
 (*c*) P—B4

33. If Black to move played . . . . R—R1*ch*, and White replied with K—Kt3?, then Black would win by playing:
 (*a*) Q × Kt
 (*b*) Q—Kt1*ch*
 (*c*) R—B2

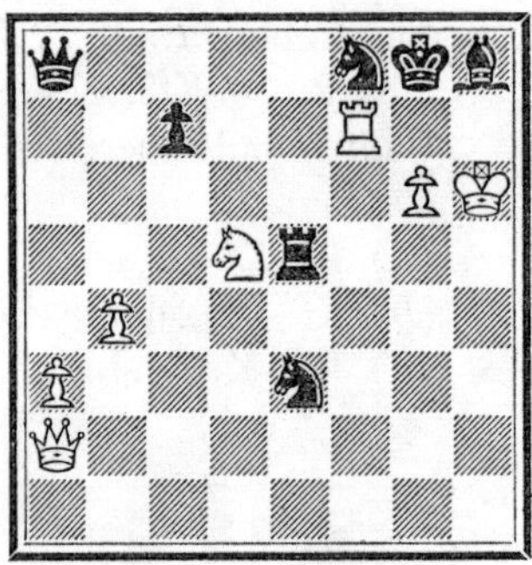

34. Black will mate in this position if he can play:
 (*a*) B—Kt2 (*b*) Kt—B4 (*c*) Kt—Kt5

35. White cannot prevent the mate by playing Kt × Kt because Black would then win after:
 (*a*) R × Kt (*b*) R—K3 (*c*) Q—R8

36. However, White to move plays Kt—K7*ch!* Black must reply . . . . R × Kt, and White now mates with the help of his Queen by:
 (*a*) R × R (check by the Queen)
 (*b*) R—KKt7 (double check)
 (*c*) R × Kt check by the Queen and Rook)

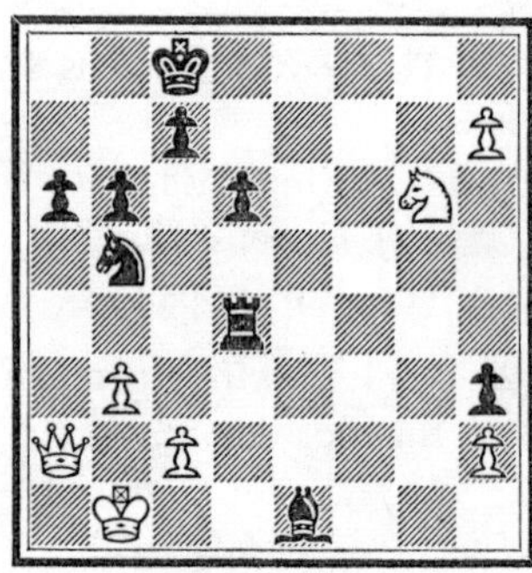

37. White is lost, for Black mates in two moves, beginning with:
 (*a*) Kt—B6*ch*
 (*b*) R—Q8*ch*
 (*c*) B—B6

38. Black would lose after *1.* . . . . Kt—B6*ch; 2.* K—Kt2, Kt × Q; because:
 (*a*) White Queens his Pawn with check and the win of Black's Rook.
 (*b*) White plays K × Kt and Black cannot prevent the Queening of the White Pawn.

(*c*) White plays P—B3 and attacks Black's Rook.

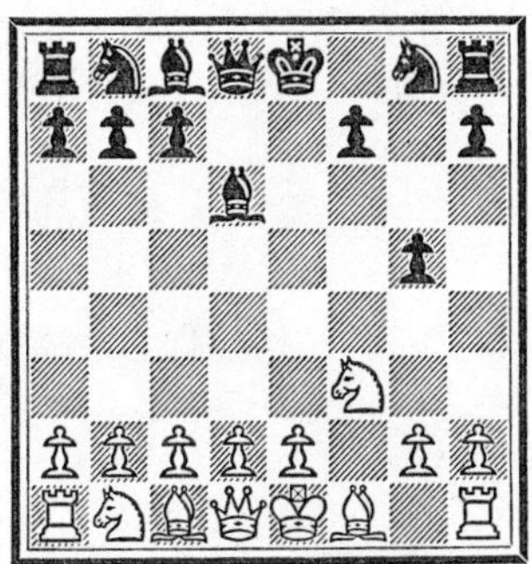

39. This position arises after the moves *1.* P—KB4, P—K4; *2.* P × P, P—Q3; *3.* P × P, B × P; *4.* Kt—KB3, P—KKt4. Black's threat is now:
   (*a*) Q—B3 (*b*) P—Kt5 (*c*) P—KR4

40. If White plays P—KR3 in this position, he loses at once, because of a move by Black's:
   (*a*) KKtP (*b*) Queen (*c*) Bishop

41. From this position, assume that the play is *5.* P—Q3?, P—Kt5; *6.* Kt (B3)—Q2. Black's winning move is now:
   (*a*) P—Kt6
   (*b*) Q—R5*ch*
   (*c*) B—Kt6*ch*

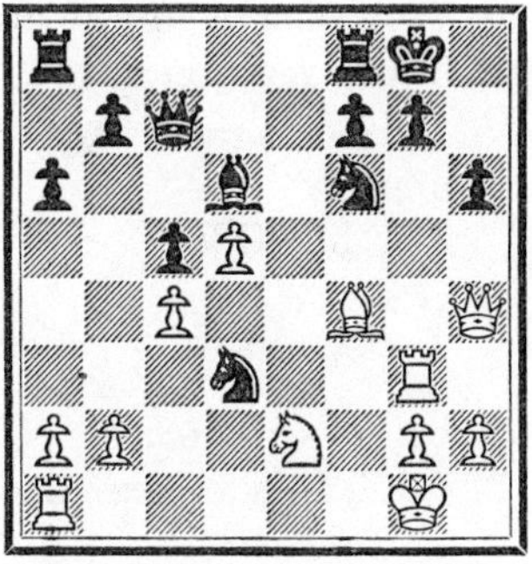

42. White to play in this position will win with:
   (*a*) Q × Kt
   (*b*) R × P*ch*
   (*c*) R × Kt

43. After *1.* Q × Kt, B × B in the above position, White wins *at once* with:
   (*a*) P—Q6 (*b*) Q × KtP (*c*) Kt × B

44. If White played *1.* R × Kt in this position, Black's best reply would be:
   (*a*) B × B
   (*b*) P—KKt4
   (*c*) P—QKt4

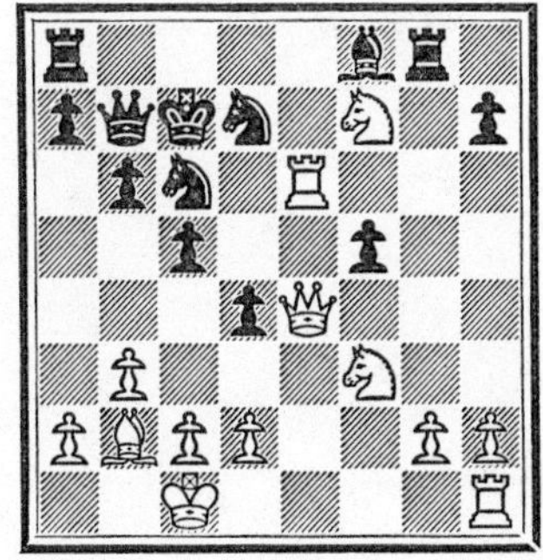

45. White has a forced mate in this position after *1.* Q—B4*ch,* K—B1; by playing:
    (*a*) Kt—Q6*ch*
    (*b*) Q × BP
    (*c*) R—K8*ch*

46. On *1.* Q—B4*ch,* Kt(Q2)—K4; White's best move is:
    (*a*) Kt(B3) × Kt
    (*b*) R × Kt(B6)*ch*
    (*c*) R × Kt(K5)

47. Black probably just played:
    (*a*) K(Q3)—B2
    (*b*) R—Kt1
    (*c*) P—KB4 (or a capture on KB4)

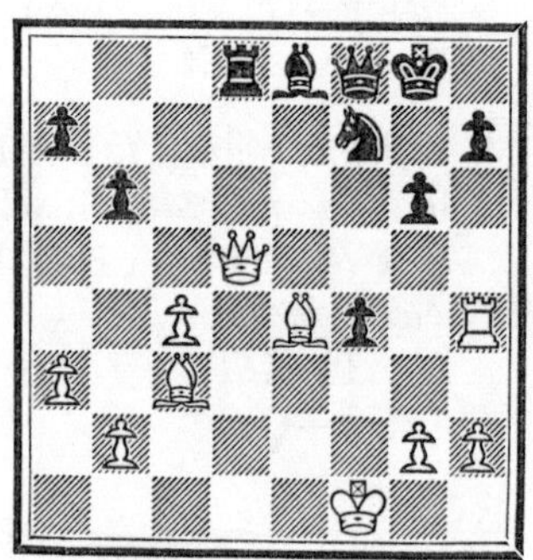

48. White's best move in this position is:
    (*a*) R × P (*b*) B × P
    (*c*) Q—K6

49. If *1.* B × P, R × Q; in the above position, White wins by:
    (*a*) R × P (*b*) B × P
    (*c*) P × R

50. If *1.* B × *P,* P—KR3; White's winning move is:
    (*a*) Q—K4 (*b*) Q—K6
    (*c*) Q—KB5

Part Four

Answers to Quizzes

Answers to Quizzes

Quiz 1

1. P—B5
2. R × R
3. B × Kt
4. B × Kt
5. Kt—B4 (discovered check)
6. Kt—B8 mate
7. P—R7*ch*
8. B—Q5*ch*
9. R × B, followed by B—B2
10. B—Kt6*ch*

Quiz 2

1. B—B6 mate **2.** R—Q8 mate **3.** Q × R mate **4.** Kt—R6 mate **5.** R—K3 mate **6.** P—B4 mate **7.** Kt—Kt4 mate **8.** Q—Q8 mate **9.** Q—Kt4 mate **10.** Kt—R5 double check and mate

Quiz 3

1. *1.* Kt—B5*ch,* K—B3; 2. P—Kt5 mate
2. *1.* Kt—Q5*ch,* K—Kt1; 2. Q × B mate
3. *1.* Kt × Kt*ch,* P × Kt; 2. Q—R4 mate
4. *1.* R × P*ch,* K × R; 2. Q—R5 mate
5. *1.* Q × P*ch,* K—B1; 2. Q—R8 mate
6. *1.* Q—Q4*ch,* K × Kt; 2. Q × P mate
7. *1.* Kt—B5*ch,* K—Q3; 2. Kt—B7 mate
8. *1.* R—K8*ch,* Q × R; 2. Q × P mate
9. *1.* R—K8*ch,* R × R; 2. R × R mate
10. *1.* Kt—K7*ch,* Q × Kt; 2. Q × P mate

Quiz 4

1. (*c*) is the best answer. The Pawn on KR5 will soon become a Queen, giving White an advantage of at least a Rook. *Advance passed Pawns!*
2. (*b*) is the best answer. Although each of the other moves is strong, the advance of the passed Pawn is stronger. REMEMBER: *Try to promote a passed Pawn!*
3. (*b*) is the best answer. Q—Kt4 threatens a discovered check, which would win quickly. For example, if Black plays . . . . B—Q3, White wins at once with Kt × B (discovered check), K × Kt; R—Q1*ch* (winning the Queen), followed by the advance of the KRP. If Black tried to escape the discovered check by playing . . . . K—K1 at once, then White mates by Kt—Kt7. *Look for discovered attacks in any position!*
4. (*b*) is the best answer. White wins at least a Bishop, for Black does not have time to recapture the piece. If the Bishop were recaptured, White would mate at once by playing Q—R7 (or, if the Black Pawn remains on R7, Q × P mate). *Attack or capture the enemy piece that protects against your threatened mate!*
5. (*a*) is the best answer. By playing . . . . Q—Q3 Black is really protecting his KR2 square, for if White played B × B, the answer . . . . Q × B would permit the Black Queen to protect against the threatened mate on White's KR7. *Protect against threatened mate by supporting the piece that is preventing the mate!*
6. (*a*) is the best answer. White wants to remove the Black Bishop. *Attack the piece that defends the enemy King position!*
7. (*b*) is the correct answer. In any position where mate in one seems possible, *seek the move that prevents the enemy King from escaping!*
8. (*c*) is the correct answer. If White plays Q—Kt4*ch*, Black can block the attack on the King by advancing the QBP. If White plays Q—Kt8*ch*, Black can play . . . . B—B1. The winning line, leading to the quickest mate, is: *1.* Q—Q8*ch*, B—K1; 2. Q—K7*ch*, K—Kt1; *3.* Q × B*ch*, K—R2; *4.* Q—R8 mate. *In a mating attack, watch for enemy moves that interpose pieces to break your attack.*
9. (*b*) is the correct answer. White threatens mate by P—Kt7. Black must therefore play . . . P × P. White then wins by

P × P, followed by P—Kt7*ch* and P—Kt8(Q)*ch*, and then Q—Kt6 mate. P—R6 and K—B8 would be errors because they permit Black to make a Queen by . . . . P—R7 and . . . . P—R8. This Queen would then control the Black QKt2 square. White would lose. *Remember to count the number of moves you and your opponent require to reach an objective in the endgame.*

10. (*a*) is the correct move. *1.* . . . . P—R7; 2. P—Kt6, P—R8(Q); and White's key attacking move, 3. P—Kt7*ch* fails because the new Black Queen now controls the checking square. *Try to Queen first in a King and Pawn endgame.*

11. (*c*) is the best answer. The Black King is hopelessly trapped. B—R5*ch* forces the quickest win: *1.* B—R5*ch*, Q × B; 2. Q—B6*ch*, R—Q2; 3. Q—B8*ch*, R—Q1; *4.* Q × R mate. *Always look for the quickest way to win!*

12. (*c*) is the correct answer. The combination of a Queen and a Rook usually mates quickly on an open board. The key to this position is that the Rook on White's K1 protects the queening square, K8. *Try to place a Rook behind a passed Pawn to protect it as it advances to the eighth rank!*

13. (*b*) is the correct answer. In fact, each of the other moves loses for Black. But . . . . Q—R1 is mate! White's 3. K—R7 was an error. He should have played winning line beginning with Q—B6*ch*, as shown in the answer to Question 12. *Once you see a winning attack, do not change it just because it seems possible to win a piece instead of mating!*

14. (*b*) is the correct answer. If either *1.* . . . . Kt × B or *1.* . . . . B × B, Black wins, as shown in the answer to the next question. However, Kt—Kt6*ch* wins the Black Queen, for the Black King cannot move to Kt1, a square covered by White's Queen. *When you have a choice of winning one of several pieces, consider first the winning of the most valuable of these pieces.*

15. (*a*) and (*b*) are correct.

(a) *1.* . . . . R—Kt8*ch*; 2. B—B1, Q—R8 mate.

(b) *1.* . . . . Q—R8*ch*; 2. B × Q, R—Kt8 mate.

Mate is possible because Black's Bishop controls the long diagonal. *Try to control the holes along the long diagonal that result when your opponent plays moves like P—KKt3 and P—K3.*

16. (*c*) is the answer, and a terrible move! White wins at once with Q—Kt8 mate. Black has blocked the defensive power of his Rook at QKt1. *Avoid moves that limit the scope of your pieces.*

17. (*c*) is the correct answer. The Black King has no escape moves, and will be mated by White's next move, Kt × P mate. *Look for a check when your opponent's King cannot move. It might be mate!*

18. (*c*) is the correct answer. Black's next move will be . . . . Kt × P, giving his King escape squares at KR1 and KB1. *Always try to have escape squares for your King.*

19. (*c*) is the correct answer. The mating attack is *1.* Q × P*ch*, K × Q; 2. B × Kt*ch*, K—Kt1; 3. Kt—R6 mate. *Memorize this mating position. It appears frequently in any chess player's career!*

20. (*b*) is the correct answer. *1.* . . . . Q × P mate shows the power of Queen and Bishop on the same diagonal. *Count the number of pawns or pieces defending any attacked square. Then count the number of attackers. If the number of attackers is greater, consider the capture or movement of a piece to the square.*

21. (*b*) is the correct answer. Black must lose the Knight, or the Rook on QR1 if the Knight moves away. Black has permitted a double attack. *Always seek moves that attack two pieces or a piece and a Pawn at the same time!*

22. (*c*) is the correct answer. After White plays P × P *e.p.*, Black is still threatened by Q × Kt and Q × P mate. *Avoid placing an unprotected piece in the center of the board. You may find yourself subject to a double attack!*

23. (*b*) is the correct answer. White is not attacking the Black Rook in the diagramed position. But he discovers an attack against the Rook if the Black Knight moves. *Undeveloped positions permit your opponent to find double attacks and discovered attacks.*

24. (*b*) is the correct answer. This is one of the possible positions in the Slav Defense to the Queen's Gambit, or in the Queen's Gambit Accepted. *Learn the opening moves of each of the important openings!*

25. (*c*) is the answer. White can now play Q—Kt3, with a double attack, B × P*ch* and Q × P. Black must lose at least a Pawn. *Play opening lines that contain threats of double attacks!*

26. (*a*) is the correct answer. The move . . . . B—B4 permitted White's Q—Kt3, with the double attack explained in the answer to Question 25. The move . . . . B—B4 may have its place in this opening, but should probably have been delayed. *Learn the correct order of moves in each opening line you decide to play!*

27. (*c*) is the correct answer. White wins quickly after *1.* . . . . R × Q; 2. R—K8*ch,* R × R; 3. R × R mate. *Double your Rooks on the open file, especially when your opponent's King does not have an escape square!*

28. (*b*) is the correct answer. *1.* . . . . Q × R wins at least a Rook. White should learn this lesson: *As a general rule, do not offer the sacrifice of a piece when other pieces are already under attack. Your opponent then has the choice of more than one capture.*

29. (*a*) is the correct answer. After *1.* Q × R White has two winning threats, Q × R and R—K8*ch.* Black should resign after *1.* Q × R. *Do not play on and on in a clearly lost position.*

30. (*c*) is the correct answer. On *1.* Kt—K7*ch* White must win Black's Queen. If *1.* . . . . K—R1 or *1.* . . . . K—B1; 2. Kt × Q*ch. Watch out for Knight forks!*

31. (*b*) is the correct answer. The mating attack is *1.* Kt × Kt*ch,* Q × Kt; 2. Q—Q6*ch,* Q—Q2; *3.* Q (or R) × Q mate. *Try to post a Rook on the seventh rank!*

32. (*b*) is the correct answer. It prevents the mate, but it cannot save the game. White should still win after *1.* . . . . Q × Kt; 2. Q × B, R—B2; 3. R—Q1*ch,* K—B1; *4.* R × *Rch,* Q × R; 5. P—B6. *Seek the line that gives you the longest defense. Your opponent must then make the best move every time—or you can begin a counterattack!*

33. (*b*) is the correct answer. After *1.* . . . . R—R1*ch;* 2. K—Kt3, Q—Kt1*ch;* 3. K × B, R—R6*ch* wins the Queen. After 3. K—B2, R—R7*ch; 4.* K—K3, Q—K4*ch* leads to mate. White could have avoided this attack by playing *1.* . . . . R—R1*ch;* 2. R—R7! *Do not permit your opponent's Rook to control an open file! If possible, contest such control by placing your own (protected) Rook on the same file!*

34. (*c*) is the correct answer. Note that White's King has *no* escape squares. Therefore, a check results in mate so long as this check does not itself create escape squares. If Black played . . . . Kt—B4*ch,* the White King could escape at KR5 or KKt5. *Do not make moves that give an attacked King escape squares!*

35. (*c*) is the correct answer. Note again that White's King has no escape squares. The check by the Black Queen is therefore mate! White's Kt × Kt gave Black's Queen a sudden powerful mobility. *Avoid moves that open lines for your opponent's pieces!*

36. (*b*) is the correct answer. A double check can be escaped only by a King move. Black is mated because his King has no squares to which it can move. *Look for double checks when the enemy King is not protected by a wall of Pawns!*

37. (*b*) is the correct answer. The mate is similar to the one you saw in the answer to Question 19. *1.* . . . . R—Q8*ch*; 2. K—Kt2, B—B6 mate. *Be ready to occupy holes in your opponent's King position!*

38. (*a*) is the correct answer. After *1.* . . . . Kt—B6*ch*; 2. K—Kt2, Kt × Q; *3.* P—R8(Q)*ch,* White has a winning double attack. Black is in check, and must play *3.* . . . . K—Kt2, after which White plays *4.* Q × R with an easy win. Black neglected a key rule: *Do not try to win material when you have a mating attack instead!*

39. (*b*) is the correct answer. This is a well-known line in the opening called the *From Gambit.* It is one of the most complicated of all gambits, and should not be played unless its chief lines have been memorized. Black now threatens to drive the White Knight away by . . . . P—Kt5. *Advance Pawns in the opening only when doing so gains time or space!*

40. (*c*) is the correct answer. On P—KR3, Black mates at once by . . . . B—Kt6 mate. White's King has no escape squares. White cannot capture the Bishop. White cannot interpose a piece at KB2. It is mate. White has ignored two rules by the blunder, P—KR3. *Do not create holes in your King position! Make certain your King has escape squares!* A proper White move in the diagramed position would be P—Q4.

41. (*b*) is the correct answer. The play from the diagramed position would be *5.* P—Q3?, P—Kt5; *6.* Kt(B3)—Q2, Q—R5*ch; 7.* P—KKt3, Q × KtP*ch!*; *8.* P × Q, B ×P mate. This is the basic Black attack in the From Gambit. White must block it by a move that creates escape squares for the King: P—Q4. If Black then plays . . . P—Kt5, White can block the attack with Kt—K5 or Kt—Kt5. *Learn the chief lines of every opening you play!*

42. (*a*) is the correct answer. Black's KKtP is pinned. Mate cannot be prevented, for the combination of Queen, Rook, and Bishop is too much for Black's undefended King position. White's earlier R—Kt3 had pinned the Black KKtP. *Pin the defenders of your opponent's King!*

43. (*b*) is the correct answer. Q × KtP is mate! Black can prevent the mate by playing . . . . P—KKt3 instead of . . . . B × B. White would then win after *1.* Q × Kt, P—KKt3; *2.* B × B,

Q—Q1; *3.* B—K7, Q—Q2; *4.* B × R, when he is a Rook ahead. White would be following an important rule: *If your opponent can prevent a threatened mate only by surrendering material, take that material!*

44. (*a*) is the correct answer. . . . . P—KKt4 would lose after White's reply QXRP. A possible line of play would be *1.* . . . . P—KKt4; 2. Q × RP, B × B; *3.* Kt × *B*, Q × Kt; *4.* R—KR3 and mate follows. If Black plays *1.* . . . . P—QKt4, White replies 2. B × P, with the threat of 3. B × P, K × B; *4.* Q—Kt5*ch*, K—R1; *5.* Q × Kt*ch*, K—Kt1; *6.* Q—Kt5*ch*, K—R2; 7. R—R3 mate. But *1.* . . . . B × B removes the White Bishop from the game. White would have to develop a new attack against the Black position. *When your opponent is attacking your King position with several pieces, try to exchange one or more of these pieces!*

45. (*c*) is the correct answer. Mate then follows after *1.* Q—B4*ch*, K—B1; 2. R—K8*ch*, Kt—Q1; 3. R × Kt mate *When your opponent's King has no escape squares, seek the check that leads to mate!* In this position, Black can interpose a Knight—but only to a square where it is attacked twice.

46. (*a*) is the best answer. White wins a piece, and keeps attacking. An amusing finish after *1.* Q—B4*ch*, Kt(Q2)—K4; might be: 2. Kt(B3) × Kt, Kt × Kt; 3. Q × Kt*ch*, K—B1; *4.* R—K8*ch*, K—Q2; *5.* Q—K6*ch*, K—B2; *6.* Kt—K5, R × R; 7. Q—Q7*ch*, K—Kt1; *8.* Kt—B6*ch*, K—R1; 9. Q × R*ch*, Q—Kt1 (or Q—B1); *10.* Q × Q mate. Play this one out on your chessboard. It illustrates the points of this position: *Do not give an attacked enemy King escape squares! Do not make moves that give your opponent time to bring new material to the defense of his King!*

47. (*c*) is the correct answer. Otherwise, Black would have captured White's Queen on his last move. White would then have been guilty of the most serious error that can occur during an attack. *Do not leave pieces* en prise (*subject to capture*) *if you need them for your attack!*

48. (*b*) is the correct answer. White is attacking with two Bishops and a Rook against an exposed King. If Black played *1.* . . . . P × B; 2. R—R8 is mate! The Black Knight cannot take the Rook, for it is pinned by the White Queen. *Open your opponent's King position—with a sacrifice if necessary—if several of your pieces are bearing down on it!*

49. (*b*) is the correct answer. White was able to leave the Queen *en prise* because B × P is mate! The White Rook protects this Bishop; the other White Bishop prevents the Black King from moving to KR1 or KKt2. Black has failed to follow a critical rule: *Do not grab at pieces while you are under attack unless you have first examined your opponent's threats!*

50. (*c*) is the correct answer. White still threatens mate by B—R7. Black has two possible replies—both of which lose.

From the diagramed position:

(1) *1.* B × P, P—KR3; *2.* Q—KB5, Kt—Kt4; *3.* Q × Q*ch*, K × Q; *4.* B × B, K × B; *5.* R × RP, with an easy win.

(2) *1.* B × P, P—KR3; *2.* Q—KB5, Q—K2; *3.* B—R7*ch*, K—B1; *4.* B—Kt4, R—Q3; *5.* R × RP wins the Rook.

This final position can remind us of the single most important group of RULES TO REMEMBER:

—*Learn the ways in which your pieces can combine their efforts to attack an enemy King!*

—*Seek open lines along which to attack!*

—*Look ahead to see how you can continue your attack!*

—*Always be ready to simplify by exchanging to reach an easily won ending!*